TOWARDS A MORE EQUAL SOCIETY?

Poverty, inequality and policy since 1997

Edited by John Hills, Tom Sefton and Kitty Stewart

JOSEPH ROWNTREE
FOUNDATION

This edition published in Great Britain in 2009 by

The Policy Press
University of Bristol
Fourth Floor
Beacon House
Queen's Road
Bristol BS8 1QU
UK

tel +44 (0)117 331 4054
fax +44 (0)117 331 4093
e-mail tpp-info@bristol.ac.uk
www.policypress.org.uk

North American office:
The Policy Press
c/o International Specialized Books Services
920 NE 58th Avenue, Suite 300
Portland, OR 97213-3786, USA
tel +1 503 287 3093, fax +1 503 280 8832, e-mail info@isbs.com

British Library Cataloguing in Publication Data
A catalogue record for this book is available from the British Library.

Library of Congress Cataloging-in-Publication Data
A catalog record for this book has been requested.

ISBN 978 1 84742 201 9 paperback
ISBN 978 1 84742 202 6 hardcover

Cover design by Qube Design Associates, Bristol
Front cover: image kindly supplied www.alamy.com
Printed and bound in Great Britain by Hobbs the Printers, Southampton

Contents

List of figures, tables and boxes

Figures

Figures (continued)

Figures (continued)

Figures (continued)

Tables

Tables (continued)

Tables (continued)

Boxes

Acknowledgements

This book was made possible by the Joseph Rowntree Foundation, whose funding supported all of its writing and the research behind it. Parts of the book, particularly in Chapter Six, also draw on research previously carried out within the Centre for Analysis of Social Exclusion (CASE) which was supported by the Economic and Social Research Council and the Nuffield Foundation. The opinions and views expressed here are, however, those of the contributors and not those of any of our supporting bodies.

Several of the contributions draw on analysis of data supplied by the UK Data Archive at the University of Essex and by government departments. In particular, the analysis presented in Chapters Two, Three and Eight of this volume using the POLIMOD model from the Institute for Social and Economic Research at the University of Essex is based on data from the Family Resources Survey which are made available by the Department for Work and Pensions (DWP). Part of the analysis in Chapter Five is based on data from the DWP's Lifetime Labour Market Database, also kindly made available by that department. Material from the Labour Force Survey used in Chapter Ten is also Crown Copyright, and has been used with permission. None of the Data Archive, National Statistics or the government departments involved bear any responsibility for the analysis or interpretations of the data reported here. Crown Copyright material, including Figure 6.2, is reproduced with the permission of the Controller of HMSO and the Queen's Printer for Scotland.

As well as this being a collective enterprise, where we have benefited from one another's advice, many people have helped the authors and editors in preparing this book. We would particularly like to thank Paul Gregg, Liz Richardson, Jane Waldfogel, and Liz Washbrook, who also contributed to our earlier book, *A More Equal Society?*, on which we have drawn throughout. Particular parts of the book have been greatly helped by advice and assistance including from: Mike Brewer and Lisa Harker (Chapters Two and Three); Caroline Paskell, Laura Lane and Helen Willmot (Chapter Six); Michele Cecchini for assistance with analysis of data on health inequalities (Chapter Seven); Greg Barrett and Pratima Rao (Chapter Nine); Laura Chappell (Chapter Ten); Paulina Terrazas (Chapters Eleven and Thirteen); Peter Matejic (Chapter Twelve); and Steve Leman, John Micklewright and Hilary Steedman (Chapter Thirteen). Chapter Six was informed by evaluation evidence and information kindly supplied by Communities and Local Government. Howard Glennerster and Anne Harrop gave invaluable advice and support throughout the whole project. We have also been greatly helped by our colleagues in STICERD and CASE in being able to complete this project, particularly Abenaa Owusu-Bempah, Jane Dickson, Joe Joannes, Laura Lane, and Nicola Serle. Lastly, Anna Tamas master-minded the preparation of the manuscript for publication against a tight timetable and our sometimes unreasonable demands, for coping with all of which we are more than grateful.

John Hills, Tom Sefton and Kitty Stewart
London School of Economics and Political Science
September 2008

Notes on contributors

Tania Burchardt is a senior research fellow at the Centre for Analysis of Social Exclusion (CASE), London School of Economics and Political Science. Her research interests include theories of social justice, definitions and measurements of inequality and social exclusion, and welfare and employment policy. She is editor of *Benefits: The Journal of Poverty and Social Justice*.

Maria Evandrou is Professor of Gerontology and Director of the Centre for Research on Ageing at the University of Southampton. She is also Co-Director of the Economic and Social Research Council (ESRC) Centre for Population Change. She has written widely on social policy and older people. Recent published work includes: with Jane Falkingham, a chapter in *The Futures of Old Age* (Sage Publications, 2006) entitled 'Will the baby-boomers be better off than their parents in retirement?'; and, with Karen Glaser and Cecilia Tomassini, an article in *The International Journal of Aging and Human Development* entitled 'The relationship of multiple role occupancy on social participation among mid-life wives and husbands in the UK' (2006, vol 63, no 1).

Jane Falkingham is Professor of Demography and International Social Policy within the School of Social Science at the University of Southampton, and Co-Director of the ESRC Centre for Population Change. She has written widely in the field of population ageing and social policy. Recent published work includes: with Asghar Zaidi, Karen Rake and Björn Gustafsson, a chapter in *Mainstreaming Ageing: Indicators to Monitor Sustainable Policies* (Ashgate, 2007) entitled 'Welfare indicators of income experience during old age'; and, with Maria Evandrou, a chapter in *The Futures of Old Age* (Sage Publications, 2006) entitled 'Will the baby-boomers be better off than their parents in retirement?'.

Natalie Heath is a research officer at the Institute of Education, University of London and a teaching associate at the Faculty of Education, University of Cambridge. Her main research interests are school choice processes and educational inequalities.

John Hills is Professor of Social Policy and Director of CASE at the London School of Economics and Political Science. His research interests include the distributional effects of tax and welfare systems, social security, pensions and housing finance. Recent publications include: *Inequality and the State* (Oxford University Press, 2004); *A More Equal Society? New Labour, Poverty, Inequality and Exclusion* (co-editor, The Policy Press, 2005); and *Ends and Means: The Future Roles of Social Housing in England* (CASE, 2007). He was a member of the Pensions Commission from 2003 to 2006.

Holly Holder is a research officer at CASE and is currently studying for an MSc in social policy and planning at the London School of Economics and Political Science. With a research background in social housing, her most recent work includes a project to develop a national equalities measurement framework.

Maria Latorre is a research assistant in the migration team at the Institute for Public Policy Research where she specialises in the economic impacts of migration as well as the quantitative analysis of social policy. Her previous work experience was in Colombia, where she worked with a non-governmental organisation in projects related to local development, with the government in the Social Development Office and with a think tank focused on the economic impact of the Colombian public policy.

Ruth Lupton is a research fellow at CASE, where her research centres on relationships between poverty, place and education, and on the interaction of urban, neighbourhood and housing policy with educational policy and outcomes. She was a specialist adviser to the House of Commons Select Committee on Education and Skills in its inquiry into the 2006 schools White Paper. Recent relevant publications include: editing a special issue of the *Journal of Education Policy* on 'Schools and the urban renaissance' (2008, vol 23, no 2); and an article, with Martin Thrupp, in the *British Journal of Educational Studies* entitled 'Taking school contexts more seriously: the social justice challenge' (2006, vol 54, no 3).

Abigail McKnight is a senior research fellow at CASE. She is a labour economist and her research interests include low-wage employment, inequality in earnings and unemployment, evaluation of active labour market programmes designed to help the most disadvantaged in the labour market, and asset-based welfare. Recent publications include: *The Impact of Policy Change on Job Retention and Advancement* (CASE, 2008) and *Assimilation of Migrants into the British Labour Market* (CASE, 2008), both with Richard Dickens.

Coretta Phillips is a senior lecturer in social policy at the London School of Economics and Political Science. Her research interests focus on ethnicities, racism, crime and criminal justice. Recent publications include: an article in *Theoretical Criminology* entitled 'Negotiating identities: ethnicity and social relations in a young offenders' institution' (2008, vol 12, no 3); and, with Ben Bowling, an article in *Modern Law Review* entitled 'Disproportionate and discriminatory: reviewing the evidence on police stop and search' (2007, vol 70, no 6).

Anne Power is Professor of Social Policy at the London School of Economics and Political Science. Her research interests include cities and sustainable development; disadvantaged and run-down neighbourhoods and communities; UK, European and international urban problems, housing and social change. Recent publications include: *City Survivors: Bringing Up Children in Disadvantaged Neighbourhoods* (The Policy Press, 2007); and, with John Houghton, *Jigsaw Cities: Big Places, Small Spaces* (The Policy Press, 2007).

Jill Rutter is a senior research fellow in the migration team at the Institute for Public Policy Research (ippr). Prior to ippr, Jill was a university lecturer and from 1988 to 2001 she was a policy adviser at the Refugee Council, London. Her recent research has included studies on the Congolese community in the UK, on migrant integration and on the impact of migration on public services in the UK. Her publications include: *Refugee Children in the UK* (Open University Press, 2006); and *From Refugee to Citizen* (Refugee Support, 2007).

Emma Salter is a research officer at the Institute of Education, University of London. Her main research interests include the impact of physical and personal environments on young people's decisions and later life outcomes, health literacy and the benefits of education on social and personal development.

Franco Sassi is a senior lecturer in health policy in the Department of Social Policy at the London School of Economics and Political Science, and a health economist at the Organisation for Economic Co-operation and Development (OECD). He is a former Harkness Fellow in Health Care Policy (2000-01) and adviser to the European Office of the World Health Organization. His research interests include the economic evaluation of health interventions, inequalities in health and in access to healthcare, and tradeoffs between equity and efficiency in healthcare. He has recently been the author of a number of publications on the economics of chronic disease prevention, as a result of his work at the OECD.

Tom Sefton was formerly a research fellow at CASE and now works for the Church Urban Fund. His research interests include the distributional impact of government spending, public attitudes to the welfare state, pensions and fuel poverty. Recent publications include a chapter in the *British Social Attitudes 22nd Report* entitled 'Give and take: attitudes to redistribution (NatCen, 2005) and a chapter in the *Oxford Handbook of Public Policy* entitled 'Distributive and redistributive policy' (Oxford University Press, 2006).

Kitty Stewart is a lecturer in social policy at the London School of Economics and Political Science and a research associate (and former research fellow) at CASE. Her research interests include child poverty and disadvantage, international comparisons of policy and outcomes relating to poverty and inequality, and employment trajectories for the low skilled. Recent published work includes: a chapter in *Blair's Britain* (Cambridge University Press, 2007) entitled 'Equality and social justice'; and an article in the *Journal of European Social Policy* entitled 'A share of new growth for children? Policies for the very young in non-EU Europe and the CIS' (2009, vol 19, no 2).

Holly Sutherland is a research professor at the Institute for Social and Economic Research at the University of Essex. She coordinates the development and use of the European Union tax-benefit microsimulation model, EUROMOD. Her recent research interests include developing microsimulation as a tool for international comparative research, understanding the distributional and gender effects of social policies, and child poverty measurement and analysis. Her recent publications include a co-authored chapter with Horacio Levy and Christine Lietz entitled 'A guaranteed income for Europe's children?' in *Inequality and Poverty Re-examined* (Oxford University Press, 2007) and an article entitled 'Swapping policies: alternative tax-benefit strategies to support children in Austria, Spain and the UK' in the *Journal of Social Policy* (2007, vol 36, no 4).

Polly Vizard is a research fellow at CASE. Her research interests include poverty, inequality, the capability approach and human rights. Recent publications include *Poverty and Human Rights: Sen's Capability Perspective Explored* (Oxford University Press, 2006).

ONE

Introduction

Kitty Stewart, Tom Sefton and John Hills

Soon after it was elected in 1997, Tony Blair's 'New Labour' government became embroiled in a row about the implementation of cuts in benefits for lone parents that had been set in train by the outgoing administration. The decision to press ahead with the cuts prompted condemnation from those who had expected a Labour government to hold the reduction of poverty and inequality as a central aim, and led to a backbench rebellion of 47 Members of Parliament (MPs) just seven months after the 1997 General Election. In the late spring of 2008, another huge row broke out over the treatment of those with low incomes, as it became visible that the abolition of the initial 10 pence rate of Income Tax, announced the year before, was leading to losses in the pay packets of low-paid workers who were not protected by offsetting changes in the tax-benefit system. This time the backbench revolt led to an emergency announcement of increased tax allowances to come later in the year, but public opinion polls and lost by-elections suggested that huge damage had been done to the government's – and particularly the new Prime Minister, Gordon Brown's – reputation for being on the side of the poor.

These two events bracket the period that we cover in this book – one of sustained economic growth and low unemployment, which at the time of writing appears to have come to an end. Are these events symbolic of an era of missed opportunities, even betrayal? Or are they moments of aberration for a government that has made a concerted effort to counter the forces that had led to huge growth in inequality, relative poverty and other aspects of social exclusion in the 1980s and early 1990s?

Shortly after the 1997 General Election, one of New Labour's architects, Peter Mandelson, challenged the 'doubters' to 'judge us after ten years of success in office. For one of the fruits of that success will be that Britain has become a more equal society' (Mandelson, 1997, p 7). We now have evidence allowing us to examine outcomes for those 10 years – the whole of Tony Blair's premiership and Gordon Brown's period as Chancellor of the Exchequer. Have policy initiatives had an impact, been adequate for the challenges, and when successful, have they been sustained? Looking across a wide range of indicators and policy areas affecting poverty, inequality and social exclusion, this book asks whether Britain has indeed become a 'more equal society' than it was when New Labour was elected.

The scale of the problem

The Labour government that came to power in 1997 inherited levels of poverty and inequality unprecedented in post-war history. More than one in four UK children lived in relative poverty, compared with one in eight when Labour had left office in 1979 (DWP, 2004). Poverty among pensioners stood at 21%.[1] Income inequality had widened sharply: in 1979 the net incomes of the top tenth of the income distribution were about five times that of the bottom tenth; by the mid-1990s, that ratio had roughly doubled (Hills, 2004, table 2.5).

Figures 1.1 and 1.2 place the changes in poverty and inequality that Labour inherited in the perspective of longer-term historical trends. Levels of poverty and inequality fluctuated during the 1960s and declined in the 1970s before the sustained increase of the 1980s. By the early 1990s the lines on both figures had flattened out at what appeared to be a new plateau high above the original plain. Unlike every other post-war decade, in which the gains of economic growth were shared across income groups, growth in the 1980s benefited the richest most and the poorest least. Indeed, on one measure, the incomes of the very poorest were *lower* in real terms in 1994/95 than they had been in 1979 (Hills, 2004, figure 2.7).

Figure 1.1: Poverty in the UK: share of the population with below half average income by household type, 1961-97

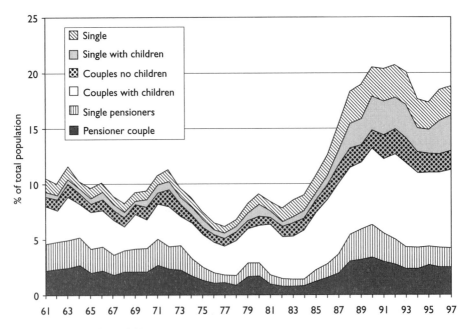

Source: Hills (2004, figure 3.1)

Figure 1.2: Inequality in the UK: the Gini Coefficient, 1961-97

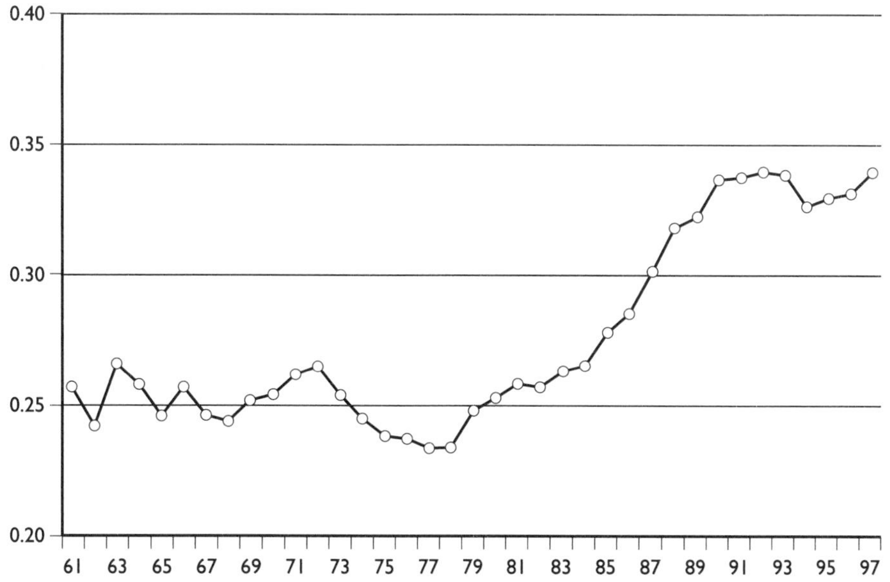

Note: The Gini takes a value of zero for a completely equal distribution and 1 if one person has all
the income and the rest none.
Source: IFS Inequality and Poverty Spreadsheet.

Several factors contributed to this sharp rise in income inequality and poverty,
including higher rates of household worklessness, widening earnings disparities,
and the impact of certain government policies. Unemployment was already
high by historical standards in 1979, but rose sharply during the early 1980s
(see Figure 1.3), passing the three million mark in 1983, as Margaret Thatcher's
government sought to bring down inflation with higher interest rates and taxes,
even at the cost of deepening recession. After falling during the late 1980s boom,
International Labour Organisation (ILO) unemployment peaked at nearly 11% in
1993, before another period of growth brought it down to around 7% in 1997,
approaching its 1979 level. However, the allocation of jobs across households had
changed markedly over the period, with growing polarisation between households
with two earners and those with no one in work, partly driven by the growing
incidence of lone parenthood. By 1997, more than 16% of households had no
member in work, more than twice the 1979 level (Gregg et al, 1999a), and the
share of children in workless households was higher than anywhere else in the
industrialised world (OECD, 1998; Gregg et al, 1999a). Long-term unemployment
was also a continuing problem: around a quarter of the unemployed had been
out of work for more than two years, a share only slightly lower than that at the
height of the 1990s recession. And youth unemployment was still substantially
above the average at 13% in 1997. Both long-term and youth unemployment

Figure 1.3: UK unemployment rate (ILO definition), 1971-97

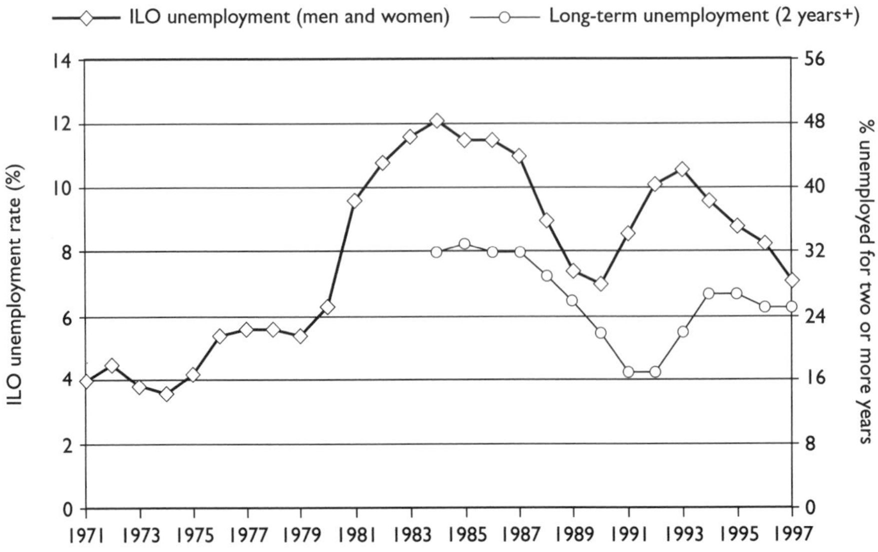

| ——◇—— ILO unemployment (men and women) | ——○—— Long-term unemployment (2 years+) |

Source: Office for National Statistics

were of particular concern because of the scarring effects of persistent or early unemployment on future employment prospects.

Another striking phenomenon of the 1980s and early 1990s was the rapid growth in earnings disparities: while the top tenth of male earners saw their wages rise by around 40% or more in real terms over this period, wages for the bottom tenth stagnated. In part, these developments were linked to a decline in the demand for unskilled labour and increased premiums for skills and qualifications, in turn linked to technological change. These same pressures were evident in many countries, but the UK was affected more than most. The high proportion of the workforce with low qualifications made the UK particularly vulnerable, but the effects were exacerbated by government action to curb trade union powers and abolish minimum wage protection. The impact on household incomes was reinforced by discretionary changes in the tax–benefit system. Benefits were made less generous with the aim of reducing welfare dependency and encouraging personal responsibility by making life on benefits less attractive. Higher rates of tax on top incomes were cut to reward high earners, and there was an increased reliance on indirect taxation, by its nature regressive.

The UK's relative performance on poverty and inequality deteriorated sharply during this period. Figure 1.4 shows the change in income inequality between the start of the 1980s and the mid-1990s for the UK and 10 other industrialised countries with available data. The most equal countries saw slight increases in the Gini coefficient, but the biggest increases were in Australia, the US and – most strikingly – the UK. By the mid-1990s, inequality was higher in the UK than

Figure 1.4: Changes in the Gini coefficient across countries during the 1980s and early 1990s

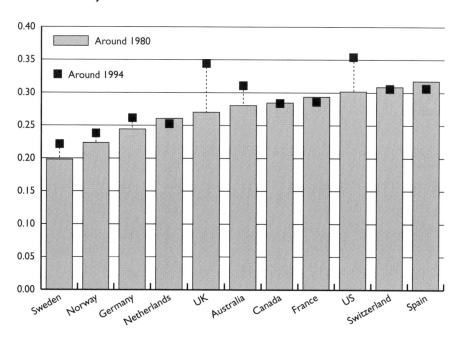

Note: Data for each country as follows. France and the US 1979, 1994; Norway and of the UK 197 1995; Spain 1980, 1990; Australia, Canada and Germany 1981, 1994; Sweden 1981, 1995; Switzerland 1982, 1992; Netherlands 1983, 1994.
Source: Luxembourg Income Study (www.lisproject.org, 23 May 2004)

in any other country represented except the US. A comparison of child poverty in 15 Organisation for Economic Co-operation and Development (OECD) countries placed the UK third from bottom: only the US and Italy had a higher percentage of children living in relatively poor households in the mid-1990s (UNICEF, 2000).

In addition, public services had suffered from two decades of declining investment and relatively low spending growth, especially on education. The explicit goal of the Conservative Party's social policy in the 1980s and early 1990s had been to 'roll back the state' as high levels of public spending were held largely responsible for Britain's economic difficulties in the 1970s. The average growth in total expenditure during the Conservative years was 1.5% per annum, significantly below the long-term trend of 2.6% per annum for the whole period since 1963-64, and net public sector investment was cut drastically (see Table 1.1). Relative public sector pay was also allowed to fall significantly, with nurses, teachers and manual workers hardest hit, contributing to low morale, staff shortages and high rates of staff turnover in some of the most important areas of the public sector (Nickell and Quintini, 2002). Ironically, given the aim of reducing welfare dependency, one of the fastest-growing areas was social security transfers: these

Table 1.1: Long-term trends in public spending in the six main areas

	Annualised average real increase (%)		% of GDP	
	Long-term trend[1]	April 1979- March 1997	1978-79	1996-97
NHS	3.7	3.1	4.5	5.3
Education	4.0	1.5	5.3	4.7
Social security	3.7	3.5	9.8	12.5
Defence	−0.3	−0.3	4.4	2.9
Transport	n/a	0.5	1.7	1.3
Public order and safety	n/a	4.1	1.5	2.1
Total Managed Expenditure	2.5	1.5	45.2	40.8
of which:				
Net investment	−0.9	−4.3	2.4	0.8
Current spending	2.8	1.7	42.8	40.0
GDP	2.4	2.1	100.0	100.0

Notes: [1] Long-term trends cover the following periods: NHS: April 1950 to March 2004; Education: January 1953 to December 1996; Social security: January 1949 to December 2000; Defence: January 1954 to December 1996; TME, net investment, current spending and GDP: April 1964 to March 2004.

Source: Emmerson et al (2004, tables 4.1 and 4.2)

increased as a share of total spending from around 22% in 1979 to nearly 31% in 1996-97, largely due to high levels of unemployment and economic inactivity and rising social sector rents.

As well as spending cuts, public sector reforms aimed to increase the role of the market, even in areas that had previously been firmly in the public domain, such as health and education. Presented in terms of promoting choice and efficiency, reforms encouraged greater use of privately funded or provided welfare services and paid little heed to, and arguably exacerbated, inequalities in health and education outcomes. The social class gradient in life expectancy, child mortality and smoking steepened in the 1990s, while the rapid expansion in higher education in the late 1980s and 1990s mostly benefited children from better-off families. The strengthening of the link between parental income and educational attainment was one factor behind a marked decline in intergenerational income mobility in the UK between the cohorts born in 1958 and 1970 (Blanden et al, 2005). Other social changes associated with growing inequality were also becoming increasingly evident, for example high levels of homelessness among families, and a rise in drug offences and suicide rates among young men (Bradshaw, 1999).

To add to the scale of the challenge New Labour faced, several of the underlying drivers of rising inequality showed no sign of slowing down. Earnings inequality was still rising, albeit perhaps more slowly than in the 1980s, and lone parenthood continued to increase. On the other hand, the macro-environment was strong: the economy was growing relatively fast, unemployment was falling and inflation was relatively low. This promised the economic stability and resources for a concerted attack on poverty and for increased public sector investment, although past experience suggested that strong economic growth could exacerbate underlying inequality as those dependent on state benefits are left behind.

Finally, it is important not to underestimate the actual and perceived constraints on the Labour Party resulting from the prevailing political climate after 20 years of Conservative rule. The dominant economic orthodoxy had moved away from Keynesianism, demand management and a belief that government could ensure full employment to embrace a more US-style laissez-faire capitalism, which gave prominence to efficiency considerations with almost no regard to equity. As noted above, many of the corporatist relations between the state, firms and unions were swept away as the Thatcher government sought to create an unfettered free market. As part of a concerted effort to 'roll back the state', public spending was constrained, top tax rates reduced and market reforms introduced in the provision of public services such as health, education and prisons. Benefit recipients, in particular lone parents and the unemployed, were negatively portrayed by government ministers and in the press and held increasingly responsible for their own circumstances. Redistribution was not a concern, because it was implicitly assumed that those lower down the income distribution would benefit from a more dynamic and efficient economy as the fruits of economic growth would 'trickle down' from top to bottom.

The responses of Conservative ministers and MPs to a Joseph Rowntree Foundation report that charted the sharp increase in poverty and inequality since 1979 (Barclay, 1995) provide an insight into the way these issues were viewed by the government of the time. In a House of Commons debate, Peter Lilley, then Secretary of State for Social Security, and his party colleagues strongly rebutted the report's analysis, arguing that real poverty in Britain did not exist; that ownership of household appliances showed that living standards were rising even for the lowest-income households; and that high-income mobility ensured that those on low incomes did not remain so for long (subsequently challenged by research; see Jenkins and Rigg, 2001). Low out-of-work benefits were defended as crucial to maintaining incentives to work, which in turn was seen as the best or only route out of poverty. Income inequalities were argued to be a fair reward for talent and hard work and to be good for competitiveness and therefore for everyone including the poor, while 'traditional' approaches to tackling poverty and inequality were dismissed as unaffordable and outdated.[2]

By the mid-1990s, many of the attitudes and assumptions espoused by successive Conservative governments had become part of the prevailing wisdom, strongly influencing both the rhetoric used by the Labour leadership to frame any discussion of welfare reform and the means by which they pursued their social justice agenda, even though they rejected the more extreme ideological beliefs of their predecessors.

The next section looks at how the incoming government faced up to the challenges sketched out above, and how its approach has evolved across a decade in power.

The government's strategy

A radical dawn?

In an interview shortly before the 1997 General Election, Tony Blair claimed that he was going to be 'a lot more radical in government than many people think' (*The Observer*, 27 April 1997), underlining the cautious promises with which the Labour Party had approached the election. Given Labour's electoral history in the 1980s and early 1990s its attitude was understandable. After the 1992 defeat, the need to reposition the party had grown in urgency, and when Tony Blair took over the leadership on John Smith's death in 1994 he made it clear that he intended to 'build a new coalition of support, based on a broad national appeal that transcends traditional electoral divisions' (Blair, 1994, p 7).

By 1997 Labour had abandoned its traditional tax and spend commitments, distanced itself from the unions and shed any commitment to securing full employment. Its 1997 election manifesto contained just six references to poverty and two (very general) references to inequality. The biggest changes proposed were arguably the constitutional reforms, including the reform of the House of Lords and devolution for Scotland and Wales. On the other hand, the manifesto did strongly emphasise the need to address educational disadvantage, promised the introduction of a National Minimum Wage and pledged to tackle long-term unemployment, particularly among young people.

Blair's rhetoric prior to the election contained only the occasional reference to poverty. In January 1996, he proclaimed that 'for the new Millennium we need a war on exclusion and a determination to extend opportunity to all' (Levitas, 2000, p 363). In July of the same year, he wrote in the *Independent on Sunday*: 'If the next Labour Government has not raised the living standards of the poorest by the end of its time in office, it will have failed' (Blair, 1996). Under some definitions, the living standards of the poorest had risen slightly even under Thatcher, so this was a modest ambition. However, as Labour minister Margaret Hodge would put it in 2000, 'in the latter days of Opposition, few Labour politicians chose to promote equality for fear of losing electoral support' (Hodge, 2000, p 34). 'Have faith' was Blair's message to his critics on the Left (Blair, 1996). It was impossible to know whether Labour's goals would become more ambitious once it was safely in office.

New Labour in office: the first term

In their analysis of New Labour's first term, Toynbee and Walker (2001) point to Blair's visit to a Peckham estate in June 1997 as the first clear indication that poverty and disadvantage were on the government's agenda. In what was particularly significant for being his first major speech as Prime Minister outside the House of Commons, Blair promised 'no forgotten people and no no-hope areas', committing the government to addressing 'the dead weight of low expectations, the crushing belief that things cannot get better' (Toynbee and Walker, 2001, p 10).

Within months, social exclusion had become a central government concept. In August 1997, Peter Mandelson announced the creation of the Social Exclusion Unit (SEU), denouncing the 'scourge and waste of social exclusion' as 'the greatest social crisis of our times' (Mandelson, 1997, pp 6 and 9). Social exclusion was never formally defined, but it was clear from the series of attempts to explain the concept that the government's concern was with multiple deprivation. At the SEU launch in December 1997, Blair described it as 'about income but ... about more. It is about prospects and networks and life-chances' (quoted in Fairclough, 2000, p 52). Later, he would define it as 'a short-hand label for what can happen when individuals or areas suffer from a combination of linked problems such as unemployment, poor skills, low incomes, poor housing, high crime environments, bad health and family breakdown' (DSS, 1999, p 23). The SEU was seen as important precisely because of the interrelations between these different problems: it would coordinate policy across departments to provide 'joined-up government for joined-up problems'.

The announcement of the SEU's programme for the first six months made it clear that income poverty was not part of its brief: the first areas to be looked at were school exclusions, rough sleeping, and poor areas, followed by teenage pregnancy and 16- to 18-year-olds not in education, training or employment. In a letter to the *Financial Times*, 54 social policy and sociology professors welcomed the establishment of the SEU but argued that, by ignoring the need for income redistribution, the government was trying 'to tackle social exclusion with one hand tied behind its back' (Lister and Moore, 1997).

However, the fact that redistribution was not part of the SEU's brief did not necessarily mean that material poverty was being ignored. The Treasury kept firm control of tax-benefit policy from the start, and the SEU agenda was consistent with a strict division of labour between the two bodies. One of Gordon Brown's first priorities at the Treasury was a welfare-to-work programme. As promised in New Labour's election manifesto, the first Labour Budget in July 1997 announced that a windfall levy on privatised utilities – the only major source of additional funds available during the first two years in office – would be used to fund a New Deal for Young People, with part of the money set aside for a New Deal for Lone Parents. On the day after the election, Brown told the Treasury to start developing plans for a tax credit scheme for the working poor (*The Guardian*, 26 November 1997), formally announced in the March 1998 Budget as the Working Families' Tax Credit (WFTC). A commission to investigate a starting level for the National Minimum Wage was also established in these first few weeks. In his 1997 conference speech, Brown announced that full employment would be a government goal – a demand that had been ridiculed by Conservative ministers and the press when made by the Trades Union Congress (TUC) just three years earlier (TUC, 2007) and which had been dropped as a Labour objective in the 1990s. In practice, it would soon become apparent that by 'full employment' Brown meant 'employment opportunity for all' (HM Treasury, 1997).

The emphasis on work-based policies reflected Brown's belief (not an original belief, as the *Hansard* records of the 1995 House of Commons debate mentioned on page 7 above make clear) that 'the most serious cause of poverty is unemployment' (Brown, 1997). But while the WFTC proposals received a cautious welcome as a means of boosting the incomes of low-paid workers, they did not allay the concerns of those worried about people unable to work for a wide range of reasons. The row that broke out in late 1997 over cuts in benefits for lone parents reinforced the initial impression that work was considered the only solution to poverty.

The March 1998 Budget was therefore significant, as it represented the first move to raise benefits for those out of work; further increases for non-working households with children would follow. Then, shortly after Budget Day 1999, at a lecture to commemorate William Beveridge, Tony Blair made his now famous pledge to eradicate poverty among children: 'Our historic aim will be for ours to be the first generation to end child poverty. It is a 20-year mission, but I believe it can be done' (Blair, 1999, p 17). Sources inside the Treasury suggest that not even the civil servants who wrote the speech were expecting this and that it was a last-minute and unilateral decision taken by Blair. This was followed up with concrete interim targets – to reduce child poverty by a quarter by 2004-05 and by half by 2010 – with poverty defined in relative terms and set at 60% of contemporary median income; a difficult target to meet while incomes are rising.

Despite the gentle overtures of the 1998 and 1999 Budgets, it is widely agreed that Blair's Beveridge speech marked a sea-change in both the government's language and its policy approach (Lister, 2001; Deacon, 2003). There is less consensus about where this change came from (see Deacon, 2003). The announcement coincided with the end of the commitment to stick to Conservative spending plans: Blair may have felt free to announce openly a goal he had had all along. Alternatively, it may have been a reaction to the rebellion over lone-parent benefit cuts.

A third factor is likely to have been a growing recognition of the extent to which opportunities available to adults are diminished by the experience of poverty in childhood. In a pamphlet on the 'Third Way' in 1998, Blair had declared the four values 'essential to a just society' to be 'equal worth, opportunity for all, responsibility and community' (Blair, 1998, p 3), and since then opportunity had become a government watchword. At about the same time as the Beveridge speech, the Treasury released a report based on research into the dynamics of opportunity (CASE and HM Treasury, 1999). The message that emerged about the long-term scarring effects of child poverty was clear.

Beyond the child poverty pledge, 1999 saw the opportunities agenda developing into a wider strategy, with the announcement of an annual audit of poverty and social exclusion – *Opportunity for All* (OFA) (DSS, 1999). *Opportunity for All* summarises government thinking on these issues in 1999 – a sort of second manifesto, and one offering a vision hugely different from and more ambitious than the manifesto for the 1997 election. The key features of the 'complex, multidimensional problems' of poverty and social exclusion were listed as:

- lack of opportunities to work;
- lack of opportunities to acquire education and skills;
- childhood deprivation;
- disrupted families;
- barriers to older people living active, fulfilling and healthy lives;
- inequalities in health;
- poor housing;
- poor neighbourhoods;
- fear of crime; and
- disadvantage or discrimination on grounds of age, ethnicity, gender or disability (DSS, 1999, p 2).

The report promised 'an integrated and radical policy response' to these combined problems (DSS, 1999, p 23), and emphasised the importance of long-term solutions, and of flexible action geared to local needs. At its heart, it put forward four policy priorities:

- tackling childhood deprivation;
- promoting employment;
- alleviating the plight of pensioners; and
- pursuing area-based solutions to social exclusion.

Many of the OFA themes were echoed in New Labour's election manifesto for 2001. In contrast not just to the 1997 manifesto, but also to election manifestos throughout the 20th century (see Kenway, 2003), poverty was mentioned 20 times in a domestic context; all were references to children and pensioners. Opportunity or opportunities (in the relevant sense) were mentioned no less than 42 times. The manifesto also pledged to tackle the 'long-standing causes of ill-health and health inequality' (Labour Party, 2001, p 21) – one of just two references to inequality, the second relating to the gender pay gap.

Into a second (and third) term: New Labour 2001-07

The opportunities agenda remained central for New Labour as it embarked on a second term. In 2001, the National Strategy for Neighbourhood Renewal set out a vision that 'within 10-20 years, no-one should be seriously disadvantaged by where they live' (SEU, 2001, p 8). This followed up on the introduction of 'floor targets' in 2000 – for the first time, government departments would be judged on the areas that were doing worst, not on the national average (see Chapter Six). At the 2002 Labour Party Conference, Gordon Brown made a pledge to abolish pensioner poverty. This was not accompanied by explicitly quantified targets, but the second term saw both a number of key reforms to current provision for pensioners (such as the introduction of Pension Credit in 2003) and the establishment of the independent Pensions Commission to look forward. The 2007 and 2008 Pensions Acts, which implemented many of the Commission's recommendations, are described in Chapter Eight as 'the most radical overhaul of the pensions system since 1948'. Among the goals were the reduction of future pensioner poverty and the achievement of fairer outcomes for women and carers.

In 2003 the Department for Work and Pensions (DWP) reported on the child poverty measure to be used for the 2010 and 2020 targets – measures of absolute poverty and material deprivation had been added, but, crucially, the central relative poverty target remained (DWP, 2003). Further changes to the benefit system were introduced, including the switch to Working Tax Credit and Child Tax Credit in April 2003. New and more ambitious targets for reducing health inequalities were introduced as part of the 2004 Spending Review.

Opportunity for All update reports continued to be published annually up to and including 2006, along with progress in the most recent year and since the baseline on a wide range of indicators (see Chapter Sixteen). In 2007, the indicators were published but not the report, with the DWP explaining on its website that 'many challenges still remain' and that 'tackling these challenges requires a new focus' (www.dwp.gov.uk/ofa/indicators).

New Labour's 2005 manifesto gave significant prominence to equality and human rights issues, announcing major new policy initiatives to introduce a Single Equality Act and an Equality and Human Rights Commission (the new Commission assumed its responsibilities in 2007; see Chapter Fourteen). These commitments signalled a significant increase in the momentum of Labour's programme of equality and human rights reform, following the passing of the Human Rights Act early in its first term. The manifesto also pledged to take forward the Strategy for Race Equality.

However, while in many respects this is clearly a rich and ongoing agenda, it is possible to identify a slowing in momentum from 2003-04 onwards, with other concerns – domestic and international – taking centre stage. The fate of the SEU is perhaps symbolic of a gradual shift in priorities over New Labour's second and third terms. In 2002, the SEU was moved out of the Cabinet Office to the new Office of the Deputy Prime Minister; in the Cabinet Office it had reported directly to Tony Blair and the subsequent move was a clear shift away from the centre of power. In 2006, it was closed altogether and its work transferred to a smaller taskforce, back in the Cabinet Office, but with a much narrower focus on the most severely excluded. The government's adoption of the term 'high cost, high harm' to describe the families of concern caused considerable consternation and was soon dropped (see, for example, House of Commons Treasury Committee, 2007).

Three main issues can be identified that affected progress in the second half of the Blair era. First, foreign affairs increasingly dominated the government's attention – and resources – as the build-up to the Iraq war began in 2003. The conflict would outlast Blair's premiership and while its impact on domestic policy is impossible to measure, it is likely to have been substantial.

Second, a gradually slowing economy placed an increasing constraint on public finances. Strong economic growth during New Labour's first two terms financed rapid growth in public expenditure (Chote et al, 2008). But gross domestic product (GDP) growth fell to a 13-year low of 1.8% in 2005, rallied slightly in 2006 and 2007 and then dipped sharply (ONS, 2008f). Spending growth slowed from around 2005-06 by enough to allow Gordon Brown to narrowly meet his own 'golden rule' assuming a 10-year economic cycle (all current spending to be financed from tax and other revenues over the cycle) (Chote et al, 2008, table 3.1). But the current account balance was in deficit every year from 2002-03 to 2006-07, with large and growing deficits predicted for 2007-08 and 2008-09; a very different outlook to that a decade earlier (Chote et al, 2008, figure 3.4).

Third, Blair devoted increasing attention to reforms aimed at expanding choice and competitiveness in the public sector. He described the 2005 Queen's Speech as 'quintessentially New Labour: economic prosperity combined with social justice' (*Hansard*, House of Commons Debates, 17 May 2005, column 45) but the public sector reform agenda was given far greater emphasis during the third term than policies to tackle disadvantage. In May 2005, in his first press conference after New Labour's third election victory, Blair argued that:

> [O]ur task is to deepen the change, accelerate reform and address head-on the priorities of the British people in the NHS [National Health Service], schools and welfare reform…. [Reform] means driving innovation and improvement through more diverse provision and putting people into the driving seat. (BBC news website, 12 May, http://news.bbc.co.uk/1/hi/uk_politics/4540723.stm)

Quite a contrast from the Peckham speech of 1997. Towards the end of his leadership, in April 2007, it was on public sector reform, not social justice, that his close friend Lord Falconer said that Blair wished he had moved more quickly

(*The Guardian*, 30 April 2007). Some have argued that these reforms were not merely a distraction from, but actively counterproductive to, the goal of widening opportunities, and acted to increase inequalities in access to health services and education (see Chapters Four, Seven and Nine).

In addition, we can point to areas that were never given a place on the agenda. There has been little attention given to workless adults without children who are not registered disabled, discussed in Chapter Two. Burchardt (2005) has described the increasing exclusion of asylum seekers and their children from benefits, employment, local authority housing and education.

Perhaps most striking, however, has been the explicit avoidance of any focus on overall income inequality, and in particular the growing gap between average living standards and those of the very rich. The pursuit of greater equality has frequently been dismissed by the Labour leadership as seeking to place an arbitrary cap on individuals' aspirations, although not everyone in the Labour Party has been so relaxed. In 2003, for example, Labour minister Peter Hain called for a public debate about raising Income Tax for those with very high incomes, but was quickly slapped down, and the issue also surfaced briefly during the 2007 deputy leadership contest. The establishment of a National Equality Panel in September 2008 may signal a renewed interest in inequality, although it is too early at the time of writing to assess the significance of this development.

The failure to engage with what is happening at the top end of the income distribution was also justified by some Labour politicians on the basis that it is more important to help the poorest, given economic and political constraints (for example Miliband, 2005). This, of course, presupposes that there is a trade-off between the two goals – that putting more effort into reducing inequality might jeopardise progress in reducing poverty or divert resources away from that goal. Two leading thinkers on the Left – Diamond and Giddens – lent their support to a slightly different proposition: that inequalities of income and wealth should only be limited if they are hindering the realisation of other social justice goals, including fighting poverty (Diamond and Giddens, 2005). In effect, inequality should be treated as a possible constraint on the achievement of other objectives, rather than as a goal in its own right. The following statement by Yvette Cooper, now Chief Secretary to the Treasury, suggests that this view had support within government:

> We should do more to address wealth inequality in Britain, not least because we don't want it to become a brake on progress in other areas. But we should not let up in the bigger battle to cut poverty and raise family incomes and opportunities to build a fairer society. (*The Guardian*, 22 March 2005)

In response to the question of whether inequality is impeding progress in other areas, there is good evidence that inequality per se is associated with poorer health outcomes, lower levels of interpersonal trust, higher rates of violent crime and other negative social outcomes (see, for example, Hsieh and Pugh, 1993; Kawachi et al, 1997; Wilkinson and Pickett, 2006) – and that, although harder to establish, reducing poverty and increasing opportunity is more difficult where there are large disparities in income and accumulated wealth (see, for example, Jackson and Segal, 2004; Esping-Andersen, 2005). As Lister (2001, p 438) puts it, 'equality of opportunity in the context of economic and social structures that remain profoundly unequal is likely to remain a contradiction in terms'. Furthermore, there is growing recognition that inequality affects those in the middle, as well as those at the bottom. Robert Frank (2007), for example, argued that rising inequality puts pressure on the middle classes to work harder and spend increasing amounts on 'positional' goods, such as larger houses, in an 'arms race' that leaves them worse off.

The Labour government under Brown

The start of Gordon Brown's era as Prime Minister in June 2007 brought with it high hopes of a renewed emphasis on social justice and perhaps a more overtly egalitarian agenda. In his first speech as Labour Leader, he described himself as a 'conviction politician' and emphasised the values that had led him to join the Labour Party: 'Wherever we find opportunity denied, aspirations unfulfilled, potential unrealised; wherever and whenever we find injustice and unfairness, there we must be also – and it is our duty to act' (Brown, 2007a).

One of Brown's first acts was to abandon well-developed plans for a new super-casino, a surprise move that cheered those who had seen Labour's support for casinos as placing the priorities of big business above the interests of vulnerable individuals.

But what followed in Brown's first year fell short of those expectations. The 2008 Budget contained the biggest increase since 2004 in tax credits for families with children, and given tight fiscal conditions the additional annual £0.9 billion committed was interpreted by some as a signal that reducing child poverty was still a high priority. However, the sum was only a quarter of that needed to keep the 2010 target in sight: the Institute for Fiscal Studies estimated that a further £2.8 billion a year would need to be announced in autumn 2009 for an evens chance of meeting the target (Brewer et al, 2008a). At the same time, 2008 saw a shift in the language used to talk about child poverty, with an increased focus on parental responsibility – Brown introduced the notion of a 'contract out of poverty' – and on the role of local authorities and the voluntary sector. This has been interpreted by some as an abdication of central government responsibility, especially given the limited increases in tax credits in recent years and the absence of a wider strategy for reducing in-work poverty.

In keeping with the 'contract out of poverty', there have been indications of a move towards much greater conditionality in the provision of state benefits. A new welfare reform Bill announced in July 2008 included proposals to remove Incapacity Benefit from drug users who refuse to take part in treatment and to abolish Income Support in favour of Jobseeker's Allowance. The proposals also pointed to a greater continuity of thinking and approach with the Blair era than might have been expected. But two issues had already delivered more serious blows to Brown's egalitarian credentials.

The first was the abolition of the 10 pence tax rate. Its introduction in 1997 had been one of Gordon Brown's early pro-poor moves as Chancellor and its abolition a decade later (purportedly to simplify the system) would overshadow the first year of his premiership as it became apparent that not all those affected had been adequately compensated in the initial plans, and with still only partial compensation through higher tax allowances added from October 2008.

Second were the changes to Inheritance Tax in autumn 2007. In reaction to Conservative proposals to raise the threshold for Inheritance Tax from £300,000 to £1 million, the government did not argue the case for a tax that in 2007 only affected the top 6% of estates, but announced an increase in the threshold to £600,000 at an estimated cost of £1.3 billion per annum by 2010-11.

It was only by November 2008, in its plans for recouping some of the budget deficits following from the financial crisis of that autumn, that there was a clear break with the 'New Labour' period. Contrasting with commitments in the last three elections not to raise rates of Income Tax, if the government is re-elected, a 45% rate will apply from 2011-12 on incomes above £150,000, while tax-free allowances will be reduced or phased out for those above £100,000 from 2010-11. Together, the government hopes these will raise £2 billion per year from the top 2% of taxpayers (HM Treasury, 2008d, table B5).

Outline of the book

As sketched out above, the period since 1997 has not seen an all-out war on poverty, inequality and exclusion. There have been moments of great hope and inspiration for those hoping that a Labour government would herald a move towards a more equal and inclusive society, and moments of extreme disappointment and frustration. However, amid the highs and lows, the government has delivered an extensive and sustained policy effort across a wide range of areas. A broad and ambitious social policy programme has attempted to tackle child and pensioner poverty, unemployment and worklessness, area and neighbourhood deprivation, inequalities in health and educational attainment and inequalities by ethnic background. This book brings together evidence on each of these domains from an extensive range of sources – government and independent documents and reports, secondary analysis of large-scale datasets and, in Chapter Six, qualitative evidence collected by researchers at the Centre for Analysis of Social Exclusion (CASE) – with the aim of providing a balanced assessment of more than a decade of New Labour government.

Following this introduction, the book is divided into three parts. The chapters in Part One examine policy and outcomes in a particular area. Authors of chapters in this part of the book were asked to consider four questions in particular. First, did the original policies match the scale of the challenge faced by New Labour in 1997? Second, how did policy develop over the decade – was momentum maintained or intensified, or did policy change direction or run out of steam? Third and fourth, were the original objectives met, and if not, why not: was it perhaps because problems were greater than anticipated or because policies were inappropriate, inadequate or not carried through?

Chapter Two, by Tom Sefton, John Hills and Holly Sutherland, sets the scene for the rest of the book by examining what is perhaps the bottom line – the evidence on income poverty and income inequality. Their assessment includes the results of micro-simulation, which allow them to separate the effects of tax-benefit policy from the effects of demographic and labour market changes, addressing the tricky question of the counterfactual: what would have happened in the absence of policy changes. They also look at the distributional impact of public expenditure on benefits in kind such as health and education. Inequality measures generally exclude benefits in kind, but as public spending tends to be higher on poorer households, increases in spending can make a significant difference to the state's overall redistributive impact.

The remaining eight chapters in Part One focus on either a particular group or policy area. In Chapter Three, Kitty Stewart looks at the government's efforts to improve living standards and opportunities for the poorest children. She assesses progress towards the child poverty targets as well as the impact of early years policies, intended to stop a class divide in child development from being established long before children reach school. In Chapter Four, Ruth Lupton, Natalie Heath and Emma Salter examine the success of education policy – Labour's top priority in every manifesto – in reducing inequalities in educational attainment in compulsory and post-compulsory education.

In Chapter Five, Abigail McKnight considers the impact of New Labour policies on inequalities in the labour market, focusing in particular on the experiences of previously disadvantaged groups: younger and older workers, the long-term unemployed, lone parents, disabled persons, and women. Chapter Six, by Anne Power, considers the government's attempts to regenerate poor neighbourhoods and inner cities, drawing on extensive work carried out by CASE researchers in 12 low-income areas across much of New Labour's period in office.

In Chapter Seven, Franco Sassi examines health inequalities, an area subject to considerable prominence, a number of targets and several government inquiries, but where policy action has been less clear. In Chapter Eight, on older people, Maria Evandrou and Jane Falkingham assess New Labour's progress towards its twin goals of tackling poverty and social exclusion among today's pensioners and ensuring that more of tomorrow's pensioners retire on a decent income.

In Chapter Nine, Coretta Phillips examines New Labour's strategies to reduce ethnic inequalities. She evaluates the impact of general policies and specifically targeted initiatives on longstanding inequalities between ethnic groups in education, employment and income, and policing. In the final chapter in Part One, Jill Rutter and Maria Latorre discuss challenges for poverty and inequality arising from higher levels of immigration. They examine both how migrant communities are faring in terms of labour market experiences and educational outcomes and possible effects of immigration on the employment prospects and wages of non-migrants.

The chapters in Part Two take a cross-cutting approach, each revisiting from a different viewpoint some of the policies and outcomes covered in Part One. In Chapter Eleven, Tom Sefton looks at public attitudes to inequality, poverty and redistribution, using quantitative and qualitative sources to ask whether public opinion has become more or less progressive since 1997 and whether New Labour's attempts to redefine the party have influenced the way people think about these issues. In Chapter Twelve, Tania Burchardt and Holly Holder explore the consequences of devolution for inequality. They discuss whether and why devolution might have been expected to have an impact on inequality within and between the four UK nations, and then look at the evidence, focusing on income and educational inequalities. In Chapter Thirteen, Kitty Stewart takes a wider cross-national perspective, asking whether a decade of Labour government has improved the UK's international standing on indicators of poverty, inequality and child well-being.

The first two chapters in Part Three are forward-looking. In Chapter Fourteen, Polly Vizard discusses equalities and human rights reform since 1997, arguing that recent legislation and the Equality and Human Rights Commission may herald a new era in the battle against persistent horizontal inequalities across gender, ethnic background, disability and sexuality. But Chapter Fifteen is less optimistic about the future for income inequality. In this chapter John Hills discusses four key factors that may make progress towards greater income equality increasingly challenging: the intergenerational transmission of advantage; wealth and inheritance; demographic change; and environmental sustainability.

Finally, Chapter Sixteen pulls together the threads of the book with the aim of reaching an overall assessment of the government's record since it came to power in 1997. Does the evidence of the previous chapters add up to a picture of substantial change, a serious assault on inherited levels of poverty, inequality and social exclusion? After more than a decade in government, how much of a difference can New Labour be said to have made? *Is* Britain a 'more equal society' than it was in 1997?

Notes
[1] In both cases, the poverty line is 60% of the equivalised contemporary median, and both are given for a 'before housing costs' income measure. After housing costs, child poverty was 34% in 1996-97 and pensioner poverty was 27%.

[2] House of Commons *Hansard* Debates for 14 February 1995 (columns 803-894).

Part One
Dimensions of policy and outcomes

TWO

Poverty, inequality and redistribution

Tom Sefton, John Hills and Holly Sutherland

Introduction

The previous Conservative government presided over a period of sharply rising income inequality: between 1979 and 1996-97, the median income of the richest tenth increased by more than 60% in real terms, but that of the poorest tenth rose by just 11% (or fell by 13% if incomes are measured after housing costs). Ultimately, many people's judgement of New Labour will rest on whether it has made progress towards reversing this trend towards greater inequality. This chapter focuses specifically on what has happened to income inequality and poverty and on the impact of the government's tax-benefit and spending policies, which are its most direct instrument for influencing the distribution of incomes.

New Labour's emphasis has been firmly on raising the living standards of the poorest, encapsulated in Blair's historic pledge in 1999 to end child poverty within a generation, rather than on seeking to reduce income inequality. Poverty was, however, to be defined in relative terms – and specifically in relation to median income, which rises over time in line with living standards in the rest of society. Although New Labour has rarely emphasised the redistributive impact of its tax-benefit policies, these have always been a vital component of its anti-poverty strategy in combination with a range of other policies designed to improve the life chances of the poorest, including the early years agenda, targeted measures to raise educational standards in the most deprived neighbourhoods, and welfare-to-work programmes (see Chapters Three, Four and Five).

New Labour's tax-benefit policies

From 1998, every Budget has included a section on 'building a fairer society' (or variants of this) from which it is possible to identify a fairly consistent set of principles underpinning the government's efforts to tackle poverty through the tax-benefit system. The first theme is work as the best route out of poverty and, therefore, the need to ensure that work pays. In its first Budget, New Labour announced its intention to introduce a National Minimum Wage (which came into effect in April 1999) as well as a more generous system of in-work tax credits for low-paid workers. The Working Families' Tax Credit (WFTC) replaced Family

Credit in 1999 for families with children (with much higher maximum awards and a more gradual taper) and was itself replaced by the Child Tax Credit (CTC) and Working Tax Credit (WTC) in 2003, which created a more integrated system of financial support for children and extended in-work benefits to families without children (though at a lower rate). Early changes in Income Tax were also designed to favour low earners, including a new 10 pence tax band and the removal of the entry charge for National Insurance contributions (both in 1999). The abolition of the 10 pence tax band in April 2008 was clearly a step in the opposite direction and only partially compensated for by increased tax credits and (at great cost) by the reactive increase in personal allowances announced in May 2008.

Another theme of New Labour's Budgets that emerged very early on was the strong emphasis on supporting families with children in recognition of the 'costs and responsibilities which come with parenthood' and the impact of child poverty on eventual adult outcomes. Financial support for children was initially to be built on universal Child Benefit (which was increased substantially for first or only children in 1999), but with extra resources targeted at families on low incomes in and out of work, largely through the tax credits system. The Married Couple's Allowance and its equivalent for lone parents were replaced by the Children's Tax Credit and then by the family element of the CTC, which were worth around twice as much as the Married Couple's Allowance, but restricted to families with children and tapered away for those on incomes taxed at the top rate. This approach was described as 'progressive universalism', giving (almost) everyone a stake in the system while offering more help to those who need it most. In practice, the progressivity of tax-benefit reforms has been more evident than their universalism, with most of the increase in child-contingent support concentrated on the income-related elements, presumably to maximise the impact on child poverty. One policy that went the other way was the decision to go ahead with the Conservative's plans to phase out One Parent Benefit and lone-parent premiums (1998), although lone parents have benefited substantially from subsequent increases in child-related benefits and tax credits.

A specific feature of the government's tax-benefit reforms has been the use of selective benefits to help parents or children at key stages, including more generous maternity grants (in 1999), higher and extended Statutory Maternity Pay (2002 and 2003 in particular), higher tax credits for families in the first year of their child's birth (2002) and higher benefits for parents with severely disabled children (from 2001). More recently, older children have been targeted with Education Maintenance Allowances (nationwide from 2004) and more generous benefits (2006) for those continuing in education and training. The cost of these measures is relatively small, but their impact is potentially significant for certain target groups.

A third objective has been to 'help pensioners share in the prosperity of the nation'. As with children, the emphasis has been on helping the poorest pensioners, with large increases in Income Support for older people (renamed Minimum

Income Guarantee in 1999 and then Pension Credit in 2003). The Savings Credit element of the Pension Credit extended support to many more pensioners with moderate incomes and savings. Apart from a step increase in the universal Basic State Pension in April 2001 (in response to the outcry over the 25 pence increase in the previous year), the Basic State Pension has risen broadly in line with prices (although with a commitment to earnings indexation probably from 2012). But, the government has introduced various universal cash payments and in-kind benefits for pensioners, including Winter Fuel Payments (introduced in 1999 and now worth up to £400 per year), free eye tests (1999), free television licences for those aged 75 or over (2001) and free local and nationwide bus travel (2006 and 2008 respectively). The government has also made several one-off payments, mainly to older pensioners, to help with their Council Tax bills (2003-04 to 2005-06 and again in 2008-09). In addition, age-related personal allowances have been raised by more than indexation, initially to compensate pensioners for the removal of the Married Couple's Allowance, but then as a stated policy to remove more pensioners from Income Tax.

The government has identified people with disabilities as a priority group in some Budgets and introduced the Disability Income Guarantee in 2001 to provide greater security for people with severe disabilities who cannot work. But the additional cost of this and other measures is very small by comparison with those targeted at children and pensioners – and, in its first year, the government implemented rules that made Incapacity Benefit less generous for some people receiving occupational pensions. For most working-age adults without children, benefits have only been raised in line with prices.

Taxation policy has not been used explicitly to redistribute incomes other than through tax credits. Through the period we cover, government kept its manifesto commitment not to raise the higher rate of Income Tax, although changes to National Insurance contributions have been progressive, including the additional 1% contribution rate on earnings above the Upper Earnings Limit (in 2003) and the step increase in the Upper Earnings Limit (in 2008).[1] But, other measures have been highly regressive, in particular changes in the taxation of capital gains in 1998 (only partly redressed in 2008) and higher and now transferable Inheritance Tax allowances (from 2005 onwards), both of which were of greatest benefit to the wealthiest individuals. In monetary terms, the most significant changes to direct taxation were the cuts in the basic rate of Income Tax from 23% to 22% (in 2000) and to 20% (in 2008), which disproportionately favoured middle- and higher-income groups.

Last, but not least, successive Budgets have emphasised the need to ensure that everyone has access to high-quality public services as an important component of the anti-poverty strategy. It is important, therefore, to consider the overall redistributive impact of fiscal policy, which we do later in the chapter.

Changes in inequality and poverty under New Labour

Trends in inequality

As in most studies of inequality and poverty, our analysis focuses on snapshots of the income distribution at different points in time. So, for example, we compare the incomes of those in the poorest tenth of households at the beginning of the period with the poorest tenth of households at the end of the period, while recognising that these are not the same people in both years. There is, however, good evidence that cross-sectional income inequality mirrors other more dynamic measures of inequality, such as lifetime income inequality and intergenerational income mobility (Esping-Andersen, 2005).

Most of the analysis presented in this chapter is based on the official Households Below Average Income (HBAI) dataset, which consists of a representative sample of UK households (DWP, 2008a). The income measure covers all the main sources of income, including earnings and state benefits, net of direct taxes and adjusted for differences in household composition. It does not include the value of benefits in kind from free or subsidised services or the effect of certain tax reforms, such as changes in capital gains taxation or Inheritance Tax. The latest HBAI publication covers the period up to 2006-07. Later in this chapter, we use a tax-benefit model to simulate the impact of government policies up to 2008-09.

Looking at the long-term picture, income inequality has been relatively flat since the early 1990s, but remains high by historical standards (see Figure 2.1). On the most common measures, there has been a small and statistically significant

Figure 2.1: Changes in overall income inequality, 1961 to 2006-07

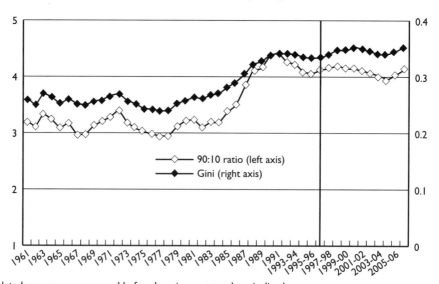

Note: Incomes are measured before housing costs and equivalised.
Source: IFS Inequality and Poverty Spreadsheet

rise in the Gini coefficient between 1996-97 and 2006-07 and no significant change in the ratio between the incomes of those 10% from the top and those 10% from the bottom (Brewer et al, 2008a). Inequality did fall on both measures for three consecutive years between 2000-01 and 2003-04, but rose in the two most recent years.

Across most of the distribution, however, incomes have become more equally distributed in the last 10 years, so this is very different to what happened in the 1980s when incomes diverged across the whole distribution. On average, the real growth in the incomes of the second decile group was greater over this period than that of the ninth decile (see Figure 2.2). The small increase in overall inequality during the last decade has therefore been driven by changes at the very top and bottom of the income distribution.

One of the main drivers behind rising inequality in the 1980s was the rapid growth in earnings differentials between more and less educated workers. There are at least three reasons why the pattern in the decade 1996-97 to 2006-07 has been different. First, the increase in the returns to education appears to slow in the 1990s and flatten out around 2000 as the supply of educated workers catches up with rapidly rising demand for them (Machin and Vignoles, 2006, table 4). Second, skill-based technological change – in particular the computerisation of routine non-manual tasks – may have depressed wages in the middle of the wage distribution more than at the top or bottom, which are dominated by non-routine

Figure 2.2: Real income growth by decile group, 1996-97 to 2006-07 and previous period

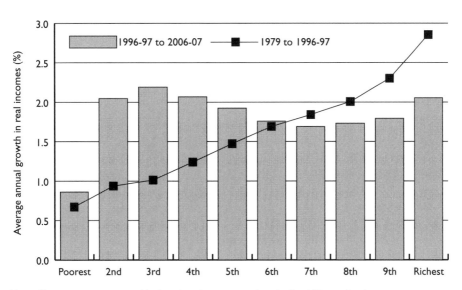

Notes: [1]Incomes are measured before housing costs and equivalised. [2]Annualised percentage increase in decile medians.
Source: IFS Inequality and Poverty Spreadsheet

analytical or manual tasks, respectively (Machin and Van Reenen, 2007). This could explain why the earnings of low-paid full-time employees are no longer falling behind median earnings, although the general slowdown in earnings growth in the last five years is striking (see Table 2.1). Third, changes in tax-benefit policies since 1997 have been more progressive than in the 1980s when rising inequality was exacerbated by discretionary changes in taxes that favoured the rich, price-indexation of most state benefits, and a weakening of the institutional structures that had previously constrained pay differentials.

Table 2.1: Real changes in hourly wages of full-time employees in the UK

	Annualised percentage increase in gross hourly pay				
	1980s	1990s	2000s	1997-2002	2002-07
5th percentile	1.8	1.0	1.3	2.6	0.6
10th percentile	1.6	1.1	1.0	2.2	0.3
25th percentile	1.8	1.2	0.8	1.9	0.1
50th percentile	2.3	1.5	0.8	1.9	0.1
75th percentile	3.0	1.9	0.9	2.2	0.0
90th percentile	3.5	2.1	1.1	2.7	0.0
95th percentile	3.8	2.2	1.5	3.6	−0.1

Notes: Data for the 1980s and 1990s are based on the New Earnings Survey (from Machin and Van Reenen, 2007, table 1). Data for the 2000s (and for 1997-2002 and 2002-07) are from the Annual Survey of Hours and Earnings (ASHE) and are derived by the authors, using published data and a special request to ONS for additional data on the 5th and 95th percentiles. Figures are converted into constant prices using the Retail Prices Index (all items). The time periods used are: 1980s: 1979-89; 1990s: 1989-99; 2000s: 1999-2007.

The very top

As already noted, inequality at the top of the income distribution has continued to rise since 1997. Brewer et al (2008b) use administrative data collected for Income Tax purposes to analyse the incomes of 'high-income' individuals in more detail than is possible using household surveys. They show that between 1996-97 and 2004-05, the top 10% of the income distribution experienced faster growth in net incomes than the rest of the population, the top 1% experienced still faster growth and the top 0.1% the fastest growth of all.

Other research shows that the pay of chief executive officers (CEOs) grew at an even faster rate than the top 0.1%. According to Tatton (2007), the total earnings of FTSE 100 CEOs grew by more than 11% per annum in real terms between 1999 and 2006, compared with 1.4% for the median of all full-time employees (see Figure 2.3). In 2006, the average earnings of a top 100 CEO was more than £2.2 million per annum or nearly 100 times the average for all full-time employees. A large and rising share of these earnings is accounted for by non-cash payments, including share options and incentive schemes. Pay growth for top CEOs is greater than in the 1990s and comparable with the 1980s.

Frank and Cook (1996) attribute this phenomenon to a growth in 'winner takes all' markets, whereby rewards have become increasingly concentrated on a small number of people at the peak of their respective occupations. Technological developments have enabled the magnification of audiences on a huge scale, favouring a select group of talented people (for example musicians and sports stars) with global appeal. Top lawyers, accountants and other professionals have also benefited from the dramatic increase in trading and business restructuring stimulated by electronic media and the opportunities this provides for value-skimming on very large flows of revenue and profit (see, for example, Erturk et al, 2006). At the same time, the institutions and social norms that previously helped to constrain pay differentials between the highest-paid directors or partners and their employees appear to be weakening (Picketty and Saez, 2003).

Although a small group, even among the super-rich, top CEOs have come to symbolise the polarisation of incomes and the government's reluctance or inability to intervene (Ramsay, 2005). Academic studies find that the majority of firms have complied with various recommended changes in corporate governance, such as the disclosure of executive pay and the setting up of remuneration committees, but that this has done very little to moderate executive pay levels or to strengthen the relationship between pay and performance (see, for example Gregg et al, 2005a).

Figure 2.3: Real growth in median earnings of FTSE 350 chief executives, 1999-2006

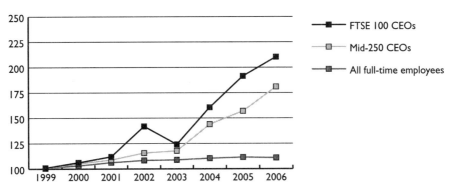

Notes: CEO earnings include salary, benefits, annual bonus, share options and Long term Investment Plans. All earnings are converted into constant prices using the Retail Prices Index (all items) and indexed (1999=100).
Source: Income Data Services (for CEO pay) and ASHE (for all full-time employees)

Trends in poverty

Over the decade up to 2006-07, overall poverty fell by 1.4 percentage points on the 'before housing costs' (BHC) measure and by 3.0 percentage points on the 'after housing costs' (AHC) measure. Relative poverty has fallen significantly among children, working-age parents and pensioners, but rose between 2004-05 and 2006-07. Poverty has also risen marginally among working-age adults without children over the period as a whole, although this group still has the lowest incidence of poverty (see Table 2.2). The decline in pensioner poverty on the AHC measure is particularly large, because many single pensioners are concentrated around the poverty threshold, so relatively small changes in their incomes have a substantial impact on poverty rates (as in the way the withdrawal of a lump-sum payment to pensioners contributed to a sharp rise in poverty in 2006-07). The reduction in child and pensioner poverty since 1997 is a significant achievement, especially when set in a historical context. Rates of child poverty doubled between 1979 and 1996-97 (from around 13% to nearly 27% on a BHC basis), while pensioner poverty fluctuated widely over the economic cycle, reaching over 40% during the last period of sustained economic growth at the end of the 1980s.

Table 2.2: Changes in relative poverty, 1996-97 to 2006-07[1]

	% of individuals below 60% of median income				Change: 1996-97 to 2006-07[2]
	1996-97	2000-01	2004-05	2006-07	
Before housing costs:					
Children	26.7	23.3	21.3	22.3	−4.4
Working age with children	20.2	18.1	16.9	17.9	−2.2
Working age without children	12.0	12.8	12.6	13.2	+1.2
Pensioners	24.6	24.8	21.3	23.2	−1.4
All	**19.4**	**18.4**	**17.0**	**18.0**	**−1.4**
After housing costs:					
Children	34.1	31.1	28.4	30.5	−3.6
Working age with children	26.6	24.7	23.0	25.2	−1.4
Working age without children	17.2	16.2	16.1	17.6	(+0.4)
Pensioners	29.1	25.9	17.6	18.9	−10.2
All	**25.3**	**23.1**	**20.5**	**22.2**	**−3.0**

Notes: [1] Figures for 1996-97 and 2000-01 are for GB; figures for 2004-05 and 2006-07 are for the UK. [2] Brackets indicate that the change is not significantly different from zero.

Source: Brewer et al (2008a, tables 4.1 and 4.2)

A more detailed analysis of the poverty statistics shows that the risk of poverty for children and their parents has fallen most among lone-parent families (in or out of work) with smaller reductions among workless couples and couples where one parent is not working or both are working part time. These groups are most likely to have benefited from the increased generosity of tax credits. The reduction in pensioner poverty up to 2005-06 was greatest among single pensioners and older pensioners, but these groups have also seen the sharpest increase in 2006-07, because they are heavily concentrated around the poverty threshold. For working-age adults without children, the incidence of poverty has risen among workless households (although there are now fewer of them) and some couples with only one full-time employee (DWP, 2008b).

There has been a significant reduction in the proportion of children living in households with incomes below 50% of the median and a significant increase in those with incomes above 70% of the median. For pensioners, the movements from below to well above the poverty line are even more marked (see Table 2.3). The reductions in poverty seen in the last 10 years do, therefore, appear to reflect a significant improvement in the relative incomes of some of the poorest households,

Table 2.3: Changes in distribution of incomes by income band, 1996-97 to 2006-07[1]

	Equivalised income as % of median					
	<40%	40-50%	50-60%	60-70%	70-80%	80%+
Before housing costs:						
Children	+1.3	−3.0	−2.5	+1.3	+1.4	+1.6
Working age with children	+1.2	−1.5	−1.8	+0.4	+0.7	+1.0
Working age without children	+1.2	+0.5	−0.5	−0.6	+0.2	−0.9
Pensioners	+1.6	−1.3	−1.6	−3.8	+1.2	+4.0
All individuals	**+1.3**	**−1.1**	**−1.5**	**−0.6**	**+0.7**	**+1.2**
After housing costs:						
Children	+0.8	−5.5	+1.0	+1.0	+1.9	+0.8
Working age with children	+1.2	−3.1	+0.4	+0.2	+1.3	+0.0
Working age without children	+0.4	+0.4	−0.4	+0.6	−0.1	−0.8
Pensioners	+1.2	−3.2	−8.5	+1.9	+1.4	+7.2
All individuals	**+0.8**	**−2.5**	**−1.4**	**+0.8**	**+0.9**	**+1.5**

Note: [1]Change in the percentage of individuals in each equivalised income band. Using OECD equivalence scale to adjust household incomes for differences in household size and composition.

Source: Own analysis using HBAI datasets for 1996-97 and 2006-07

contradicting the assertion that almost all the reduction in child poverty has come from raising households from just beneath the poverty line to just above it (see, for example, Conservative Party, 2008).

However, Table 2.3 shows that there has been a small rise in the proportion with incomes below 40% of the median. These figures are not generally seen to be reliable,[2] but there are reasons for supposing that some of this increase in 'severe poverty' may be a genuine phenomenon for certain groups, due either to non-take-up of benefits and tax credits or as a side-effect of selective tax-benefit policies that have given less priority to working-age adults without children.

Table 2.4 shows maximum levels of Income Support for different family types in relation to a relative poverty threshold. This shows a decline in the relative incomes of those working-age adults without children who are wholly dependent on state benefits. A single person aged over 25 and without children whose only income is from Income Support would have seen their income fall from around two thirds to half of the relative poverty threshold. Workless families with one child have maintained their position relative to the poverty line, while pensioners

Table 2.4: Income Support levels in relation to poverty thresholds and Minimum Income Standards (MIS) by family type, 1997 to 2008-09

	% of poverty line[1]				% of MIS[2]
	1997-98	2000-01	2004-05	2008-09	2008-09
Single, aged 18-24, no children	52	47	42	40	–
Single aged 25+, no children	65	59	53	50	42
Couple, working age, no children	60	54	49	46	42
Couple, 1 child aged 3	67	67	68	66	62
Couple, 2 children aged 4, 6	67	70	75	75	62
Couple, 3 children aged 3, 8, 11	71	72	80	81	61
Single parent, 1 child aged 3	81	79	81	81	67
Pensioner couple, aged 60-74	83	83	92	94	106
Single pensioner, aged 60-74	93	93	105	107	109

Notes: [1] The poverty threshold is 60% of contemporary median incomes (AHC). The 2008-09 threshold is projected from 2006-07 in line with the growth in the (whole economy) average earnings index. [2] Income Support/Pension Credit levels in April 2008 (including Winter Fuel Payments for pensioners) as a % of the MIS for each family type (excluding rent, Council Tax and childcare costs). MIS budgets are based on the analysis in Bradshaw et al (2008) and taken from their Ready Reckoner (available on www.minimumincomestandard.org). MIS budgets for single childless adults assume an older adult (aged 25+) and so may not be applicable to younger single adults.

Source: Except where stated below, own analysis using information on benefit and tax credit rates in April of various years and poverty thresholds from DWP (2008b) and its equivalent for earlier years.

and larger families have experienced a significant increase in means-tested entitlements both in absolute terms and in relation to the poverty line. In the case of single pensioners, the guarantee element of Pension Credit is now above the poverty line (AHC), which accounts for the sharp reduction in the poverty rate among single pensioners over this period. Separate research by Bradshaw et al (2008) shows that the incomes of pensioner households in receipt of Pension Credit now exceed a 'consensual' estimate of the income needed to achieve a minimum acceptable standard of living, whereas Income Support levels for other family types are well below this Minimum Income Standard, which is higher than the poverty threshold for these groups (see final column of Table 2.4). The large and widening differential in means-tested support for different family types raises serious questions about the horizontal equity of the benefits system and, in particular, the sustainability of further selective increases in benefits for pensioners and families with children.

HBAI data for 2006-07 showed that child poverty rose for the second year running and that poverty also rose among pensioners (see Table 2.2), leading many commentators to argue that the government's anti-poverty strategy had stalled (see, for example, Field and Cackett, 2007; Palmer et al, 2008). The largest year-on-year reduction in child poverty took place between 1999-00 and 2000-01 – a reduction of 2.3 percentage points. And while there were significant reductions in child poverty in 2002-03, 2003-04 and 2004-05 (0.6, 0.5 and 0.8 percentage points respectively), these were smaller than the one percentage point reduction that would have been required each year to achieve the government's target of halving child poverty by 2010-11 (from its 1998-99 level). Having increased in the last two years, child poverty would need to fall by around 2.3 percentage points per year between 2006-07 and 2010-11, matching the previous highest annual reduction in poverty for four consecutive years.

The slow progress on child poverty in recent years is partly a reflection of the government's target being a relative one. In order to reduce poverty, the incomes of low-income families need to rise by more than median incomes, which have grown by around a quarter in real terms over the period up to 2006-07 (although this had nearly all occurred by 2004-05). As one commentator put it, reducing child poverty is like 'running up a down escalator' (*The Guardian*, 14 March 2003). Substantial increases in spending on tax credits or other targeted benefits are, therefore, needed every year simply to stand still. As many commentators noted at the time, it was a very ambitious target.

Figures 2.4a and 2.4b show changes in net incomes for hypothetical family types on the assumption that they claim all the benefits and tax credits to which they are entitled. The biggest beneficiaries of tax credit reforms over this period were families with children on below average earnings. While the WTC extended in-work benefits to families without children, only those on very low earnings – at or around the National Minimum Wage – are entitled to WTC and take-up rates are very low.

Figure 2.4a: Net incomes for hypothetical family types on half average earnings relative to the contemporary poverty threshold

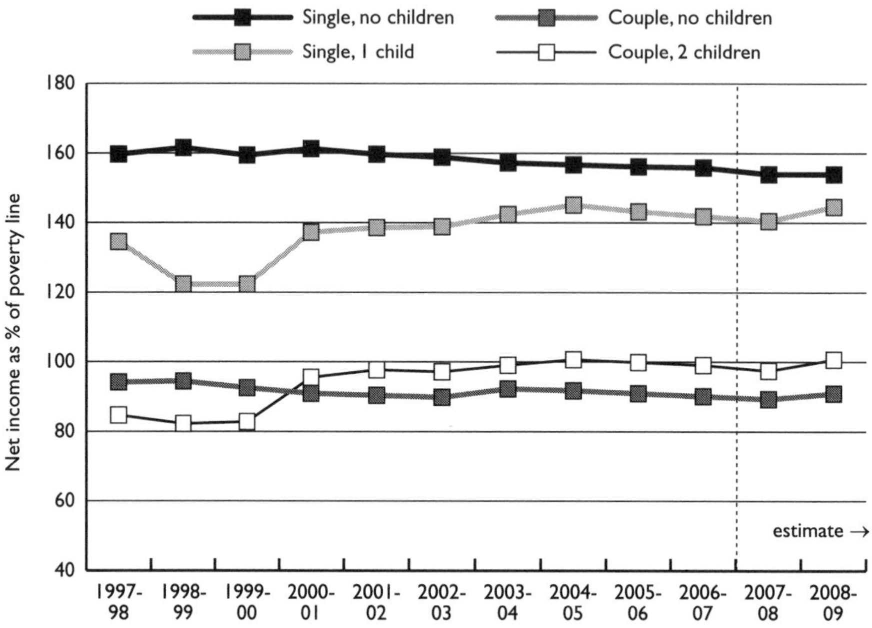

Notes: The assumptions used to calculate net incomes (AHC) at different earnings levels are the same as in DWP (2008a), except that we use ASHE earnings throughout: gross weekl wages of full-time female employees (for lone parents) or full-time male employees (for other family types). 2008-09 earnings are projected in line with the ONS (whole economy) Average Earnings Index between April 2007 and April 2008. Poverty thresholds up to 2006-07 are from DWP (2008b) and projected to rise in line with the AEI in 2007-08 and 2008-09 with an additional upward adjustment in 2008-09 for changes in the basic rate tax allowance in May 2008. The value of benefits and tax credits is based on the rates applying in April of each year.
Source: Own analysis based on methodology used in DWP (2008a)

Perhaps of greater interest here is the phasing of these changes over the period. For families with children and below average earnings, there was a large step increase in net incomes following the introduction of the WFTC in October 1999. Subsequent increases in tax credits were only sufficient to broadly maintain their position relative to a rising poverty threshold. For a hypothetical couple with two children and one full-time worker on half average earnings, the WFTC lifted them close to the poverty threshold, where they have remained for the rest of the period, even though the maximum award has been raised from around £6,000 in 2000-01 to around £9,000 in 2008-09. The pattern is similar at different levels of earnings, although the step increase in 2000-01 was less marked for those with higher earnings (because tax credits are withdrawn at higher incomes) and for those with very low earnings and/or higher rents (because tax credits are offset against other means-tested benefits).

Figure 2.4b: Net incomes for a couple with two children, by level of earnings relative to the contemporary poverty threshold

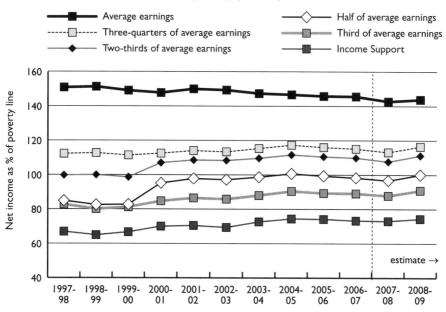

Notes and *Source:* See Figure 2.4a

The step increase in the generosity of tax credits between 1999-00 and 2000-01 coincided with the biggest year-on-year reduction in child poverty. When the government has increased the child element of the CTC by more than earnings, as it did in April 2004 and 2008, this does have a noticeable impact on the net incomes of low earners. But, to maintain the early progress on child poverty, increases of this magnitude would have to be implemented every year. That this did not happen in 2005, 2006 or 2007 is surely one of the reasons why child poverty rose in 2005-06 and 2006-07 – and seems likely to rise again in 2007-08. The other main reason is that unemployment bottomed out around 2000, so overall changes in employment are no longer contributing to a reduction in poverty as they did during New Labour's first term (Sutherland et al, 2003).

This raises the question as to whether the government's anti-poverty strategy is fundamentally flawed, being over-reliant on ever-increasing amounts of tax credits. By undermining work incentives and increasing benefit dependency, the Conservative Party (2008) has argued that this approach could increase poverty in the long term. However, the evidence to support this claim is rather weak. In a review of five previous studies, Brewer and Browne (2006) concluded that the introduction of the WFTC had a positive impact on the labour market participation of previously workless families and that large negative effects on second earners do not appear to have materialised. The Institute for Fiscal Studies' own estimates are that the combined impact of all tax and benefit reforms between 1999 and

2002 was a small net *increase* in employment, even though the WFTC was part of a package of anti-poverty measures that incorporated large increases in out-of-work benefits (Brewer et al, 2006a).[3] For those families already in work, the expansion of tax credits substantially increased the number of families entitled to income-related benefits and facing high marginal effective tax rates (although it reduced the numbers facing the highest rates). While in theory this reduces their incentive to work harder and longer, Brewer et al (2008c) conclude that the responsiveness of hours worked to the tax system is likely to be very low for most groups and 'perhaps even zero'. That the government has managed to reduce child poverty significantly with apparently no adverse impact on employment suggests that it has successfully negotiated the 'poverty trade-off' described in Adam et al (2006).

Looking ahead, simulation work commissioned by the Joseph Rowntree Foundation shows that the 2010 target to halve child poverty could plausibly be achieved through further increases in tax credits. The amount of money is large – the Institute for Fiscal Studies' latest estimate is that an extra £2.8 billion per year would be needed (Brewer et al, 2008a) – but not impossible in relation to other recent spending announcements. However, further progress beyond that – and towards the 2020 goal of reducing child poverty to 'among the lowest in Europe' – would be very hard to achieve through the tax-benefit system alone. The required increase in tax credits and Income Support for families with children would involve a dramatic increase in the differential treatment of families with and without children; it is in this sense that a strategy reliant on tax credits would appear to become unsustainable much beyond 2010 as the system would become so distorted as to be 'ultimately unjust' (Hirsch, 2006). In the longer term, the anti-poverty strategy will depend on the effectiveness of education, employment and other policies in ensuring that future parents have the necessary skills and earnings capacity to keep their families out of poverty (see Chapters Four and Five).

Isolating the impact of tax-benefit policies

Changes in the income distribution since 1997 have resulted from a wide range of factors, many of which are not directly under the government's control. This section seeks to isolate the impact of one of the most important factors that is directly controlled by government – the structure and generosity of the direct tax system and of cash benefits and tax credits. It draws on modelling results from the tax-benefit model, POLIMOD (Redmond et al, 1998). This allows us to investigate what the income distribution *would have* looked like if different decisions had been made about the system from those actually implemented – and described earlier in this chapter. The results do not allow for any behavioural differences between the population under the actual systems that emerged and these 'counterfactual' worlds with which it is compared.[4]

The results compare the system as it had emerged by 2008-09 with those of 1996-97, 2000-01 and 2004-05. But to make such comparisons, assumptions have to be made about how the earlier systems would have been adjusted over time in the absence of 'policy change'. One assumption – and the one generally used in official analysis – is that an 'unchanged' 1996-97 system would involve all of its elements adjusted for *price inflation*. We then compare the actual 2008-09 system with the structure of taxes and benefits as they were in the past, on the assumption that the values of benefits, tax allowances and so on would have been constant in *real* terms since the earlier date.

However, if the main concern is with the impact of government policy on inequality and on *relative* poverty, this kind of comparison will be misleading. A benefit or tax allowance that is unchanged in real terms will have fallen behind other contemporary incomes – considerably so, if the comparison is looking back as far as 12 years. A system adjusted only for price inflation would imply increasing direct taxes as a share of gross domestic product (GDP) ('fiscal drag'), but falling benefit and tax credit spending as a share of GDP and increased relative poverty (as a result of 'benefit erosion').[5] We therefore also show the results of comparing the actual 2008-09 system with the counterfactual of earlier systems if all of their components had been adjusted in line with average *earnings growth*. Other things being equal, this assumption is consistent with 'unchanged policy' being neutral in terms of income distribution and relative poverty rates, and as these are our main concerns, it is results on this basis that we think are most enlightening.

First, we consider the effect on the public finances of the reforms introduced since 1996-97. On the price-indexed basis, the public finances would be improved by £14 billion if the actual 2008-09 system were replaced with that of 1996-97. On this basis the government could claim – and indeed has done so over time – to have 'given away' a net amount of £14 billion, with particularly large generosity in the middle period between 2000-01 and 2004-05. Average disposable incomes are thus 2.5% higher than they would have been. However, on the earnings-indexed basis, the aggregate difference between the systems is much smaller. Indeed, the actual 2008-09 system raises *more* than the earnings-linked earlier ones, £11 billion more than that of 1996-97, for instance. But these differences are relatively small in the context of Income Tax and National Insurance revenues projected at £260 billion in 2008-09, for instance. The earnings-linked comparisons shown below therefore show the distributional effects of a system that has changed in ways that leave *average* net incomes only a little changed (reduced by under 2% by comparison with the 1996-97 system).

Figure 2.5 shows, however, that the effects of the reforms have differed greatly between income groups, and between the three time periods examined. In the upper panel, against a price-linked base, the top two-tenths of the distribution can be seen to be slightly worse off under the 2008-09 system than they would have been under the 1996-97 system. However, income groups lower down the distribution are gainers, with the largest percentage gains at the bottom – by more than 25% for the bottom-income group. Although there was some gain at the bottom from the changes between 1996-97 and 2000-01, the bulk of it came

Figure 2.5: Overall distributional effect of tax-benefit policies, 1996-97 to 2008-09

(a) Relative to price indexation of policies

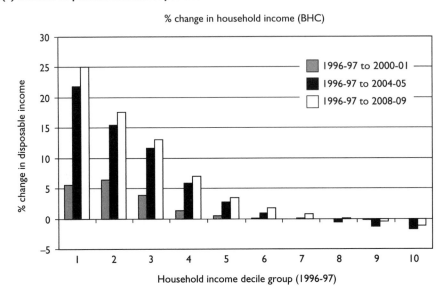

% change in household income (BHC)

(b) Relative to earnings indexation of policies

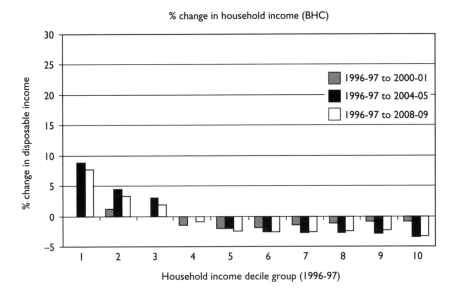

% change in household income (BHC)

Note: People are ranked into decile groups according to their equivalised household income under 1996-97 policies.
Source: Own analysis using POLIMOD

between 2000-01 and 2004-05. The improvement in real terms for the bottom of the distribution since 2004-05 has been fairly slight.[6]

The lower panel of Figure 2.5 shows an alternative view of the way in which policy has been redistributive. Against an earnings-linked base, the top seven-tenths of the distribution emerges as losers – by 3% for the top tenth. The gains for the bottom-income groups are much smaller than against the price-linked base, with the bottom tenth 8% better off and the next two-tenths less than 5% better off than they would have been under an unreformed, but earnings-linked, version of the 1996-97 system New Labour inherited. This shows more starkly the difference between the time periods. For the lowest-income groups, the 2008-09 system is *less* generous than the 2004-05 system had been, when the comparison is made in this way.

Figure 2.6 shows how this process translates into the relative poverty rates implied by the different systems, compared in price- and earnings-linked terms. The overall relative poverty rate is modelled to be 17% under the 2008-09 tax-benefit system.[7] By comparison, if the 1996-97 system had been left in place, but with its parameters linked to price growth, the poverty rate would have been 23% – or 21% against an earnings-linked base. This gives a key measure of the impact of policy over the period: the results suggest that without the reforms, relative poverty in 2008-09 would have been between four and six percentage points higher than the actual outcome (unmeasured at the time of writing). It should be noted, however, that this 'policy effect' is larger than the likely *actual* reduction in the overall poverty rate over the period (see Table 2.2). Between 1996-97 and 2006-07 this only fell by 1.4 percentage points. In other words, other factors, such as demographic and household composition, changed in a way that would have led to an *increase* in poverty without the tax and benefit reforms. Most of the redistribution shown in Figure 2.5 was needed to stop relative poverty worsening; only a part of it led to an actual fall in the poverty rate. The implications are discussed further in the concluding chapter as an indication of what might have happened under a continuation of previous policies.

Figure 2.6 shows how the poverty rates for different groups have been affected by the reforms (shown here on the BHC income measure). By far the largest effect is for children living in lone-parent families, whose poverty rate is 14 percentage points lower than it would have been had the system Labour inherited been left unchanged, but uprated with earnings growth reduction (the bottom panel). For other families with children, the reduction is seven percentage points, and for pensioners, three percentage points. Pensioner and, particularly, child poverty have been the government's priorities. However, for working-age adults *without* children, the effect of the policy reforms has been a slight *increase* in poverty against this benchmark.

Figure 2.6 also shows a stark difference between the three time periods. Between 1996-97 and 2000-01, and between 2000-01 and 2004-05, the policy effect was a reduction in poverty overall, with greater reductions for children as a whole

Figure 2.6: Changes in poverty due to tax-benefit policies, 1996-97 to 2008-09

(a) Relative to price indexation of policies

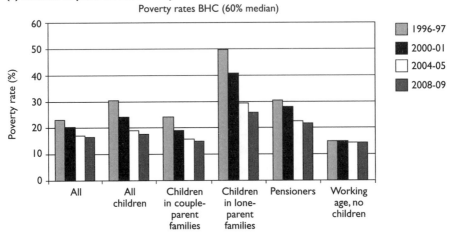

Poverty rates BHC (60% median)

(b) Relative to earnings indexation of policies

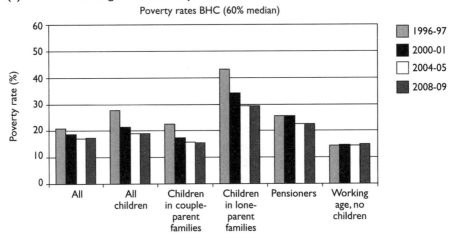

Poverty rates BHC (60% median)

Note: This figure shows simulated poverty rates in the base year for analysis, 2004-05, under the tax-benefit systems prevailing in 1996-97, 2000-01, 2004-05 and 2008-09. The systems in earlier years are uprated in line with prices (in the top panel) or earnings (in the bottom panel).
Source: Own analysis using POLIMOD

in the first subperiod and for pensioners in the second subperiod. But between 2004-05 and 2008-09, this process stalled, and the poverty rates for all subgroups were virtually unaffected by policy, even against a price–indexed counterfactual. There have been some changes since the major tax credit reforms of 2003-04, but none has had a very large impact, and through most of the last subperiod the indexation of most benefits and tax allowances only with prices put upward pressure on relative poverty rates, balanced by the overall effects of the reforms that took effect in 2008-09.

Even though Figure 2.5 shows a gain from policy over the whole period for most income groups on a price-linked basis, and for the bottom three decile groups on an earnings-linked basis, even within these groups some households have been losers. The upper panel of Figure 2.7 shows that, relative to price indexation, most households are gainers, although there are some losers, even

Figure 2.7: Net gainers and losers from tax-benefit policies, 1996-97 to 2008-09

(a) Relative to price indexation of policies

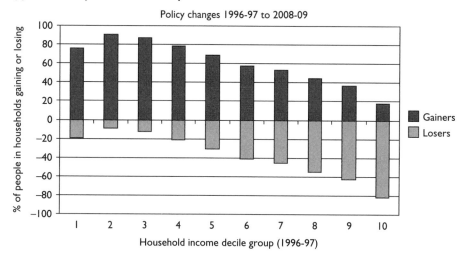

(b) Relative to earnings indexation of policies

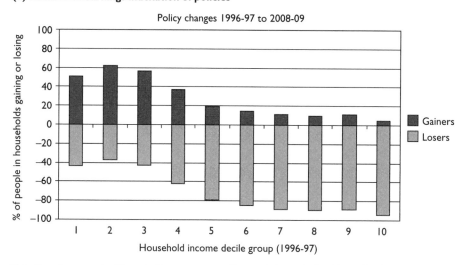

Note: People are ranked into decile groups according to their equivalised household income under 1996-97 policies. A change in income of 10 pence per week or more is counted as a gain or a loss.
Source: Own analysis using POLIMOD

on this basis, within the bottom-income groups.[8] By the top three-tenths more people are worse off than better off. But relative to an earnings-linked base, the lower panel shows that the number of losers is more than double the number of gainers. These include more than half of households in the bottom half of the income distribution and most households in the top half of the distribution. For the subperiod since 2004-05 (not shown here), this position is reversed: the majority of poorer households are losers and the majority of better-off households are gainers. Nevertheless, three-quarters of the gainers over the whole period of reforms are located in the bottom four-tenths.

Impact of public spending

Although most inequality measures do not take into account public spending on benefits in kind, like healthcare and education, their inclusion is potentially very significant in monitoring the overall impact of government policies on the poorest households (Sefton, 2002). The government itself has highlighted the important contribution of public services to tackling poverty and the need for redistribution through public service programmes, as well as the tax and benefit system. Subsequent chapters consider the impact on inequalities in education, health and employment outcomes. In this chapter we consider the distributional impact of public spending on the assumption that the amount of expenditure is a reasonable measure of its worth to recipients, using estimates produced by the Office for National Statistics (ONS) of the effects of taxes and spending on household income (Jones, 2008).

Public spending was initially tight as New Labour stuck to its electoral commitment to match the Conservative government's spending plans for two years. Thereafter, public spending grew rapidly for six successive years – by more than 4% per year in real terms – but started to slow down from around 2005-06 (Chote et al, 2008). In 2008-09, total managed expenditure was more than four percentage points higher as a share of GDP than when Labour came to power, although still lower than in 1991-92.

Table 2.5 shows the growth in spending on the three largest spending areas. Spending on cash benefits and tax credits ('social protection') grew more slowly than average and has fallen by two percentage points as a proportion of GDP since 1996-97. Falling unemployment and the linking of certain benefits to prices, as opposed to earnings, has freed up resources to spend on tax credits and on public services. It could be argued that Tony Blair has succeeded in his stated objective to reduce 'spending on failure'. However, spending less on unemployment benefits, for example, is not necessarily a good thing if it is achieved by restricting benefits, which in part it has been; some of the consequences for working-age adults without children have already been noted. The main priorities for higher spending were health and education. The first part of the decade saw the largest sustained increase in National Health Service (NHS) funding since its inception

---

Table 2.5: Growth in UK public spending in real terms, 1987-88 to 2008-09[1]

	1987-88 to 1991-92	1991-92 to 1996-97	1996-97 to 2000-01	2000-01 to 2004-05	2004-05 to 2008-09 (plans)
Annual growth (%)					
Health	3.9	3.8	3.8	8.1	4.6
Education	2.8	1.4	2.8	6.1	3.7
Social protection[2]	2.5	3.8	0.6	2.3	1.2
Total managed expenditure	1.4	1.6	1.4	4.9	2.8
TME, excluding social protection	1.0	0.7	1.7	6.1	3.5
% of GDP (end of period)					
Health	5.2	5.5	5.6	6.9	7.5
Education	5.0	4.7	4.6	5.3	5.6
Social protection[2]	12.5	13.2	11.8	11.8	11.2
Total managed expenditure	42.5	40.6	37.5	41.2	41.9
TME, excluding social protection	30.0	27.4	25.7	29.4	30.7

Notes: [1] Figures up to 2007-08 are from HM Treasury's Public Expenditure Statistical Analyses (PESA) 2008. Planned expenditure for 2008-09 is from tables D2 and D6 of the 2007 Pre-Budget Report and Comprehensive Spending Review (for education and health) and table C9 of Budget 2008 (for social security and tax credits and for total managed expenditure). All figures are price-adjusted using HM Treasury's GDP deflator (at 28 March 2008). [2] Excluding personal social services in those years where it is incorporated under this heading.

in 1949: spending grew by over 8% per annum between 2000–01 and 2004–05 and increased from 5.5% of GDP in 1996–97 to a projected 7.5% in 2008–09. Education spending also grew faster than overall spending and as a percentage of GDP, although year-on-year increases in spending have been quite volatile.

Figure 2.8 shows the impact of adding the value of public spending on benefits in kind – largely healthcare and education – to people's cash incomes. The impact of indirect taxes is also incorporated, as these are deducted by the ONS in calculating 'post-tax income' prior to the addition of benefits in kind to give 'final income', but these results are not discussed here.[9] The bottom tenth benefited most from the rapid growth in public spending during New Labour's second term, because health and education spending is pro-poor. Households in the bottom tenth have more than twice as much spent on them, on average, as the top tenth, largely due to demographic factors: lower-income groups contain more children and older people, who are the most intensive users of these services. The growth in 'final incomes' of the poorest tenth is higher than the average for all households and only exceeded by the third decile group.

Figure 2.8: Real growth in disposable, post-tax and final incomes, 1996-97 to 2006-07

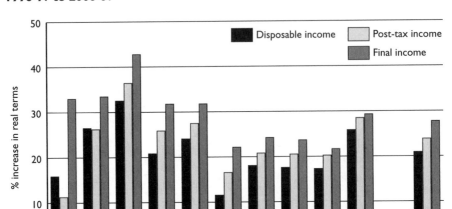

Notes: Disposable income comprises earnings, other private sources of income and cash benefits, less direct taxes, employees' National Insurance contributions (NICs) and Council Tax payments. Post-tax income deducts VAT, indirect taxes and estimates of intermediate taxes (including employers' NICs). Final income adds in estimates of benefits in kind, mostly state education and the NHS. All incomes are converted into constant prices using the Retail Price Index (all items). *Source:* Own analysis using data published by the Office for National Statistics (Jones, 2008, and previous reports in the same series)

For several reasons, these estimates may underestimate the redistributive effects of public spending. First, they omit the value of personal social services and understate the economic value of social housing,[10] both of which are strongly pro-poor. Second, the ONS estimates take into account differences in usage by age and gender, but not the independent effect of income and other socioeconomic characteristics. According to Sefton (2002), around half the pro-poor bias in the distribution of the benefits in kind is attributable to non-demographic factors – and this latter effect is likely to have strengthened over time, because the government has purposively skewed spending towards poorer areas (Sefton, 2004; see also Chapter Four on the distribution of schools funding).

Finally, the ONS data can be used to assess the overall redistributive impact of the government's tax-benefit and spending policies by comparing the level of inequality – as measured by the Gini coefficient – before and after the inclusion of taxes, cash benefits *and* benefits in kind. This analysis shows that fiscal policy has been strongly counter-cyclical over the last 30 years, being more strongly redistributive when unemployment is highest and vice versa. But, there was a clear change in this pattern between 2000-01 and 2005-06 when the redistributive impact of the welfare state increased significantly even though unemployment remained at historically low levels (see Figure 2.9). This was due to a combination of more generous tax credits, slightly more progressive taxation and increased

Figure 2.9: Redistributive impact of tax-benefit and spending policies, 1979 to 2006-07

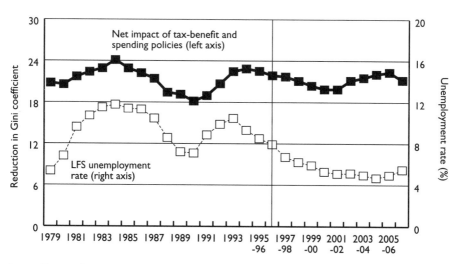

Source: Own analysis using data kindly provided by the ONS for the purposes of its annual report on the effects of taxes and benefits on household income (for example Jones, 2008). Unemployment rates are taken from the ONS Time Series MGSX, based on the Labour Force Survey.

spending on public services. The subsequent decline in the redistributive effect in 2006-07 was driven by changes in the distribution of cash benefits and taxation and is consistent with the micro-simulation results discussed above. The overall redistributive effect of the welfare state is still broadly equivalent to what it was during the recession of the early 1990s when unemployment was nearly twice the current level. In crude terms, pro-poor spending on in-work benefits and public services has substituted for pro-poor spending on out-of-work benefits over the period as a whole.

Conclusion

Labour's benefit and tax credit policies have favoured families with children and pensioners, especially those on low incomes. In-work tax credits (for low earners) and savings credits (for pensioners) have sought to strike a balance between redistribution, on the one hand, and maintaining or improving incentives to work and save, on the other. With a few significant exceptions, these objectives were pursued consistently throughout the period. However, the number of Budget measures with a substantial impact declined in the period between 2004 and 2008 and became increasingly selective. Tax policy was not used explicitly to reduce inequality and some measures were highly regressive.

New Labour has not reversed the dramatic growth in income inequality over the previous 20 years, but nor has income inequality worsened significantly. Incomes have become a bit more equal across most of the distribution, due to changes in the distribution of earnings and redistributive tax-benefit and spending policies that targeted some of the poorest households. But, income growth slowed across the whole distribution from 2003 and growing differentials at the very top and bottom of the income distribution led to a small rise in overall inequality. The government did little to address the rapid rise in top incomes – and where action was taken, this proved largely ineffective.

On a more positive note, child and pensioner poverty fell significantly under New Labour, which is a considerable achievement compared with what happened in the preceding 20 years and what would have happened if the inherited tax-benefit system had been uprated with prices or even earnings growth. Over the period as a whole, tax-benefit policies were strongly redistributive and poverty would have worsened substantially in their absence. We estimate that overall poverty in 2008-09 would have been up to six percentage points higher and child poverty up to 13 percentage points higher under a continuation of the previous government's tax-benefit policies. Adding in the value of health and education spending strengthens the redistributive impact of fiscal policies and substantially improves the relative position of the poorest.

However, poverty rose among all groups between 2004-05 and 2006-07 and among working-age adults without children over the period as a whole. The lack of progress in recent years is due to several factors. First, falling unemployment is no longer contributing to reductions in poverty. Second, the government's tax-benefit policies have largely neglected certain groups, most notably workless adults without children who continue to fall further behind. Third, the government has failed to build on the initial success of the WFTC, which would have required large increases in tax credits to be implemented consistently every year. In the four years since 2004-05, changes in tax-benefit policies have had virtually no impact on relative poverty, even among the government's priority groups, and growth in spending on public services has started to slow. The anti-poverty strategy appears to have run out of steam not because it is fundamentally flawed, but because the government has taken its foot off the pedal. However, there are limits to what can be achieved through further increases in tax credits without the system becoming overly distorted as the wide variation in out-of-work benefits raises serious concerns about horizontal equity between different family types. Nevertheless, tax credits have been effective in reducing child poverty and are still the government's best hope of coming near to its 2010 target. The resources committed to reducing Inheritance Tax thresholds could have been used for this purpose, but were instead used in a way that will disproportionately benefit higher-income groups. The very much tougher economic outlook at the time of writing will limit the scope for redistribution and force the government to make difficult policy trade-offs if it is to get back on track in its ambitious goals for reducing poverty.

Notes

[1] However, in November 2008, the government announced that it would introduce a new top rate of income tax of 45% on incomes over £150,000 per year from 2011-12 and progressive changes to personal tax allowances from 2010-11 if elected for a fourth term.

[2] Brewer et al (2008a), for example, found that children in households with less than 40% of median income are less materially deprived, on average, than those in households with between 40% and 60% of median income.

[3] Incentives to work may be somewhat weaker now than in 2002, because the WTC has not been increased as much as the CTC, which is also available to workless families with children.

[4] The source data for the modelling is the Family Resources Survey carried out in 2003-04, but adjusted to be consistent with levels of earnings and housing costs in 2004-05. Non-take-up of means-tested benefits and tax credits is modelled using latest estimates from DWP (2007c) and HMRC (2007), but is assumed to be unaffected by changes in entitlements. The results are compared with the tax and benefit system of 2008-09, *including* the increase in personal allowances announced in May 2008.

[5] See Chapter Fifteen and Sutherland et al (2008) for more detailed discussion.

[6] As a result of tax-benefit changes since 1996-97, households would change their relative position within the income distribution. Some of those gaining in the bottom-income group would move into higher-income groups to be replaced at the bottom by others not targeted by reforms. Thus, the distributional effect of changing from the system of 2008-09 to that of 1996-97 would not be the mirror image of that shown in Figure 2.5. For example, if people were ranked according to household income under the 2008-09 system then, relative to price indexation of the 1996-97 system, the bottom-income group would be better off by 10% of their income and the second income group by 16% (contrasted with 25% and 18% respectively using the ranking under 1996-97 policies).

[7] Different tax-benefit systems are applied to a market income distribution as it was in the base year for analysis – 2004-05 – so this is not a forecast of actual poverty rates in 2008-09.

[8] One of the main explanations for low-income losers is the non-take-up of benefits and tax credits, as well as the policy of only indexing to prices most of the benefits received by working-age adults without children.

[9] See Sutherland et al (2003) for an analysis of the distributional effects of indirect taxes.

[10] For housing, net expenditure is a poor guide to the value of housing subsidies. See Sefton (2002) for estimates based on an economic valuation of submarket rents in the social rented sector and Right To Buy discounts.

THREE

'A scar on the soul of Britain': child poverty and disadvantage under New Labour

Kitty Stewart

Background and inheritance

The number of children living in poverty in the UK increased dramatically in the two decades to 1997. When Labour came to power, 25% of children lived in households with income below 60% of the median before housing costs (BHC), up from 12% in 1979 (DWP, 2004). After housing costs (AHC), the rise was even greater, from 14% in 1979 to 34% in 1997. The increases were much sharper for children than for the population at large. In 1979, children had the same poverty risk as the general population, but by 1997, they were twice as likely to live in poverty as childless working-age adults. In the mid-1990s, child poverty was higher in relative terms in the UK than in all but two other industrialised countries – Italy and the US (UNICEF, 2000).

One important explanation is the rising level of household worklessness: one in five children lived in a household with no member in work in 1997, compared with just 8% in 1979 (Gregg and Wadsworth, 2001). This in turn was partly driven by the rising share of children living with a single parent, up from 10% in 1979 to 22% in 1995-96 (Gregg et al, 1999b, table 1). But the 1980s and 1990s had also seen polarisation of work among two-parent households, with growing numbers of both two-worker and no-worker families (Gregg and Wadsworth, 2001).

While worklessness was increasing, poverty rates were rising for households in and out of work. Among workless households, poverty rose between 1979 and 1997 even against a fixed real poverty line, as most benefits were adjusted only in line with prices (Gregg et al, 1999b). At the same time, low pay and increasing wage inequality meant that a job was not always enough to provide for a family: even children in two-parent households with both parents employed experienced an increase in relative poverty risk between 1985 and 1991 (Bradshaw, 2000).

This was the situation that Labour faced when it was elected in 1997. Meanwhile, growing evidence emphasised the importance of childhood poverty for later outcomes. Children growing up poor appeared to have lower self-esteem, were less likely to be successful in education and employment and were at increased risk of early childbearing, low income, benefit dependency and homelessness (Hobcraft, 1998; Ermisch et al, 2001). These findings were not lost on a government that had declared itself committed to 'opportunity for all'. In November 1998, the Treasury organised a workshop for academics and policymakers to review the evidence on the causes of persistent poverty and lifetime inequality (Hills, 1999; HM Treasury, 1999). The conclusions, which underlined the central importance of childhood, were published just as Tony Blair made his 'Beveridge speech' in March 1999, and can be seen as a key motivation behind his unexpected pledge to eliminate child poverty: 'Our historic aim – that ours is the first generation to end child poverty forever.... Life chances should depend on talent and effort, not the chance of birth' (Blair, 1999, pp 7-8).

The Treasury had also been exploring a second stream of evidence. The Comprehensive Spending Review set up in 1997 included a review of young children's services, stimulated by a UK study showing that social class begins to affect educational development before a child is four (Feinstein, 1998), as well as interest in US evidence about the long-term impact of preschool interventions (see Waldfogel, 1998). This review led to the development of Sure Start and to substantial investment in services for preschool children for the first time.

New Labour's attack on childhood poverty and disadvantage can therefore be seen as two-pronged – it aimed to reduce (and eventually 'eradicate') income poverty among children, while also improving public services – in particular education, health and parenting support – to try to reduce the wider disadvantages associated with poverty, starting in the earliest years. This chapter examines both aspects of the strategy, concentrating for the latter on services for preschool children. Education services for older children are examined in the next chapter. While tax-benefit policy affects the whole of the UK, responsibility for early years education and childcare rests with the devolved administrations, and these parts of the chapter focus on England. See Wincott (2006) for discussion of early years policies in Scotland and Wales.

Policies

Since 1997, Labour has introduced a raft of policies aimed at raising incomes and improving early years services. However, while children have remained conspicuous on the legislative agenda through all three terms of office, the rate of increase in spending slowed sharply after 2003-04.

Labour's first term: 1997-2001

Labour's child poverty strategy aimed from the start to encourage employment and make it pay. Two key early policies aimed to increase employment: the New Deal for Lone Parents provided lone parents with advice and support in looking for jobs, while the National Childcare Strategy aimed to deliver 'good quality, affordable childcare for children aged 0 to 14 in every neighbourhood' (DfEE, 1998, p 6). The National Childcare Strategy was a turning point: for the first time, government took on formal responsibility for an area that had previously been considered a parental problem. The approach was market based, with partial three-year funding for new providers in deprived wards (for example the Neighbourhood Nurseries Initiative), and business support to private providers elsewhere (for example a loan guarantee scheme for nurseries). Low-income parents could apply for a subsidy through the Childcare Tax Credit, initially worth up to 70% of formal childcare costs. New rights to request part-time and flexible working, more generous Statutory Maternity Pay, and the introduction of two weeks' paid paternity leave (albeit at a low flat rate) can also be seen as part of the plan to make employment easier for parents.

Policies to make work pay aimed both to improve work incentives and to reduce poverty for those already working. The National Minimum Wage and tax and National Insurance reforms benefited all low-income workers. Other policies – the Working Families' Tax Credit (WFTC) and the Children's Tax Credit – boosted incomes for families with children in particular (see Chapter Two).

While employment was considered central to reducing poverty, living standards also improved for workless households. Income Support allowances for children under 11 were increased (see Figure 2.4b and Table 2.4 in Chapter Two) and low-income households became eligible for a £500 Sure Start Maternity Grant. Universal Child Benefit rose for the eldest children, and children born after September 2002 received a Child Trust Fund payment (doubled for those in lower-income households), to be drawn on when the child reaches 18. On the other hand, in 1997 the new government implemented Conservative plans to phase out One Parent Benefit and the lone parent premium in Income Support, but other changes described above eventually compensated most households.

There were three main aspects to investment in early years services in Labour's first term. First, all three- and four-year-olds were guaranteed a free part-time nursery place (12.5 hours per week). Second, attempts were made to improve the quality as well as the quantity of childcare, with the introduction of Office for Standards in Education (Ofsted) regulation, legally enforceable quality standards, funding for childminder training, and the establishment in 1997 of the first Early Excellence Centre as a model of good practice in providing integrated childcare and early education. The idea was that there could be a 'double dividend' (Strategy Unit, 2002, p 29) – childcare benefiting children while also allowing their parents to work. Finally, Sure Start Local Programmes (SSLPs) were introduced for under-fives in the most deprived 20% of wards. Each programme was different, designed locally to meet local needs, but all offered five core services:

- outreach and home visiting;
- parenting support;
- play and learning opportunities;

- healthcare and advice;
- support for parents and children with special needs.

Labour's second term: 2001-05

Labour's second term saw the publication of *Every Child Matters* in 2003 (DfES, 2003b), in response to the inquiry into the death of eight-year-old Victoria Climbié. This Green Paper and the Children Act that followed in 2004 aimed to strengthen children's preventative services using a joined-up approach, with schools and Children's Centres acting as coordinating hubs to improve overall outcomes and narrow inequalities.

In April 2003, the Child Tax Credit (CTC) and Working Tax Credit (WTC) replaced the WFTC and Children's Tax Credit. The new tax credits were described by then Paymaster General Dawn Primarolo as 'the biggest single change in the way government provides financial support for families since the Beveridge reforms of the 1940s' (BBC, 2004) and were to become the government's main anti-poverty tool. In creating a single system of support for families in and out of work, they aimed to remove most of the benefit disincentives and uncertainty surrounding the move into a job. As almost all families with children would be eligible for the CTC, the system sought also to remove any stigma associated with tax credit receipt.

The introduction of the new system was bumpy. In particular, it soon became clear that the systematic overpayment – and subsequent 'clawing back' – of tax credit entitlements was contributing to income instability for low-income households. Tax credits are paid out each year on the basis of the previous year's income, then adjusted once actual income information becomes available; potentially up to a year later. If income rose sharply from one year to the next then a family could find itself required to return a payment it had already spent. A total of £2.2 billion was 'overpaid' in 2003-04, with 1.9 million families facing repayments (NAO, 2008a). The government's failure to predict that this lagged system – administered smoothly for Income Tax payments – would cause problems for households on low and fluctuating incomes was a major error. In 2006, it responded to growing criticism with a series of measures including a 10-fold increase in the extra income allowed before tax credit entitlement is cut (from £2,500 to £25,000), thus protecting almost all families with rising incomes from repayments. In 2006-07, overpayments were significantly down, but £1 billion was still overpaid to 1.3 million families (nearly one in four households in receipt) (NAO, 2008a).

Unlike other parts of the benefit system, largely linked to prices (see Chapter Fifteen), the child element of the CTC was linked at least to average earnings until 2007-08, later updated to cover the full third Parliament. An above-earnings increase followed in April 2004, in response to widespread predictions that the government would miss its first interim child poverty target (see discussion below).

Between 1999, when the pre-election commitment to stick to Conservative spending plans came to an end, and the end of New Labour's second term, spending on child-related benefits and tax credits rose by 60% in real terms (£11 billion, or an extra 0.6% of gross domestic product; GDP). Most of this increase was delivered by 2003-04 – spending peaked in that year as a share of GDP – and most came from targeted benefits (see Table 3.1). Means-tested support for in-work families had nearly trebled by 2004-05, while that for non-working families had risen by 80%; in contrast, spending on universal Child Benefit was up by 14%. Spending on early years education and childcare started rising from 1997-98 and had risen by 133% by 2004-05, an increase of nearly £3 billion.

Labour's early third term: 2005-07

Two central pieces of legislation affected children in Labour's third term. The 2006 Childcare Act made local authorities responsible for ensuring sufficient childcare provision, and pledged 3,500 Children's Centres by 2010, to be developed from SSLPs, Neighbourhood Nurseries and Early Excellence Centres and to provide integrated early education, childcare, health services, and family and childminder support. The idea was to spread the benefits of Sure Start to every community, although concerns were immediately raised about funding and about the dilution of parent and community involvement (discussed below).

The Childcare Act also contained a commitment to Extended Schools – by 2010 all schools would provide some out-of-school childcare from 8am to 6pm – and to stretch free nursery places for three- and four-year-olds to 15 hours per week from 2010, with pilots for two-year-olds in disadvantaged areas. Further, the Act introduced a single quality framework across all Ofsted-registered settings, in principle removing the distinction between education and childcare settings.

The second major legislation of this period – the 2007 Welfare Reform Act – introduced benefit conditionality for the first time for lone parents from October 2008. Drawing on a report by David Freud (2007), it moved non-working lone parents onto Jobseeker's Allowance – the same financial support but with a job-search requirement – once their youngest child reached the age of 12, to be reduced to age seven from 2010.

Other changes included the extension of Child Benefit to pregnant women in their third trimester from April 2009 – a principle long campaigned for by children's charities – and a weekly credit for lone parents in their first year in work. However, despite widening concern that the first child poverty target would be missed, there were no above-inflation increases in wider benefits or tax credits beyond the CTC child element, meaning that their value would fall increasingly behind rising incomes. Table 3.1 shows that child-contingent support rose by only 7% between 2003-04 and 2006-07. Spending on early years and childcare

Table 3.1: Expenditure on child-contingent tax credits and benefits and early years education and childcare (£million, 2006-07 prices)

	1996-97	1997-98	1998-99	1999-2000	2000-01	2001-02	2002-03	2003-04	2004-05	2005-06	2006-07
Spending on child-contingent support, of which:	**18,306**	**18,145**	**18,125**	**19,175**	**20,459**	**24,100**	**25,172**	**28,588**	**29,160**	**29,622**	**30,655**
Child Benefit[1]	8,880	8,810	8,844	9,843	10,146	10,064	9,925	10,163	10,065	10,035	10,062
Other non-income related benefits[2]	837	859	886	919	1,024	1,016	1,071	1,034	1,003	1,071	1,066
Family Credit, WFTC, CTC for in-work families[3]	2,630	2,850	2,894	3,395	5,067	5,998	6,567	8,847	9,327	9,667	10,462
MCA, Children's Tax Credit, CTC family element[4]	2,060	2,001	1,964	1,319	–	2,403	2,552	2,451	2,445	2,385	2,317
IS, JSA, CTC for out-of-work families[5]	3,390	3,083	2,988	3,173	3,661	3,984	4,377	5,499	5,617	5,623	5,732
Other income-related benefits[6]	509	542	549	526	560	635	680	594	703	841	1,016
Spending on early years and childcare, of which:		**2,204**	**2,478**	**2,859**	**3,413**	**4,088**	**4,367**	**4,854**	**5,293**	**5,889**	**6,399**
Local authority spending on under fives, excl. Sure Start[7]		2,156	2,202	2,458	2,696	3,180	3,154	3,373	3,537	3,671	3,801
Sure Start, of which:		5	223	260	443	550	776	800	995	1,311	1,385
Sure Start Local Programmes		–	–	9	68	158	247	405	613	789	–
Childcare Tax Credit		42	52	140	275	358	437	680	762	907	1,213
Child contingent support (% of GDP)	1.84	1.76	1.71	1.74	1.80	2.08	2.12	2.33	2.32	2.31	2.31
Early years and childcare (% of GDP)		0.21	0.23	0.25	0.29	0.34	0.36	0.38	0.41	0.45	0.47

Notes:

2006-07 is provisional outturn. Price conversion carried out using GDP Deflator from 27 June 2008.

[1] Figures for 2003-04 onwards for Child Benefit are taken from *Hansard* in response to parliamentary questions from Justine Greening (10 October 2006) and Paul Goodman (17 January 2007).

[2] Includes disability benefits for children (mostly Disability Living Allowance for children under 16) and child dependency increases.

[3] Family Credit: total expenditure on Family Credit (including element allocated to working age adults in the DWP Benefit tables); WFTC: net expenditure from Inland Revenue annual reports; WTC/CTC: total entitlement of in-work recipients excluding family element of CTC (previously delivered through the Married Couples Allowance and the Children's Tax Credit) and childcare element of CTC.

[4] Includes estimated cost of Married Couples Allowance (MCA) and Additional Persons' Allowance to families with children prior to abolition in 2000, which are provided in various Budget reports (in a table showing the estimated cost of main tax expenditures). Half of MCA is assumed to go to married couples with children. Estimates of expenditure on the Children's Tax Credit is from HMRC's 'Tax Expenditures and Ready Reckoners' (T1.5). Estimated spending on family element of CTC is estimated by multiplying its value per family (£545) by the total number of in-work families with children in receipt of CTC (from table 1.1. of HMRC's 'Child and Working Tax Credit Statistics: Finalised annual awards 2006-07'.

[5] Includes CTC payments to out-of-work families, which was previously included within the child premia for Income Support. From 2003/04, expenditure estimates are from table 1 of HMRC's 'Child and Working Tax Credit Statistics: Finalised annual awards 2006-07'.

[6] Includes Housing Benefit, Council Tax Benefit and the Social Fund.

[7] Includes expenditure on under-fives in nursery schools, in primary schools and in the private, voluntary and independent sectors.

Sources:

Top half of table from Tom Sefton, using the Department for Work and Pensions' Benefit Expenditure tables, which have been adapted and supplemented in the case of certain benefits where responsibility has been transferred to other departments. Expenditure on children is determined by estimating what expenditure on each particular benefit would be if the household or benefit unit did not contain any children.

Early years spending from the Department for Children, Schools and Families Annual Report 2008 and (earlier years and Sure Start breakdown) House of Commons Public Accounts Committee (2007); except Childcare Tax Credit from HMRC 'Child and Working Tax Credit Statistics': Finalised annual awards 2006-07' and earlier equivalents, and Working Families Tax Credit Quarterly Enquiry for November 2002.

grew at a much faster pace, with particularly large increases (75% over these three years) for Sure Start and the CTC.

Gordon Brown 2007+

Gordon Brown's arrival at Number Ten brought high hopes from the child poverty lobby. As Chancellor, he was credited with much of the progress towards meeting Blair's child poverty pledge, and he had spoken frequently of the moral obligation to address child poverty, describing it as 'a scar on the soul of Britain' (*The Guardian*, 17 March 2000). In his first speech as Labour Party Leader in June 2007, he called for the child poverty cause to be placed 'at the heart of building a better Britain' (Brown, 2007a). The new Department for Children, Schools and Families (DCSF) was intended to give children a single champion in Whitehall.

In practice, Brown's first year in office was disappointing, bringing relatively modest increases in spending and no major new initiatives. The Children's Plan (DCSF, 2007a) pledged investment in playgrounds and resources for childcare for parents undertaking training in disadvantaged areas. The 2008 Budget announced the largest increases to the CTC since 2004 and changed Housing and Council Tax Benefit rules to improve work incentives, but the additional £0.9 billion per year that was committed was only a step towards the extra annual £4 billion believed necessary to meet the 2010 child poverty target (Hirsch, 2006).

Tight economic conditions clearly created constraints, but there were also signs of a shift in thinking about the burden of responsibility for tackling child poverty. The report that accompanied the 2008 Budget was entitled *Ending Child Poverty: Everybody's Business* (HM Treasury, 2008a), and this and the series of Child Poverty Pilots announced later in 2008 emphasised the role of local authorities and the need for local solutions. The report also set out 'the beginnings of a contract out of poverty', calling on 'families to make a commitment to improve their situations where they can and to take advantage of the opportunities on offer' (HM Treasury, 2008a, p 55). It pledged that 'the Government will provide all families with a clear *route out* of poverty' by 2020 (p 3, emphasis added); a small but significant change in language. On the other hand, in his September 2008 party conference speech, Brown reiterated that 'we are in this for the long haul – the complete elimination of child poverty by 2020', and surprised everyone by announcing his intention to enshrine the child poverty pledge in law (*The Telegraph*, 24 September 2008).

Outcomes: child poverty

The child poverty targets

Two interim targets were set as milestones on route to ending child poverty (itself defined from 2003 as reaching a poverty rate 'amongst the best in Europe';

DWP, 2003, p 20). The first target was to reduce the number of children living in households with an income below 60% of the contemporary median by a quarter between 1998-99 and 2004-05. The rate of child poverty fell steadily over this period but not by enough to meet the target (see Figure 3.1). Measured AHC, the number of poor children fell by 700,000 out of a total 4.3 million, or 16% (18% on a BHC basis). After 2004-05, poverty began to rise – perhaps unsurprising given the sharp slowing down in additional expenditure highlighted in Table 3.1. The total reduction in the number of poor children between 1998-99 and 2006-07 was just 400,000 AHC, or 9% (12% BHC), leaving a long way to go to reach the second target, halving child poverty on the BHC measure by 2010.

Of course, the story is more complicated than one headline can convey. Three points stand out. First, recent evidence shows a very large decline in persistent poverty – measured as the percentage of children living below the poverty line in at least three out of four consecutive years – down from 17% for four-year periods between 1993 and 2002 to 11% between 2002 and 2005 (DWP, 2008b, table A3.3). This is important as research shows that negative outcomes are more likely for children who are persistently poor (Barnes et al, 2008).

Second, the government's task has been made harder by the choice of a relative income target, as benefits and tax credits need to rise faster than average earnings to have an impact. Expenditure on benefits for out-of-work families grew by nearly 80%, as recorded in Table 3.1 (reflecting increases in benefit levels, not an increased caseload), but made only small gains on the poverty line for some family types and no gains at all for others (see Table 2.4 in Chapter Two). Similarly, the

Figure 3.1: Child poverty 1979 to 2006-07[1]

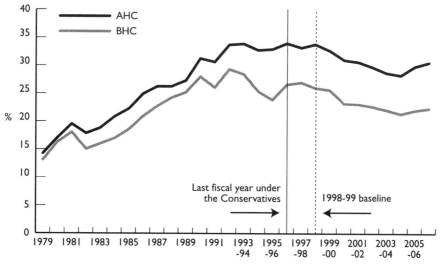

Note: [1]The percentage of children living in households with income below 60% of the contemporary median (before and after housing costs)
Source: Family Expenditure Survey and Family Resources Survey data from IFS website (www.ifs.org.uk)

enormous changes in spending on tax credits delivered substantial growth in net incomes as a share of average earnings only between 1999-00 and 2000-01, when tax credit spending increased by 47% year on year (see Table 3.1 in this chapter and Figure 2.4 in Chapter Two).

Figure 3.2 shows that child poverty has fallen much more dramatically if measured in 'absolute' terms, against a fixed income standard (60% of the 1998-99 median, updated to reflect only changes in prices). On this measure, the numbers in poverty have fallen by 42% AHC and 48% BHC. In contrast, between 1979 and 1997 (a period more than twice as long), the number of children in households with incomes below the same fixed standard fell by just 12% AHC or 24% BHC, despite average annual median income growth only slightly lower (1.6% under the Conservatives compared with 1.9% under Labour; Brewer et al, 2008a). In 2004, almost certainly to ensure at least some good news in the future, the government announced two additional targets for 2010: it would (a) halve poverty against 60% of the 1998-99 median; and (b) halve the number of children living below 70% of the contemporary median with a high material deprivation score. As suggested by Figure 3.2, the first of these two extra targets was met well ahead of time, in 2004-05. However, even against the fixed income standard, child poverty rates rose after 2004-05.

Table 3.2 gives further evidence both of rapid improvement in real living standards – here among lone parents in particular – and of faltering progress in recent years. Between 1999 and 2002, we see striking improvements in financial security and in lone parents' ability to afford the sorts of things listed in the table that most families in 21st-century Britain take for granted. Research has found

Figure 3.2: Children living in households with income below 60% of the 1998-99 median (%)

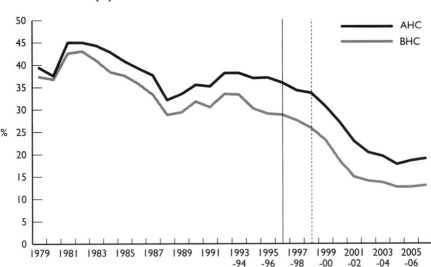

Source: Family Expenditure Survey and Family Resources Survey data from IFS website (www.ifs.org.uk)

Table 3.2: Material deprivation and financial stress among lone parents: evidence from the Families and Children Survey (FACS)

	1999	2002	2005	2006
% unable to afford selected items				
Fresh fruit on most days	17	8	6	
Best outfit for children	20	13	10	
Toys and sports gear for each child	24	12	7	7
Celebration with presents at special occasions	27	14	11	10
Friends/relatives for a meal once a month	34	20	18	16
One-week holiday (not staying with relatives)	74	58	53	53
Indicators of financial stress				
Problems with debts almost all the time	15	12	14	
Always runs out of money before end of week	27	19	19	18
Worries about money almost always	45	30	27	29

Sources: Author calculations from FACS; and Conolly and Kerr (2008) for 2006 figures.

that the extra money received by low-income households in this period really was spent on items such as these, with expenditure shares on fruit and vegetables, children's clothing and toys and games all increasing more than proportionately (Gregg et al, 2005b). But Table 3.2 shows more modest progress since 2002.

The government's own combined material deprivation and income measure continued to fall between 2004 and 2006, although it is not on track to halve by 2010 – the total fall between 1998-99 and 2006-07 was just under a quarter (Brewer et al, 2008a) – and the indicator is sensitive to the deprivation threshold chosen. The same measure with a wider deprivation threshold (more children classified as deprived) shows virtually no decline after 2004-05 (Brewer et al, 2008a).

The third important point was made in Chapter Two: quite aside from the rise in average earnings (which has meant a constantly shifting poverty line), other factors are also changing in ways that would, tax-benefit policy remaining equal, have led to increases in the poverty rate. Figure 2.6 showed that poverty for children in both lone-parent and couple families was far lower in 2004-05 (more than a one-third reduction) than it would have been had 1996-97 tax-benefit policies remained unchanged but uprated with earnings. Once again, however, we see only negligible gains from policy change in New Labour's third term. These gains are driven by the large increases to tax credits announced in the 2008 Budget, which should offset small rises in poverty from 2004-05 to 2007-08.

The failure to reach the 2004-05 target even by 2006-07 is deeply disappointing, and the slowdown in spending recorded in Table 3.1 shows that there are clear reasons why progress stalled at the end of Labour's second term; it was neither inevitable nor driven by forces beyond government control. However, it remains true that the gentle slopes presented in Figure 3.1 do not reflect the full force of the government's policy effort. Labour also deserves credit for adopting a very tough target, for getting it accepted, at least as 'an aspiration' (Letwin, 2006), even by the Conservative Party (unthinkable in 1997), and for not ditching it entirely when the going got tough: the 2010 target is the *only* quantified target in a reduced set of Public Service Agreements (PSAs).

Which children have moved out of poverty?

Table 3.3 shows changes in child poverty by family type and employment status. Children in lone-parent households – where poverty rates were highest to start with – saw much bigger improvements over the decade than children living with two adults. Children living with a lone parent working part time benefited most, with poverty falling by at least 25% measured both before and after housing costs. Child tax credits have been particularly effective for lone parents because the family element does not increase with the number of adults, and for part-time workers because lower earnings mean a higher payment.

Children living in households with a single full-time earner (either a lone parent or one half of a couple, especially with a second member working part time) saw large falls on the BHC indicator but no change (or a rise) once housing costs are accounted for. Among workless households, poverty fell by 3-4% for children living with couples and 9-10% for those with lone parents; in both cases, the risk of poverty remains very high at 77% AHC. No family type recorded falls in poverty in the first part of New Labour's third term, and most saw poverty rise, with a particularly sharp increase for children in couple households with one full-time worker and one adult at home. Nearly one in three children in such households lived below the poverty line AHC in 2006-07, higher than the share in 1996-97.

Worklessness

As well as reducing the risk of poverty in particular employment situations, a central aim has been to move parents into work. Table 3.4 shows that the share of children living in workless households has fallen but not dramatically, from around 19% in 1997 to around 16% in 2007. Most of this fall is due to a rise in lone-parent employment, and most was delivered in New Labour's first term. As discussed in Chapter Five, the government now looks very unlikely to meet its target of 70% employment among lone parents by 2010. The overall task of reducing worklessness has been made harder by the rising share of children living with only one parent (from 20.1% in 1997 to 22.5% in 2007).

The failure to deliver more rapid improvements in parental employment has led to the introduction of greater benefit conditionality for lone parents from 2008, following the recommendations of the 2007 Freud report. A second report from

Table 3.3: Child poverty, by household composition and employment status (AHC), and changes 1996-07 to 2006-07 BHC and AHC

	% of children living in households below 60% median income AHC				% point change 1996-97 to 2006-07 BHC	% point change 1996-97 to 2006-07 AHC	% change 1996-97 to 2006-07 BHC	% change 1996-97 to 2006-07 AHC
	1996-97	2000-01	2004-05	2006-07				
Lone parent	67	58	52	52	-12	-15	-24	-22
of which								
Lone parent, full time	16	15	15	16	-4	0	-36	0
Lone parent, part time	44	35	32	33	-8	-11	-30	-25
Lone parent, no work	86	82	76	77	-6	-9	-9	-10
Couple	25	22	21	23	-3	-2	-14	-8
of which								
Couple, at least one self-employed	28	31	28	30	+1	+2	+5	+7
Couple, both full time	2	2	2	4	+1	+2	+100	+100
Couple, one full time, one part time	6	6	6	6	-1	0	-25	0
Couple, one full time, one no work	28	27	23	30	-2	+2	-9	+7
Couple, one or more part time	61	56	48	54	-6	-7	-11	-11
Couple, no work	79	74	74	77	-3	-2	-4	-3
All children	34	31	28	30	-5	-4	-19	-12

Note: Percentage and percentage point changes are calculated on the numbers presented, which have been rounded.

Source: DWP (2008b, table 4.12ts)

Table 3.4: Percentage of children living in workless households, by family type

	Couple households	Lone-parent households	All household types
1997	8.7	58.0	18.8
1999	7.2	55.3	17.8
2001	6.6	51.4	16.3
2002	6.8	51.0	16.8
2003	6.0	51.1	16.2
2004	6.2	49.3	16.0
2005	6.3	47.9	15.8
2006	6.5	46.7	15.6
2007	6.5	48.0	15.9

Note: Figures refer to the spring quarter, April-June, each year.
Source: ONS, Work and Worklessness among Households, Latest Release August 2007

the Department for Work and Pensions (DWP), specifically on child poverty, proposed a series of more supportive measures to make Jobcentre Plus work more effectively for parents; some of these are being tested as Child Poverty Pilots (Harker, 2006). It remains to be seen whether these new approaches will manage to boost employment further. Here we consider the most obvious key constraint – the availability and affordability of childcare.

Childcare

The number of formal childcare places doubled between 1997 and 2006 (see Figure 3.3) – a substantial increase in a short timeframe, although well short of the government's ambitious goals: the National Childcare Strategy pledged 900,000 new places by 2004 plus a further 250,000 by 2006 (DfEE, 1998). There is evidence of larger increases in more deprived areas, but concerns about their sustainability: the share of nursery places in the 30% most deprived areas rose from 24% in 2003 to 37% in 2005, but dropped back to 29% in 2006; with similar trends in out-of-school places (Butt et al, 2007). This may well reflect both the success of the Neighbourhood Nurseries Initiative and New Opportunities Fund in expanding supply in the short run, and the problems that arose when start-up funding finished in 2005. The Neighbourhood Nurseries Initiative evaluation highlighted uncertainty among providers about their long-term funding strategy (NNI Research Team, 2007). In 2005, settings in deprived areas were no more likely to have made a loss than settings in other areas, but by 2006 they were significantly more likely to have done so (Butt et al, 2007). By 2007, despite the government falling short of its own targets, there was evidence of an oversupply of nursery places: occupancy rates were down from 95% in 2002 to 79% in 2007, with vacancies higher in deprived areas (Butt et al, 2007).

Figure 3.3: Registered childcare places in England, 1997-2006

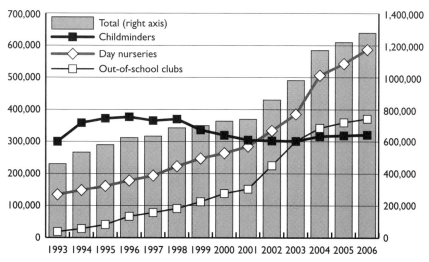

Sources: 1993-2003 from Ofsted figures provided by Daycare Trust; 1997 and 2004-06 from Butt et al (2007). 1997 figures are the same in the two sources, so the series should be consistent.

Figure 3.4, from an ongoing survey of parents, confirms the view that take-up of formal childcare has largely stopped rising. The only statistically significant change since 2004 is for five- to seven-year-olds, and this appears to reflect a change in the survey's timing and the anomaly that reception classes are counted as formal childcare (Kazimirski et al, 2008). Use of out-of-school clubs has not increased since 2004, which may reflect relatively slow growth in places (see Figure 3.3), despite the roll-out of the Extended Schools Programme. The very high use by three- to four-year-olds reflects free early years places, which at 2.5 hours per day are not childcare.

The lack of change is broadly reflected across employment, income and ethnic background categories, such that wide disparities in the use of formal childcare remain, as illustrated in Table 3.5. Survey numbers are too small to break down by age and ethnic background, but overall 33% of children from Black African and white backgrounds used formal care, compared with 24% from Black Caribbean, 25% from Indian and 18% from Pakistani/Bangladeshi backgrounds. It is a PSA target for the DCSF to increase take-up of formal childcare by working households with an annual income below £20,000 from 615,000 in 2004 to 735,000 by 2008. The share of children increased slightly (but not significantly) from 26% in 2004 to 27% in 2007 but as the share of children both overall and in these two bands has fallen, the actual number of children has fallen to 544,000.

One interpretation of these figures is that there is now sufficient childcare available for those who want it. Hakim et al (2008) note that, in 2004, 66% of those using informal care said it was because they could trust the provider, compared

Figure 3.4: Use of formal childcare in the last week, 1999-2007 (%)

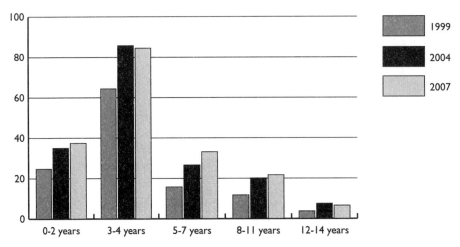

Notes:

(1) Includes day nurseries, playgroups, nursery classes and nursery schools, reception classes, breakfast and after-school clubs, childminders, nannies, au pairs and babysitters.

(2) The numbers for five- to seven-year-olds should be read with caution – the increase is likely to reflect a change in the date of fieldwork. Children in reception class (but not later school years) are automatically included as using formal childcare. The 2004 survey was carried out in the autumn when most of the reception class were only four; the 2007 survey was carried out in the spring when the majority were five, boosting the share of this age group classified as using childcare.

Source: Parents' Childcare Survey Series, 1999 and 2004 reported in Butt et al (2007, table 5.4); 2007 from Kazimirski et al (2008)

Table 3.5: Use of formal childcare, by household and area characteristics, 2007 (%)

	0-2	3-4	5-7	8-11	12-14
Annual income below £10,000	25	80	23	12	4
£20,000-£29,999	38	88	35	22	8
£45,000+	63	92	50	38	10
Couple, both work	59	94	37	27	7
Couple, one works	25	79	30	16	6
Couple, no work	23	71	16	14	4
Lone parent, works	50	89	50	25	10
Lone parent, no work	27	81	35	20	8
Most deprived area quintile	26	76	28	17	6
Middle area quintile	46	92	34	22	6
Least deprived area quintile	50	93	44	30	10

Notes: As for Figure 3.4.
Source: Kazimirski et al (2008)

with 7% citing the cost of formal care and 2% saying they had no other choices. In 2007, the most commonly cited reason for not going to work was 'I want to stay with my child(ren)' (46%), compared with 22% mentioning the cost of childcare (Kazimirski et al, 2008). However, this still leaves more than one household in five explicitly discouraged by childcare costs – significantly down from 31% in 1999 but slightly up from 20% in 2004 (Butt et al, 2007). Furthermore, when non-working parents were asked whether they would work if they could arrange 'good-quality childcare which was convenient, reliable and affordable', 51% said they would, including 65% of those with a household income below £10,000 and 66% of lone parents (Kazimirski et al, 2008). Overall, the 2007 survey found that perception of availability and affordability of local childcare improved slightly between 2004 and 2007, but 36% thought that affordability was fairly or very poor and 37% that there were not enough childcare places in their local area.

Part of the reason why overprovision can sit alongside unmet need may be a mismatch between supply and demand, both across areas and across childcare types. Barnes et al (2006) point to a preference for childminders for very young children, but childminder numbers have fallen since 1997 (see Figure 3.3), probably as a result of tighter regulation. There is also evidence of underprovision outside regular hours and for disabled children (Waldfogel and Garnham, 2008).

Another obvious explanation is that costs are still too high for many families to consider, even with the subsidy available through the childcare element of CTC. Take-up has increased since the childcare element was introduced, and the government spent over £1 billion on it in 2006-07 (see Table 3.1). By April 2008, 30% of eligible families were benefiting, up from 23% in 2004, including 55% of single parents with a child under five (Sefton: forthcoming). However, this still leaves a large share of families relying on friends or family or facing market prices for childcare. The fact that not all costs are covered has been found to be a disincentive (see discussion in Waldfogel and Garnham, 2008). For families on the lowest incomes, 80% of childcare costs are covered, but the taper begins early. That the credit is conditional on employment also presents difficulties for families considering entering work, requiring two big leaps at once.

Kazimirski et al (2008) conclude that the National Childcare Strategy has not had as much impact as intended, particularly in relation to the most disadvantaged children, and this assessment seems fair. New nursery places carry uncertainty about sustainability, while not always meeting parents' requirements – not everyone wants this type of provision, while for others cost is still prohibitive. After-school and holiday provision have not expanded at the same rate as nursery places, despite the 2010 deadline for Extended Schools.

The high take-up of early years places for three- and four-year-olds indicates that where provision is both free and good quality, parents will use it. This may be partly because places are part time and partly because parents feel differently about group care once a child is three years old. But the strength of the response does suggest that the model of (limited) demand-side subsidy for younger and older age groups may not have been the most effective.

At the same time, however, it is important to remember that childcare issues are just one part of the equation for low-income families. The majority of poor children now live in working households. The concept of a 'contract out of poverty' implies that parents are failing to take up good opportunities to improve their children's circumstances, but where the choice is between being working poor (even before childcare costs are deducted) and being poorer still but at home with the children, the right decision in the best interests of the child is not obvious. The issue of low pay is discussed further in Chapter Five.

Outcomes: early child development

Childcare was discussed above in the context of facilitating parental employment to reduce income poverty. We now turn to government policies focused on early child development, including action to improve the quality of formal childcare places as well as wider policies aimed at giving disadvantaged children a better start.

To begin at the beginning, however, changes to Maternity Allowance should not be overlooked – up from 18 to 39 weeks by April 2007, with a pledge of 52 weeks by 2010; and up by 60% in real value by 2008. Research finds that lower-income women return to work when paid leave ends (Tanaka, 2005), meaning that more children in low-income households should now be benefiting from more time with their mothers in the first year, with important benefits for health, cognitive development and social and emotional well-being (for a review of this evidence, see Waldfogel, 2006).

Childcare quality

Despite the government's stated objective of childcare that provides a 'double dividend' – improving outcomes for children as well as enabling parental employment – Butt et al (2007, p 96) assess its strategy on raising childcare quality as 'extraordinarily unambitious'. Childcare quality is a difficult concept to pin down, but affection, communication and responsiveness are generally agreed to be crucial features, particularly for those aged under three, with learning opportunities also becoming important as children get older (Melhuish, 1993). The first three aspects appear impossible to measure consistently, and equally hard to legislate for, but several structural features have been found to make a quality experience more likely for children; in particular, staff qualifications and conditions, child–staff ratios and continuity of caregivers (see Sylva et al, 2003; Melhuish, 2004; Waldfogel, 2006).

The government goal is for a graduate leader in every setting by 2015, with the full workforce at National Vocational Qualification (NVQ) Level 3, or A-level equivalent. (In contrast, New Zealand is working towards an entire graduate workforce in the sector by 2012.) A Transformation Fund was set up in 2006 to support training, and small improvements in qualification levels (and also turnover) have resulted. In 2005, 56% of childcare staff were supervisors – qualified to work with children on their own – up from 50% in 2003, while 72% had at least a Level 3 qualification, representing a 'substantial increase' on earlier years (Butt et al, 2007). But only 7% had post-secondary (Level 5 or 6) qualifications, compared with 60-80% in nursery and primary schools.

The approach to improving quality has instead relied heavily on regulation. The single Ofsted framework seeks to eliminate the disparity in experience of a three-year-old in day nursery compared with nursery school with a wave of targets for each child. These require a burden of reporting that has been criticised for having a negative impact on quality by taking up staff time and, by some, for being too regimented and learning oriented (for discussion, see Tanner et al, 2006). Seeking to improve quality by tightly regulating 'output', rather than allowing more freedom to a more highly qualified staff, certainly seems an inferior strategy, but it has the advantage that it is lower cost. Improving staff qualifications and wages would raise the question 'who pays?', and under the current market-based system few parents could afford to pay more. Table 3.1 showed large increases in early years expenditure, but the total (0.48% of GDP) remains well short of spending in the Nordic countries (from 0.9% up; OECD, 2007d). The unwillingness to go further and faster in increasing expenditure placed serious constraints on the government's ability to improve childcare quality.

Nursery education

Table 3.6 records considerable success in ensuring that three- to four-year-olds have access to early education: in 1999 nearly one-quarter of parents said that their child did not use an early years provider; by 2004 this had fallen to just 6%, although progress since then has stalled. All income and ethnic groups have benefited, but significant disparities remain. Table 3.6 also shows that around 8% of children attend an eligible setting but – according to their parents – pay a fee. In part, this may be due to parents paying for extra hours on top of the free entitlement and not realising that the fee has been reduced, but it is worrying that non-working households appear equally affected. A new code of practice introduced in April 2006 should in principle ensure that parents are not charged for the basic entitlement, but as many settings only offer sessions longer than 2.5 hours per day, charging is likely to continue.

Perhaps more disappointing is recent evidence from a study by researchers at Durham University, which assessed development and skills of children starting school between 2001 and 2006 in 124 primary schools (Merrell et al, 2008). The study found no evidence of either improved average scores or a narrowing gap between poor children and others, despite the increase in nursery attendance.

One potential explanation is that expansion has taken place entirely in private and voluntary sector day nurseries and preschools, not in nursery schools and nursery classes, where quality is highest (West, 2006). Funding for the part-time place (currently £457 per child per term) is much less than what is spent by both state and private nursery schools, leaving settings without other support at a severe disadvantage. But the Durham results are also disappointing given wider early years initiatives (discussed below) and increased income and expenditure in poorer households (discussed above).

Sure Start

Hugely ambitious, Sure Start aimed to change the long-term developmental trajectories of young children. Its full impact would by definition only become clear in the long term, but it was hoped that early positive signs would be visible

Table 3.6: Share of eligible three- and four-year-olds not using any early years education, 1999-2007 (%)

	1999	2004	2007	Received 'eligible childcare' but not free entitlement 2007
All	23	6	6	8
Working household	21	5	5	8
Non-working household	33	11	9	8
Income <£10,000	35	9	8	8
£10,000-£19,000	20	8	10	8
£20,000-£31,999*	19	5	5	6
£32,000+*	17	2	3	7
Two-parent family	21	5	6	7
Lone-parent family	33	10	7	8
White family			5	7
Black family			5	13
Asian family			15	11
Other family			8	8

Base: All three and four-year old children eligible for the free entitlement.

Notes: Coverage higher than in Figure 3.4 because that includes all three- and four-year-olds; here three-year-olds are only included in the term after their third birthday.

*slight change in top two income categories for 1997: £20,000-£29,000 and £30,000+.

Sources: Parents' Childcare Survey Series (table 5.2 in Butt et al. 2007 for 1999 and 2004; Kazimirski et al, 2008 for 2007)

sooner. While the programme was popular with parents from the start (Power, 2007), initial results from the National Evaluation of Sure Start were disappointing: the most disadvantaged three-year-olds and their families (teenage parents, lone parents and workless households) were doing *less* well in SSLPs than outside them, scoring lower on verbal ability and social competence and higher on behavioural problems (NESS, 2005). Somewhat less disadvantaged households within the areas did seem to be benefiting, suggesting that the new programmes were less well targeted than those they had replaced.

However, the most recent results tell a different story. Half the outcomes assessed showed positive effects: SSLP children displayed more positive social behaviour and greater independence, and their parents less negative parenting and a better home environment (NESS, 2008). This time there were no differences across subgroups. The effects identified were modest in size, but the results nevertheless encouraging, particularly given the difficulty of influencing these variables and the fact that the evaluation is 'unusually thorough' in seeking to avoid a false positive (albeit according to an evaluation board member; Rutter, M., 2006). There are some methodological differences between the studies, but the key difference appears to be that the three-year-olds in the later study benefited from more developed programmes that were there for their entire lives, and that were able to learn from earlier findings, especially regarding the need for more effort to reach the most vulnerable. This is perhaps a lesson in the importance of giving programmes time to establish themselves before expecting measurable results.

Sure Start Local Programmes can also be assessed against PSA targets. Success on these has been mixed, with good progress against early targets to reduce the share of children re-registered on the child protection register and to reduce smoking in pregnancy, but less success on smoking in the middle period, and consistent underperformance in terms of reducing worklessness. Early targets (to 2001-02) to reduce the percentage of low birthweight babies and emergency hospital admissions in the first year were not met, and did not reappear in later PSAs.

Children's Centres

By April 2006, the majority of SSLPs were operating as Children's Centres – abolished in their existing form just as they started to show benefits, a victim in effect of their own popularity. Children's Centres are ostensibly an attempt to mainstream Sure Start and bring the benefits of joined-up playgroups, healthcare and parenting support to the whole of England. Of the 3,500 planned Centres, over one-third (1,400) were in operation by September 2007, reaching over a million children, mostly in disadvantaged areas.

The incorporation of SSLPs into Children's Centres has been met with concern on several fronts. First, Children's Centres are funded through and run by local authorities, with more specific guidelines about the services to be offered. Sure Start Local Programmes were run by local boards, which included parents and members of the community as well as representatives from statutory authorities. Norman Glass, one of the founders of Sure Start, has argued that the boards were crucial to the project's success, not only because they ensured responsiveness to local need but also because they gave local people ownership; Sure Start was not just another Whitehall initiative 'being done to, or for, them' (Glass, 2005).

A second concern is that Children's Centres represent the capture of Sure Start by the 'employability agenda', with a much greater emphasis on childcare (Glass, 2005; Hakim et al, 2008). It is not clear that this is the case – many Children's Centres do not provide onsite childcare, and PSA targets have always included reductions in worklessness. On the positive side, Children's Centres offer the potential to become permanent and universal features of the landscape, more difficult to dismantle in the future than the SSLPs.

Perhaps the most serious worry regards funding. The average expenditure per child in SSLPs that had been operational for three years was £900 at 1999-2000 prices, or £1,070 at 2006-07 prices (NESS, 2006); in 2006-07 funding for Children's Centres was down to £540 per head and is set to fall further to £405 by 2010.[1] There are also questions about whether this funding will continue to be ringfenced within local authority budgets.

Conclusions

Labour's agenda for tackling poverty and disadvantage among children was serious and wide-ranging, but with the benefit of hindsight, it is clear that policies did not match the scale of the challenge. The strategy began well and ambitiously, and by 2004 there were positive signs that it was succeeding in improving the daily reality and future prospects of poor children. However, it was noted in 2005 that this success should be considered just a start: 'If the government is to leave a lasting legacy, progress to date will need to be only the first step' (Stewart, 2005a, p 163).

In reality, very little has changed since 2004. Expenditure on tax credits and benefits, which had risen sharply in each year since 1999, has flattened out, with the expected impact on child poverty. Progress in reducing worklessness has also stalled. The government has continued to increase the number of formal childcare places available, but there has been little change since 2004 in the number of parents using them, suggesting that more should have been done to ensure affordability and/or that other factors are creating disincentives for parents to enter work. While government has turned to conditionality to try to beat the deadlock, high levels of in-work poverty suggest that the failure to 'make work pay' may be a key culprit.

Meanwhile, nearly every three- and four-year-old receives some preschool education, but this has not had a measurable impact on school readiness, perhaps due to varying quality. For children attending formal childcare, quality appears improved relative to 1997 thanks to tighter regulation, but there has been little change in the factors that are believed to make an important difference to a child's experience – staff qualifications and pay. Sure Start is proving itself now it has had time to bed in, with impacts on parenting that may reap long-term rewards. But while the new Children's Centres have built a long-term future for Sure Start out of bricks and mortar, funding per head has been cut dramatically.

We should not lose sight of the fact that poor children are far better off, both in absolute and relative terms, than they would have been had policies been left unchanged from 1997. Perhaps it was unrealistic to expect that the damage done during the 1980s to the life chances of today's parents could be undone in the same timeframe. But as economic times get tougher, and with Labour facing probable defeat in the next General Election, it is difficult not to look back on a decade of economic growth and huge parliamentary majorities as a rare opportunity only partly grasped to restructure society in the interests of the poorest children.

Note

[1] These estimates are based on a response by Beverly Hughes to a parliamentary question about expenditure on Sure Start Children's Centres – £604 million in 2006-07 and £1,135 million in 2010-11 (*Hansard* written answers, 12 June 2008). Figures were divided by 1,400 Children's Centres in 2006-07 and 3,500 in 2010-11, and by 800 children covered by each Centre.

FOUR

Education: New Labour's top priority

Ruth Lupton, Natalie Heath and Emma Salter

Introduction

Education has been central to the New Labour mission – its top priority in every election manifesto. The government has focused on raising school standards and on expanding opportunities for post-compulsory education and training in order to tackle what Gordon Brown (2007b) has referred to as the problem of 'no room at the bottom' – the disappearing demand for unskilled and low-skilled jobs in Britain's economy. Reducing inequality has been a central theme for economic as well as social reasons. 'For generations', New Labour has argued, 'our country has been held back by an education system that excelled for the privileged few but let down the majority' (Labour Party, 2005). In the 2004 Comprehensive Spending Review, tackling the attainment gap between more and less advantaged groups became a specific government target and Gordon Brown has since reaffirmed this commitment, emphasising its importance to the achievement of 'social justice for all'.

The overall picture is one of investment and expansion. UK public expenditure on education has risen as a percentage of gross domestic product (GDP) from 4.7% in 1996-97 to 5.5% in 2006-07, and is now at its highest level for 30 years (DCSF, 2008a), rising on average by 4.3% per year in real terms, compared with 1.4% under the Conservatives (Sibieta et al, 2008), and nearly reaching the Organisation for Economic Co-operation and Development (OECD) average. In England, per capita spending on schools rose 84% from 1997-98 to 2007-08 (DCSF, 2008b), including a big increase in capital expenditure with a commitment to renew the buildings of every secondary school by 2020. There are now over 35,000 (9%) more teachers and many more support staff, leading to a large reduction (from 27.9% in 1997 to 10.8% in 2008) in the percentage of primary school classes with more than 30 pupils (DCSF, 2008c). The total number of students (home and overseas) in higher education (HE) increased by nearly a third between 1997 and 2005-06.

New Labour has presided over an expansion of education policy 'through the day and through the lifecourse' (Ball, 2008). For schools, the initial focus was on standards in primary schools, shifting to an emphasis on secondary schools in the second term and more tailored and individualised provision in the third.

Adult education has been a priority throughout, albeit with a shift in focus from 'lifelong learning' to 'skills for life'. In 2001, the government turned to HE with a 'historic commitment' to open it to half of all young people before they are 30 (Labour Party, 2001). In 11 years there have been nine Acts of Parliament covering education and skills as well as countless non-legislative changes: a relentless programme of intervention and change.

In this chapter, we look at what has happened to educational inequality during this period of investment, growth and reform. We adopt a conventional approach used in education research, looking at the differences in attainment between different social groups rather than simply at the overall distribution of attainment, thus reflecting historic welfarist aspirations for universal state education as an equalising force in society. We focus primarily on social class inequalities in England; inequalities between ethnic groups are covered in Chapter Nine, and differences in policy in Scotland, Wales and Northern Ireland in Chapter Twelve. Space constraints require us to leave analysis of the intersections between social class, ethnicity and gender to others (for example Cassen and Kingdon, 2007). Finally, although education has now been subsumed under the broader children's agenda, we keep it separate here. Other aspects of children's welfare were covered in Chapter Three. We return to the importance of their integration with education in our conclusions.

Background and inheritance

New Labour inherited a legacy of relatively high attainment and low equity. Primary, GCSE (General Certificate of Secondary Education) and A-level results were all rising, albeit amid media controversy about whether this was a result of allegedly easier examinations. England's 15-year-olds ranked eighth in mathematics and seventh in reading among OECD countries (ONS, 2002). Success was apparently achieved with relatively low investment: education spending as a proportion of GDP was low by OECD standards and falling (McKnight et al, 2005).

However, at the same time, socioeconomic inequalities in attainment were high relative to comparable industrialised nations, and a disturbing report from the Office for Standards in Education (Ofsted) had shown that the social class attainment gap was growing wider as standards rose (Ofsted, 1993). There were particular problems in disadvantaged urban areas. Three-quarters of inner-city schools did not reach the national target of 50% of students getting five or more GCSEs at grades A*-C (DfEE, 1999a). Moreover, nearly three times as many inner-city secondary schools as other schools were judged by Ofsted to have 'serious weaknesses' or require 'special measures'. According to New Labour's first Education Secretary David Blunkett (1998), 'the traditional solutions [were] not working in these areas'.

High levels of inequality in school achievement were reflected in relatively low rates of participation in education and training for 17- to 19-year-olds, lower than in any other major industrial nation. Two-thirds of the workforce lacked vocational qualifications (Labour Party, 1997), and a government taskforce led by Sir Claus Moser reported that seven million adults (one in five) were not functionally literate and up to 40% had problems with numeracy – more than in most other leading economies. Only 250,000 of those seven million adults were undertaking any relevant courses of study (DfEE, 1999b).

Further, while HE had rapidly expanded since the early 1980s and participation among students from lower socioeconomic groups had risen, more affluent groups had benefited disproportionately from university expansion (DfES, 2003a; Blanden and Machin, 2004). Shortly before New Labour came to power, the National Committee of Inquiry into Higher Education under Sir Ron Dearing recommended a new focus on widening participation, backed by additional funding (Dearing, 1997).

New Labour responded to educational inequalities with a combination of system-wide and targeted policies, expecting that the most disadvantaged pupils and students would benefit from general improvements, but also that they would need additional help. Here we divide policies into those affecting compulsory schooling (ages 5-16) and those aimed at post-compulsory education and training. We first review the interventions made, then assess their impact on outcomes and inequalities.

Policies for compulsory schooling

System-wide policies

New Labour's initial focus was on the primary phase of schooling, where it set an ambitious target that by 2004, 85% of 11-year-olds would reach the expected level (Level 4) in the Key Stage 2 tests, rising from 64% in English and 62% in mathematics in 1997. The principal mechanism was to be stronger central government intervention in curriculum and pedagogy. National strategies for literacy and numeracy were introduced, prescribing a mandatory hour per day on these subjects, along with frameworks for teaching, guidance materials, and teacher training. Concerns that this made the curriculum too narrow were reflected in a new primary strategy in 2003, covering all subjects and emphasising school and teacher autonomy. In 2006, the original frameworks for literacy and numeracy teaching were revised, with greater emphasis on the teaching of synthetic phonics, following a review of the teaching of early reading (DfES, 2006a).

After 2001, central intervention in teaching and learning was extended to secondary schools, with the introduction of the Key Stage 3 strategy (later Secondary National Strategy), offering consultancy, guidance and teaching materials across all subjects and on whole-school approaches to assessment and monitoring, behaviour and attendance. The government set a target that the proportion of students attaining qualifications equivalent to five GCSEs at grades A*-C should rise by two percentage points each year between 2002 and 2006 and to 60% by 2008, and that all schools should have at least 20% of students at this level by 2004, rising to 25% by 2006 and 30% by 2008.[1]

Reforms in teaching and learning were supplemented by initiatives to improve behaviour and attendance, and backed by investment in the school workforce. More teachers and support staff were recruited and a national workforce agreement in 2003 aimed to free teachers from administrative tasks and excessive cover, giving them guaranteed time for planning, preparation and assessment.

All of these programmes support an early claim that the government would focus on 'standards more than structures as the key to success' (Labour Party, 1997, p 7). However, structural changes in the secondary school system have been far-reaching. Most controversial has been the introduction of Academies: state-funded independent schools with private sponsors, with control of their own admissions and (for the first Academies but not later ones) curriculum. The first Academies were announced in 2000, and the government's goal is to open 400. Trust schools (foundation schools supported by a charitable trust) were also established in 2006, and there has been a massive expansion of the Conservative-initiated specialist schools programme, moving towards all secondary schools having a specialism by 2008.[2] More faith schools have also been encouraged. These choice and diversity policies, combined with the government's failure to abolish grammar schools, have been widely seen as a move to the Right – so much so that the government, supported by the Conservatives, only narrowly survived a backbench revolt over its 2005 schools White Paper (DfEs, 2005a). Concerns that the result will be a more socially stratified system in which middle-class children will be educationally advantaged are supported by research evidence that demonstrates that middle-class parents are better equipped to exercise school choice (Gewirtz et al, 1995), that faith schools have more advantaged intakes than their surrounding areas (Allen and West, 2007) and that more able pupils do better than less able pupils in specialist schools (Levacic and Jenkins, 2004). Moreover, within schools, the government has encouraged setting by ability, despite evidence that this is likely to result in working-class and some minority ethnic students being consigned to lower sets (Gillborn and Youdell, 2000). A new emphasis on personalised learning announced in the 2005 White Paper raises similar concerns. While potentially offering the chance of relevant, engaging curriculum and appropriate teaching, it also presents opportunities for 'differentiation and social advantage-seeking that interested parents will undoubtedly pursue' (Ball, 2008, p 204).

Targeted policies

At the same time as these system-wide reforms, interventions targeted towards the most disadvantaged areas and schools have been stepped up under New

Labour. Early Education Action Zones were quickly incorporated into a bigger programme – Excellence in Cities (EiC) – targeted on all secondary schools (and later on about a third of primary schools) in selected urban authorities. Funding of about £120 per pupil per year was provided to support specific interventions: learning mentors, learning support units, City Learning Centres and provision for students identified as 'gifted and talented'. A plethora of other ringfenced grants was also targeted on schools in disadvantaged areas, including the Ethnic Minority Achievement Grant (EMAG), the Leadership Incentive Grant (LIG) and, perhaps most importantly, Pupil Learning Credits (PLCs), an additional grant to 260 secondary schools in EiC areas with 35% or more pupils on Free School Meals (FSM), aimed at the 11-14 age group.

Later policies have substantially reinforced this early targeting. Since 2006, many of the individual grants and programmes, including EiC, have been mainstreamed as part of the School Development Grant, embedding them more firmly and giving schools more freedom over spending. The emphasis on targeted interventions in primary schools has also been stepped up, with a new emphasis on targeting individual disadvantaged pupils, not just schools and areas (Whitty, 2008). Since 2005, there have been three new programmes of intensive individual support: Every Child a Reader, Every Child a Writer and Every Child Counts. More attention is now also being given to the organisation, resourcing and functions of schools, in ways that should equip them better to meet the needs of disadvantaged pupils. London Challenge – a central government-led, city-wide approach to improving education – was a significant development in 2003, as it emphasised structural issues, including teacher recruitment, professional development and accreditation, and support for leadership, as well as interventions aimed at pupils. It was extended in 2008 to Greater Manchester and the Black Country. There has been a new emphasis on social and emotional aspects of learning (SEAL). Extended schools, first announced in 2001 and expected to include all schools by 2010, gave more emphasis to support services and out-of-school activities. Most significantly, the introduction of *Every Child Matters* in 2003 (DfES, 2003b) and the integration of education within the Children's Plan of 2007 signalled a much broader vision of a 21st-century school that 'actively contributes to all aspects of a child's life – health and wellbeing, [and] safety … because they help children achieve, but also because they are good for children's wider development and part of a good childhood' (DCSF, 2007a, p 146).

This approach offers much greater prospects than hitherto that schools might contribute to breaking down the barriers to learning for children in poverty, if of course they can give sufficient priority to these issues while also responding to government pressure on attainment targets.

All in all, there is no doubt that more money has been directed towards schools with disadvantaged intakes and that recent policies are accentuating this redistribution.

Figure 4.1, showing change between 1997-98 and 2005-06 in the total funding per pupil that local authorities receive, shows a clear, although not dramatic, redistribution towards those that are more disadvantaged. Sibieta et al (2008) estimate that the extra amount in the secondary school funding settlement for FSM pupils (the 'FSM premium') has risen in real terms by nearly 13% per year since 2003-04, faster than the base per pupil amount, such that in 2006-07, schools received an extra 77% over the base amount for each FSM pupil, up from 61% in 2003-04. These are significant changes, but their effect will be locally variable, since each local authority has its own formula for distributing school funds and many put less of a premium on deprivation than does the government. Whether *all* disadvantaged schools have seen a generous increase in funding is less clear than the overall redistributive effect of policy. Moreover, there is no incentive in the system for schools to spend all their additional money on disadvantaged pupils: performance targets have focused on higher-grade GCSE attainment, not the progress or achievement of the least advantaged.

Outcomes from compulsory schooling

Overall outcomes

We assess outcomes of these policies through the standard mechanism of national test results. This approach has some limitations. Achievement in tests is only one

Figure 4.1: Change in per pupil funding (age 3-19) for local authorities, by FSM level 1997-98 to 2005-06

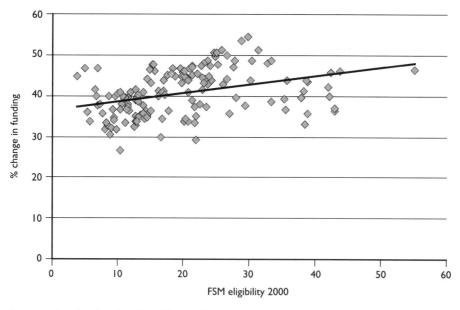

Source: Authors' analysis based on FSM data from Statistics of Schools in England 2000 and DCSF Per Pupil Funding Series, October 2007

outcome of education, and one that can be particularly affected by performance targets. There is a time lag between policy change and results, as learners building on stronger foundations move gradually through the system, and this makes it difficult to assess the full impact of policies that have only recently been introduced. Furthermore, all tests measure knowledge and understanding in particular ways. As Kitty Stewart points out in Chapter Thirteen, some international tests for 15-year-olds show a rather different picture than national tests, possibly a function of the tests themselves. However, we use national test results here because this is the only source of standardised annual data over time, enables trends among different groups to be identified and allows evaluation of the government's performance in relation to its own targets.

Overall impacts on attainment have been relatively modest, but with a greater improvement since 2004-05. Between 1997 and 2004, the proportion of students achieving five higher-grade GCSEs (A★-C) or equivalent rose by about one percentage point per year, the same as under the Conservatives in the 1990s. From 2004-05, it rose by over two percentage points per year, taking it over the 60% target (to 60.8% in 2006-07). The proportion of young people achieving any passes is not currently a target but is a better indicator of progress at the bottom. This did not reduce at all under the Conservatives, but fell by about one-third between 1997 and 2007 – a significant improvement. Again the greatest gains were from 2004-05 onwards, a change that may reflect the arrival of cohorts of GCSE students better equipped by their primary education. Although attainment at primary level has fallen short of the government's target, rising only to 80% in English and 77% in mathematics by 2007, there were very substantial gains in 1998-99 and 1999-2000, after the introduction of the national strategies. Children taking Key Stage 2 tests in 1999-2000 were the first cohort for whom subsequent GCSE results improved markedly (Figure 4.2). However, the improvement also coincides with the inclusion in school performance measures of a wider range of vocational qualifications. Improvements since 2004-05 in the proportions achieving five GCSEs at grades A★-C including English and mathematics have been considerably smaller than the proportions getting five A★-C grades overall.

Progress in tackling inequalities

Turning now to the question of *whose* results have improved, it is immediately clear that disadvantaged schools and areas have shown more rapid improvement than the average. By 2005 (the latest available analysis), there had been a marked closing of the gap between schools with 35% of FSM pupils and others (Figure 4.3). In fact, the most disadvantaged schools had overtaken those with moderate FSM levels.[3] An evaluation of EiC has shown that the percentage of pupils achieving five A★-C grades increased by around 11 percentage points from 39.8% in 2001 to 50.6% in 2005, compared with five percentage points for non-EiC schools (from 52.2% to 57.5%), thus closing the gap from 12.4 percentage points to 6.9 (DCSF,

Figure 4.2: Change in attainment levels at Key Stage 2 and GCSE, 1997-98 to 2006-07

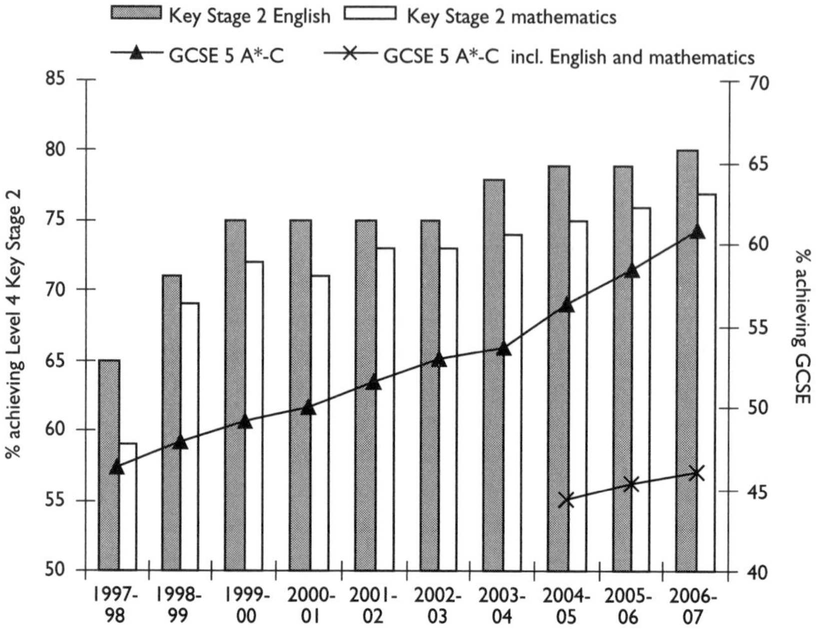

Source: DCSF (2008c)

2008d). In general, the lowest-attaining schools have caught up but in 2007, 638 (about one-fifth) were still adrift of the target of 30% attaining five A*-C grades (including English and mathematics), resulting in the announcement of a new programme, 'National Challenge', a funding offer of £400 million for intensive tuition and for support to school leaders, backed by the threat of swift closure and reopening as an Academy or trust school if no progress is made.

Progress is less impressive when we look at individual-level data. The Youth Cohort Study[4] enables analysis by social class from 1989 to 2004. It shows a slight closing of the gap between highest and lowest social class groups, but not nearly as great as the change at school level, and only sufficient to return the gap to its 1992 level (Table 4.1). These data are not available beyond 2004. If the downward trend had continued since 2004, the gap would be at 38% by 2007, the lowest recorded figure. From 2002 onwards we can compare the attainment of pupils on FSM with those not – thus measuring the relationship with family poverty rather than social class. These data show the FSM gap closing more sharply from 2004-05, suggesting that part of the uplift in overall GCSE attainment has been due to the relatively greater progress of disadvantaged pupils (Table 4.2).[5]

One possible reason that individual measures do not show as much progress as school measures is that targeted policies have enabled poor pupils in the most disadvantaged schools to improve more rapidly than their counterparts elsewhere.

Figure 4.3: Change in attainment levels at GCSE, by FSM level of school, 1999-2005

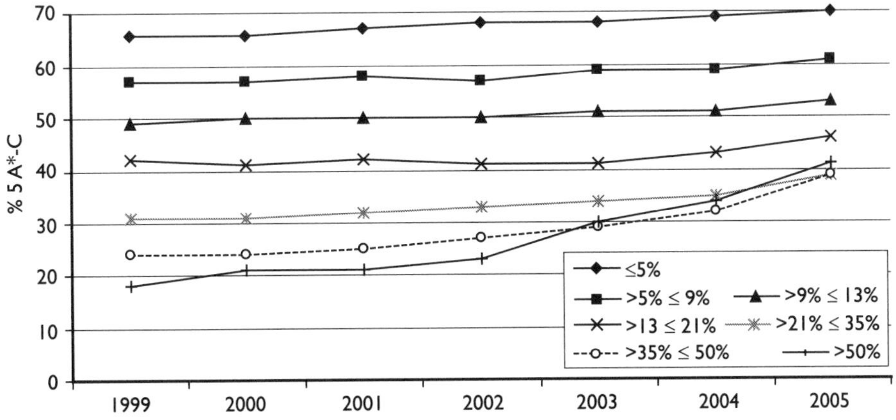

Source: DCSF Statistics of Education: Trends in Attainment Gaps: 2005

Table 4.1: Attainment of five GCSE grades A*-C in Year 11, by social class, 1989-2004, England and Wales

Parental occupation (socioeconomic group)	1989	1991	1992	1994	1996	1998
Managerial/professional	52	58	60	66	68	69
Other non-manual	42	49	51	58	58	60
Skilled manual	21	27	29	36	36	40
Semi-skilled manual	16	20	23	26	29	32
Unskilled manual	12	15	16	16	24	20
Other/not classified	15	18	18	20	22	24
Gap between highest and lowest (excluding other)	40	43	44	50	44	49
Ratio of highest to lowest categories	4.3	3.9	3.8	4.1	2.8	3.5
Parental occupation (National Statistics Socio-Economic Classification)	**2000**	**2002**	**2004**			
Higher professional	74	77	77			
Lower professional	62	64	65			
Intermediate	49	51	53			
Lower supervisory	35	34	40			
Routine	26	31	33			
Other/not classified	24	26	33			
Gap between highest and lowest (excluding other)	48	46	44			
Ratio of highest to lowest categories	2.8	3.0	2.3			

Source: DCSF Youth Cohort Study SFR04/2005

This is plausible, as qualitative evaluations of these interventions have generally been good (Braun et al, 2005; Ofsted, 2005). However, only small independent effects on attainment have been shown (Machin et al, 2007). Alternatively, disadvantaged students in very disadvantaged schools may be characteristically different from those in more advantaged schools, in ways that make them more likely to succeed. Ethnicity may be a factor (Lupton and Sullivan, 2007). There is also some evidence (DfES, 2006b; Machin et al, 2007) that it is the more advantaged pupils in disadvantaged schools who have benefited most from targeted policies, suggesting the need for greater targeting of support to disadvantaged pupils *within* schools.

What is clear is that an enormous social class attainment gap remains. The social class gap between highest and lowest groups at the end of compulsory schooling is around 40 percentage points (44 in 2004 but possibly lower now). The gap between the most and least advantaged schools is nearly 30 points (Figure 4.3), and that between non-FSM and FSM pupils 27 points (Table 4.2). New area-level data for 2007 show that four-fifths of young people in the most advantaged 10% of areas leave compulsory schooling with five GCSEs at grades A*-C compared with only two-fifths in the poorest areas. Gaps are greater at the higher than at the lower levels of attainment (Table 4.3 and Figure 4.4). Moreover, primary school trends do not indicate that a more rapid closing of the gap is on the horizon. Between 2001-02 and 2006-07, the FSM gap at Key Stage 2 closed by about one percentage point per year for English and less for mathematics.[6] The trend is in the right direction but there is a very long way to go.

Table 4.2: Attainment of five GCSE grades A*-C or equivalent passes, by FSM status, 2002-07

	2002	2003	2004	2005	2006	2007
FSM	23.0	24.4	26.1	29.9	32.6	35.5
Non-FSM	54.0	55.2	56.1	58.9	60.7	62.8
% point annual increase FSM		1.4	1.7	3.8	2.7	2.9
% point annual increase non-FSM		1.5	0.9	2.8	1.8	2.1
% point gap FSM: non-FSM	31.0	30.8	30.0	29.0	28.1	27.3
Ratio	2.3	2.3	2.1	2.0	1.9	1.8

Source: DCSF SFR04/2004, SFR 08/2005, SFR 09/2006, SFR46/2006, SFR38/2007

Table 4.3: Attainment at Key Stage 2, Key Stage 3 and GCSE levels in most and least deprived areas (%)

	Decile of deprivation		
	Most deprived	Least deprived	Gap
Key Stage 2 Level 4 average of English and mathematics	67.0	89.5	22.5
Key Stage 3 Level 5 average of English and mathematics	58.5	89.0	30.5
GCSE five A*-C	42.3	78.6	34.3
GCSE five A*-C including English and mathematics	25.3	68.4	43.1

Source: DCSF Statistical First Release SFR 38/2007

Figure 4.4: Highest Year 11 qualification, by social class, 2004 (%)

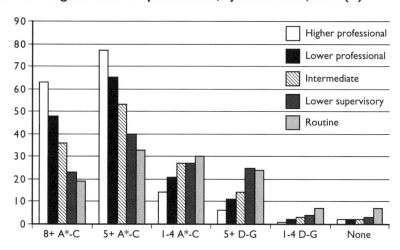

Source: DCSF Youth Cohort Study SFR04/2005

Post-school policies and outcomes

Ages 16-19

A key goal that New Labour inherited from the Conservatives was to increase participation after the age of 16. The government aimed to reduce the numbers of so-called NEETs (16- to 18-year-olds not in employment, education or training) from 9.1% in 2002 to 8.2% in 2004. In 2007 it announced a new goal that by

2015, 90% of 17-year-olds would be in education or work-based learning, along with proposals to support this not only with a restructuring of financial support but also with attendance orders and other sanctions.

New initiatives were directly targeted at the post-16s: Connexions, a new integrated service incorporating careers advice, youth services and other support, and the Education Maintenance Allowance (EMA), a weekly cash allowance for 16- to 19-year-olds from low-income families remaining in full-time education. Changes have been made both to the 14-16 curriculum, including the introduction of applied GCSEs, and to A-levels. Moreover, since 2003, the government has been attempting to bridge the gap between pre-16 (compulsory) and post-16 (non-compulsory) education, with a single 14-19 phase that would increase the status of vocational education and enhance post-16 participation and skills. The Tomlinson Committee, which was set up to review 14-19 education, recommended a single new diploma framework that would gradually subsume all existing qualifications (DfES, 2004), including GCSEs, A-levels and all vocational qualifications, but this key proposal was rejected in the 2005 *14-19 Education and Skills* White Paper (DfES, 2005b), which introduced new vocational diplomas (which have subsequently been criticised for being too academic) but also retained GCSEs and A-levels, thus reinforcing the academic/vocational divide. From 2007, the government guaranteed a learning place in the following September for all 16-year-olds finishing school (the 'September Guarantee'), and extended this to all 17-year-olds from 2008. It has also put increased emphasis on apprenticeships, and in 2008 promised to introduce the entitlement to an apprenticeship place for every 'suitably qualified young person' (DCSF and DIUS, 2008).

These policies have had mixed results. There is clear evidence that the EMA has encouraged some young people to stay in education or training. The EMA pilot resulted in an increased participation rate at age 16 of 5.9 percentage points among 16- to 17-year-olds, and particularly among young men, those with unskilled, semi-skilled or unemployed parents and those who were not high achievers at the end of Year 11 (Middleton et al, 2005). It was estimated that just over half of those staying on in education and receiving EMA would have been inactive (NEET) rather than in work (Dearden et al, 2005). Moreover, students with EMA were more likely to stay in their courses than similar non-EMA students, and, among those from the most deprived areas, had higher achievement rates than their peers without EMA (Aitken et al, 2007).

Provisional figures for 2007 show that the proportion of 16- to 18-year-olds in education or training was at its highest ever (78.7%) (Figure 4.5), although this is only a 1.9% increase since 1997. Efforts will have to be stepped up to reach the 2015 target. Moreover, the rise in the overall rate has not been achieved by a reduction in NEETs but by an increase in the proportion in education or training (particularly education) – a positive trend, but not for the most disadvantaged group. The NEET proportion is now higher than when New Labour first came to power, hovering stubbornly around 9-10%, leading the government to revise

Figure 4.5: Participation in education and training for 16- to 18-year-olds, 1994-2007

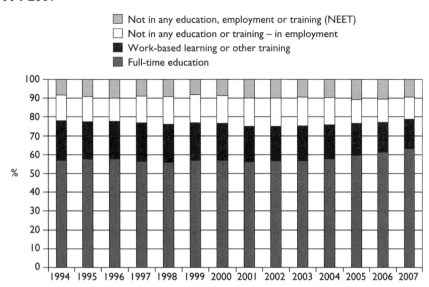

Source: DCSF Statistical First Release SFR13/2008

its target in the 2007 Comprehensive Spending Review (to reduce the NEET proportion by 2% by 2010).

Adult learners

Adult basic skills have been a particular focus, following the Moser (DfEE, 1999b) report. In 2001, the Skills for Life strategy established an Adult Basic Skills Strategy Unit within the Department for Education and Employment, and new national standards, curriculum and training for further education teachers, in a concerted attempt to improve the quality of teaching and professionalise the adult education workforce. A national promotion campaign was launched, and free courses were made available to people without a Level 2 qualification. The target was to equip 750,000 adults with better basic skills by 2004, 1.5 million by 2007 and 2.25 million by 2010. Throughout there has been a strong emphasis on the achievement of qualifications, including the removal of the duty on local authorities to provide adult and community learning not leading directly to qualifications. Additional financial support has been made available to adult learners initially through Individual Learning Accounts (later withdrawn) and from 2004 through Adult Learning Grants, a means-tested allowance aimed at full-time adult learners studying for the first full Level 2 or Level 3 (for young adults) qualification.[7] Personal lifetime skill accounts are also being trialled in 2008 (see Chapter Five). The fact that government funding has been concentrated on the development of skills and qualifications for people of working age has led to some criticism that wider learning has been underemphasised, and with it the more indirect routes to and through learning for those who missed out on opportunities at school. The government has responded with a consultation on informal adult learning, with a policy paper expected later in 2008, or 2009.

Attempts to improve adult basic skills appear to have been successful, particularly in relation to literacy. A national survey of basic skills in 2003 found 5.2 million adults below the baseline level (a D–G grade at GCSE), considerably fewer than the seven million estimated in 1997 (DfES, 2003a), although these data are not strictly comparable. In 2008, the government announced that over two million adult learners had achieved a first qualification in literacy, language or numeracy since 2001, in excess of its target (DCSF, 2008e). A longitudinal study of Skills for Life participants has shown a very positive impact on progression to further training and education and on self-esteem, health and net earnings (Meadows and Metcalf, 2007). Adult Learning Grants also seem to have made a significant impact (LSC, 2006), although recent evidence also suggests high and increasing levels of attrition after initial enrolment (Bathmaker, 2007), emphasising that the challenge is not just getting people into learning as adults, but also supporting them to continue despite domestic, economic and social pressures. In respect of the value of qualifications to those who do attain them, evidence is mixed. Wolf et al (2006) found that the increases in attainment for adult learners had very little positive impact on earnings, although De Coulon and Vignoles (2008) report a different picture, with strong positive returns to NVQ qualifications.

Higher education

Perhaps one of the government's most ambitious targets has been to increase the rate of participation in higher education for 18- to 30-year-olds towards 50% by the year 2010,[8] and particularly to increase participation by low-income families and low-participation areas. To expand the system, New Labour has persisted with the Conservative policy of shifting the cost burden of HE away from general taxation and onto students and their parents, introducing fixed fees in 1998 and variable – or 'top-up' – fees from 2006. At the same time, it has attempted to reduce the expected deterrent effect for potential students from low-income families (Callender and Jackson, 2005), by reducing the cost of HE for them. Grants, abolished in 1998, were reinstated from 2006 for low-income students, who are also exempt from fees, significantly increasing the value of financial support available. Furthermore, ministers have 'practically fallen over themselves' (Brown, 2002, p 75) to emphasise that expansion must be driven by the increased participation of underrepresented groups. The government has adopted Dearing's recommendations that HE institutions should implement strategies to widen participation, monitored by a new Office For Fair Access (OFFA). It also introduced, in 2004, a national programme – Aimhigher – to raise aspiration, attainment and HE participation among non-traditional groups by a series of interventions including master classes and mentoring schemes, information, advice and guidance and university visits.

Overall, participation seems to have been rather resilient to government efforts. The Higher Education Initial Participation Rate (HEIPR) for 17- to 30-year-old English-domiciled students shows very little progress towards the target of 50% by 2010. By 2006-07, participation had increased by just over half a percentage point (from 39.2% to 39.8%), and actually decreased for men (from 37.1% to 34.8%) (Figure 4.6). The rise in 2005-06 and drop the following year may have been due to the introduction of variable fees – some students may have decided to enroll in 2005 rather than taking a year off. 2007-08 may be a better indicator of the 'normal' position, and indeed university applications are up on 2006-07 levels (UCAS, 2008a). Participation rates are below the OECD average (OECD, 2007a).

Progress on reducing inequalities seems rather better, with an improvement in recent years. Analysis by the Higher Education Funding Council for England (HEFCE) for the period 1994-2000 actually showed a slight widening of the gap between disadvantaged areas and others. Regional inequalities significantly widened, with participation rates in London rising by 22 percentage points (to 36.4%), compared with four in the North East (to 24%) (HEFCE, 2005). Galindo-Rueda et al (2004) also suggested a widening of the already large socioeconomic gap in HE participation after the introduction of tuition fees in 1998. However, more recent data (DIUS, 2008)[9] suggest a closing of the gap in participation rates (Table 4.4). At least in the period 2002-04, for which more

Figure 4.6: Higher education initial participation rate, by gender, 1999-2000 to 2006-07

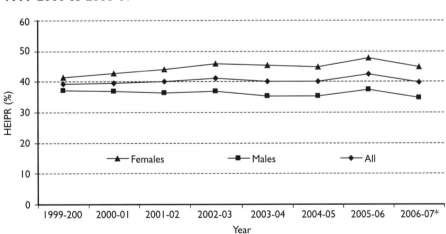

* indicates provisional figures.
Source: DIUS SFR 02/2008

Table 4.4: Participation rates for English-domiciled 18- to 20-year-olds, by National Statistics Socio-Economic Classification (NS-SEC), 2002-06 (%)

NS-SEC	2002	2003	2004	2005	2006
NS-SEC 1,2,3	44.1	40.9	41.2	42.8	39.5
NS-SEC 4,5,6,7	17.5	17.8	17.4	19.8	19.0
Difference	26.5	23.1	23.7	22.9	20.5

Source: DIUS (2008)

detailed data are available (Kelly and Cook, 2007), this appears to arise chiefly from a decline in participation among the highest social class groups, rather than widening participation among lower groups. From 2005 onwards, participation among lower groups appears to increase. Data from the Higher Education Statistics Agency also show a slight recent increase in the proportion of young HE entrants from National Statistics Socio-Economic Classification groups 4-7 (up from 27.9% in 2002-03 to 29.8% in 2006-07) and from low participation neighbourhoods (up from 12.5% to 13.5% from 2002-03 to 2005-06). This is an encouraging recent trend.

It is not clear how much of this improvement is due to HE policy and how much to the effect of the closing social class gap at GCSE level, which could have impacted from 2004 onwards (see Tables 4.1 and 4.2). Certainly, progress in HE depends largely on the reduction of inequalities at earlier stages: there is very little socioeconomic gap in HE participation rates once achievement at A-level is taken into account (Marcenaro-Gutierrez et al, 2007; Chowdry et al, 2008). Nevertheless, evaluation shows some positive impact of central government widening participation activities, with a third of HE institutions estimating that Aimhigher activities have resulted in an increase in applications from the target groups (Bowers-Brown et al, 2006).

As with school-age outcomes, progress so far can only be seen as a start. Higher education remains dominated by more affluent groups, with those from lower socioeconomic backgrounds making up just 29% of new young full-time entrants (NAO, 2008b). Inequalities also persist *within* HE. Students from lower social classes and poorer neighbourhoods remain relatively underrepresented in pre-1992 universities, and in fact this gap appears to have widened a little in recent years as older universities have been less successful in widening participation than newer ones. In 2006-07, 36.9% of young (18- to 20-year-old) full-time first degree entrants at post-1992 universities were from NS-SEC groups 4-7, up from 34.9% in 2002-03, while 22.4% of entrants at pre-1992 universities in 2006-07 were from these same social groups, up from 21.4% in 2002-03. Students from lower social classes are more likely to study close to home and to be on courses with lower entry requirements (UCAS, 2008b) and less likely to be awarded 2:1s (RGCC, 2008). Much of this is also due to prior attainment, but it does suggest that efforts to widen participation should address the type and quality of course and university attended, as well as the fact of going to university per se (Chowdry et al, 2008).

Discussion and conclusion

Overall, the government's efforts to tackle educational inequalities have been extensive, expensive and sustained. The increases in per-pupil spending have been highly significant given near-stable figures in the 1990s, and progressively more money has been directed to the least advantaged. A wide range of additional initiatives have been aimed at the poorest pupils, students and schools, and with few exceptions, evaluations demonstrate their success. Investment in, and reform of, the further education sector has made a major contribution to the provision of 'second chances' for adults and young people who did less well at school. Over time, closing the attainment gap has become more of a priority, not less, and the period since 2005 has seen some significant new developments:

- more programmes targeted at the least advantaged pupils within schools;
- the mainstreaming of additional grants;
- the rolling out of extended schools;
- City Challenge; and
- reforms of HE funding.

These efforts have yielded rewards. Attainment is rising and attainment gaps are narrowing. Moreover, key indicators (GCSE results and participation in HE) show a greater narrowing of the gap since 2004-05 than previously, suggesting that some of the earlier investments are beginning to bear fruit. Youth Cohort Study data suggest that the widening of the social class gap that opened up during the late 1980s and early to mid-1990s has been reversed – a significant achievement. It seems clear that inequalities in educational outcomes are now lower than they would have been without New Labour's additional investment and targeting: that is, had the policies of the Conservatives in the mid-1990s simply persisted.

However, in relation to the overall scale of the problem, the change is small. Social class attainment gaps remain very large – in the order of 30 to 40 percentage points at GCSE level depending on the indicator used, and 20 for HE participation. Middle-class children and young people continue to distinguish themselves in national examinations and enjoy privileged access to elite universities. From this perspective, 11 years of New Labour government have only just begun to impact upon the problem, and with planned increases in education spending now slowing down (Sibieta et al, 2008), further gains will have to come through smarter rather than greater spending.

What accounts for the fact that progress has not been greater in this, the government's number one priority area? One key point is that we could not expect education policy alone to erase educational inequalities: family income, health, housing, job prospects and the opportunity to participate and be valued are all vitally important. Another is that educational improvements take time to impact, as learners move through the system. The full impact of more recent policies is yet to be seen, and the situation in 2008 should not be the final measure of New Labour's performance.

However, we argue that more could still have been achieved, had the government acted differently. First, we suggest that New Labour started too late with some of the policy directions it is now pursuing, in particular with interventions targeted at particular children within schools (such as reading recovery) to prevent those starting education at a disadvantage from falling further and further behind. It persisted too long with a managerial approach to school improvement, focusing on improving leadership and pedagogy and largely neglecting the organisational demands that make it hard for schools in disadvantaged areas to improve (Lupton, 2005). More redistributive funding, extended schools and the recent roll-out of London Challenge are all moves in the right direction in this respect. Perhaps most importantly, the government has taken too long to recognise the need to take an integrated approach to social inequalities and education. Ironically, its insistence that poverty *should not* cause educational disadvantage, and its focus on driving up academic standards through internal school improvements and targets for higher-grade GCSEs has made it more difficult for schools to take a more rounded view and address the social and economic disadvantages that *do* hold children back (Ainscow et al, 2008). Every Child Matters, the integration of education within the Children's Plan, extended schools and SEAL all signal the beginnings of a new approach that could start to make a much bigger difference to the most disadvantaged pupils. They must now be reflected in the curriculum and qualifications, in the organisational design of schools and most of all in performance measures, to remove the current pressures on schools to focus on learners who, with a little extra help, can pass the tests, at the expense of those whose learning journey will be slower and more complex.

Second, we point to inherent ambiguities in the government's account of what education is for and how it should be provided. Despite its insistence that greater educational equality is critical for social inclusion, social mobility and economic success, New Labour has embraced many aspects of a system in which longstanding social divisions in education are constantly reinforced. One example is its retention of the academic/vocational divide. Some grammar and secondary modern schools have been retained, with selection at age 11. The idea of greater curriculum flexibility and continuity from ages 14 to 19 is a positive development, but the government's failure to take up the Tomlinson recommendations is a missed opportunity to deliver a genuinely more inclusive system, in which all learning is valued. The format of university education also remains largely unchanged. Perhaps most important is the tension between New Labour's commitment to marketisation, privatisation, choice and diversity in schooling and the egalitarian direction of its targeted policies. The former create a system in which access is increasingly determined by parental resources of economic, social and cultural capital, within which, as Whitty (2008) has pointed out, targeting a proportion of resources towards the more disadvantaged is likely to have limited effect. The new National Challenge initiative illustrates this tension perfectly. It gives a fresh injection of resources to the lowest-attaining schools, while failing to acknowledge the structural constraints on their performance: many are in disadvantaged areas and/or are secondary modern schools. Policy responses that might really help, such as ending selection at age 11 or introducing admissions systems that allocate pupils more evenly to schools, have been rejected as contrary to the choice agenda. In fact *more* choice and diversity, in the form of Academies and trust schools, is proposed for schools that fail to improve. Educational commentators persistently call for less emphasis on choice and more support for existing schools to respond to their local contexts. As Harris and Ranson (2005, p 584) state:

> The stubborn relationship between social disadvantage and underachievement is more likely to be broken through localised and community based action rather than through the external, dispassionate and disengaged forces of competition, control and choice.

We conclude, therefore, that education is unquestionably more equal than it was in 1997, and certainly more equal than it would have been without the extensive and persistent commitment that the government has made, but it is less equal than it could have been with more radical change. Current policies promise much. Whether they can deliver within a marketised education system resting on higher-level academic achievement as the marker of success remains to be seen.

Notes

[1] This target was subsequently strengthened to count five A*-C grades including English and mathematics (all schools are to have more than 30% by 2011).

[2] Except those with Academy status and those not providing an acceptable standard of education.

[3] One explanation is that schools with very high rates of FSM tend to have high proportions of students from Bangladeshi or Pakistani backgrounds, who are making more rapid progress than similarly disadvantaged White British students (see Chapter Nine).

[4] The Youth Cohort Study covers England and Wales. The socioeconomic classification changed in 2000, making data before and after this not strictly comparable. For this reason we refer simply to highest and lowest social class groups.

[5] FSM is a problematic indicator of disadvantage, as families move in and out of eligibility and many who are on low incomes are not eligible (or are not known to be). Eligibility for FSM in secondary schools has fallen from 17.5% in 1998 to 12.8% in 2008, which might lead us to conclude that the closure of the FSM gap is particularly impressive, since the FSM group is becoming relatively more disadvantaged. However, there is a spread of economic circumstances within both the FSM and non-FSM groups and it is not clear whose results are driving changes. Youth Cohort Study data show that within the FSM category, those from higher social class groups have higher attainment than people from lower social class groups (DfES, 2006b).

[6] DCSF Statistical First Releases SFR 04/2004, 08/2005, 09/2006, 46/2006, 38/2007.

[7] Level 2 qualifications include five or more GCSEs at grades A*-C, National Vocational Qualification (NVQ) Level 2 and other qualifications such as Business & Technician Education Council (BTEC) first diplomas. Level 3 qualifications include two A-levels, NVQ Level 3 and other qualifications such as the International Baccalaureate and BTEC nationals.

[8] This target was updated for the 2007 Comprehensive Spending Review to include an additional aim of growth of at least one percentage point every two years to the academic year 2010-11.

[9] This is based on a new measure (Full-time Young Participation by Socio-Economic Class) that calculates full-time participation rates of 18- to 20-year-olds using socioeconomic data from the Labour Force Survey in order to reflect contemporary class structure. The authors (Kelly and Cook, 2007) argue that some of the previous 'widening gap' evidence (for example DfES, 2003a) has been distorted by a failure to take account of changing social class structure.

FIVE

More equal working lives?
An assessment of New Labour policies

Abigail McKnight

Introduction

This chapter examines how New Labour policies have had an impact on inequality in people's lives derived from their experience in the labour market. For most individuals, their income and social status is derived directly through their employment; when children, through their parents' employment; for some adults, through their partner's employment; for retired people, through their own and/or their partner's work histories. While New Labour did not set out to reduce inequality in the labour market as a main policy objective, it has tackled inequality in employment rates as a result of a number of major policy objectives and through setting a range of targets. The three main targets are:

- to achieve 'full employment' through the Employment Opportunity for All agenda (defined as an 80% employment rate);
- to eradicate child poverty by 2020 (with a strong focus on facilitating families to work their way out of poverty; see Chapter Three); and
- to reach a 70% employment rate among lone parents by 2010.

While policies designed to meet these targets have had an impact on the unequal distribution of work across individuals and households, they have not addressed labour market inequality in terms of earnings inequality. The National Minimum Wage introduced in April 1999 has benefited many low-paid workers but has had little impact on inequality. There have also been some changes to Income Tax and National Insurance schedules (see Chapter Two) but not enough to have a noticeable impact on inequality. As discussed in Chapter Four, New Labour has tried to tackle education inequalities (which are the largest determinants of earnings inequality) but it is unlikely that these policies will be enough to have a large impact on inequality in the labour market and it will be some time before the impact will be noticed (although change for younger cohorts should be detectable 10 years on). Much of the 'making work pay' agenda addresses inequality in individual/family income, rather than pay, such as tax credits, in-work credits and back-to-work bonuses.

Background and inheritance

When New Labour came to power in 1997 it inherited a labour market that had experienced a great deal of turbulence since 1979. Two large recessions had seen claimant unemployment reach highs of around 10% in the early 1980s and early 1990s. Although by 1997 unemployment had fallen to a more respectable 4.5%, a simple extrapolation based on the length of previous business cycles would have predicted unemployment to shortly be on the rise again.

High unemployment rates translated into a very unequal distribution of work across individuals and households. Unemployment was often of long duration and repeat spells of unemployment were common (Teasdale, 1998). Not only did individuals and their families suffer when unemployed but research evidence suggested that the scars of unemployment were carried into subsequent employment experience with a greater likelihood of low-paid work and cycling between low pay and no pay (Stewart and Swaffield, 1999). In response, the Conservative governments had started to tighten up Unemployment Benefit entitlement and reform job search assistance for those claiming benefits. The introduction of Jobseeker's Allowance (JSA) in 1996 was a fairly radical change in benefit entitlement in terms of both conditionality (work search criteria) and duration of entitlement (contribution-based benefits were cut from lasting up to 12 months to lasting six months).

The virtual collapse of the youth labour market, which accompanied the decline of the manufacturing sector in the UK, meant that young people leaving school had difficulty finding jobs, apprenticeships or other forms of high-quality training. The Conservatives had attempted to tackle youth unemployment through the introduction of a variety of youth training schemes and latterly with the introduction of Modern Apprenticeships. Young people were increasingly staying on at school post 16 years – between 1979 and 1997 the proportion of school leavers who continued into full-time education increased from around 0.4 to around 0.7 (Clark, 2002) – although this had flattened out by the mid-1990s (Figure 4.5) – and unemployment-related benefits had been abolished for 16- and 17-year-olds.

Changes in the labour market, no doubt affected by changes on both the supply side and the demand side, led to some fairly dramatic increases in earnings inequality. Between 1979 and 1997, the ratio of the hourly earnings of the highest 10% of employees relative to the lowest 10% increased from 2.75 to 3.9 – an increase of nearly 42% (McKnight, 2000).

Social change had led to large increases in labour force participation of women, delayed motherhood, smaller family sizes, increases in lone parenthood and a divergence in employment rates between single mothers and married mothers. This led to an increase in the number of lone parents and their children dependent on social security benefits (see Chapter Three). The gap between women's and men's pay was narrowing, partly helped by the 1975 Sex Discrimination Act and partly due to narrowing in the gap in educational attainment and human capital gained through work experience and work-based training. The growth of the service sector and continuing demise of the manufacturing sector also played a contributory role.

There had also been a large increase in the number of people who were inactive and claiming sickness and disability-related benefits. Expenditure on benefits for disabled people almost trebled between 1974 and 1997 and alongside an overall increase in welfare expenditure between 1979 and 1997 the share of expenditure on disability-related benefits increased from 16 to 27% (Burchardt, 1999). Employment rates among disabled men and women were much lower than among their non-disabled counterparts, fluctuating around 40%. Over the 1980s and 1990s, employment rates among disabled women increased while there was little change in the rates for disabled men (Burchardt, 2000).

Over the Conservative administration (1979-97) there appeared to be a cultural shift towards early retirement. Employment rates among older men aged 50-64 fell by 16 percentage points and remained stable among older women aged 50-59, despite large increases in employment among younger women (see Figure 5.14 later in this chapter). Relatively low and falling employment rates among older workers was causing considerable concern as demographic change alone was putting pressure on pension systems (see Chapter Eight).

Policies and objectives

When New Labour came into power in 1997 it rapidly put in place a raft of labour market policies designed to increase employment. It defined 'employment opportunity for all as the modern definition of full-employment' and set full employment as one of its key long-term objectives (defined as an 80% employment rate) (DWP, 2007e, p 5). A large active labour market programme known as the New Deal programme, was introduced early on. Tailored programmes were introduced for, among other people, young people (aged 18-25), lone parents, disabled people, the long-term unemployed and older workers. Once these programmes had settled in and had become part of the mainstream, increased emphasis was placed on individuals claiming benefit who traditionally had not been required to actively search for work to meet entitlement criteria. Now, at a minimum, work-focused interviews and back-to-work plans are the norm for the majority of out-of-work benefit recipients.

In April 1999, for the first time in the UK, a National Minimum Wage was introduced. Although lower than many campaigning organisations would have liked, the National Minimum Wage increased the wages of a considerable number of low-paid workers. Continuing evaluation of the impact of the National Minimum Wage suggests that it has done this without having a detrimental impact on employment (Stewart, M.B., 2004).

The introduction of the National Minimum Wage was part of a package of policies that were collectively known as the 'making work pay' agenda. The keystone was the introduction of tax credits in October 1999. The Working Families' Tax Credit (WFTC) was more generous than its predecessor – Family Credit – and more individuals qualified as it reached further up the earnings distribution. The WFTC was designed to improve the financial incentive for low-wage workers to find and remain in work. Research evidence suggests that the WFTC increased employment retention among male recipients (Dickens and McKnight, 2008a). Tax credits have also played an important part in reducing child poverty and working towards Labour's pledge to eradicate child poverty in a generation (see Chapters Two and Three). The WFTC was superseded by the Working Tax Credit (WTC) and the Child Tax Credit in April 2003.

It was increasingly apparent that one of the greatest challenges that lay ahead was tackling low rates of economic activity and high rates of poverty among individuals claiming disability-related benefits. In the early years of Labour's return to power, it piloted and introduced a number of initiatives. A New Deal targeted at disabled people was piloted in 1998-99 and introduced nationally on a voluntary basis in 2001 (with services provided by the public, private and voluntary sectors) but with limited success. A Disabled Person's Tax Credit was introduced in 1999, replacing Disability Working Allowance and later subsumed into the WTC in 2003, but take-up was very low. Gradual enforcement of the 1995 Disability Discrimination Act has benefited disabled people as has Pathways to Work – piloted and gradually rolled out since 2003, providing a package of support to help individuals prepare for work and, for some, gain access to an additional in-work credit when they find work.

As Chapters Two and Three discussed, lone parents have been the focus of many policy developments since 1997. They came under the spotlight during the 1990s due to an increase in lone parenthood and the number of children being raised in lone-parent families, relatively low rates of employment of lone mothers compared with married mothers and lone parents in some other European countries (see Table 13.2). Increasing expenditure on supporting lone parents and their children drew attention to this group and there was a growing concern that non-employment among lone parents was having a negative impact on their children. Policies initially focused on lone parents with older children but have gradually targeted lone parents with younger children.

To help lone parents find and remain in employment, an active labour market programme for the first time targeted at lone parents was introduced in April 1998. The New Deal for Lone Parents (NDLP) is a voluntary programme providing assistance with searching for and preparing for work, help with benefit and tax credit applications and advice on childcare. While participation in NDLP remains voluntary, from April 2003[1] all lone parents making a new claim for Income Support (IS) have had to attend a work-focused interview at the start of their claim, as have existing claimants since April 2004. Lone parents claiming

IS have to attend compulsory review meetings at six months, at 12 months and then annually. Lone parents with older children who are nearing the end of their entitlement to IS have to attend quarterly review meetings.[2]

The New Deal for Partners was introduced on a voluntary basis in April 1999 and, since March 2001, some couples without children have been treated as joint claimants rather than previously where one adult was classified as the main claimant and only that person had to meet JSA eligibility criteria. Under a separate initiative, since April 2004, JSA claimants' partners (without children) have been required to attend work-focused interviews every six months. In the most recent Green Paper, *No One Written Off* (DWP, 2008g), the government is proposing that, for couples with children over the age of seven, both individuals should have to meet the conditions of JSA entitlement.[3]

In the past there was a lower expectation of older benefit recipients finding work. Since 1997, greater assistance has been offered to older claimants with a gradual move towards aligning active labour market programmes with those that apply to 30- and 40-year-olds. The New Deal 50 plus (ND50), introduced in 2000, offers assistance on a voluntary basis to individuals aged 50-59/64 who have been in receipt of unemployment-related benefit for six months or longer. Individuals who find work of over 16 hours a week through ND50 can qualify for WTC and an additional credit for the first 12 months (previously known as Employment Credit). They can also qualify for additional financial assistance towards training.

In October 2006, new legislation regulated against workplace discrimination on the basis of age – the Employment Equality (Age) Regulations. A number of regulations extended employment rights to older workers, banned age discrimination in terms of recruitment, promotion and training and gave individuals the right to request working beyond retirement age.

Recent and proposed reforms to labour market policy

Gordon Brown has always been actively involved in developing New Labour's welfare-to-work policy agenda. The two main areas of policy development since he became Prime Minister are (a) new approaches to increasing employment among lone parents, disabled people and partners of benefit recipients who previously were not required to search for work as a condition of benefit receipt and (b) an attempt to improve basic skills among jobseekers. The New Deals have been fully integrated and are now collectively known as the Flexible New Deal. There are proposals and moves towards streamlining out-of-work benefits to a single benefit regime.

Gordon Brown is attempting to make his mark by refocusing the welfare reform agenda to one where there is a much greater emphasis on the acquisition of skills. This appears to represent a shift away from the 'work first' model, largely followed under the Blair government, in the direction of the 'human capital' model.[4] It has been justified in terms of identifying the current problem as one of lack of skills while previously it was claimed that it was a problem of lack of jobs. This is clearly an oversimplification as lack of skills has always been a problem. A major review of the UK's long-term skills needs (Leitch, 2006) recommended, among other things, the creation of an integrated employment and skills service and a programme to improve the basic skills of jobseekers with the aim of increasing sustainable employment and progression. Leitch's review highlighted the UK's poor performance on skills, with the exception of high-level skills, relative to other advanced economies. Although the number of individuals with no skills has halved since 1997, half of this group are not working.

Under new welfare reform plans (DWP, 2008g), people claiming JSA who have gaps in their basic skills will have to attend training to help them find a job. Personal Skill Accounts will be introduced in 2010; trials began in September 2008. These accounts will enable individuals to access training to develop and improve their skills and assist them in finding a job and to progress in the labour market. Personal Skill Accounts will be lifetime accounts and will be offered to all adults, in and out of work, whatever their qualification level. Identifying the training needs of individuals and businesses will be aided through the work of the new Adult Advancement and Careers Service and the expansion of Train to Gain (run by the Learning and Skills Council).

Despite all the changes made to in-work benefits, there remain (real and perceived) financial disincentives for some individuals to find work, particularly those receiving Housing Benefit. The range of benefits available and their interplay make it difficult for some individuals to assess how their income will change when they find a job. In addition, despite considerable effort, there remain administration problems in the application processes, and real concerns on the part of individuals that starting work will be accompanied by a drop in income over the difficult transitional period (Freud, 2007). The introduction of benefit run-ons and in-work credits (for some), back-to-work grants and bonuses and Jobcentre Plus personal advisers trained to help with claim applications have all attempted to ease this problem. There are also pilots in London during 2008 to test the effect of covering upfront childcare costs. 'Better Off In Work Credits' are being piloted in 2008, to be extended in 2009 if successful for lone parents and long-term benefit claimants. This credit is designed to ensure that the recipient is at least £25 per week better off for the following 26 weeks.[5]

There are major changes being introduced and planned for the treatment of disability-related benefit claimants and the administration of these benefits. Since October 2008, all individuals applying for out-of-work benefits on the basis of disability or incapacity to work have to apply for the new Employment and Support Allowance (ESA). All applicants have to undergo a Work Capability Assessment. Individuals who qualify for ESA are split into two groups, depending on the outcome of the assessment. The most severely disabled people receive higher levels of benefit, while other disabled people and those with long-term health problems who could work receive greater help to find employment. Those who do not qualify for ESA can instead apply for JSA. From April 2010, all Incapacity Benefit claimants will be required to take a Work Capability Assessment.

Changes have also been made to lone parents' entitlement to IS. Lone parents were previously entitled to IS until their youngest child was aged 16. This was reduced to age 12 in October 2008 and will be reduced to age 10 in October 2009 and age 7 in October 2010. When entitlement to IS expires, lone parents who remain out of work will be entitled to claim JSA and will be required to meet JSA eligibility criteria. Exceptions will be made for difficulties in finding and remaining in work associated with childcare.

Two further developments are the moves to improve employment retention and progression, and the use of benefit histories to identify jobseekers in need of extra help and early intervention. Two elements of the Employment Retention and Advancement project will be rolled out nationally as a result of favourable initial evaluation: In-Work Advisory Support and the In-Work Emergency Fund (Riccio et al, 2008). In addition, new claimants with a recent history of long-term unemployment will be fast tracked and will receive supported job search early in their claim (DWP, 2008g). From April 2009, young people with six months or more experience of inactivity between the ages of 16 and 18 will be fast tracked to the intensive, Jobcentre Plus-led, support and sanctions regime. Following recommendations made in a recent report on options for the future of welfare to work (Freud, 2007), the delivery of services assisting long-term unemployed people will be contracted out to private and voluntary sector organisations.

The government has also put forward proposals for tackling drug use among benefit claimants (DWP, 2008g). These proposals include requiring claimants to report drug use, receive medical treatment to tackle drug dependency and take active steps to return to work. Individuals who do not comply will face benefit sanctions. How successful such a regime will prove to be for this client group remains to be seen.

Outcomes

In this section, a range of labour market indicators are examined to assess the impact of labour market policies. Macro-economic trends and specific groups that have been the focus of labour market policies due to poor labour market outcomes in the past are examined.

Unemployment

The turbulent years of the 1980s and 1990s, which saw unemployment peak at around 10% (12% for men), looked set to continue after 1997 but instead were replaced by an unprecedented period of falling unemployment that continued until 2008. The rate of unemployment defined by the number of economically active working-age people claiming unemployment-related benefit had fallen to 2.5% by early 2008, a rate not observed since the beginning of 1975 (see Figure 5.1). The government's preferred measure (the International Labour Organisation [ILO] measure)[6] had fallen to 5.3% (up a little from 4.8% in 2004), lower than any rate recorded during the 1979-97 Conservative government, although this had risen to 5.8% by the third quarter of 2008. With the exception of a small rise in 2006, unemployment declined from 1997 until the financial crisis of 2008. Probably as a result of increased labour market participation of women, unemployment rates for men and women have been converging, although unemployment rates for men remain above those for women.

The divergence in the ILO and claimant-based measures of unemployment since 1997 suggests that there is a significant, increasing proportion of the unemployed who are not entitled to unemployment benefits. They are likely to be mainly made up of partners of benefit claimants, lone parents and disabled people. The higher ILO unemployment rate compared with the claimant rate among men is a marked break from past trends where previously rates have been very similar.[7]

McKnight (2005) has shown that, from 1990 to 2004, economic inactivity increased steadily from 12% to 16% among men and fell from around 29% to 26% among women. There has been very little change since then. The overall inactivity rate was 20.8% over the three months to April 2008, down 0.4% over the year, 16.2% among working-age men and 25.8% among working-age women.

Figure 5.1: Unemployment, 1971-2008 (first quarter)

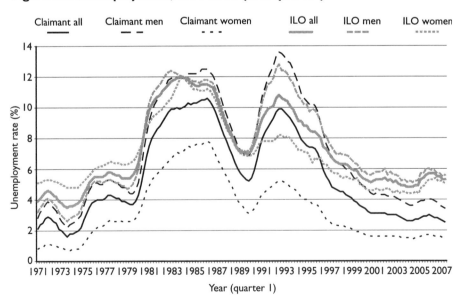

Source: Labour Force Survey and claimant data, ONS time series data

Employment

Official statistics show that the employment rate for people of working age was 74.9% for the three months up to April 2008; 79.0% for men and 70.4% for women. The number of people in employment had reached the highest level since comparable records began in 1971 (29.55 million in April 2008). Figure 5.2 shows the share of working-age men and women in employment 1971-2008. For women, employment has largely followed an upward trend since 1971 while the rate for men fell over the 1970s. The overall employment rate increased from 1993 to 2001 but has remained virtually unchanged since then. Between 1971 and 2008, the female employment rate increased 14 percentage points but it fell by 13 percentage points for males. Therefore, the overall employment rate was roughly the same in 2008 as it was in 1971 (75%).

The number of workforce jobs has consistently increased since 1997. In contrast to earlier periods, where the gains were all made by women, this increase in jobs has been shared equally between men and women. For men this meant that by 2003 the number of jobs had finally returned to the level inherited by the Conservative government in 1979. Since 1997, the number of workforce jobs has increased by 4.3 million.[8] However, Figure 5.2 shows that the continuing increase in the *numbers* in employment (for both men and women) has not been mirrored in employment *rates*, which have flattened out. This suggests that the size of the working-age population has continued to increase over this period, which is likely to have been fuelled by migrant workers (see Chapter Ten).

Figure 5.2: Working-age employment, 1971-2008 (first quarter)

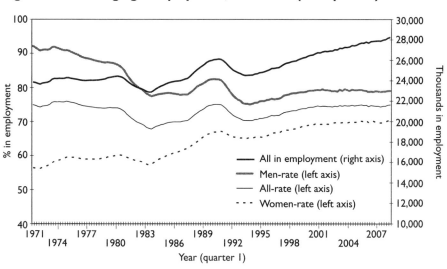

Source: Labour Force Survey, ONS Time Series Data

Earnings inequality and earnings mobility

Many studies have measured changes in earnings inequality using hourly, weekly or even monthly measures of pay. These provide snapshots of the distribution of earnings at a point in time. Annual earnings give a more complete measure as they incorporate intensity and continuity of work over a complete year. This section draws on research conducted by Dickens and McKnight (2008b) using the Lifetime Labour Market Database (LLMDB).[9]

Figure 5.3 shows annual earnings inequality among all employees from 1978-79 to 2003-04.[10] The large increases in inequality of hourly and weekly earnings in the 1980s and early 1990s, which have been reported elsewhere (Dickens, 2000; McKnight, 2000), are also seen in annual earnings. There have been larger increases in the widening in the bottom half (50:10 ratio) of the distribution than the top half (90:50 ratio) but very little change in the bottom half since 1997.

These figures are for all employees irrespective of the number of hours they worked in a given year. Unemployment will therefore have the greatest impact on the bottom half of the distribution. Figure 5.3 shows that the large increases in inequality in the 1980s and 1990s stopped around 1996-97 and, with the exception of a rise in the 90:10 ratio since 2002, the other measures show fairly stable rates of inequality since then.

Figure 5.3: Changes in annual earnings inequality, decile ratios, 1978-79 to 2003-04

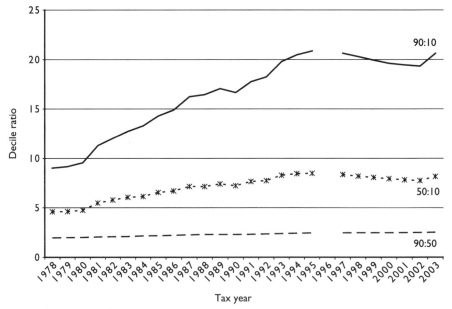

Source: Lifetime Labour Market Database

Figure 5.4 plots summary measures of annual earnings inequality between 1979–80 and 2004–05. Two inequality measures are shown: the Gini coefficient, which is sensitive to changes in the middle of the earnings distribution, and the General Energy Measure, GE(1) (see Dickens and McKnight, 2008b, for more details), which is more sensitive to changes at the top and bottom of the distribution. The figure shows that annual earnings inequality is higher among female employees than male employees until around 2004–05.

Over the 1990s, increases in the inequality of annual earnings were greater among male employees than female employees. In contrast, inequality in hourly wages has been shown to be greater among men employed full time than women employed full or part time and increases in hourly wage inequality were higher among women than men over this period (McKnight, 2000). These contrasting findings suggest that the greater inequality in annual earnings than hourly wages among women is due to greater variability in their hours of work. It is also most likely that the greater increase in annual earnings inequality among men was driven by an increase in inequality of annual hours worked; probably due to the experience of unemployment in the 1990s recession translating into lower annual earnings for years in which individuals spent some time unemployed.[11] Likewise, increases in employment among women, and particularly women working full time, have no doubt affected changes in their distribution of annual earnings. Since 1997, annual earnings inequality has been gradually falling among female employees but has continued to rise, albeit at a slower rate, among male employees.

Figure 5.4: Changes in annual earnings inequality, 1979-80 to 2004-05

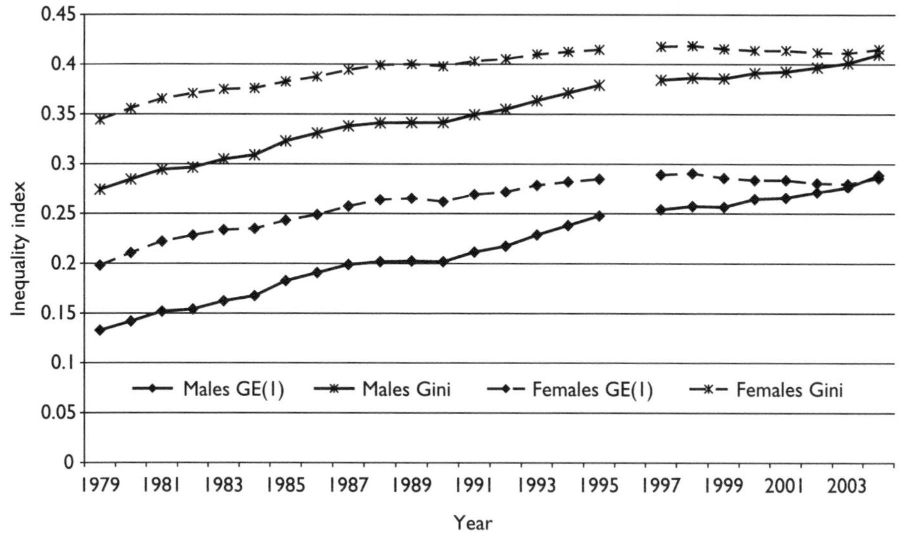

Source: Lifetime Labour Market Database

Figure 5.5 shows inequality in earnings and employment between 1979-80 and 2004-05 through the inclusion of individuals with no earnings in a particular year.[12] This demonstrates very clearly how earnings from employment have become more equal among economically active working-age women since the early 1990s. Increases in employment among women more than counterbalanced increases in earnings inequality after the late 1980s, so that in 2005-06 inequality returned to 1979-80 levels. Overall inequality in earnings and employment has increased among men, with the biggest increases taking place between 1979 and 1986. The early 1990s recession does not appear to have had a big impact on this measure of inequality. Since 1997, inequality according to this measure has been gradually falling among men. Overall inequality among economically active men increased by 38% between 1979 and 1997, but fell by 4% between 1997 and 2005.

A further progression is to consider a longer-run view by measuring the inequality of individuals' earnings aggregated over a number of years. This allows an assessment of the extent to which increases in year-to-year mobility can ameliorate increases in cross-sectional inequality. The results show that mobility among male employees fell between 1979 and around 1994 (Figure 5.6). This implies that cross-sectional measures of earnings inequality are now more representative of long-run differences in individuals' earnings – there is less averaging out through year-to-year changes – than in the past. There is also evidence that mobility has started to rise a little since around 2000. For women earners there is less variability

Figure 5.5: Inequality in annual earnings across the working-age population, 1979-80 to 2004-05

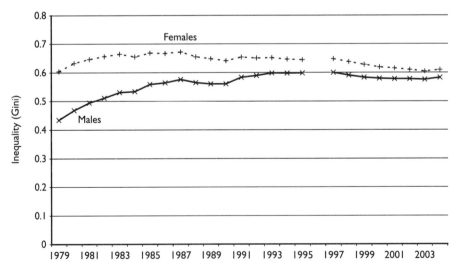

Source: Lifetime Labour Market Database

Figure 5.6: Changes in earnings mobility among male and female employees

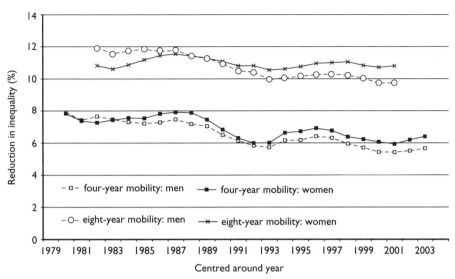

Source: Lifetime Labour Market Database

in mobility than for men over the same time period. While there are some changes over time, mobility rates are quite similar in the late 1970s and the mid-2000s. Again there is some evidence that equalising mobility among women started to increase after 2000 (Figure 5.6).

In this section it has been shown that inequality in annual earnings increased over the 1980s and the first half of the 1990s but has been fairly stable since 1997. Overall inequality among men and women has been converging. Increases have been higher among male employees while increases in the number of women working and their work continuity have meant that increases in inequality have been lower among women. In addition, earnings mobility has also fallen more among male employees, indicative of an increase in lifetime earnings inequality.

16- to 18-year-olds

Except in exceptional circumstances, young people under the age of 18 do not qualify for social security benefits when they are unemployed. As a result, young people aged 16 and 17 fall out of the remit of active labour market programmes that are largely restricted to welfare recipients. Staying-on rates in post-compulsory education have been increasing since 2003 (see Chapter Four) and the government plans to raise the compulsory age of remaining in education or training to 17 by 2013 and 18 by 2015. Some additional information on young people who are not in employment, education or training (NEET) can be found in Chapter Four. Figure 4.5 showed that despite political awareness of this group and a number of initiatives designed to target them, their share of the age group has hovered around 9–10% since 1997.

Since 1997, the recorded unemployment rate among economically active 16- and 17-year-olds has increased quite dramatically; from 20% in the second quarter of 1997 to a high of 29% in the third quarter of 2007. The latest data show that rates have subsequently started to fall, although more data are required to judge if this is a trend. Figure 5.7 also shows trends in the levels of activity and unemployment. It shows that the increase in the unemployment rate has been driven by both a fall in the number of economically active young people and an increase in the number of this group who are unemployed. Between 1997 and 2008, the main change was a fall in the number of economically active young people, with the number of this group who are unemployed roughly the same at the start and end of this period. With around one-fifth to one-quarter unemployed, there are clearly significant numbers of young people struggling to find work. It is some time before the government plans to raise the compulsory age for remaining in education or training to 17/18 and clearly more could be done in the meantime to help this group.

18- to 25-year-olds

The New Deal for Young People (NDYP) (for 18- to 24-year-olds) was the flagship of New Labour's New Deal programmes. It was heralded as a major investment

Figure 5.7: Economic activity and ILO unemployment among 16- to 17-year-olds in the UK

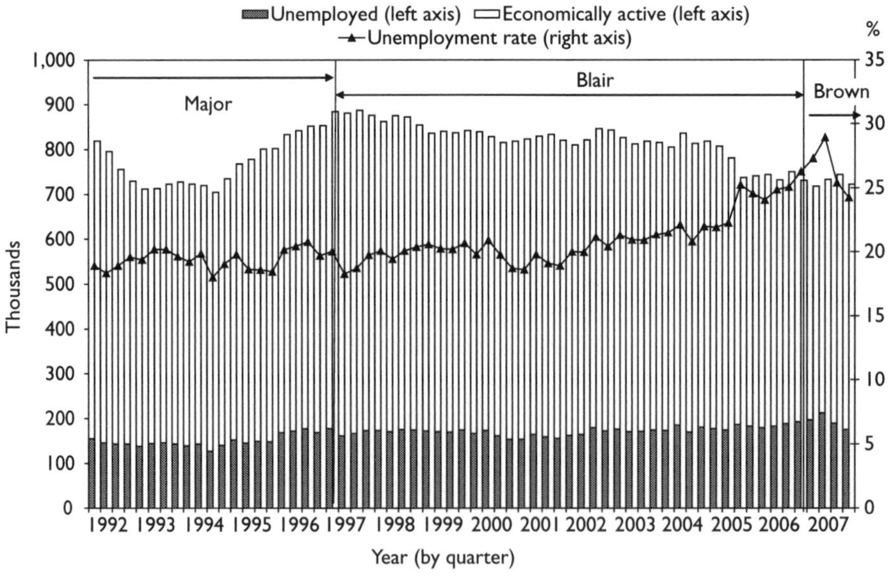

Source: Labour Force Survey, ONS Time Series Data

programme designed to turn around the unemployment experience of this age group. When it was introduced in the spring of 1998, it was the first compulsory New Deal programme. After participating in a series of work-focused interviews with personal advisers and intensive work search assistance, any young people who remain unemployed after three months have to choose from a limited range of work/training options; remaining unemployed is not an option. Young people refusing to participate fully face benefit sanctions. Any jobseekers still without work at the end of an option then re-enter the programme. An evaluation of the first five years of NDYP (De Giorgi, 2005) showed that NDYP had a small but positive impact on increasing transitions off Unemployment Benefit, increasing the employability of young men by 4.6%.

Figure 5.8 shows the ILO unemployment rate among 18- to 24-year-olds between summer 1992 and spring 2008.[13] During this period the unemployment rate among young men peaked in spring 1993 at 21.5% (13.9% for young women in summer 1993). Unemployment rates were already falling when New Labour came to power in May 1997 and they continued to fall until towards the end of 2000 when they appeared to plateau at around 10% until 2005, before beginning to rise again to around 12%. By the first quarter of 2008, unemployment rates among this group were again equivalent to those observed when NDYP was first introduced 10 years earlier.

The long-term unemployed

Long-term unemployment (LTU) became a problem in the 1980s and 1990s (Machin and Manning, 1999). It was shown in McKnight (2005) that the share

Figure 5.8: ILO unemployment rates, 18- to 24-year-olds

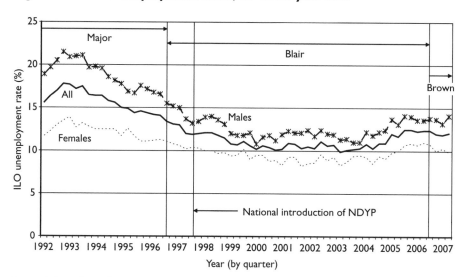

Source: Labour Force Survey, ONS Time Series Data

of unemployed 25- to 49-year-olds who had been unemployed for 12 months or longer had fallen since 1997. The share fell from around 40% to around 25%. The New Deal for 25+ (compulsory for individuals aged 25 or over and unemployed for 18 months or longer) was introduced in June 1998 to tackle the problem of LTU among this age group. Figure 5.9 shows that the share of the unemployed (ILO measure) who are long-term unemployed has increased since 2006 – this increase ties in with the increase in the overall unemployment rate shown in Figure 5.1. These figures suggest that although LTU has fallen, the New Deal has not been able to build on early successes.

Figure 5.10 shows changes in the number of 25- to 49-year-olds unemployed and claiming benefit for 12 months or longer and their share of all 25- to 49-year-old claimants between May 1997 and April 2008. Both these series follow a similar trend over this period and although the share of LTU is considerably higher in the ILO series (nearly 10 percentage points higher) the evolution over time is very similar. The ILO measure is likely to be more reliable because after approximately 22 months of unemployment these individuals have to stop claiming JSA and instead have to claim a New Deal Allowance during the Intensive Activity Period. If they are still unemployed around 13 weeks later they have to reapply for JSA. However, even the claimant series shows a plateau after 2002 and an increase in LTU after 2005 but unlike the ILO series the number and share of claimants who are long-term unemployed fell from the beginning of 2007.

Figure 5.9: Unemployed 25- to 49-year-olds who have been unemployed for 12 months or more (%)

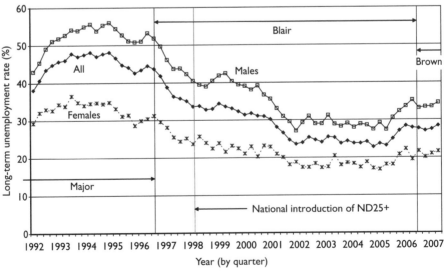

Source: Labour Force Survey, ONS Time Series Data

Figure 5.10: Unemployed 25- to 49-year-olds who have been claiming benefit for 12 months or more (%)

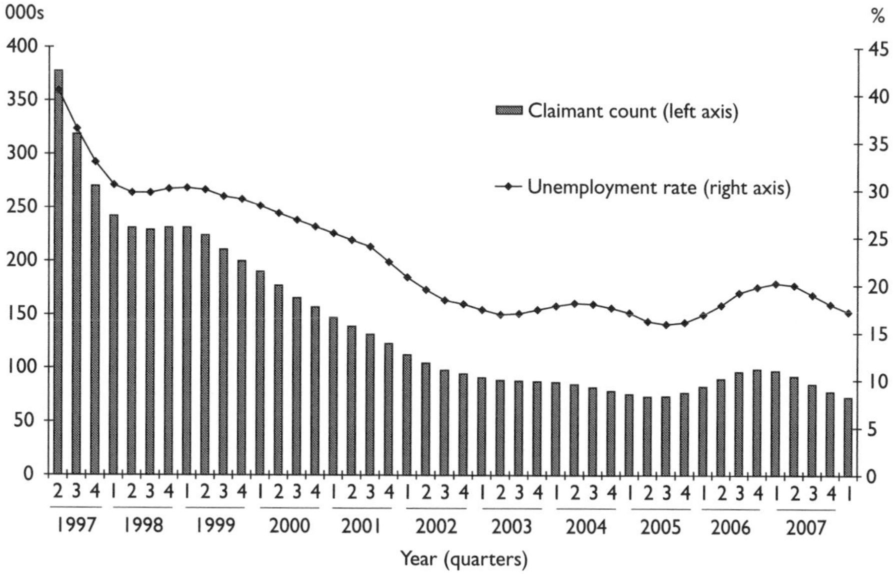

Source: Claimant data, ONS Time Series Data

Lone parents

While employment rates among lone parents have clearly been rising under New Labour, it looks extremely unlikely that the government will reach its 70% target in 2010 (57.1% in 2007). It would take a very radical policy or combination of policies and the rate of increase between 2007 and 2010 would have to be higher than anything achieved so far (requiring an over 10 percentage point increase in only three years, equivalent to the increase in the 10-year period between 1997 and 2007) to achieve this target. While the NDLP and the introduction of WFTC both had a significant positive impact on lone parents' employment rates, they have jointly achieved nothing like the size of the effect required. It is not clear if the government has dropped this target as in the latest Green Paper (DWP, 2008g) it is not mentioned. Instead, it is stated that it has a goal to help 300,000 more lone parents into work but there is no mention of a timescale.

Much of the policy focus on lone parents has been motivated by the fact that their children are more at risk of living in poverty than children in couple families, and those at greatest risk live in workless households. While New Labour has increased the real value of out-of-work benefits, it has continued to promote work as the best form of welfare. However, due to the high prevalence of low-paid jobs, work is not a guarantee against poverty.

Figure 5.11 shows the official statistics on poverty rates among lone parents by employment status and for workless couples with children from 1994-95 up to

Figure 5.11: Poverty rates among families with children (% living in households below 60% median income)

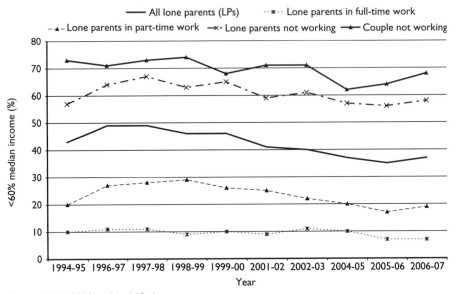

Source: DWP (2008b, table 4.12ts)

the most recent statistics for 2006-07 (see also Table 2.2). Poverty rates among lone-parent families have declined since 1997, bucking the previous upward trend. The most recent year for which statistics are available (2006-07) shows an increase in poverty rates for lone parents working part time and lone parents without work. Also shown in Figure 5.11 are the poverty rates among workless couples with children. It is interesting to note that poverty rates among this group are higher than among workless lone parents but they have not come under the same scrutiny. The number of children living in workless lone-parent households remained fairly stable between 1994-95 and 2006-07 at around 1.7 million while the number of children living in workless couple families has roughly halved from 1.2 million to 0.6 million.

Disabled people

One of the main challenges that the government has set itself is to increase employment rates among disabled people. The increasing rates of disability in the working-age population, the relatively low and decreasing rates of economic activity and high poverty rates have brought this group under the policy spotlight. The major changes to benefit entitlement and employment promotion for this group are, at the time of writing, yet to come.

Figure 5.12 shows the activity and employment status of individuals defined as disabled according to the 1995 Disability Discrimination Act definition since 1999.

Figure 5.12: Employment and activity rates among disabled people

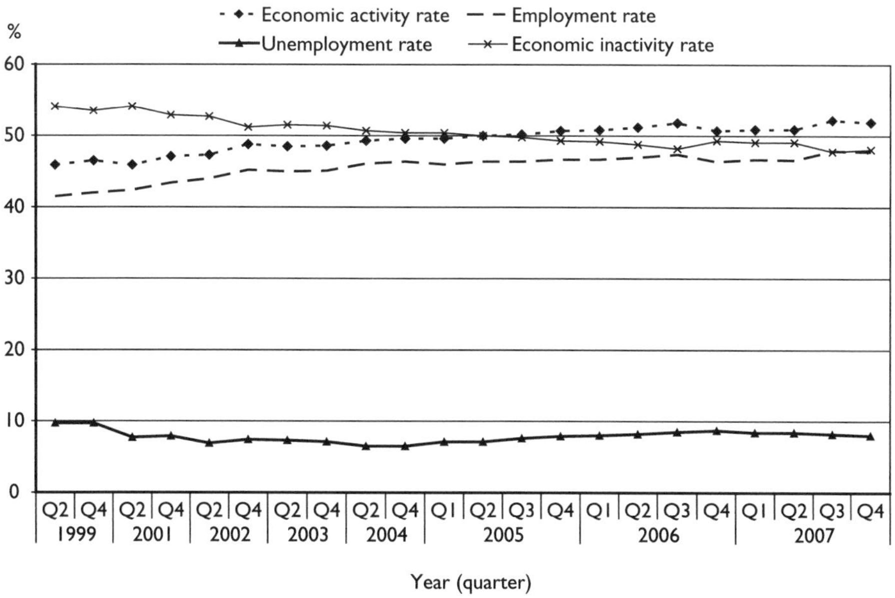

Source: Labour Force Survey, ONS Time Series Data

It is difficult to produce a longer historical picture due to inconsistent definitions of disability used in different datasets and within the same dataset over time. Data are shown for all individuals as trends over this time period are very similar for men and women; employment and activity rates are a few percentage points lower among women. This shows that employment and activity rates for disabled people are lower compared with the non-disabled working-age population. Employment rates among disabled people have continued to rise up to 2008 (albeit at a slow rate) while it is shown in Figure 5.12 that employment rates flattened off after 2001 among the whole working-age population.

Women and gender pay inequality

Despite the Equal Pay Act being in force since 1975 there remains a large gender pay gap in the UK. In 2006, the UK had the fourth largest hourly pay gap out of the 27 European Union (EU) member states, one-third higher than the EU average (Council of the European Communities, 2008). Since 1997, some progress has been made but it has been slow. Figure 5.13 shows the percentage gap in average hourly earnings between men and women working full time and between men working full time and women working part time, all on adult rates. Pay gaps are shown according to mean and median pay (mean pay is more sensitive to very high and very low rates of pay). The gaps according to these two measures are a few percentage points apart (and the rank is different for full- and

Figure 5.13: Gender pay gap (hourly earnings of adult employees)

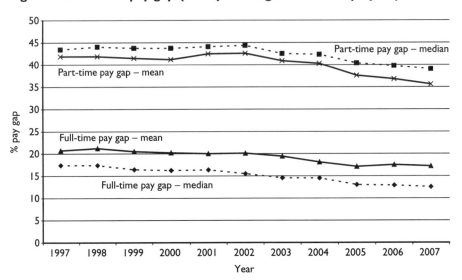

Source: ONS (2007c, table 1.6a)

part-time employees) but the relative difference has remained fairly stable over time. Changes to the data series[14] make precise comparisons difficult for the full 10-year period but the findings do suggest that little progress has been made since 2005 among full-time employees (and the latest figures show a slight widening of the gap in 2008).

A recent synopsis of the position of women in the labour market demonstrates that while women's employment rates have been increasing and inactivity rates falling, many remain segregated in low-paid jobs (TUC, 2008). The considerable disadvantage women face in the labour market due to a combination of the undervaluation of 'women's work', occupational segregation, high levels of part-time working and limitations derived from caring responsibilities undertaken by women, significantly increases women's chances of living in poverty and exposes their children to poverty. While the government views employment as the surest route out of poverty, over half of children living in poverty live in a household where at least one adult is in work.

Older workers

Trends in employment rates among older workers diverged over the 1970s with falling rates among older men and stable rates among older women. Employment rates among older men (aged 50-64) fell dramatically from around 90% in the early 1970s to 70% in the early 1980s (Figure 5.14). In contrast, employment rates among older women (aged 50-59) remained fairly stable at around 60%. The recessions of the early 1980s and early 1990s took their toll on older workers'

Figure 5.14: Employment rates for men and women aged 50-59/64 years

Sources:
Pensions Commission (2005, Fig 8.4); 2005-07 Labour Force Survey updated from ONS series;
1973-96 General Household Survey (GHS); 1993-2007 Labour Force Survey (LFS)

employment rates but the continuing increase in labour force participation of women offset rates among older women. Since the early 1990s, employment rates have steadily increased but at a faster rate among women than among men. Since 2005, employment rates among older men have remained virtually the same but have continued to increase among older women. This has meant that the gap between the two rates has narrowed further and in 2007 they were separated by only three percentage points. Overall, there appears to have been more sustained success in improving employment rates among this age group compared with young people and the long-term unemployed. There is little evaluation evidence on how much of the observed increase can be attributed to government policy.

Conclusions

New Labour's first 10 years were marked by falling and exceptionally low unemployment rates and the New Deal programmes were undoubtedly played a contributory role. However, early successes have stalled among some groups (such as the long-term unemployed) and, for other groups, unemployment rates have returned to pre-New Deal levels (18- to 24-year-olds). How high unemployment would be among these groups in the absence of the New Deals is unknown. Unemployment has certainly increased among 16- and 17-year-olds for whom no programme of assistance is available. The evidence appears to suggest that for active labour market programmes to remain effective they have to continue to evolve, to adapt to changing circumstances and to remain fresh and imaginative. The majority of individuals making a claim for JSA are now repeat claimants (Carpenter, 2006), which means that there is a high likelihood that participants have previous experience of active labour market programmes. Programme fatigue affects both those individuals who cycle through the programmes and those responsible for delivering the service. Time will tell if the proposed evolution of the New Deal will be sufficient to refresh it. It is unclear whether the New Deal has become less effective due to individuals cycling through the programme or if Jobcentre Plus resources and efforts have been diverted to new client groups such as disabled people, partners of claimants and lone parents.

In addition to falling and historically low unemployment rates, the number of people in employment continued to rise until 2008. This has not always translated into higher employment rates as the workforce has expanded. More lone parents have found employment and more generally women's position in the labour market has improved through a gradual narrowing of the gender pay gap, signs of falling inequality and increasing mobility. Overall, men's and women's working lives are more equal but there remains a considerable degree of inequality in the labour market.

Some groups have not fared so well and a refocus and increased emphasis is required. While the number of people with low levels of skills has been on the decline, their labour market position has deteriorated (Leitch, 2006). The government is tackling the problem of low skills through the introduction of Personal Skill Accounts for all, basic skills screening and skill acquisition plans for jobseekers in need.

Unemployment among economically active 16- and 17-year-olds is a major problem, with around one-quarter of this group unemployed. The government plans to extend compulsory education and formal training to age 18 but this will not come into force until 2015. Even then the most disadvantaged young people in need of help will be hardest to reach. These young people do not qualify for social security benefits and therefore they cannot be sanctioned. In addition, unless vocational options are of high quality there is a danger that they will act as a form of warehousing and provide a negative view of adult education and training.

As the economy turned down in the wake of the credit crunch. the claimant count of unemployment had already reached nearly one million by October 2008. According to the ILO measure, the number was 1.82 million, the highest for over 10 years. These figures will get worse as the fall-out from the financial crisis takes hold in the real economy. Perhaps the biggest challenge that lies ahead is how the active labour market programmes will cope with, and effectively respond to, a severe economic downturn.

Notes

[1] These interviews were introduced progressively from April 2001.

[2] The point at which quarterly review meetings become mandatory is dependent on the age of the lone parent's youngest child. The qualifying age is being gradually brought down.

[3] There is some variation if one of the couple claims Incapacity Benefit or Employment Support Allowance.

[4] These two models are self-explanatory. The 'work first' model is based on the notion that any job is better than no job at all. The emphasis is on moving unemployed people into work as fast as possible. In contrast, the 'human capital' model emphasises the need to improve jobseekers' skills to find a job, remain in work and progress in the labour market.

[5] They will need to work 16 hours per week if a lone parent (24 hours if a partner in a couple). How much of an incentive this will prove to be remains to be seen as it amounts to marginally over £1.50 per hour for those working 16 hours.

[6] The ILO definition of unemployment identifies people who are: out of work, want a job, have actively sought work in the previous four weeks and are available to start work within the next fortnight; or out of work and have accepted a job that they are waiting to start in the next fortnight.

[7] Prior to 1991 the quarterly series has been imputed by the Office for National Statistics (ONS) drawing on information from the annual Labour Force Survey (1984-91) and the biennial Labour Force Survey 1979-83 and the estimated relationship between the Labour Force Survey ILO series and the claimant count (Lindsay, 2005). The estimated higher rates of ILO unemployment among women compared with men over the 1970s warrants further investigation.

[8] This figure relates to the number of jobs and not their full-time equivalent, which will be lower.

[9] This is an administrative dataset where the information on earnings has been compiled from tax records. Information is available for a 1% random sample of people living in Britain with a National Insurance record.

[10] There is a break in the series at 1996-97 due to a change in the administrative system under which these data were collected and compiled. The series are consistent before and after this date.

[11] If an individual was unemployed for the complete year, that is, had zero earnings, they do not appear in this data series.

[12] This sample excludes the self-employed, for whom there is no record of earnings, and individuals who are abroad.

[13] Data based on receipt of unemployment-related benefit show a similar trend.

[14] Changes to the methodology and sampling design have been made to the data series – Annual Survey of Hours and Earnings – over this period. For more details, see www.statistics.gov.uk/statbase/product.asp?vlnk=13101

SIX

New Labour and unequal neighbourhoods

Anne Power

Introduction

When New Labour came to power in 1997, there was great enthusiasm within government for tackling deprivation, particularly area concentrations of problems. There were several important reasons. First, the growth of inequality during Thatcher's years had not been reversed (Chapter One). Second, social housing (still making up over a fifth of all homes) had become far poorer as a result of targeting access more systematically at the most deprived and vulnerable households. Third, levels of worklessness, benefit dependency and lone parenthood had all risen steeply and became more concentrated in the poorest areas, particularly in large council estates (Power and Tunstall, 1995). Overlaid on these problems were physical decay within older urban areas, lack of investment in infrastructure, high crime and evidence of a fast-growing gap between conditions in the poorest areas and the average. Repeated initiatives in the 1980s and 1990s in the poorest areas and efforts at estate renewal had not overcome problems of multiple disadvantage.

Area-based initiatives

With a strong commitment to reducing inequality and shrinking the gap between the poorest areas and the average, the new government pledged to improve the performance of public services in education, health, crime reduction and prevention, access to work, training and skills development. It carefully targeted programmes at the most disadvantaged areas, setting up Health and Education Action Zones, welfare-to-work programmes, and Drug and Youth Action Teams. It continued the Single Regeneration Budget, initiated by the Conservatives, focusing government reinvestment through local partnerships on many of the poorest areas. It also announced initiatives for literacy and numeracy hours in primary schools, anti-crime initiatives and a new regime of 'Tsars', such as 'Drug Tsars'. It was not always clear what the multiple zones and the hyperactivity of overlapping initiatives would do or who was really responsible for them, but they seemed to respond to a need and generate an atmosphere of change. This chapter sets out findings from area-based research carried out by the Centre for Analysis of Social Exclusion (CASE) over the 10-year period from 1998 to 2008 alongside those from five major government-funded evaluations of area-based initiatives (Lupton, 2003; Power and Lupton, 2005; Power, 2007).

Two expensive and long-run area-based initiatives quickly followed the first period of 'instant action'. The New Deal for Communities, announced in 1998, aimed to 'put communities at the helm' of £50 million regeneration programmes for each of 39 areas of around 4,000 homes, while Sure Start was announced in 1999 to help infants, preschool children and their parents in up to 500 very poor neighbourhoods located within the 80 most deprived local authority areas (see Chapter Three).

Both the New Deal for Communities and Sure Start were hastily constructed with generous funding and targets for achieving 'lasting change', but they were building on earlier long-run experience and evidence of what works (Foster and Hope, 1993; Power and Tunstall, 1995; Love et al, 2002). They were quickly passed down, below local authority levels, to community-based partnership boards, pulled together from scratch and at speed, to deliver action on the ground within a year or two. These expensive leaps of faith were to be closely monitored with costly and complex evaluations (CRESR, 2005, 2008; NESS, 2007). In the very poor areas that CASE was following, both programmes quickly appeared on the ground, sending expectations sky-rocketing among residents and local staff (Power, 2007).

Social exclusion and Neighbourhood Renewal

There was a bigger argument within government about how to tackle complex interactive pressures on people and places. Time-limited special initiatives would not be enough to change overall patterns of deprivation. There was an urgent need both to understand the full scale and complexity of neighbourhood-based problems, and to generate more permanent, more mainstream solutions. The Social Exclusion Unit (SEU) was set up in 1998 directly under the Prime Minister, with two main purposes: to understand the complex problems of specially vulnerable and excluded groups, such as rough sleepers, truanting teenagers and teenage mothers; and to tackle the worst areas based on all available evidence of deeply entrenched problems disproportionately concentrated in the poorest areas.

The SEU's first report, *Bringing Britain Together* (SEU, 1998), confirmed that deepening inequality affected all major aspects of life chances in the worst areas: education, health, income, employment, housing, crime, security, environmental conditions, quality of services, anti-social behaviour, family stability and so on. This catalogue of disadvantage was extremely conspicuous; the report demonstrated that the poorest areas suffered more than double the average level of problems, creating a 'geography of misery' that could only harm child development, hamper parents' efforts at betterment and consume disproportionate remedial resources (Mumford and Power, 2003).

Bringing Britain Together presented convincing evidence of deeply unequal conditions in around 3,000 small areas spread all over the country, almost entirely urban. The government believed that it needed multi-pronged, 'joined-up' action to ensure a mutually reinforcing programme of renewal. The SEU organised 18 innovative Policy Action Teams to look more closely at the specific aspects of the problem, drawing on experts from the ground, academia and government (SEU, 2000b). The Neighbourhood Renewal Programme was launched in 2000 to deliver the resulting National Strategy for Neighbourhood Renewal covering the 88 most deprived local authority districts in England (SEU, 2000a).

The broad-based and expensive Neighbourhood Renewal Programme, with a budget of £800 million for the first three years, gave the 86 'most deprived' local authorities an allocation of Neighbourhood Renewal funding that they could spend broadly within their own priorities, as long as they could show long-term benefits in the disadvantaged areas the programme was aimed at. Several linked programmes within this broad-based approach emerged, such as Neighbourhood Management and Neighbourhood Warden pilots. The Neighbourhood Renewal Programmes have been extensively evaluated.

Alongside these somewhat flexible, service-oriented programmes, the government recognised the major investment deficits – not only in potentially equalising services such as education, health and policing – but also in capital investment and the renewal of physical assets. Council housing became a prime target and the Decent Homes Programme was launched with the aim of upgrading all socially rented homes to a minimal decency standard by 2010. This programme eventually became very significant within the Neighbourhood Renewal approach because of the intense concentration of council and other social housing in the most deprived areas as shown in Figure 6.1.

Throughout the entire period of intense government focus on Neighbourhood Renewal in the poorest areas, CASE's 10-year study of area-based disadvantage was tracking 12 representative small areas of high multiple deprivation and interviewing 200 representative low-income families every year about what it is like to bring up children in such areas. This gave us extensive evidence of what conditions were really like, how they were changing and what measures introduced by government had a noticeable impact.

This chapter assesses the direction of change in poor areas, drawing on five government evaluations, comparing their findings with our own two longitudinal area studies. The views of the 200 families we visited annually over eight years proved startling. Their experiences of bringing up children in poor areas span almost the whole of New Labour's time in government to date and cover the whole Neighbourhood Renewal period. They reported what was really changing in their eyes and whether it was for better or for worse. First we examine evidence from the government's five evaluations; then we examine evidence from CASE's wider neighbourhood study of 12 highly disadvantaged areas; finally, we look at the assessment of change made by the 200 families in 2006.

Figure 6.1: Distribution of social housing in England, by 2004 level of deprivation of area, 1991 and 2004

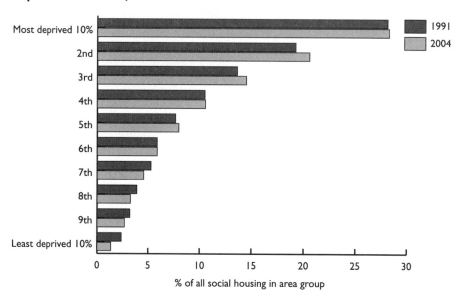

Note: Deprived areas are based on the 2004 Index of Multiple Deprivation ranged decile groups of Lower Layer Super Output Areas.
Source: Hills (2007), based on data from the English Housing Conditions Survey

What government evidence shows about the scale of area-based problems

In *Bringing Britain Together*, the SEU drew on the 1991 Census and local authority-level evidence up to 1997 to highlight just how big the gap between the 5% poorest wards, their surrounding local authorities and the national average had grown over the 1980s and 1990s in concentrations of lone-parent households, the unemployed and the proportion of children in poor households. There were over two-and-a-half times the concentrations of children living in poverty in the poorest areas, as Figure 6.2 shows. The report also showed the much more rapid rise in worklessness among council tenants than the average. Between 1983 and 1997, worklessness rose by 6 percentage points among owner-occupiers but, at two-and-a-half times that rate, by 15 percentage points among social housing tenants.

The SEU showed that 40% of all crime happened in just 10% of areas. Violent crime was at least three times as common in the most deprived as the least deprived areas (SEU, 1998). Similar variations applied to drug use and drug-related crime. Figure 6.3 shows over double the concentrations of total crime and other anti-social behaviour.

Figure 6.2: Comparison of the 44 local authority districts, the rest of England and the 5% most deprived wards in England

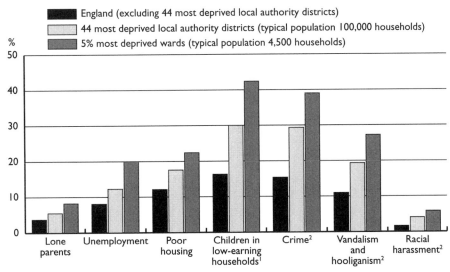

Notes: [1] 'Children in low-earning households' is defined here as the percentage of children in households that rely on Income Support. [2] Perception of whether issues are a serious problem in respondents' local area.
Source: SEU (2000a)

Figure 6.3: People and place factors interact to impact on quality of life and undermine life chances

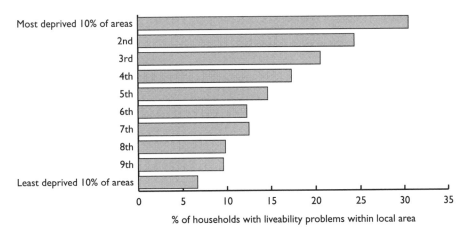

Source: English House Conditions Survey (*Why Place Matters* presentation at CLG People and Place seminar 17 October 2007)

Secondary schools in the 10% poorest areas showed different outcomes, with a quarter of all children leaving school with no GCSEs at all, five times the national average, and truancy affecting four times the average proportion of children (see Chapter Four).

An underlying problem, often compounding social exclusion, was the disproportionate concentration of minority ethnic residents in the poorest areas, four times their share of the population as a whole. This meant that their housing, education, work opportunities, experience of crime and policing fell far behind the average. Alongside this ethnic dimension to the problem, many of the poorest areas were almost exclusively white, particularly large, peripheral council estates, and some older industrial areas that began to decline before the Second World War (Power and Mumford, 1999).

Further evidence of area inequality comes from repeated government surveys of how residents feel about conditions and services in places where they live (see Figures 6.3 and 6.4). These have shown much higher levels of dissatisfaction in poorer areas on many indicators. At the advent of New Labour's area-based initiatives, these levels of dissatisfaction were intense. Area dissatisfaction with basic conditions, repair, the local environment, sense of safety, neighbourliness, useable open space, local services and so on seemed stubbornly higher in the poorer areas than the average, and six times higher in the poorest areas compared with the richest, as Figure 6.3 shows. On a broad range of measures, the government found evidence of very large differences in quality of life between areas dominated by social housing (mainly large urban estates) and others. Poorer areas suffered up to four-and-a-half times the intensity of 'liveability' problems, a broad term encompassing most aspects of neighbourhood life that affect people's views of where they live.

What government evidence shows of closing the gap

The government set its sights on closing the gap between the poorest areas and the average, eventually including the ambitious goal of ensuring that 'no one is seriously disadvantaged by where they live' (SEU, 2001, p 8). The National Strategy for Neighbourhood Renewal adopted the bold idea of 'floor targets' for all basic services and conditions, a level below which no area should fall, since wider service improvements with particular efforts directed towards the most needy areas were expected to close the gap.

The Conservatives' earlier efforts at area targeting had been undermined by wider negative trends. Therefore, the New Labour government combined area-based targeting with wider public service reform and redistribution measures. Somewhat to the surprise of sceptics, these overarching efforts have had greater impacts in poorer areas, thereby in reality closing the gap in conditions, as the government set out to do. The different strands of research we have examined confirm this positive trend, even though they also show that the gap is still wide and much remains to be done. Figure 6.4 shows that both the 86 local

Figure 6.4: Comparative performance – Neighbourhood Renewal Fund (NRF) 10% worst Lower Layer Super Output Areas (LSOAs) and NRF local authority districts (LADs) vs national average, 2001-05

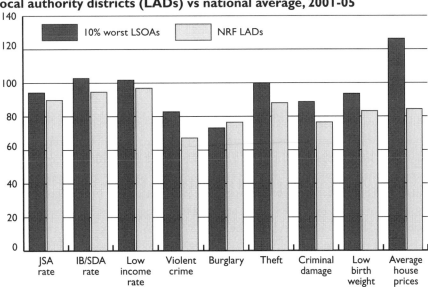

Notes: Scores above 100 show widening gap with national average. Scores below 100 show narrowing gap with national average. JSA = Jobseeker's Alliance; IB = Incapacity Benefit; SDA = Severe Disablement Allowance
Source: NCRA Narrative, Expert Panel Meeting, June 2007 (Michael Parkinson and Jean Parry, LJMU)

authorities receiving Neighbourhood Renewal funding and the 10% poorest areas within them have closed the gap with the national average on key measures of disadvantage. Scores below the 100 line show the gap narrowing.

Sure Start and the New Deal for Communities

The Sure Start and New Deal for Communities evaluations are based on large resident surveys as the programmes evolved. In both programmes it took up to five years for direct improvements to show through clearly. But the latest evidence from 150 Sure Starts in the 5% most deprived areas (NESS, 2008) measures both child development and parental gains among the most disadvantaged families in comparison with similar families not participating in Sure Start (see Chapter Three). Through direct involvement in Sure Start services, parents and children show improvements in health, child development, sociability, levels of immunisation and general access to other services. The families also benefit from a more general growth in social capital through greater social contact and support. This leads to families coping better.

The New Deal for Communities evaluation (CRESR, 2005) collected evidence of changes in services and neighbourhood conditions in the 39 targeted areas.

Ipsos Mori surveyed a large sample out of the quarter of a million households in the 39 areas, collecting their views of area change (DCLG, 2007c). Progress in services was significant, beyond the general service gains under New Labour. Resident satisfaction with the areas as places to live rose significantly and the gap in satisfaction between the targeted areas and the average closed (Figure 6.5). The gains in the New Deal areas were significantly higher than control areas or the national average. Nonetheless, although the gap closed by 11 percentage points between 2002 and 2006, the New Deal areas were still 16 percentage points behind the average in 2006.

Progress was not smooth and the 'community-led' emphasis of the New Deal for Communities sometimes generated more conflict than 'empowerment'. In some New Deal areas, community-level problems, disagreements over delivery of programmes and conflicting priorities between resident spokespersons and official 'pay masters', prevented or seriously delayed action on the ground, the very purpose of the highly localised and targeted programme. However, a major lesson from the evaluations is both the time it takes to develop local delivery and the benefits of tuning programmes to community needs and priorities (NESS, 2007; CRESR, 2008).

The New Deal for Communities evaluations underlined the need for physical and environmental upgrading alongside social and community programmes. Both programme evaluations confirm that targeted resources, local delivery, locally prioritised improvements in services and conditions and direct participation by local residents can work together to change area conditions and 'narrow the gap'. The corollary may be that more diluted, less targeted effort does not work as well,

Figure 6.5: How satisfied are you with this area as a place to live?

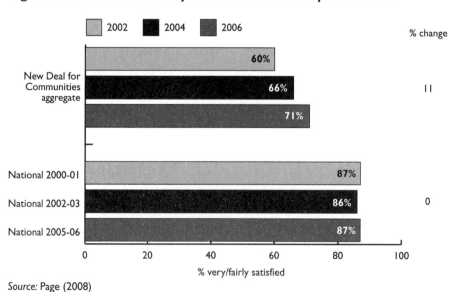

Source: Page (2008)

and does not close the gap. This is because the 'mainstream' method of service improvement effectively pushes up standards everywhere, and because the worst areas need more effort to catch up.

The Neighbourhood Renewal Fund and the National Strategy for Neighbourhood Renewal

The evaluations of the Neighbourhood Renewal Fund, the National Strategy for Neighbourhood Renewal, Neighbourhood Management and the Neighbourhood Warden pilot were not as detailed or as long run as the Sure Start and New Deal for Communities evaluations. Nonetheless, they collected detailed ground-level evidence of change and impacts, including resident surveys before and after the programmes. The Neighbourhood Renewal Fund targeted the 86 most deprived local authority areas, covering the bottom 20% of the population, and containing a large majority of the 10% most deprived small areas within their boundaries. Local authorities are responsible for, and play a large part in, delivering most main services and are directly responsible for area conditions, open spaces, the local environment, council housing, social services and youth and child provision. This makes local authorities major public actors in ensuring and maintaining local conditions and 'liveability'. The evaluation of the Neighbourhood Renewal Fund showed that wider changes and reforms in service delivery at local authority level could be measured, alongside small area impacts.

The National Strategy for Neighbourhood Renewal had broader but shallower ambitions than Sure Start or the New Deal for Communities. By allowing struggling local authorities discretion as to how they spent the average of £30 million per annum that went to each council, the government was experimenting with a new policy emphasis on 'freedom and flexibility' in *how* local services managed resources to achieve agreed targets and outcomes. Many practitioners were doubtful that this more loosely targeted approach would work in the distressed urban areas with the poorest performance records and the worst outcomes in schools, health, the police and economic activity – the 'floor targets' of the SEU – given the neighbourhoods with multiple deprivation within their boundaries.

In Birmingham, Liverpool, Manchester, and Tower Hamlets, Hackney and Newham in East London, a third or more of the city's population lived in the nationally highest poverty wards (Lupton, 2001, 2003). Targeting a broad band of disadvantaged areas with relatively modest and low-cost improvements that were immediately visible inspired area clean-ups, tackling local 'eye sores', street supervision, wardens, and upgrading open space, parks and play areas. This broad local management approach was dubbed later by the government as the 'cleaner, safer, greener' agenda (ODPM, 2002). Councils also used the Neighbourhood Renewal Fund to support additional or more intensive mainstream services for children, young people, the low skilled, unemployed, lone parents and older people within deprived areas or within vulnerable groups.

The Neighbourhood Renewal Fund evaluation shows that the rate of claiming Jobseeker's Allowance fell faster in two-thirds of the target local authorities than nationally, and almost all the poorest areas within them (97%) closed the gap with the local authority average. This also applied to incapacity and social security claims. The wider gains already shown in Figure 6.4 on most of the floor targets are confirmed by this progress in closing the gap both within the most disadvantaged local authorities and with the national average. There is one important caveat to this – the areas and local authorities where the gap has not closed are mostly in London and the greater South East where the extremes of wealth and poverty are greater and where the economic progress is more heavily based on the knowledge economy (DCLG, 2007b).

The success in closing the gap also suggests three other important outcomes: first, it is possible to 'bend' mainstream services to help more disadvantaged areas, at both district and more local levels; second, relatively modest programmes across many poorer areas within a framework of improved performance of public services have an effect; third, Neighbourhood Management – a coordinated and localised effort to tackle basic area conditions and environments – achieves visible improvements that can restore confidence, encourage investment and signal wider progress. The Neighbourhood Management evaluation (ODPM, 2006) tells us more about this approach.

Neighbourhood Management

Neighbourhood Management, an idea trialled in the 1980s on the Broadwater Farm estate in North London and through tenant management initiatives (Power, 1997), became a pivotal part of Neighbourhood Renewal from 2000 because it offered a relatively low-cost and easy to set up local management system for ensuring ground-level delivery of essential services, and for organising dedicated street-level care. Every successful model of progress uncovered by the SEU prior to the National Strategy involved some kind of Neighbourhood Management (Power, 2004). Thirty-five Neighbourhood Management pilots in some of the poorest areas outside the 86 targeted local authorities aimed to spread the Neighbourhood Renewal Fund more widely and to trial a low-cost model of area improvement. A dedicated, locally based management team with a dedicated local budget were the hallmarks. Places like Chester, a prosperous city with two large, highly disadvantaged council estates, was one successful pilot.

Neighbourhood Management showed real gains in conditions and services (ODPM, 2006; DCLG, 2007a), as well as significant rises in satisfaction and a closing of the gap in conditions between the pilots and the control areas. The cost of organising this additional layer of supervision below the local authority level was relatively modest – around £150,000 per year for 4,000 homes, but it was vulnerable to budget cuts once the special government funding was withdrawn in 2004. When the local teams had to cover much larger areas, the scheme lost its hallmark quality of familiarity and close, direct supervision. While Neighbourhood Management was easily replicable and produced tangible benefits to the local authorities, the evaluation highlighted that wherever local authorities have widened the approach they have spread staff too thinly and shrunk budgets. They have done this on grounds of cost and 'efficiency' savings, but by losing its core qualities of focus, local coordination and resident involvement and confidence, it may well be a false economy. Dilution, when the worst problems have abated, may result in the loss of gains (NAO, 2007).

Neighbourhood Wardens

Wardens provide a level of visible street supervision that is uncommon in most of Britain's built-up areas, but is increasingly popular in cities, particularly in poorer, more decayed areas. The intensive caretaking approach of social housing estates is a top resident priority; close supervision of communal areas and local involvement helps ensure its success (Birmingham City Council, 2003). This approach was therefore used as a model for many warden schemes. Wardens often form part of a wider Neighbourhood Management initiative. Interestingly, the evaluation of Neighbourhood Wardens (ODPM, 2004) shows similar improvements in general environments and rises in satisfaction.

Unlike the other area programmes, it proved impossible to detect higher gains in the Neighbourhood Warden pilot areas being evaluated than in the similar control areas, where it seemed that the Neighbourhood Warden programmes had also been adopted. Warden schemes are cheaper than Neighbourhood Management, are quicker to set up and are straightforward to run. They bring immediate gains, are extremely popular and fundable within council budgets, so they have been widely replicated in low-incomes areas (ODPM, 2004).

A major lesson from the overall Neighbourhood Renewal approach is that some basic frontline services, withdrawn in the era of public service cuts and privatisation of basic cleaning and environmental services, were vital to the viability of established urban areas. Their almost total withdrawal and replacement with inadequate, hard-to-supervise mobile services led to a rapid deterioration in conditions and a chain effect in attitudes and behaviour (Power, 1987; Mumford and Power, 2003). Lack of continual maintenance and oversight quickly causes decay, rubbish accumulation and disrepair. Negative environmental signals (rubbish, graffiti, vandalism, broken windows) cause withdrawal, loss of informal control, fear and the emergence of crime and anti-social behaviour (Power and Mumford, 1999). The converse, shown through the Neighbourhood Management and Neighbourhood Warden pilots, is that increased environmental care not only creates greater satisfaction, it also pays for itself in reduced vandalism, and generates a form of self-policing by making streets and open spaces people-friendly again, attracting people and activities back.

Summary

Overall, we can draw several conclusions from government evaluations of area-based initiatives. First, the gap between the poorest areas (the bottom 10%) and the average had grown unacceptably wide in physical, social and economic conditions. Second, locally targeted, broad-based initiatives, combining different services (health, education, the police, housing and income) could respond to local priorities and make a measurable difference to outcomes. Third, relatively low-cost replicable Neighbourhood Management, warden supervision and street-care services have a significant impact if they are sufficiently local and sufficiently intensive (DCLG, 2008a).

The government now faces the challenge that most of its targeted initiatives are ending, or reducing significantly, both in spending and in small-area focus. Local authorities carry the responsibility for targeting their resources on deprived areas and there are worries about whether they will do this, given overall resource constraints and more pressing priorities. It is easy to overlook the most marginal areas, which divert resources from the mainstream, if a council is trying to improve its overall performance. We return to the issue of follow-through in area-based programmes in our concluding section.

Evidence from CASE's 12 areas – the gap

Government evaluations have shown fairly consistently that services and conditions improved to a point where the gap was closing between the poorest areas and the average. CASE's area-based research focuses on the ground-level impacts of changes in policy conditions and social composition. It addresses the impact of improving conditions on the overall viability of the most deprived and marginal areas. We chose 12 areas to represent differences in urban and regional characteristics in order to reflect as wide a range as possible of types of deprived areas. The areas are: Birmingham, Blackburn, Caerphilly, Hackney, Knowsley, Leeds, Newcastle, Newham, Nottingham, Redcar, Sheffield, and Thanet. The poorest 3% of wards were heavily clustered in the poorer, older parts of cities, in former industrial areas and in large outer estates built to replace industrial slums, separate from existing built-up areas. Over four-fifths of these high-poverty areas were adjacent to other highly deprived wards in extended clusters of poverty. Only one of our areas – Thanet – a Southern coastal area, had isolated poverty wards. The concentration of the worst areas within much larger deprived areas made it easier for the government both to target programmes and to justify the special efforts. Therefore, the areas we studied all experienced a boom in area-based initiatives, which we were able to monitor closely.

Prior to New Labour, the 12 areas had already gone through every kind of special programme, totalling 74 in the 12 areas over the 1980s and 1990s, up to New Labour. In 1998, they were poised for a new burst of activity. Three areas had the New Deal for Communities, 10 were targeted by Neighbourhood Renewal Funds and Sure Start appeared in all areas, except Caerphilly, which came under Welsh regeneration schemes. By 2002, there were between three and four new initiatives in each area. By 2006, 11 of the 12 areas had some form of local management. All received Decent Homes Programme investment. This expensive programme has not yet been evaluated by the government, but we gathered extensive feedback, both from our visits to the 12 areas, and from the 200 families, on the £10,000 per social rented home invested.

Our assessment of 10 years of change since 1998 shows the greatest gains in environmental quality, in general cleanliness and tidiness, in the care and upgrading of existing homes and open spaces and in resident involvement. These changes reflected:

- Neighbourhood Management approaches (including wardens);
- more intensive and more community-oriented policing (including the introduction of community support officers);
- direct housing reinvestment through stock transfer, take-over by arm's length management organisations and the Decent Homes Programme;
- new services (including Sure Start, school and health programmes); and
- a constant attempt to involve community representatives.

All the new initiatives attempted to sound out residents' priorities, using their 'eyes on the ground' to target the most immediate problems quickly. Between 1999 and 2003, there was a 50% reduction in environmental damage and visible degradation of property in the 12 areas (Paskell and Power, 2005). This trend was further confirmed when we revisited the areas in 2006.

The government's long-run, slowly evolving and broad-based efforts and investments had a measurable impact in reducing environmental problems, improving the popularity of difficult areas and, in a majority of the areas, increasing their viability and prospects. However, gains were not even across services and much depended on local leadership (for example a dynamic school head, police chief or neighbourhood manager), as well as on location and the overall regional economy. Areas and services could do well for a time with the right ingredients and a charismatic boss but might still not be viable.

Some areas still have weak economies after a decade-and-a-half of wider recovery (for example Redcar and Teesside). Some have an oversupply of council housing, albeit transferred to alternative non-profit landlords, in cities where too much clearance was replaced with peripheral post-war estates (for example Liverpool and Knowsley). Some have lost their original rationale (such as Caerphilly, a former coalmining valley). However, even the most marginal areas were better run and in better condition, with less dissatisfied residents, in 2006 than they had been in 1998; but they were still almost universally poor and their future was far from secure. Four of our 12 areas fell into this grouping; all are located outside the core urban area and all are far from regional growth hubs.

Outer-city areas were dominated by large pre- and post-war council estates, mixed with run-down private housing, often for rent. But they were within the main built-up area, connected by public transport to lively city centres, one or two miles away, making them accessible for jobs and amenities. Four areas fell into this grouping. These four areas were generally becoming more viable, even though in two cases the local authorities were set on 'regenerating' the areas, turning them into 'mixed communities' through wholesale, costly and disruptive clearance. The plan was for replacement with more private, more up-market and less affordable housing, but the process of regeneration was causing widespread uncertainty, general blight and long delays. According to the families we interviewed in two of the areas, they were improving significantly in general in spite of these drastic plans, which were still far off on the horizon. In the current climate, total regeneration may no longer proceed, which may actually help their future.

The four most improving and promising areas were in dense inner-city neighbourhoods adjacent to city centres. In all cases, they contained a mix of housing types, including pre-First World War terraces, inter-war blocks and post-war estates, a rich mix of uses and services and ethnically diverse, fast-changing populations. Their recovery was driven by their location, close to city centres; their greater density, allowing local shops, buses and facilities to survive; their mix of housing types, encouraging in-movers to invest and upgrade; and their diverse communities repopulating previously declining areas.

Within existing urban areas, highly disadvantaged communities appeared to recover with a combination of targeted programmes, coordinated and delivered locally, and greater supervision and maintenance of public spaces, supported by active residents. They had the key ingredients of location, a critical mass of people and activities, and a mixed working infrastructure, including public transport. This applied to the four inner core areas, and to a lesser extent, to the four outer core areas. The outer core areas were still somewhat precarious and they will almost certainly suffer from the credit crunch, but they are now at least showing many signs of recovery.

The converse applied to peripheral areas. In spite of heroic management and community efforts and significant investment, they appeared to have lost a critical mass of people and activities, making their futures increasingly uncertain. In two cases, they had been marginal from when they were built and in the other two cases, their reliance on a single large industry had made them vulnerable to collapse.

There was a strong sense of déjà-vu in the approach to these marginal areas. Demolition of surplus, abandoned and ransacked peripheral housing was being replaced in three of the four cases with large-scale private, but heavily subsidised building. Based on previous experience under the Conservatives, this approach is doomed to failure (Mumford and Power, 2002). Cheap new private and subsidised alternatives to unwanted but structurally sound council and private housing would simply compound the oversupply and rebuild low-value homes to uncertain demand. The collapse in the housing market after 2007 may delay such plans and allow time for the government to reconsider its insensitive approach to 'mixed communities' and housing numbers, based on shaky household projections.

There were also doubts about the demolition and replacement programmes in the inner and outer core areas under the same banner of 'mixed communities' and 'market renewal'. These slow-moving plans are changing because of changes in the housing market, although in at least two cases they are too far advanced to be scrapped completely. In all, eight of our 12 areas are significantly affected by demolition.

More small-scale, less dramatic, more long-term interventions, such as Neighbourhood Management, Neighbourhood Wardens, Decent Homes and Sure Start, showed more certain gains than total physical replacement. Physical replacement was vulnerable to market changes – disrupting any other improvements in community life such as schools, health or childcare – and displaced disadvantaged populations, rather than built community stability.

Our study shows that more continual smaller-scale reinvestment and area management can restore the viability of disadvantaged areas, where a low-income population, predominantly tenants, simply cannot generate the necessary resources and where landlords and local authorities have collective responsibility for area services and conditions. As current programmes wind down, the successful methods the evaluations uncovered need to be held in place in order to realise the goal of closing rather than just narrowing the gap.

Current economic trends, coupled with government funding shortages, threaten the future viability of larger-scale, more radical schemes, favouring the smaller-scale approach that we found across all areas to show most promise. A steadier hand, lower-level but more continual inputs and more long-term policies and funding would build on progress to date (Power and Willmot, 2005).

Evidence from 200 families

If the 12 areas gave us close-grained insights into how things are panning out on the ground, our tracking of 200 families in four of the 12 areas fills in the minutiae of programme delivery and its value to families with children. Over eight years of visiting the same families, we captured changes in housing and neighbourhood environments, play areas, open spaces and local facilities. Parents also talked about money, work and training, education, health provision and childcare, policing, security and safety, youth provision, inter-ethnic understanding, and community. We believe that families' sensitivity to area problems, their low incomes and struggle to survive, and their constant reliance on one or other of the main services, gave us unique feedback on how programmes have played out, and how conditions have changed.

By 2006, over half the families thought that their neighbourhoods were getting better. This view was much more common in the North (60% positive) where the problems at the outset had also seemed less stark; in London, two-fifths (40%) thought that their areas were improving, more than those who thought they were getting worse (36%) even though the East London areas were under immense development pressure, extremely rapid ethnic change and major regeneration plans in the Newham area, which thus far had failed to solve entrenched problems of poverty and multiple disadvantage.

The four family areas were within the two more viable types of area – inner-city and core urban areas – even though they all started out with intense poverty, worklessness and physical decay. As long as wider economic conditions were favourable and 'closing the gap' remained a major goal, these areas improved under the impact of many different initiatives, even though the East London areas were in the top four most deprived local authorities in the country.

Families revised their view on whether they wanted to move away from these areas over the eight years that we visited them. At the outset, nearly half the London families (45%) wanted to move away compared with 27% by 2005. In the North, far fewer (one-fifth) wanted to move away at the outset, but by 2006 this had dropped to 12%. Wanting to stay is possibly the best barometer of confidence in the areas as the parents' answers reflect their feelings about where they live and the prospects for their children, rather than their actual prospects of moving.

London families more often wanted to move away because of the housing problem, the pressure of space and the impossibility of either transferring to a bigger rented home, moving out from a flat into a house with a garden or having any future hope of buying in the area. For some, however, it was a mixture of housing and area problems. In the North, in contrast, most families already occupied houses, could transfer more easily and were generally more satisfied with their homes. Area conditions were therefore the main driver for wanting to move, albeit at a lower level of dissatisfaction.

The three most significant areas of improvement that families identified were:

- lower crime, coupled with more visible policing, supervision and sense of security;
- the upgrading of housing through the Decent Homes Programme, New Deal for Communities (in the two inner-city areas) and better, more responsive housing management (often blurring into Neighbourhood Management); and
- the upgrading of neighbourhood environments and services.

Even though crime was still much higher in these areas than elsewhere, fewer than 5% of families gave it as their main negative comment.

Overall, four out of five parents saw significant positive changes reflecting not only the visible physical improvements they valued because the place *looked* better; but also the less tangible or more service-oriented changes that made them feel better and helped their families cope. Sure Start, parent–school links, familiar faces, local 'fun events' and 'looking after things' were examples.

Yet the overwhelming majority (85%) still saw problems and gaps in the efforts to equalise conditions. As a result of these gaps, about half the parents had mixed feelings about their communities and their families' future prospects although the direction of change was overwhelmingly positive at our last interview. The parents' highest priorities for further action were more facilities and activities for children and young people, more crime prevention and more physical reinvestment, particularly in homes.

A theme that constantly recurred was 'community spirit', how much it mattered, how vulnerable it was to over-rapid change, how intangible and immeasurable it was and yet how vital it was to families. Over 90% said that it mattered a lot to them, but many felt that it was undermined by the constant inflow of strangers, the difficulty, particularly in London, of staying near family, and the feeling that incomers were constantly undermining and displacing the existing community. Competition between groups was most intense in housing, childcare and school places, particularly in the more sought-after local schools (often church schools). This tension did not prevent the majority of parents from finding their area friendly, far friendlier than the average for other areas (Mumford and Power, 2003).

Overall, the evidence from the families coincides with the findings from the 12 areas and from government evaluations:

- that the poorest areas have benefited from targeted programmes;
- that low-income families have benefited from anti-poverty and family support measures; and
- that the type of improvements that showed up in the other evaluations are more than supported by what 200 families directly experienced.

What of the future? Is progress slowing down?

The real progress made over 10 years looks increasingly precarious for the least favoured areas for several reasons:

- Most of New Labour's area-based initiatives are now ending so there will be very little targeting from 2009.
- This does not apply to Sure Start for now, but even Sure Start will be diluted by broadening the areas it covers and as its remit changes when Children's

Centres – in principle an excellent and universal service for families – take over (see Chapter Three). Hopefully, the latest positive evaluation findings will reinforce the arguments for keeping Sure Start intact in the poorest areas.

- The SEU, the Neighbourhood Renewal Unit, Neighbourhood Management and Warden Programmes are no longer central government priorities. Reinvesting in the most deprived areas will decline as things stand.
- Social housing still dominates almost all the poorest areas and there is no sign of this changing fundamentally (although the proportion of social housing has fallen steeply in 11 of our 12 areas). Social housing is still 2.5 to 3 times more concentrated than the national average in the poorest areas and social housing itself has become poorer. The recent Mixed Communities initiative (a government initiative to break up 'social ghettos', mainly poorer large council estates, and to attract more diverse incomes and uses into disadvantaged areas) has no muscle and no money (6 of our 12 areas are included but it has no obvious impact).
- As the economy declines, the poorest areas may be hit hard with 'worst first'.
- The government has devolved powers to local authorities, leaving them maximum discretion to decide what programmes they design and how much emphasis they place on the poorest areas. While this worked with the Neighbourhood Renewal Fund, the whole purpose of the National Strategy for Neighbourhood Renewal was to close the gap with the poorest areas. At government level this no longer applies.

What are the likely consequences of reduced area targeting?

The ending of special programmes and neighbourhood focus will lead to a slip in effort. Already there is evidence from the Neighbourhood Management evaluation showing a loss of focus (ODPM, 2006). Spreading the untied resources more thinly over bigger areas will not extend the value of achievements to date and may actually cancel out positive impact. Motivation at the local level is hard to sustain without the 'carrot' of extra, dedicated funding and the inspiration of being part of a bigger programme. Reinvestment problems will quickly re-emerge in rented housing and low-income owner-occupier areas with the wind-down of the Decent Homes Programme.

Until now, government-driven targets have shaped the progress we have described. Now, the move to greater 'freedoms and flexibilities' will leave some local authorities struggling without a wider framework. For local politicians, inequality may be a lower priority than re-election, upgraded town centres or prestige events and buildings.

The French experience of central government 'taking its eye off the ball' during the Chirac era and devolving responsibility for the poorest areas to local authorities struggling with multiple problems led to area inequalities accelerating out of control. This culminated in widespread riots in 2005 (Thiollière, 2007).

We should not follow that route, although there is now a serious vacuum in area-based policies. Since Gordon Brown became Prime Minister, no area programmes have been announced.

However, there are clear signs of renewed interest in the neighbourhood agenda for the following reasons:

• Some follow-through to the Decent Homes Programme linked to environmental upgrading and energy efficiency seems likely because of the urgency of tackling fuel poverty, which has risen steeply due to high energy prices.
• The threat of disorder as the economic climate deteriorates may drive new efforts to help the worst areas.
• Environmental pressures and hostility to new greenfield building are growing so poorer areas may become *much* more valuable, aiding reinvestment and recovery.
• There is an ongoing concern about the consequences for families and children in disadvantaged homes and areas of poor neighbourhood conditions. Child poverty, secondary school failures, youth disaffection and unemployment have not gone away.
• The need for low-cost services largely run by low-paid and part-time workers makes the survival of low-cost areas important to the future of cities.
• There is a growing recognition that area targeting helps address wider problems of inequality, such as housing conditions, schooling, play and ethnic disadvantage.

For all these reasons, some reconfiguration of current spending plans to help sustain the gains made in poor areas must make sense.

SEVEN

Health inequalities: a persistent problem

Franco Sassi

Introduction

The first New Labour government came to power in the same year in which a major report on health inequalities was published (Drever and Whitehead, 1997), following the *Black Report* and *The Health Divide* (both in Townsend et al, 1992), respectively, 20 and 10 years before. The evidence collated in the three reports consistently showed that while most indicators of health and longevity were on long-term trends of improvement, inequalities between socioeconomic groups and between areas in many such indicators had been increasing since the 1950s. Gaps in life expectancy at birth, as well as in infant and child mortality, between the most and the least disadvantaged in society, had been widening over time. Differences in life expectancy between the top and the bottom social classes were 4.8 years in women and 5.4 years in men in the early 1970s, and were 6.3 and 9.4 years, respectively, 20 years later. Gaps in premature mortality (before age 65) similarly increased, with rates dropping by 44% over two decades in the highest social classes, but only by about 10% among unskilled manual workers, with particularly large inequalities in deaths from respiratory diseases and in smoking rates.

The theme of health inequalities did not feature in the Labour manifesto for the 1997 General Election. However, it soon became one of the top priorities once the new government came to power. Only a few months into its first term, the government established an independent inquiry into health inequalities, under the leadership of Donald Acheson. The final report presented the following year (DH, 1998a) confirmed once again the virtually ubiquitous nature of health inequalities in Britain and presented a number of policy recommendations emphasising the need for cross-government policies, for a lifecourse approach and for policies to address poverty and social exclusion. But even before the publication of the Acheson report, the government began to address the health inequalities problem in a sequence of major policy documents. It started with the Green Paper *Our Healthier Nation: A Contract for Health* (DH, 1998b), followed in 1999 by the White Paper *Saving Lives: Our Healthier Nation* (DH, 1999a), which was published with a joint document entitled *Reducing Health Inequalities: An Action Report* (1999b) that set out planned inputs for a strategy to tackle inequalities. *The NHS Plan* (DH, 2000) had a focus on health inequalities and announced the publication of national targets, which were issued in 2001, before the General Election (DH, 2001b).

Health inequalities featured prominently in the 2001 Labour manifesto, and New Labour's second term of office was characterised by a further escalation of strategies, targets and policy documents, as well as by an increasing involvement of the Treasury in policy on healthcare and health inequalities. A cross-cutting spending review led by the Treasury in 2002 involved yet another collection of evidence on health inequalities and the identification of key strategies to deliver the national targets. A cross-government delivery plan was published the following year in *A Programme for Action* (DH, 2003) which provided an assessment of progress made since the Acheson Inquiry and a plan for further action.

The policy initiatives and documents briefly summarised here were discussed in some detail in Sassi (2005), reaching the conclusion that, despite an unprecedented focus on health inequalities, real action to tackle the problem had been very disappointing. This was also noted on more than one occasion by Derek Wanless as part if his two National Health Service (NHS) reviews, undertaken on behalf of the Treasury (Wanless, 2002, 2004). The links between goals, actions and resources were never made clear. Goals were often too general or too vague and specific targets did not seem particularly helpful; action plans were often mere lists of desirable objectives; resources were often set out as broad spending commitments. Moreover, the government had always been very explicit about its aim to improve the overall health of the population at least as much as to reduce health inequalities, failing to acknowledge the sacrifices that may have to be made on one or the other of these potentially conflicting objectives.

Policy developments on health inequalities since 2004

Although there have been no major turns in the overall direction of government policy on health inequalities since 1997, the strategy appeared to become somewhat more focused in 2004. At least three important developments occurred in 2004:

- a Spending Review that led to the formulation of new Public Service Agreements (PSAs);
- the publication of the public health White Paper *Choosing Health* (DH, 2004a); and
- the identification of a 'spearhead group' of local authorities and primary care trusts.

The 2004 PSA for the Department of Health significantly expanded the set of national health inequalities 'floor targets' set by the government in 2001. These national targets were relatively narrow in scope (they addressed only infant mortality and geographic inequalities in life expectancy); they did not look particularly ambitious (for example the infant mortality target meant averting one infant death for every 20,000 births in the manual classes, over 10 years); and they were somewhat inconsistent, as one focused on inequalities by social class, while the rest focused on geographic inequalities. However limited the original targets may have been, it was already apparent in 2004 that the government was not on track to achieving at least some of them (Shaw et al, 2005). The new set of targets in the 2004 PSA for the Department of Health was broader in scope, as it included measures of premature mortality and health-related behaviours; it was more ambitious in terms of the size of the reductions aimed for, but perhaps more achievable given past trends in some of the relevant measures. The new targets, however, were no more consistent than the original ones. Premature mortality targets focused on geographical inequalities; the smoking cessation target focused on inequalities by social class; and the child obesity and teenage pregnancy targets referred to overall improvements rather than reductions in inequalities. However, by the end of the year it was clear that the government was going to attach the highest priority to narrowing the mortality gap between more and less deprived areas of the country.

In November 2004, a 'spearhead group' of local authorities and primary care trusts was identified by selecting the fifth of local authorities that had not only the highest levels of deprivation, but also the lowest overall life expectancy at birth, for males and females, and the highest mortality for cancer and cardiovascular disease under 75 years of age. The strategy was not new, as it might be seen as a development and consolidation of the Health Action Zones experiment. Primary care trusts in the spearhead group would receive extra resources; they would be the focus of targeted initiatives and careful monitoring of progress on achieving health inequality targets. However, if it is true that geographic differences in life expectancy in England and Wales are largely explained by deprivation and associated risk factors (Woods et al, 2005), it is also true that differences in area composition by social class explain only a relatively small proportion of health inequalities across areas (Shaw et al, 1999) and that inequalities by social class are not exacerbated in more deprived areas (Pevalin, 2007). Additionally, while in spearhead areas a higher proportion of the resident population belongs to disadvantaged socioeconomic groups, at the national level most of those who belong to disadvantaged socioeconomic groups live in non-spearhead areas. Therefore, tackling geographic inequalities is not the same as tackling inequalities by social class in the overall population, and perhaps New Labour governments should have been more explicit about this distinction throughout.

A further milestone in 2004 was the publication of the public health White Paper *Choosing Health* (DH, 2004a). The contents of the White Paper follow rather closely the conclusions of the second Wanless review and the *NHS Improvement Plan* (DH, 2004c), published in June of the same year. The primary focus is on improving the overall health of the population by making healthy lifestyle choices easier and reducing the incidence and prevalence of key risk factors for health. In an effort to improve the evidence base on which public health decisions are based, the White Paper announced that the Health Development Agency would merge into the National Institute for Clinical Excellence to form a National Institute for Health and Clinical Excellence (NICE) with a plan to produce appraisals and guidelines relevant to tackling the major public health problems the country is facing. Health inequalities do come into the picture in the White Paper, but they are addressed only to a very limited extent. The key question of how overall health improvements that may be achieved through the promotion of healthy lifestyles might lead to the narrowing of health inequalities is never addressed in the White Paper. Claims are made that improvements would naturally follow on from both aspects by enabling individuals to make healthier choices, without the support of evidence or other justification. Only to provide one example, in discussing the issue of patient empowerment and patient choice, the *NHS Improvement Plan* claims that:

> Improving the population's health literacy will be a key element in realising the potential of the information revolution we have embarked on and ensuring that access to information results in reduced inequalities in health and reduced inequities in access to care. (DH, 2004c, p 73)

The implementation document *Delivering Choosing Health: Making Healthier Choices Easier*, published in 2005 (DH, 2005), listed tackling health inequalities among the priorities and indicated a number of 'big win' interventions to achieve this goal. Once again, the strategies proposed (for example, smoking reduction, improved access to primary care, high-quality family and early years support) remained very general and did not specifically address the question of how socioeconomic inequalities would be narrowed through them.

Yearly progress reports on the implementation of the 2003 *Programme for Action* (DH, 2003), including comprehensive assessments of progress in the pursuit of health inequalities targets, were published from 2005. The latest available report at the time of writing is based on 2004-06 data (DH, 2007, 2008b). This confirmed disappointing results on the original targets, which the government does not seem on track to achieving, as discussed further below. However, the report presented encouraging results on some of the targets set in 2004, showing excellent progress in achieving the cancer and cardiovascular premature mortality targets, with the former having already been achieved five years ahead of time.

The latest step in the government's policy-making efforts on health inequalities is the publication in June 2008 of the report *Health Inequalities: Progress and Next Steps* (DH, 2008c). The main goal of this document seems to be to maintain the focus on health inequalities, to show a continuing commitment to achieving the health inequalities targets and to prevent the potential demoralising effects of the most important targets appearing increasingly out of reach. The report acknowledged that '... the health of the most disadvantaged has not improved as quickly as that of the better off. Inequalities in health persist and, in some cases, have widened' (DH, 2008c, p 4).

But it also emphasised that improvements in the health of the most disadvantaged were realised, and that progress had been made on tackling the root causes of ill-health. As many such documents in the previous 10 years, this latest one dwelled on analyses of the problem more than on possible solutions. On the latter side, it stressed with unprecedented strength the 'crucial role' of local government in tackling health inequalities and appeared to propose a strategy primarily based on the 'scaling up' of local initiatives that had proven effective.

Trends in health inequalities before and during the New Labour governments

Specific aspects of inequalities in health and access to medical care have been assessed at various stages during the last 10 years. Such assessments were made by independent researchers; by the Office for National Statistics (ONS), as part of its routine data collection activities; and by the Department of Health, as part of its monitoring of progress towards the achievement of the national health inequality targets. In this section, I will draw a comprehensive picture of trends in health inequalities during a period that generally covers the years of the Major government and the first two terms of Blair governments, by providing a new series of analyses based on mortality, health status and health-related behaviour data from a range of sources.

Mortality data were obtained both from death registrations and from the ONS Longitudinal Study, comprising Census and vital event information for 1% of the population of England and Wales since 1971. Individual-level health status and health-related behaviour data were obtained from samples of individuals surveyed as part of the Health Survey for England (HSE). The latter comprises a series of household-based annual surveys beginning in 1991, designed to provide regular information on various aspects of the nation's health. The HSE is a cross-sectional survey and new individuals are sampled every year. The size of the sample has varied from year to year, partly in relation to the special focus adopted in each edition of the survey (on specific diseases, for example cardiovascular disease; or specific population groups, for example older people).

In the remainder of this section I will present trends in inequalities, mainly by socioeconomic condition, in a wide range of measures of longevity and health status. In most instances, I will present trends separately for men and women, as inequalities often tend to differ by gender. I will also provide a limited discussion of trends in health inequalities by ethnic group, for which no government targets have been set, but which have been the subject of much debate over the course of the past decade. Analyses of trends in measures of health status were first carried out through multivariate regressions including the following covariates: age, gender, socioeconomic status (five-level occupation-based socioeconomic classification, with imputation of the head of household socioeconomic category for those who did not have one of their own), ethnic group (divided into three macro-categories: white, black, Asian), education level (highest educational qualification) and working status. Quadratic (non-linear) trend lines were fitted for each population subgroup. Each of these curves provides a clear picture of the overall trend for a given subgroup (for example most disadvantaged socioeconomic group) over the period covered by the analysis and can identify a major trend reversal during that period, however, it would not identify multiple and less important changes in trends over the same period. In addition, the analyses described above do not account for possible changes over time in the relative size and composition of population subgroups. This may be a problem particularly in analyses of inequalities by occupation-based social class, in which progressively shrinking groups at the bottom of the socioeconomic scale may include increasing concentrations of less healthy individuals over time.

The multivariate regression analysis was complemented by two additional sets of analyses in order to gather further evidence in relation to the two issues illustrated in the previous paragraph. In particular, a more detailed exploration of possible changes in trends over the period 1991–2005 was made using the Joinpoint approach, developed by the US National Cancer Institute. On the other hand, in order to account for changes over time in the size and composition of population subgroups, I calculated relative and absolute inequality measures named, respectively, the relative index and the slope index of inequality, following an approach used by a number of researchers (for example, Wagstaff et al, 1991; Shaw et al, 2005; Mackenbach et al, 2008), dating back to the 1980s (Pamuk, 1985). The slope index reflects the slope of the regression line obtained by regressing levels of a given health indicator (for example cardiovascular disease rates) for different population groups (for example social classes) on the cumulative size of population groups, as a proportion of the overall population (for example from higher to lower social classes, or vice versa). The relative index reflects the ratio between the levels of the health indicator estimated for the individuals at the two extremes of the scale used to divide the population into groups (for example the social class scale), identified by calculating the intercepts between the regression line and the two vertical axes corresponding to 0% and 100% of the reference population.

Trends in mortality and longevity

Mortality and life expectancy are among the most objective aggregate health indicators, but they tend to react slowly to health policy changes. As the main determinants of health inequalities are at least partly rooted in the early stages of the lifecourse of individuals, policies aimed at tackling those determinants will only have effects on mortality in the long term and mortality rates observed today may reflect the effects of government policies adopted many years previously. However, it is possible that at least some of the changes observed, particularly in the latest years of the period covered in this analysis, may also reflect the impact of policies adopted in the early years of the New Labour governments.

I first analysed trends in overall inequality in age at death, which were reported until 2001 in Hills and Stewart (2005). Inequality in age at death, measured by the Gini coefficient on an age-standardised population, had been on a long-term decreasing trend for 20 years, from 1974 to 1994, but it stabilised in women and began to increase fairly sharply in men after 1994. As shown in Figure 7.1, inequality continued to increase in men after 2001, with a particularly large increase in 2006. The increase observed in women in 2000 and 2001 was reversed in 2002, but since 2002 inequality has been consistently increasing in women too, again with an acceleration in 2006. Of course, overall inequalities in life expectancy do not necessarily show the same patterns and trends as inequalities by socioeconomic condition because the size and composition of socioeconomic groups varies over time, and because inequalities exist also within socioeconomic groups, and these vary over time. Further exploration of trends in overall inequalities shows that these remained substantially stable over the last 10 years in the adult population (aged 15 and over), with only a modest increase in men in higher social classes (the group that gained the most in terms of life expectancy). Therefore, increases in overall inequality in age at death may be due at least in part to infant and child mortality rates declining less rapidly than rates for older age groups, possibly because of an increasing proportion of births in more disadvantaged social groups (which display higher mortality rates).

Data on life expectancy at birth by social class from the ONS Longitudinal Study indicate that inequalities markedly increased in women between 2002 and 2005, relative to between 1997 and 2001, as women in higher classes have extended their expectation of life while outcomes for women in the lowest social class have remained essentially stable over the last 15 years (Figure 7.2). However, inequalities by social class have been steadily decreasing in men since the early 1990s, with the fastest improvements observed among unskilled manual workers.

However, New Labour governments appear to have been more concerned about reducing health inequalities in life expectancy between more and less deprived areas of the country, than about reducing overall social class inequalities. In 2001, four years into the first New Labour government, average life expectancy across English local authorities showed a marked inverse correlation with deprivation, as it did previously (Sassi, 2005), and the inverse correlation was even stronger between healthy life expectancy and deprivation (Figure 7.3).

A report by Shaw et al (2005), based on mortality data up to 2003, claimed that the government was not on track to keeping its promises, as inequality in life expectancy across local authorities in Britain appeared to be increasing two years after national inequality targets had been set. I carried out a new analysis using

Figure 7.1: Trends in mean age at death by gender, and in overall inequalities in life expectancy

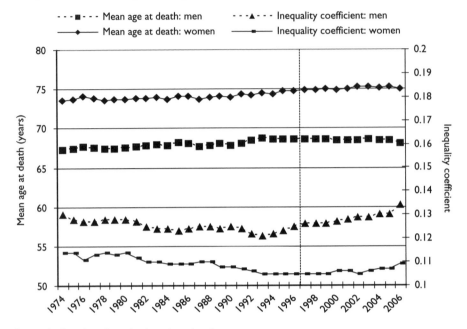

Source: Analysis based on death registration data

Figure 7.2: Trends in life expectancy at birth in the top and bottom social classes, men and women

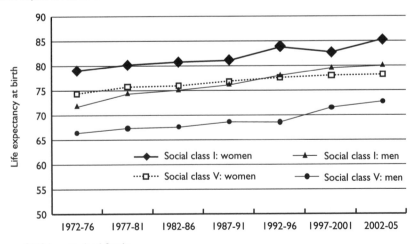

Source: ONS Longitudinal Study

life expectancy data by local authority up to 2005, ranked by level of deprivation based on the income dimension of the Index of Multiple Deprivation 2000. This analysis shows that the slope index of inequality, which reflects absolute differences in life expectancy between the most and the least deprived local authorities, has indeed been increasing in England from the early 1990s up to 2002, but it appears to have declined somewhat in the following three years, in both men and women, as shown in Figure 7.4, which represents a potentially important reversal in the underlying trend. As life expectancy has been generally increasing, a reduction in absolute differences means that relative gaps (on which national targets are based) have narrowed as well, although the latter do not appear to have narrowed to the extent the government was aiming at in the particular measure that was selected for the national target (difference between life expectancy in the spearhead areas versus the national average) (DH, 2007).

The latest available assessment of progress towards the achievement of national health inequality targets at the time of writing is based on mortality and life expectancy data up to 2006. This shows that the infant mortality target seems far out of reach. The relative gap between the most disadvantaged groups and the national average (including only births for which a socioeconomic classification is available) increased from 13% to 17%. If the government in 2001 deemed a single percentage point reduction (from 13% to 12%) over 12 years a worthwhile target, a four percentage point increase over seven years must look like a dire result.

Figure 7.3: Life expectancy and healthy life expectancy in local authorities, ordered by average level of deprivation, 2001

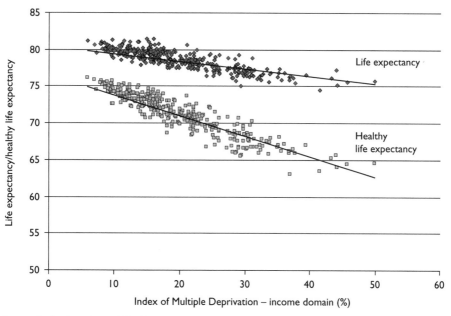

Source: Author's analysis of ONS data

Figure 7.4: Slope index of inequality in male and female life expectancy for local authorities, by level of deprivation and three-year moving average lines

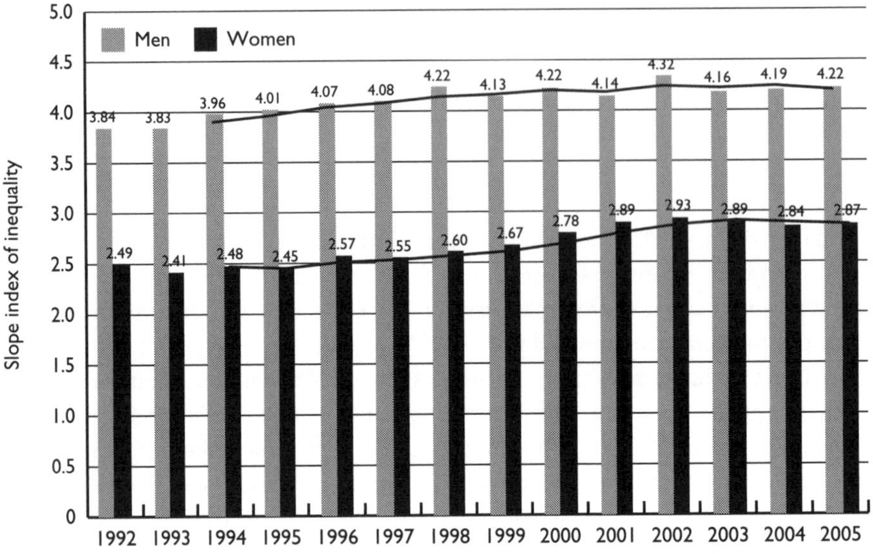

Source: Author's analysis of ONS data

Similarly, the government did not appear on track to achieving either of the life expectancy targets, as the gap between spearhead areas and the national average for England increased for both men and women in absolute as well as relative terms. The relative gap increased by 2% in men and 10% in women, relative to the baseline, while the government aimed at cutting it by 10% for both genders by 2010. Life expectancy gaps for males had widened, rather than narrowed, in 44 out of 70 spearhead local authorities, and gaps for females had widened in 48 out of 70 (DH, 2007).

Trends in health status

Measures of health status and health-related behaviour are more responsive to health policy changes than mortality measures. However, the disadvantage with the former is that they are often derived from surveys and potentially subject to a certain degree of self-report bias, which might vary across population subgroups. The HSE offers a valuable mix of self-reported and measured indicators of health status and health-related behaviour, a selection of which I used to explore trends in health inequalities since 1991. Results are reported below for general health indicators such as self-assessed health (proportion of individuals reporting their own health as 'poor' or 'very poor') and longstanding illness; disease-specific indicators such as self-reported diabetes, diagnosed severe cardiovascular disease (angina, heart attack or stroke) and mental health (assessed using the General

Health Questionaire [GHQ12]); and aspects of lifestyle and associated risk factors such as self-reported current smoking, measured obesity (body mass index of 30 or more), diagnosed hypertension (whether treated or untreated) and uncontrolled hypertension (untreated or ineffectively treated).

General health indicators

Inequalities in self-assessed health in individuals over 40 years of age appear to have significantly worsened over the last 15 years, with rates of self-reported poor health increasing in all socioeconomic groups, but at a substantially faster pace among the most disadvantaged, as shown in Figure 7.5. Breaking down these trends by subperiod and gender (Figure 7.6) leads to the observation that inequalities worsened especially in women in the last quinquennium, with roughly a four point increase in the slope index of inequality, while inequalities in men continued to increase in absolute terms, but decreased in relative terms in the latest quinquennium.

Rates of self-reported longstanding illness in different socioeconomic groups have also been consistently increasing (with a peak of 68% in unskilled manual workers in 2005) and diverging over time, but to a lesser extent than rates of poor self-reported health. Absolute gaps between the most and the least disadvantaged increased in women, while they first increased (1996-2000 over 1991-95) and then slightly decreased (2001-05 over 1996-2000) in men. However, relative gaps generally narrowed.

Minority ethnic groups reported consistently higher rates of poor self-assessed health than the white population, but rate differences remained stable in absolute terms, determining a substantial reduction in relative inequalities, given increasing overall rates. A progressive convergence of all ethnic groups was observed in rates of longstanding illness, leading to virtually identical rates in the most recent years.

Cardiovascular disease and mental health

Mortality from cardiovascular disease has been on a declining trend for some time, partly due to an increased use of effective preventive and curative medical care such as cholesterol-lowering drugs and revascularisation procedures. However, the incidence and prevalence of cardiovascular disease appear to have followed diverging trends in different socioeconomic groups and genders. The HSE provides various measures of cardiovascular disease. Figure 7.7 shows trends in the most general measure, cardiovascular disease as self-reported longstanding illness, by socioeconomic group. Rates appear to have been stable or slightly declining in the middle groups but decreasing at a significantly faster pace in the top socioeconomic group and increasing in unskilled manual workers. A more detailed measure, based on the diagnosis of specific forms of cardiovascular disease, is available for selected years starting in 1998. Rates of the most severe forms of cardiovascular disease in

Figure 7.5: Rates of self-assessed poor health, by social class (%)

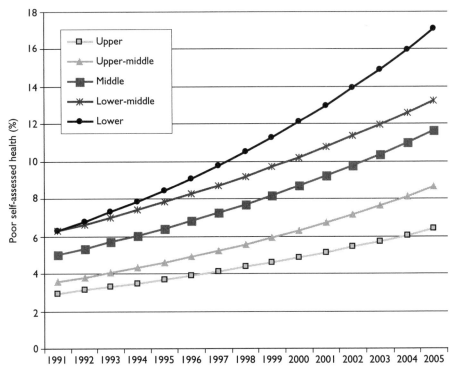

Note: Based on multivariate regression analysis. Quadratic trend lines.
Source: HSE data 1991-2005

Figure 7.6: Slope index and relative index of inequality in poor self-assessed health, by social class in men and women

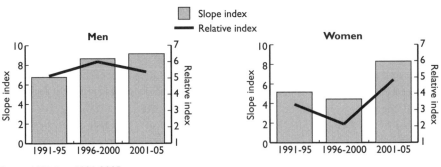

Source: HSE data 1991-2005

the population over 40 years of age do not appear to have changed in a consistent way across socioeconomic groups, but increased by over two percentage points among the most disadvantaged between 1998-2000 and 2002-05 (Figure 7.8). This is the result of an increase of more than three percentage points in women belonging to the same group, partly offset by a slight decrease in men. Over the same period, rates decreased substantially among women in higher social classes, thus generating a marked socioeconomic gradient not previously observed, while they increased among men in higher social classes.

New inequalities appear to have arisen also in relation to mental health, for which some of the most remarkable changes have taken place during the period covered by the analysis. By reference to a measure of mental health (more precisely, 'psychosocial' health) based on a score of 4 or more on the GHQ12 scale, inequalities were virtually absent among men of different socioeconomic groups in the early 1990s, while they were present, but following an inverse socioeconomic gradient, in women (lower rates of poor mental health in disadvantaged women). However, changes that have occurred over the last 15

Figure 7.7: Rates of cardiovascular disease self-reported as longstanding illness

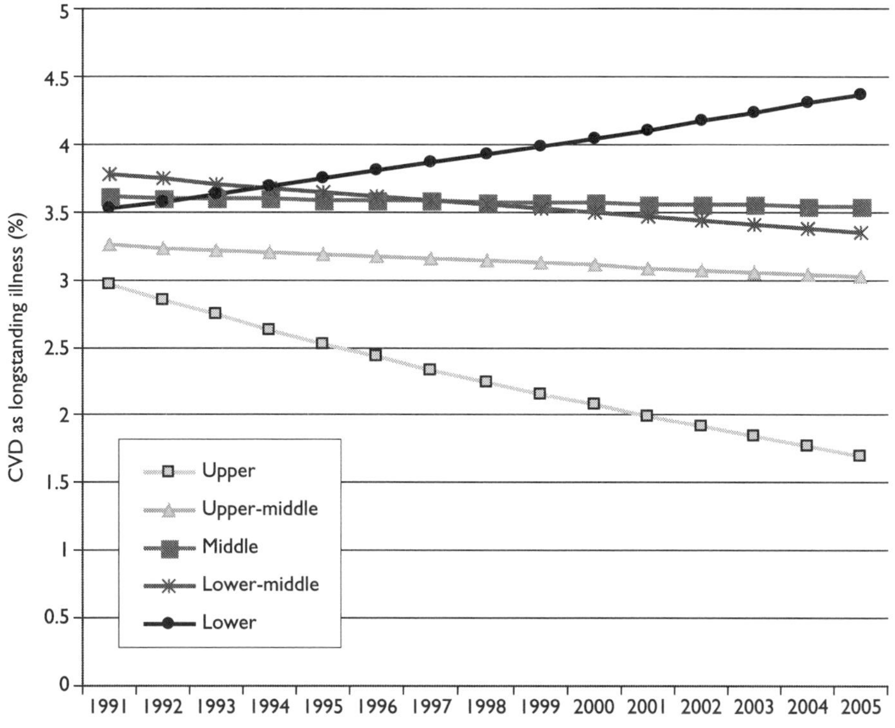

Note: Based on multivariate regression analysis. Quadratic trend lines.
Source: HSE data 1991-2005.

years have led to marked inequalities, with men and women in higher social classes displaying significantly lower rates than those in poorer socioeconomic circumstances. Figure 7.9 indicates that gradients have developed in different ways in men and women. Women in lower social classes maintained stable rates over the entire period, and inequalities were generated by women from higher and middle classes significantly improving their levels of mental health over time. Among men, higher and lower socioeconomic groups moved in different directions, the former decreasing and the latter increasing their rates of mental health. Men in more disadvantaged conditions appear to be catching up with the higher rates observed in women in the same social groups. On the other hand, women from higher social classes appear to be catching up with the lower rates observed among men in higher social classes.

Lifestyles and risk factors

Improving lifestyles has been the focus of much government action during the last few years. New Labour governments have been able to enact smoking bans in public places, to strengthen smoking cessation services and to launch a strategy to improve diets and physical activity in the population through actions aimed at providing incentives to individuals to make healthy choices (for example, a partial ban on advertising to children, guidelines on food nutrition labelling and interventions in the physical environment and transportation system).

Figure 7.8: Rates of severe diagnosed cardiovascular disease (%)

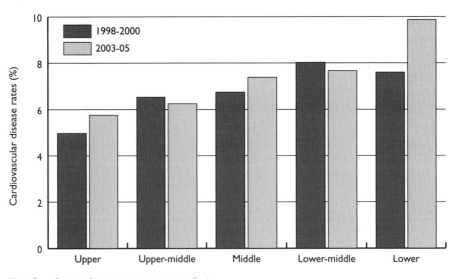

Note: Based on multivariate regression analysis.
Source: HSE data 1998-2005

Figure 7.9: Rates of poor psychosocial health in men and women (%)

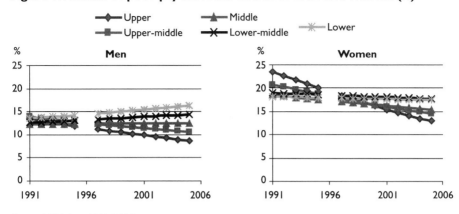

Source: HSE data 1991-2005

Smoking is a key health-related behaviour and a risk factor for a wide range of chronic diseases, responsible for a significant proportion of inequalities observed among socioeconomic groups. Smoking-related deaths in the age group 35-69 were found to account for over half of the mortality difference between the top and the bottom socioeconomic groups in England and Wales (Jha et al, 2006). Smoking-related causes of death were also found to be those most closely associated with area deprivation (Romeri et al, 2006). Smoking rates have been on a long-term declining trend in England, particularly among men. Consistently, HSE data show that rates have decreased in all socioeconomic groups over the period 1991-2005. However, smoking has provided one of the rare instances in which the Joinpoint analysis has shown a clear trend change over the period of the analysis. Smoking rates appeared to stagnate, or even increase slightly, during the period 1994-97, but a sharp declining trend resumed in both manual and non-manual classes after 1997, with the two groups achieving similar absolute reductions in smoking rates (Figure 7.10). The slope index of inequality in smoking remained virtually stable in both men and women over the entire period. Faster reductions in smoking rates and a steeper socioeconomic gradient in men led to smoking rates that are still higher among men than among women in the most disadvantaged groups, but lower among men in higher social classes in the most recent years. Smoking rates were consistently lower among minority ethnic groups than among the white population throughout the period covered by the analysis, and declined in the former groups at similar or faster rates.

Unlike smoking, other risk factors increased their prevalence in the population during the period covered by the analysis. The most important is obesity, which reached epidemic proportions during the 1990s and early 2000s, placing England among the countries with the highest rates worldwide. Obesity is mainly determined by patterns of diet and physical activity, and in turn leads to a range of chronic diseases, of which diabetes is the most closely associated. Obesity rates grew steadily in all socioeconomic groups, and so did the slope index of inequality in obesity, both by social class and by level of education, indicating that absolute differences between population subgroups widened over time. In relative terms, however, inequalities remained stable or slightly declined, as all rates were fast increasing. However, gradients are markedly different in men and women. Only modest inequalities in obesity rates are observed in men, while steep inequalities are observed in women. The slope index of inequality by social class is about four times larger in women than in men, and about twice as large by level of education. The rise in obesity was particularly dramatic in children over the last two decades, partly in relation to the increase in adult obesity, as there tends to be a strong correlation in levels of body mass between members of the same household. Government efforts, particularly with regard to improving school meals and regulating food advertising to children, may have contributed to an apparent slowdown or even halting of increases in child obesity in very recent years, as discussed in Chapter Three, but HSE data seem to indicate that the existing socioeconomic gradient has not been significantly affected.

Figure 7.10: Joinpoint analysis of smoking rates in manual and non-manual socioeconomic groups (%)

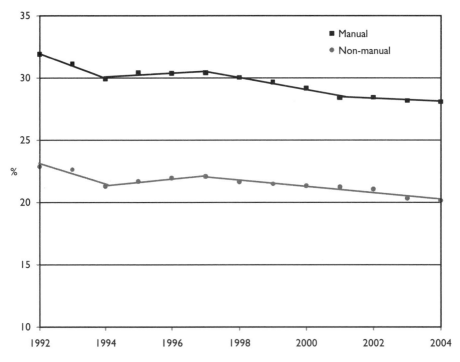

Note: Dots represent three-year moving averages. Best-fitting partial trend lines.
Source: HSE data 1991-2005

Partly as a consequence of the spread of obesity, rates of self-reported diabetes observed in the HSE also increased very rapidly over the study period. Diabetes is more prevalent among men than women, but rates have been increasing at a similar pace in the two genders. However, inequalities have been slightly decreasing in men, and rapidly increasing in women, particularly by level of education, with a threefold increase in the slope index of inequality between 1991-95 and 2001-05, as shown in Figure 7.11.

Obesity rates were particularly high in black and minority ethnic groups, especially among women, although rates increased fastest in the white population. High rates of obesity may have contributed to a strong increase in rates of self-reported diabetes in black and minority ethnic groups, particularly during the late 1990s and early 2000s.

A further important risk factor is high blood pressure, for which the HSE provides several useful indicators based on measurements taken by nurses as part of the examination schedule. The prevalence of high blood pressure, including those with normal measurements but taking anti-hypertension medicines prescribed specifically for the purpose of reducing blood pressure, decreased only marginally from 1991, but inequalities by social class increased in both genders since the early days of the New Labour governments (slope index from 0.2 to 5.1 in men between 1998-2001 and 2002-05; and from 10.9 to 14.2 in women). However, an alternative measure of high blood pressure – measured systolic pressure above 140 mm/Hg – provides a somewhat more encouraging picture. The latter measure reflects untreated, or ineffectively treated, hypertension, thus providing information not just on the prevalence of the risk factor, but also on the degree of unmet need for healthcare in different individuals and population groups. Unmet need may be due to limitations in access to appropriate healthcare, or to poor compliance to treatment schedules. Rates of this measure of high blood pressure declined rapidly during the last 10 years, with a sharp acceleration relative to previous periods and without any significant increases in absolute differences between

Figure 7.11: Slope index and relative index of inequality in self-reported diabetes, by years of full-time education in men and women

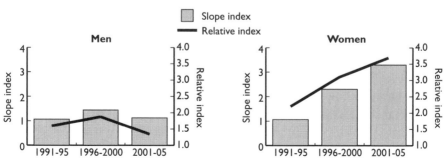

Source: HSE data 1991-2005

socioeconomic groups (relative gaps did increase, of course, because overall rates decreased). This picture appears consistent with findings on a different risk factor – high cholesterol – reported by Ramsay et al (2005), indicating that the use of cholesterol-lowering drugs (statins) increased over time with little variation across socioeconomic groups.

Black and minority ethnic groups do not appear to have enjoyed the same reduction in the prevalence of high blood pressure observed in the white population, with a resulting increase in inequalities between ethnic groups. However, untreated and ineffectively treated hypertension declined even more rapidly in black and minority ethnic groups than in the white majority.

Evidence of other changes in health and healthcare inequalities

Analyses of inequalities in access to, or utilisation of, healthcare may be substantially more difficult than those focusing on health status and longevity, because measures of access and utilisation must be adjusted for individual need, given differences in morbidity between socioeconomic groups that may cause disadvantaged groups to use more medical care than the better off. A policy-relevant concept of horizontal equity in healthcare is equal access, or equal utilisation, for equal need, rather than simply equal access or equal utilisation for everyone. The HSE provides a range of variables that can be used to adjust for differences in healthcare needs, but one existing study had an opportunity to link HSE data to small area characteristics (at the local authority ward level) leading to a more accurate and detailed adjustment for need than the HSE variables alone would permit (Morris et al, 2005). The latter study investigated the existence of possible horizontal inequity in four healthcare utilisation variables – general practitioner consultations, outpatient visits, day case treatments and inpatient stays – from the 1998-2000 HSE. The authors used a wide range of controls and assessed inequalities by socioeconomic condition, level of education and ethnicity. There appeared to be a consistent general pattern indicating that the most disadvantaged groups, including those in poor socioeconomic circumstances, the less well educated, and members of black and minority ethnic groups, made greater use of primary care and less use of secondary care than their better-off counterparts. These findings are consistent with those of other studies focusing on specific patient populations (for example Bachmann et al, 2003). However, Morris et al failed to identify statistically significant inequalities by social class, and identified few significant inequalities by level of education (low education was associated with more primary care consultations) and by ethnicity (Asian minority groups were less likely to have outpatient visits). This may be read as a relatively encouraging picture relating to the early years of New Labour governments, although it is based on relatively crude measures of healthcare use. The interpretation of the apparent greater use of primary care by disadvantaged groups remains uncertain, given that not all aspects of morbidity may have been accounted for by the needs adjustment variables. The authors reject the hypothesis that more limited use of secondary care by disadvantaged groups may be driven by a reluctance to seek contact with a general practitioner. Other studies have also shown that the quality of primary care is comparable across areas with different levels of deprivation, based on data from the UK Quality and Outcomes Framework (Ashworth et al, 2007).

Since the primary focus of government policy to tackle health inequalities, at least in the most recent years, has been on reducing geographic inequalities, resource allocation must be a key policy instrument to achieve the goal of narrowing health gaps between more and less deprived areas of the country. As discussed in Hills and Stewart (2005), successive governments have made significant efforts to improve the resource allocation formula and to make it suitable for addressing inequalities in health across areas. The formula currently in use accounts for unmet need, among other things, and leads to target allocations that are more markedly pro-poor than formulas adopted previously. Although distance-from-target statistics indicate that more deprived areas (primary care trusts; PCTs) still tend to be slightly below target in their actual allocations, while least deprived areas tend to be slightly above, the latest recurrent revenue allocations for 2007-08 are almost 42% larger on a per-capita basis in the most deprived tenth of PCTs than in the least deprived tenth. And the gap is even greater when non-recurrent allocations tied to specific public health objectives following the 2004 *Choosing Health* White Paper (DH, 2004a) are considered. For instance, allocations in relation to smoking cessation efforts under the NHS Stop Smoking Services programme were almost 70% higher, on a per-capita basis, in the most deprived tenth of PCTs relative to the least deprived tenth.

Government policies to tackle smoking provide an excellent example of the difficulties involved in improving overall population health while at the same time narrowing inequalities. Smoking is widely acknowledged to be a leading risk factor for health and one of the major determinants of health inequalities. NHS Stop Smoking Services were generously funded, with disproportionately large allocations to more deprived areas, as indicated above. However, the study that is generally deemed to provide the best empirical evidence of the impact of NHS Stop Smoking Services on health inequalities up to 2005-06 concluded that the impact has been a modest contribution towards reducing inequalities in smoking prevalence (Bauld et al, 2007). The Smoking Toolkit Study, funded by Cancer Research UK and run between 2006 and 2008 (West, 2008), showed that NHS Stop Smoking Services are very successful in helping individuals to stop smoking (the odds of successful cessation are three times larger for those attending the services relative to those not attending, although the possibility of self-selection should not be ruled out). However, only about 3% of smokers use such NHS services and the proportion has been stable over time, which may at least partly explain the modest contribution to the reduction in health inequalities, despite funding being heavily skewed in favour of the most disadvantaged areas.

The Smoking Toolkit Study also provided evidence of the impact of the smoking ban introduced in England in 2007. The rate of decline of smoking prevalence accelerated sharply in the months following the introduction of the ban, leading to an estimated 4.3% decrease in overall prevalence by April 2008. However, rates appear to have declined in similar proportions in different socioeconomic groups, maintaining a constant relative gap.

Conclusions

In the most recent years, the government has adopted a somewhat lower profile on health inequalities than it did during its first two terms of office. This may be seen as a natural development, as it became apparent over the years that it would not be possible to deliver any major breakthroughs on health inequalities. But efforts have not ceased and, if anything, they have become more focused than before. Resources have been flowing from the centre to local communities, particularly the most disadvantaged ones, and although government policies have often remained disappointingly vague on actions to be taken on the ground, initiatives have developed at the local level, which, if proven effective and efficient, may be expanded to a larger scale to reap the benefits that have so far been lacking.

The current picture of health inequalities and trends over the past 15 years should be a cause of concern to those who had hoped that the unprecedented efforts and resources devoted to tackling health inequalities since 1997 might narrow, or at least halt the progression of, such inequalities. In the overall picture described in this chapter, it is worth noting at least two aspects, in particular. First, the analysis has shown an encouraging stabilisation, or a slight decline, of inequalities in life expectancy across local authorities with different levels of deprivation, which appears consistent with evidence of closing gaps between neighbourhoods in other domains, as discussed in Chapter Six. Although the government has based its targets on a different measure, which has been progressing less favourably, the results reported here may provide an indication that the government's choice to prioritise geographic inequalities over inequalities by social class in the overall population is beginning to show some results, after initial scepticism. Of course, these may not be the results, or not the only ones, that most people would have expected from a strategy to tackle health inequalities. The primary focus on geographic inequalities will remain controversial, particularly if inequalities by socioeconomic condition continue to increase.

On a less positive note, the analysis reported in this chapter shows that inequalities have worsened among women to a significantly greater extent than among men. This is true across a wide range of indicators, from life expectancy to obesity; from mental health to cardiovascular disease. In some cases, inequalities have increased simply because better-off women have improved their health or longevity faster than any other groups. In other cases, a deterioration of the health of more disadvantaged women has been observed as well. Other European countries have observed larger increases in health inequalities among women during the 1980s and 1990s (Kunst et al, 2005). However, it is difficult to identify the precise determinants of the changes observed.

Health inequalities have been rising over many decades in Britain (Davey Smith et al, 2002) and perhaps it would have been naïve to expect a major reversal of this increasing trend over a relatively short time span, considering how deeply rooted health inequalities are in the early stages of the life cycle of individuals. The long-term effects of the policies enacted by successive New Labour governments over the last 10 years remain uncertain, but we may now confidently say that the short- and medium-term impact of those policies has been disappointing. Areas of particular concern include substantial emerging inequalities in mental health and increasing inequalities in aspects of lifestyle such as those associated with obesity. New Labour governments appear to have made genuine efforts to tackle an almost intractable problem, and deserve credit for having emphasised the importance of tackling the root causes of health inequalities through a multifaceted approach not limited to actions within the healthcare domain. However, they have probably indulged too much on analyses, consultations and target setting, and have engaged too little and too late in real action and evaluation. The government has been ambiguous and has lacked clarity of vision and transparency on at least two fronts: in assessing the implications of its choice of geographic inequalities as the top priority for government action; and in its persistent claims that overall health and lifestyle improvements would necessarily be accompanied by reductions in health inequalities.

EIGHT

Pensions and income security in later life

Maria Evandrou and Jane Falkingham

Introduction

When New Labour came to power in May 1997, an estimated 2.9 million pensioners were living in 'poverty' (DWP, 2008f).[1] The 1997 election manifesto restated the party's commitment that 'all pensioners should share fairly in the increasing prosperity of the nation' and promised to 'set up a review of the central areas of insecurity for elderly people: all aspects of the basic pension and its value, second pensions including the State Earnings Related Pension Scheme, and community care' (Labour Party, 1997, p 27). Just two months into the new administration in July 1997, the new Secretary of State, Harriet Harman, announced a review of pensions. The terms of reference for the Pension Provision Group were to look into concerns of today's pensioners and develop plans for a second pension scheme over and above the basic state pension (PPG, 1998). The next 11 years witnessed a transformation of the pensions landscape, starting with the Green Paper *A New Contract for Welfare: Partnership in Pensions* (DSS, 1998) and culminating in two White Papers – *Security in Retirement* (DWP, 2006a) and *Personal Accounts: A New Way to Save* (DWP, 2006b) – leading to the 2007 Pensions Act and 2007/08 Pensions Bill. The reforms amount to the most radical overhaul of the pensions system since 1948, with no part of the system being immune to change – from the safety-net 'floor' of means-tested benefits for pensioners, through to the 'first tier' of the basic state pension, the 'second tier' of publicly provided second (earnings-related) pensions, to the top floor of private provision of occupational and personal pensions.

In 1999, New Labour set out its blueprint for tackling poverty and social exclusion in *Opportunity for All* (DSS, 1999). Among the priorities highlighted were the twin goals of (a) ensuring that more of tomorrow's pensioners can retire on a decent income and (b) tackling the problems of low income and social exclusion among today's pensioners. This chapter discusses New Labour's policy agenda in the area of pensions and then assesses the extent to which this has been successful in improving the living standards of the poorest pensioners, now and in the future. We start, though, by considering the background and inheritance faced by New Labour, including the policy legacy and demographic context that prompted and helped to shape the government's pension reforms.

Background and inheritance

The policy legacy

The pensions system inherited by New Labour in 1997 was one of the most complex in the world, the result of decades of reform layered one after another upon previous systems (Pemberton, 2006). Table 8.1 summarises the evolution of pension provision in the UK, from the introduction of the first means-tested non-contributory pension by the Lloyd George government in 1908 through to the Pensions Bill going through Parliament a century later. From the 1920s onwards, the persistent ideology has been of a contribution-based minimum pension supplemented by additional private provision, but with a means-tested safety net and a minimal role for the state in providing earnings-related provision (Glennerster, 2006).

Table 8.1: A century of pension reform, 1908-2008

1908	**1908 Pensions Act** establishes a means-tested non-contributory old age pension of 5 shillings a week (25 pence) for people aged 70 and over of 'good moral character'. Two-thirds of recipients are women. Public expenditure on pensions accounts for less than 0.5% of gross domestic product (GDP) in 1910.
1920s	Occupational pensions begin to expand but remain the preserve of the minority (around 13% of workers), mainly civil servants and white-collar workers. In 1921, the government introduces tax relief on pensions. **1925 Old Age Contributory Pensions Act** establishes a flat-rate contributory pension scheme for manual and lower-paid non-manual workers. Initially set at 2 shillings (50 pence). Benefits are introduced for widows with dependent children and older widows of insured men.
1940s	**1940 Old Age and Widow's Pensions Act.** The state pension age for women is reduced to 60. Means-tested supplementary assistance introduced to boost the already means-tested state pension; around a third of pensioners qualify.

(continued)

Table 8.1: A century of pension reform, 1908-2008 (continued)

1940s (contd)	**1942 Beveridge Report** on 'Social Insurance and Allied Services' is published, recommending that pensions be universal, contributory, flat-rate and minimal, 'just guaranteeing the minimum income needed for subsistence'.
	1946 National Insurance Act and **1948 National Assistance Act** enact the Beveridge proposals. A new flat-rate National Insurance retirement pension is introduced for all those retiring after 5 July 1948. Pensions are set at a level even lower than envisaged by Beveridge – at 26 shillings a week (£1.30) for a single person and 50 shillings (£2.10) for a married couple. Many older people have to supplement the pension with means-tested benefits.
1950s	The basic state (BSP) pension is raised several times during the 1950s but its level steadily falls below National Assistance levels.
	1954 Phillips Report on 'Economic and Financial Problem of the Provision for Old Age' is published, highlighting pensioner poverty but also the rapid ageing of the population.
	1959 National Insurance Act creates the Graduated Pension Scheme, the first state earnings-related pension scheme – although not particularly generous.
1960s	The main feature of the decade is the growth in occupational pension coverage. Membership peaks at 12.2 million in 1967, when 66% of male workers and 28% of female workers were covered.
1970s	The BSP is indexed to growth in average earnings from 1974 to 1979; its value is around 25% of average national earnings.
	1975 Social Security Pensions Act establishes the State Earnings Related Pension Scheme (SERPS), which is implemented in April 1978 – a fully indexed earnings-related pension equivalent to 25% of the best 20 years of lifetime earnings on top of the BSP.
	1978 Home Responsibility Protection reduces the contribution requirements for those who are not in work because they are caring for children or a disabled relative.

(continued)

Table 8.1: A century of pension reform, 1908-2008 (continued)

1980s	**1980 Social Security Act** abolishes earnings indexation of the BSP. In 1984, Norman Fowler sets up the 'Inquiry into Provision for Retirement', leading to the **1986 Social Security Act**. This substantially reduces the generosity of SERPS for future beneficiaries, being based on 20% of average lifetime earnings. Individuals are allowed to contract out of the state second tier into a personal pension plan (PPP). More than five million PPPs are sold between 1984 and 1992, encouraged by generous NI rebates but also poor advice.
Early 1990s	Following the death of Robert Maxwell in 1991, it is discovered that £400 million is missing from the Mirror Group pension funds. The Maxwell Scandal raises serious concerns about the possible misuse of company pension funds. **1995 Pensions Act** puts in place stronger regulation and a compensation scheme. The Act also further reduces generosity of SERPS and raises the state pension age for women from 60 to 65 (to be phased in between 2010 and 2020).
July 1997	A fundamental and wide-ranging review of all aspects of pension provision is announced by Harriet Harman, the new Secretary of State for Social Security.
1997-2001	1998 Green Paper *Partnership in Pensions*, implemented through the **1999 Welfare Reform and Pensions Act** and **2000 Child Support, Pensions and Social Security Act**, replaces SERPS with the State Second Pension (S2P), and replaces Income Support with the Minimum Income Guarantee and subsequently the Pension Credit.
2001-05	2002 Green Paper *Simplicity, Security and Choice: Working and Saving for Retirement* puts forward proposals for the simplification of the tax treatment of occupational and personal pensions. The Green Paper is further expanded on in the 2003 White Paper *Simplicity, Security and Choice: Action on Occupational Pensions*, which includes proposals for a Pension Protection Fund and 2004 White Paper *Simplicity, Security and Choice: Informed Choices for Working and Saving*, which provides for improved information for informed choices. Culminates in the **2004 Pensions Act**. In December 2002, the government announces the formation of the Pensions Commission.

(continued)

Table 8.1:A century of pension reform, 1908-2008 (continued)

2005 onwards	**Pensions Commission** publishes comprehensive proposals for pension reform in its second report *A New Pension Settlement for the Twenty-First Century*. Reform packages are crystallised in the two 2006 White Papers *Security in Retirement* and *Personal Accounts:A New Way to Save*.
	2007 Pensions Act introduces a series of radical reforms to the state pension sector with reformed eligibility for the BSP and the system of credits for S2P. It also increases the age of retirement to 68 (phased in between 2024 and 2046) and creates the Personal Accounts Delivery Authority.
	2008 Pensions Act introduces measures aimed at encouraging greater private saving, including the establishment of a new Personal Accounts scheme. Employers must auto-enrol employees into a qualifying workplace pension scheme with a minimum employer contribution.

Source: We are grateful to Tom Sefton for producing an earlier version of this table.

As pension provision expanded during the post-war period, the average income of pensioners rose, leading to a doubling of real incomes in the 30 years from 1961 to 1991 (Johnson et al, 1996). Accompanying the growth in overall pensioner income has been a shift in the relative importance of different sources of income in later life. Table 8.2 shows changes in the share in total pensioner gross incomes from the four main sources of income in later life over the period 1951 to 2006-07. Several features stand out. Most notable are the decline and subsequent rise in the relative importance of income from employment and the growth of occupational pensions, which now account for over a quarter of total pensioner income. The drop in the share of income from state benefits from a high of 62% in 1981 reflects in part the abolition of the indexation link of the BSP with

Table 8.2: Sources of pensioners' gross incomes, 1951 to 2006-07 (%)

	1951	1961	1974	1981	1986	1991	1993	1997-98	2001-02	2006-07
State benefits	42	48	55	62	59	49	53	52	51	44
Occupational and private pensions	15	16	15	16	20	22	25	26	29	29
Savings and investments	15	15	13	13	14	20	16	14	11	11
Employment	27	22	17	9	7	7	6	8	9	17

Source: Falkingham (1997, table 6.4) up to 1993 and DWP (2008f) and previous editions for 1997-98 onwards

earnings from 1979. The effect of this has taken time to feed through. In 1981, the BSP was worth around a quarter of national average earnings (NAE) and 20% of average male earnings (AME); by the time New Labour came to power in 1997, its value had fallen to just over 14% of AME.

One important outcome of a devalued basic pension is that second-tier pensions have become increasingly important in maintaining the living standards of pensioners relative to those of the working population. From as early as 1921, successive governments have created incentives for private pension savings (Glennerster, 2006; Whiteside, 2006) and by 1967, 66% of male and 28% of female workers were members of occupational pension schemes. In the 1970s, the government introduced SERPS as a residual scheme for those not in an occupational scheme. However, at the same time, it also increased incentives to opt out through a rebate on NI contributions.

Prior to the mid–1980s, an employee could only opt out of SERPS into a final salary occupational pension. The 1986 Social Security Act permitted employees to use money purchase pensions to contract out of the state second-tier pensions. Importantly, in contrast to a final salary scheme where the employer bears the risk concerning the value of the pension that will eventually be paid, in personal pensions it is the individual who bears the risk. Moreover, money purchase schemes are typically much less generous than final salary schemes. By 1996, a quarter of men in full-time employment were members of a personal pension scheme (Falkingham and Rake, 2003). Thus, New Labour inherited a pension system where the balance of pension provision was shifting in three important ways:

- overall, from public towards private provision;
- *within* the public sector, from an income guaranteed by the contributory state pension towards one guaranteed through means testing; and
- *within* the private sector, from one where the risk was shared to one where the risk was individualised.

Furthermore, although average pensioner incomes had been growing steadily over the previous 20 years, not all pensioners had benefited equally from the growth in real incomes. For example, the median net income after housing costs (AHC) of the poorest fifth of pensioner couples grew by only 30% in real terms between 1979 and 1996-97 compared with an average increase of 61%, and an increase of 91% for the richest quintile (DWP, 2008a, table A4.1). Thus, in 1996-97, nearly three million pensioners were living in households below 60% of the contemporary median income AHC (DWP, 2008b, table 6.3tr), of whom nearly three-quarters (70%) were female and a half (48%) were aged over 75 (DWP, 2008b, table 6.4ts). New Labour therefore inherited a situation where a significant minority of the pensioner population were living in poverty and where expectations were high that Labour was the party to reverse this situation. It was notable, however, that for the first time since 1979, restoring the link between the BSP and earnings growth was absent from the 1997 election manifesto.

Demographic context

Concern over the changing demographic structure of the population, with increasing numbers of older people dependent on a shrinking population of working age, has been a consistent backdrop to pension reform throughout the last 50 years.

Past trends in fertility and mortality have resulted in a dramatic increase in the proportion of the population aged over 65 (Figure 8.1). In 1901, those aged 65 and over constituted less than 5% of the population. In 2001, they made up just over 16% and by 2041 it is expected that they will comprise over a quarter of the population, as the large birth cohorts of the late 1950s to early 1960s age (ONS, 2008a). Such figures have given rise to the notion of a 'demographic time bomb'. However, while the idea of a bomb ticking away beneath our feet remains popular with some sections of the media, most academic commentators now agree that this is a myth (Johnson and Falkingham, 1992; Warnes, 1996; Mullan, 2000). First, substantial changes in the age structure of the British population have already taken place, without any catastrophic effect. The last century saw a tripling of the share of the pensioner population at the same time as the expansion, rather than contraction, of the welfare state. Future increases in the share of the older population will be less dramatic than many mature welfare states have coped with in the past (Glennerster, 1999). Second, it is increasingly recognised that the welfare support ratio is determined by many other factors in addition to demographic change, not least the proportion of people of different ages who are in work and the design of welfare policy itself (Falkingham, 1989; Hills, 1997).

Figure 8.1: Britain's population aged 65 plus and 85 plus, 1901-2041

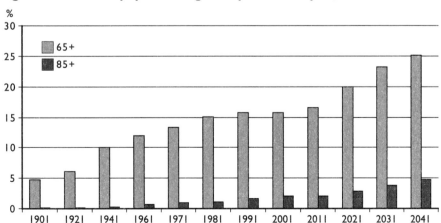

Source: ONS historical data and population projections

That is not to say that demographic change is unimportant. Recent changes in mortality at older ages have had a significant impact on longevity, with the result that more older people will spend longer in retirement than ever before. In 1961, men aged 60 could expect on average to live a further 15 years and women aged 60 a further 19 years; by 2005, this had risen to 20.8 years for men aged 60 and 23.9 years for women aged 60 (ONS, 1997, table 13; ONS 2008b, table 5.1).[2] It is the *combination* of relatively more people retiring and more people living longer in retirement that presents a challenge for policy makers, both for the provision of income in later life and for the funding of health and social care services (see Chapter Fifteen).

Recent reductions in mortality, particularly at older ages, have been faster than predicted by many demographers and actuaries, with the result that life expectancy has been consistently and substantially underprojected in national population projections (Shaw, 2007). Uncertainty about future improvements in morbidity and mortality make it difficult for pension providers to assess future liabilities. The most recent *cohort*-based projections suggest that a woman aged 65 in 2031 may expect to live on average for a further 25.5 years. However, this is the median variant projection; a more optimistic scenario regarding mortality trends suggests that she may live for a further 28.6 years while a less optimistic scenario gives a life expectancy of just 23 further years (GAD, 2008). As Hills (2006) notes, with rising expectation of life beyond retirement age, the sheer length of time pension providers are expected to enter the 'funnel of uncertainty' presents a problem of a greater order of magnitude than in the past. Thus, although the demographic context New Labour inherited was not new, it could be argued that these trends together with the changes in the pension system noted above combined to present a new set of challenges.

Moreover, just as people are surviving longer, the last 50 years have also seen a number of important changes in the labour market and working life. Since the mid-1970s, there has been a dramatic fall in the number of years of life that men spend in employment and a corresponding increase in the number of years spent in other activities such as education, unemployment and especially retirement. Analysis of economic activity rates among different birth cohorts within Britain shows that successive generations of men are both entering the labour market later and leaving earlier, and having lower overall participation rates at any given age (Evandrou and Falkingham, 2000). The shorter working lives of men will reduce the time period during which they are able to accumulate pension entitlements, and increase the period of time that they are dependent on such entitlements. At the same time, changes in the pension system and the increasing importance of private pensions in retirement incomes mean that prospects in retirement are now more closely linked to experiences during working life than previously. It is important to note, however, that changes in the labour market have affected men and women differently. Women from more recent birth cohorts experience higher rates of participation in full-time employment at any given age than earlier cohorts, although their participation rates remain lower than those of men (Evandrou and Falkingham, 2000).

In sum, in 1997 New Labour inherited a complex set of circumstances, including a pension system where the BSP was declining in value, the system was failing to provide adequate pensions for many (particularly women), membership of defined-benefit occupational schemes was falling and saving in defined-contribution schemes was being undermined by financial scandals and a widespread lack of trust in the pensions industry. Furthermore, all this was against the backdrop of demographic trends and changes in patterns of labour force participation resulting in increases in beneficiaries and reductions in the number of contributors. The time was yet again ripe for pension reform.

A decade of pension reform

Within three months of entering office, New Labour had set up a review of pension provision in the UK. A decade later, no part of the pension system has remained untouched. Table 8.1 highlights the key pieces of legislation, while Figures 8.2 and 8.3 provide a schematic representation of the UK pension system at the start and end of the decade.[3] The figures contrast the system in place in 1997 with that which will come into place as a result of the 2007 Pensions Act and 2007/08 Pensions Bill. In fact, individual pensioners' entitlements will be more complex, with rights accrued under both current and past systems. For example, people retiring in 1997 may have accrued state second-tier pension rights under both the State Graduated Pension and SERPS.[4] However, for ease of presentation, only the system in operation at that point of time is shown.

Figure 8.2: The UK pension system (pre-reform, 1997)

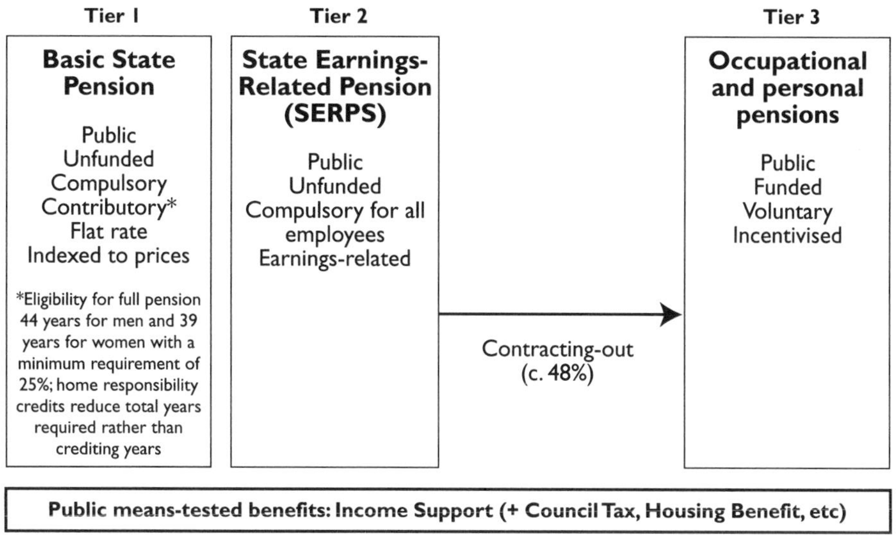

Tier 1	Tier 2		Tier 3
Basic State Pension	**State Earnings-Related Pension (SERPS)**		**Occupational and personal pensions**
Public Unfunded Compulsory Contributory* Flat rate Indexed to prices	Public Unfunded Compulsory for all employees Earnings-related		Public Funded Voluntary Incentivised
*Eligibility for full pension 44 years for men and 39 years for women with a minimum requirement of 25%; home responsibility credits reduce total years required rather than crediting years		Contracting-out (c. 48%)	
Public means-tested benefits: Income Support (+ Council Tax, Housing Benefit, etc)			

Figure 8.3: The reformed UK pension system (2008 and beyond)

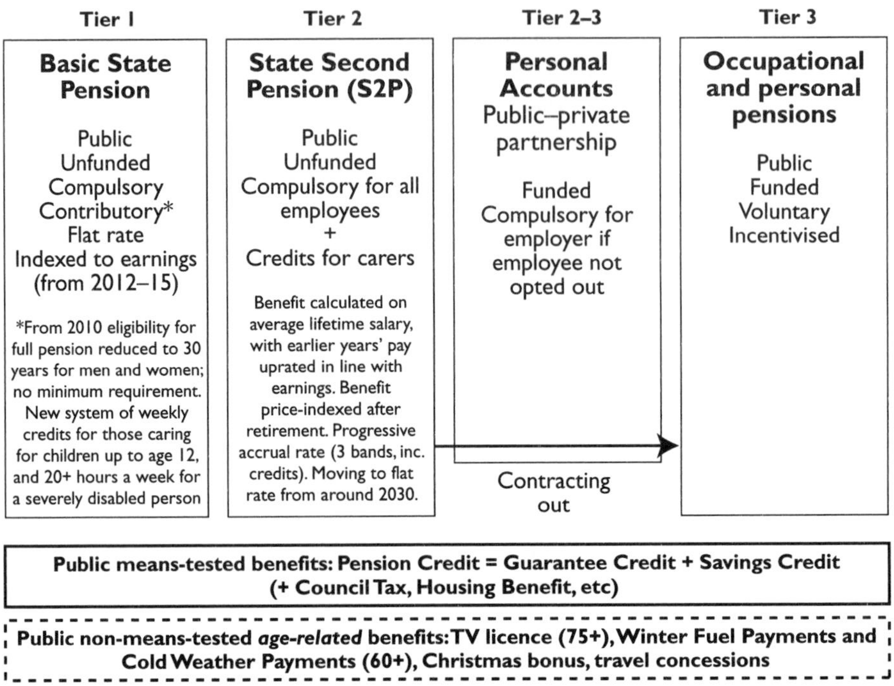

Tier I	Tier 2	Tier 2–3	Tier 3
Basic State Pension Public Unfunded Compulsory Contributory* Flat rate Indexed to earnings (from 2012–15) *From 2010 eligibility for full pension reduced to 30 years for men and women; no minimum requirement. New system of weekly credits for those caring for children up to age 12, and 20+ hours a week for a severely disabled person	**State Second Pension (S2P)** Public Unfunded Compulsory for all employees + Credits for carers Benefit calculated on average lifetime salary, with earlier years' pay uprated in line with earnings. Benefit price-indexed after retirement. Progressive accrual rate (3 bands, inc. credits). Moving to flat rate from around 2030.	**Personal Accounts** Public–private partnership Funded Compulsory for employer if employee not opted out Contracting out	**Occupational and personal pensions** Public Funded Voluntary Incentivised

Public means-tested benefits: Pension Credit = Guarantee Credit + Savings Credit (+ Council Tax, Housing Benefit, etc)

Public non-means-tested *age-related* benefits: TV licence (75+), Winter Fuel Payments and Cold Weather Payments (60+), Christmas bonus, travel concessions

An in-depth discussion of each of the reforms to the overall pension system introduced since 1997 is beyond the scope of this chapter. Here we briefly highlight the key changes that have resulted, by comparing the system at the beginning and end of the period 1997 to 2008, thereby passing over some of the early teething problems where one reform was quickly followed by another. However, before looking at each tier of the pension system in turn, we provide a brief chronological overview of the major reforms and the principles underlying them.

Principles

From the outset, New Labour highlighted that it aimed to deliver on its commitment to ensuring that pensioners share in the prosperity of the nation through a new partnership 'between public and private provision, and a balance between income sourced from tax and invested savings' (Labour Party, 1997, p 27).

The publication of the Green Paper *A New Contract for Welfare: Partnership in Pensions* (DSS, 1998) in December 1998 marked an attempt to forge a new and enduring settlement for the provision of income in retirement to carry Britain through the 21st century. The Green Paper put forward several interrelated goals including: ensuring an adequate income in later life for all; providing a reward for savings; and altering the balance between individual and state provision. A central tenet of the reforms was that where individuals were in a position to save for their own old age they should be encouraged to do so, but for those who were unable to save sufficient resources either because of low income or interrupted working lives then the state should provide an adequate safety net. The 1999 Welfare Reform and Pensions Act and the 2000 Child Support, Pensions and Social Security Act introduced changes to the state safety net, replacing Income Support with the more generous Minimum Income Guarantee (MIG) and subsequently the Pension Credit (PC), as well as replacing SERPS with a new State Second Pension (S2P). The safety net now 'taken care of', attention turned to encouraging saving, preferably in the private sector.

The idea of encouraging savings based on partnership continued to resonate throughout subsequent policy documents: 'Pensions savings should be based on partnership with employees, employers, pension providers and government all working together' (Andrew Smith, foreword, DWP, 2002) and 'we need to strike a new balance of rights and responsibilities between the State, employers, the financial services industry for provision of long-term savings and retirement income' (Alan Johnson, foreword, DWP, 2005). The 2004 Pensions Act introduced measures to simplify the tax treatment of occupational and personal pensions to further incentivise savings as well as a Pensions Protection Fund to allay the public's fears of a repeat of the Maxwell affair.

In December 2002, the government announced the establishment of the Pensions Commission to 'report on how the current voluntarist approach [to encouraging greater pension savings] is developing' (DWP, 2002, p 10). Once established, the Commission interpreted its brief more broadly, concluding that it was impossible to look at part of the system without analysing the whole (Pensions Commission, 2004). The conclusions of the first report were stark. Given demographic trends, the government faced an unavoidable choice – future pensioners will become poorer, or taxes devoted to pensions must rise, or saving rates must grow, or average retirement ages must increase. The second report put forward a series of recommendations combining the last three options, increasing pensioner poverty being felt not to be a popular or desirable option. These included further reform of the state system, in recognition that the safety net required further strengthening, automatic enrolment to encourage saving, a modest minimum level of matching employer contributions to cement the partnership and the creation of a National Pension Saving Scheme (Pensions Commission, 2005).

Prior to the publication of the Pensions Commission's second report, the government set out its own principles for reform:

> The pensions system must tackle poverty effectively; the opportunity to build an adequate retirement income should be open to all; affordability and economic stability must be maintained; the pensions system should

produce fair outcomes for women and carers; reform should seek to establish a system that people understand; and reform should be based around as broad a consensus as possible. (DWP, 2005, p 25)

A remarkable degree of consensus emerged around the Pensions Commission proposals and its report was swiftly followed by two White Papers (DWP, 2006a, 2006b), which, although not adopting the proposals in full, gave force to many of its recommendations. In particular, the White Paper *Security in Retirement* (DWP, 2006a), subsequently enacted in the 2007 Pensions Act, transformed the state pension system while the 2008 Pensions Act introduces a new public–private savings partnership through Personal Accounts along with auto-enrolment.

Reforms

The UK pension system may be thought of as being based on three tiers (or pillars), supported by a publicly funded means-tested safety net. This section provides a description of the reforms and how they affected each tier of the system. Although means-tested benefits and other social security benefits are not strictly part of the pension system, they are intimately related to it, providing a significant share of overall income in later life.

The first wave of reforms detailed in the 1998 Green Paper (DSS, 1998), legislated in the 1999 Welfare Reform and Pensions Act and the 2000 Child Support, Pensions and Social Security Act, transformed the safety net. Prior to 1999, there had been a unified system of social assistance for people of all ages whose incomes fell below a minimum level, that is, Income Support. In 1999, Income Support for people aged above state pension age was replaced by the MIG, which was subsequently replaced by the PC consisting of a Guarantee Credit (GC) payable from age 60 for those living on a low income, and a tapered Saving Credit (SC) payable from age 65 to reward those older people with small amounts of savings – minimising the so-called 'occupational pension trap'. The separation of the system of social assistance for older people from that for households headed by persons of working age meant that the government could increase the generosity of means-tested benefits to one section of the population without extending the same generosity elsewhere. This it duly did with a series of above-inflation increases in the value of MIG in 1999 and 2000. Moreover, since 2001, GC (and its predecessor MIG) has been increased in line with average earnings. As at April 2008, GC provides a minimum income of £124.05 a week for a single person and £189.35 a week for a couple. Taken together, the BSP and maximum SC are currently worth approximately 24% of NAE (PPI, 2008), which is approximately the same as the relative value of the BSP in 1979 before the link with earnings was broken.

In addition to PC, older people on low incomes may also be entitled to other means-tested benefits such as Housing Benefit and Council Tax Benefit. Furthermore, pensioners receive other benefits that could be considered part of the underlying foundation of public provision. Here, New Labour has introduced several new benefits including free television licences for those aged 75 and over, free eye tests and dental checks and most recently national travel concessions, with free swimming now promised. People aged over 60 are entitled to an annual Winter Fuel Payment of up to £250, rising to £400 for those aged 80 and over. On top of this, there have been one-off age-related payments in some years. Taken all together, the changes since 1997 have significantly increased the value of the safety net for older people. Whether this has had the desired effect of reducing pensioner poverty is discussed in the next section.

The first tier of public pension provision has also undergone radical reform, although most of the changes do not affect current generations of pensioners, with the transition to the new system beginning in 2010. There were some above-inflation increases in the BSP in New Labour's first term, but since 2001, the BSP has continued to be uprated in line with prices. Thus, its value relative to earnings has continued to fall and in 2008 it was estimated to be worth just 16% of NAE (PPI, 2008). Older people with no other incomes other than the BSP are entitled to GC. However, the 2007 Pensions Act has signalled that at some point between 2012 and 2015 the link between the BSP and earnings will be restored. Moreover, from 2010 the number of years of contributions required for a full BSP will be reduced to 30 years for both men and women (from 39 years for women and 44 years for men). In addition, the old system of Home Responsibility Protection, which reduced the contributory requirement for those providing care to dependent children or disabled adults, will be replaced with a new system of weekly Credits, recognising the valuable contribution to society of unpaid caring. The other major change is that the age at which people become entitled to the BSP will be raised to 68 for both men and women, phased in between 2024 and 2046; women's state pension age is already rising to 65 by 2010.

After half a century, the government is also abandoning its attempt to provide a state earnings-related pension. In 2002, SERPS was replaced by the S2P. However, significant payments under the S2P have yet to start and SERPS remains the most important second-tier benefit for existing pensioners. The main aim of the S2P is to provide a public second pension to the low paid and those who cannot work due to disabilities or caring responsibilities. Currently, rights to the S2P are accrued based on three earnings bands and three accrual rates, with a strong progressive element, and low earners and carers (via credits) are guaranteed a minimum level of pension. Following the 2007 Pensions Act, the S2P will be gradually converted into a flat-rate pension by about 2030, at which time it will be worth around 17% of average earnings. Thus, the reforms will effectively create a dual flat-rate pension, with BSP earnings linked and requiring 30 years of contributions or credits and S2P price linked and requiring work-based contributions or credits over a full working life from age 16 to state retirement age.

The third tier of private pension provision in 1997 was composed of occupational and personal pensions. The 1998 Green Paper (DSS, 1998, ch 2, para 19) highlighted occupational pensions as 'one of the great welfare success stories of the century', and an aspiration was to share this success story more broadly across the population. The first vehicle chosen to do this was the Stakeholder Pension (SHP), which became available in April 2001. The SHP is a form of low-charge personal pension, with management charges for those taking out a pension after April 2005 capped at 1.5% for the first 10 years, reducing to 1% thereafter. However, take-up of the SHP has been disappointing (ABI, 2003) and private savings have if anything reversed.

One of the major tasks set by the government for the Pensions Commission was to think of ways to stimulate private saving and the government's proposals to achieve this are set out in the 2008 Pensions Act. From 2012, Personal Accounts will provide a low-cost, portable individualised pensions saving scheme. All employees over the age of 22 will be auto-enrolled into either the Personal Account or an equivalent employer-based scheme. Although there will be an option to opt out, it is hoped that a combination of inertia and informed choice will result in most employees choosing not to. Incentives to remain in the scheme will be provided by a national minimum employer contribution of 3% above and up to certain thresholds. The 2007 Pensions Act established the Personal Accounts Delivery Authority to provide advice to government on the introduction of Personal Accounts and many of the details have yet to be finalised.

Delivering on 'Opportunity for All'

Tackling the problems of low income and social exclusion among today's pensioners

Tony Blair, in the foreword to the first 2006 White Paper, stated:

> I am proud of what the Government has achieved for pensioners. We said our first priority would be tackling pensioner poverty. There is more to do, but since 1997 two million pensioners have been lifted out of poverty. Thanks to measures like the Pension Credit, Winter Fuel Payments, free TV licences and above-inflation increases in the Basic State Pension, pensioners are now less likely to be poor than the population as a whole. (DWP, 2006a, p v)

John Hutton, then Secretary of State for Social Security, went further, stating that 'the immediate crisis of pensioner poverty is being successfully addressed' (DWP, 2006a, p vii). However, the evidence on trends in pensioner poverty provides a less optimistic picture. The absolute number of pensioners living in relative poverty (measured before housing costs [BHC]) has actually *risen* by 100,000 over the decade 1996-97 to 2006-07 (Table 8.3). But the size of the pensioner population has also grown across the decade. Thus, the *proportion* of older people living in poverty by this measure has *fallen* from 24.6% to 23.2% and even greater reductions in poverty rates are seen if incomes are measured AHC (the two right-hand columns in Table 8.3), from 29.1% in 1996-97 to 18.9% in 2006-07. What is striking, however, is that between 2005-06 and 2006-07, *both* the absolute number and the proportion of pensioners in poverty increased significantly regardless of the measure being used. According to analysis by the Institute for Fiscal Studies (IFS), the rise in poverty between 2005-06 and 2006-07 has undone about two-thirds of the fall in poverty measured BHC, and about one-sixth of the more considerable fall using incomes measured AHC (Brewer et al, 2008a).

The rise in poverty in 2006-07 is surprising. The value of the maximum entitlement to benefits for pensioner families with no private income has generally exceeded the growth in the poverty line since 2000-01, largely as a result of MIG then GC being uprated in line with average earnings, which tend to grow faster than median income (Brewer et al, 2008a). In fact, as shown in Table 2.4 (Chapter Two), for single pensioners, the guarantee element of PC is now above the 'AHC poverty line'. Two factors may be responsible for the rise in poverty. First, age-

Table 8.3: Pensioners living in households with incomes below 60% of the contemporary median income

	BHC		AHC	
	%	Million	%	Million
1996-97 (GB)	24.6	2.4	29.1	2.9
1997-98 (GB)	25.3	2.5	29.1	2.9
1998-99 (GB)	26.8	2.7	28.6	2.9
1999-2000 (GB)	25.1	2.5	27.6	2.8
2000-01 (GB)	24.8	2.5	25.9	2.6
2001-02 (GB)	25.1	2.5	25.6	2.6
2002-03 (UK)	24.4	2.5	24.2	2.5
2003-04 (UK)	22.9	2.4	20.6	2.2
2004-05 (UK)	21.3	2.3	17.6	1.9
2005-06 (UK)	20.8	2.2	17.0	1.8
2006-07 (UK)	23.2	2.5	18.9	2.1
Changes				
1996-97 to 2006-07	−1.4	0.1	−10.2	−0.8
2005-06 to 2006-07	2.4	0.3	1.9	0.3

Source: Brewer et al (2008a, table 4.2)

related payments, which provided between £50 and £200 to individuals aged 60 and over during the winter of 2005-06, were not repeated in the subsequent year. Second, there appears to have been a decline in the proportion of pensioners reporting receiving PC and other state benefits in the 2006-07 Family Resources Survey on which the poverty estimates are based, although there has been no accompanying fall in PC in administrative data – casting doubt on part of the rise. The sensitivity of pensioner poverty to one-off payments, or lack thereof, highlights the fact that many pensioners are living on incomes just around the poverty threshold (see Chapter Two, Table 2.3). Thus, relatively small changes in income can result in relatively large changes in poverty.

Although the reliability of the recent rise in pensioner poverty can be debated, it remains the case that the number of pensioners living in poverty has never fallen below 2.2 million (measured BHC) throughout the decade. One of the main reasons for this is the persistent problem of low take-up of means-tested benefits. In 2006-07, between 33% and 41% of entitled pensioners failed to claim PC they were entitled to (DWP, 2008c). Caseload take-up rates are higher for GC (between 72% and 82%) than for GC plus SC (between 64% and 77%) and SC only (between 42% and 49%). However, this still means that between a fifth and a quarter of those older people living on the very lowest incomes are missing out. Some non-claimants may miss out on relatively small entitlements, and so may have thought it not worthwhile claiming, but the average amounts unclaimed were non-trivial at £28 per week. In total, £1,960-2,810 million PC was unclaimed in 2006-07. Family Resources Survey data suggest that 35% of the entitled non-claimants were aged over 80, and two-thirds were living in households below the poverty line (DWP, 2008c, table 2.14). An additional £28 per week would make a big difference to their living standards.

Moreover, significant differences remain within the pensioner population. Pensioner poverty remains particularly concentrated among women, with two-thirds of those living below 60% median income being women (DWP, 2008b, table 6.3). *Persistent* poverty is also concentrated among older women, with the proportion experiencing such poverty being three times that of the whole population (DWP, 2007a). This reflects both the lower wages of women while in work – 'the wage gap' – and the fact that they are much more likely to have experienced interruptions to their earnings histories – 'the pay gap'.

Black and minority ethnic pensioners also experience an elevated risk of poverty. For example, 39% of Pakistani and Bangladeshi, 33% of Indian and 29% of Black Caribbean elders live in households with incomes below 60% of the contemporary median (BHC) compared with 21% of their white counterparts (DWP, 2008b, table 6.5). In part this reflects the fact that many of the current generation of black and minority ethnic elders entered the UK part way through their working lives and so have not had an opportunity to accumulate a full pension. This disadvantage may reduce as younger cohorts of UK-born minority ethnic groups enter retirement. Minority ethnic groups are, however, more likely to experience unemployment and are disproportionately found in low–skill, low–income employment, so differences in employment-based pensions are likely to remain.

In order to assess the impact of policy changes over the last decade, modelling results from the tax–benefit model, POLIMOD, are used to compare rates of pensioner poverty under different policy regimes (see also Chapter Two). Line (a) in Table 8.4 shows the poverty rates that *would have* resulted if the tax and benefit system of 1996-97 (uprated by prices and by earnings) had remained unchanged, while lines (b), (c) and (d) show the poverty rates under the policy regimes in 2000-01, 2004-05 and 2008-09 respectively. Comparing lines (a) and (d) shows that if there had been no policy changes, relative poverty rates would have been between 3 and 18 percentage points *higher* in 2008-09 than they were when New Labour came to power in 1997. Based on these measures, New Labour's policies to tackle pensioner poverty have met with considerable success. Table 8.4 also shows dramatic differences across time, particularly for poverty measured AHC, with the big reduction in pensioner poverty occurring between 2000-01 and 2004-05 and only relatively modest decline between 2004-05 and 2008-09.

So far, progress in reducing pensioner poverty has been assessed according to the government benchmark of 60% of contemporary median income. Brewer et al (2006b) consider an alternative measure of relative poverty, using household *expenditure* to quantify living standards. They find that pensioner poverty rates are considerably higher when measured using expenditure (excluding housing costs) rather than income (AHC) and rates of expenditure poverty have remained

Table 8.4: Simulated estimates of pensioner poverty under alternative policy regimes, Britain, 2008-09

	BHC	AHC
Price indexation		
(a) 1996-97 policy regime	30.4	29.8
(b) 2000-01 policy regime	28.0	28.1
(c) 2004-05 policy regime	22.4	14.1
(d) 2008-09 policy regime	21.6	12.2
(d) – (a)	–8.8	–17.6
Earnings indexation		
(a) 1996-97 policy regime	25.6	26.1
(b) 2000-01 policy regime	25.5	24.1
(c) 2004-05 policy regime	22.4	14.1
(d) 2008-09 policy regime	22.5	14.5
(d) – (a)	–3.1	–11.6

Source: See Chapter Two

largely unchanged since 1996-97. Research by Scharf et al (2005, 2006), using focus groups and in-depth interviews with older people, highlights how older people are often excluded from normal patterns of behaviour and consumption. Interestingly, many older people do not seem to acknowledge their own needs; for example, cutting back on food was not perceived as going without. The generally low expectations of older people in relation to their living standard 'points to the degree to which the experience of poverty has been internalised by many disadvantaged older people over the course of their lives' (Scharf et al, 2006, p 5).

In summary, New Labour has made some progress in tackling pensioners' poverty in the decade since 1997. The increased generosity of the means-tested safety net has made a real difference to some of the poorest pensioners and poverty is lower than it would have been had the policy reforms of the last decade not occurred. However, around a fifth of pensioners were still living in poverty in 2006-07, and with recent above-inflation rises in energy prices there are concerns that the number of older people living in fuel poverty will rise significantly (NEA, 2008). Thus, it appears premature to conclude, as John Hutton did, that 'pensioner poverty is being successfully addressed' (NEA, 2008).

Ensuring that more of tomorrow's pensioners can retire on a decent income

There is no doubt that the reforms of the BSP in the 2007 Pensions Act will mean that more men and women will retire with a full BSP. It is predicted that by 2025, 90% of men and women reaching state pension age will have entitlement to a full BSP compared with the current position of only 35% of women and 85% of men (DWP, 2007b). However, given that the BSP is already being paid below the level required to qualify for means-tested benefits, and that its real value relative to earnings will continue to decline until the link to earnings is restored, this alone will be inadequate to deliver a 'decent income'. It will nevertheless provide a higher floor on which people can build their own private entitlement.

Achieving the goal of delivering a secure income in retirement will depend on greater saving in second- and third-tier pensions. The S2P, particularly now that credits have been introduced for carers, will go some way to delivering for the low paid and those with interrupted work histories. It is estimated that extending credits for childcare in the S2P from age 6 to age 12 from 2010 will allow around an extra 780,000 women and 30,000 men to accrue entitlement to the S2P and a further 180,000 additional people (of which 110,000 are women) will accrue entitlements through the new carers credit (DWP, 2007b). The Institute for Fiscal Studies estimates that in 2030 the BSP will be worth around 13% of NAE and the S2P around 17% (Emmerson et al, 2006). Thus, *together*, the dual flat-rate state pension will be worth 30% of average earnings, almost achieving the 1979 Labour Party manifesto pledge of achieving 'a single person's pension of one-third gross average earnings' and providing an above-poverty-level income. However, as the

S2P is expected to continue to be linked to prices *after* retirement, the value of the state pension package relative to NAE will fall during retirement. This, combined with gaps in coverage, means that many older people will remain dependent on means-tested benefits.

The latest projections by the Department for Work and Pensions indicate that under the reform proposals in the 2007 Pensions Act around 30% of pensioner households will be eligible for PC by 2050, with around 5% pensioners being eligible for the GC (DWP, 2008d, table 1). This compares with 45% and 10% respectively today. However, analysis by the Pensions Policy Institute suggests that the government figures are a conservative estimate and that, depending on the different assumptions used, between one-third and two-thirds of pensioner households may be reliant on means-tested PC (PPI, 2006a). Both sets of analysis are, however, in agreement that dependence on PC would be much higher without the reforms, with up to 80-90% of pensioners eligible for PC by 2050 if the recent policy changes did not occur. Using a dynamic micro-simulation model, the Institute for Fiscal Studies projects that the number of pensioners in poverty in 2017-18 will be around two million, that is, similar to levels today (Brewer et al, 2007). However, without the White Paper reforms and the indexation of PC to earnings, their results suggest that pensioner poverty would be significantly higher, at around 2.4 million (Brewer et al, 2007, table 5.2).

Nevertheless, the continued reliance on means-tested benefits is problematic for a number of reasons. First, as discussed above, 30-40% of entitled pensioners do not claim PC. Second, means-tested benefits are assessed on a household rather than individual basis and, as a result, many older women with low personal incomes are not entitled to this state support due to their husband's pension provision. Recent evidence has shown that it is a mistake to assume that resources are always shared equally within a household (Rake and Jayatilaka, 2002). Thus, from a gender perspective, the optimum solution is both to ensure maximum entitlement to the BSP and the S2P and to maintain these at a level that is adequate to protect pensioners from means testing. The reforms go a long way to achieving both of these goals but there remain gaps in credits – for example carers caring for someone in receipt of lower-rate Disability Living Allowance or earning less than the lower earnings limit – and issues of adequacy. Moreover, the reforms only affect women reaching state pension age from 2010 and do not address the gaps in entitlement to state provision for women currently in retirement or retiring before then.

Improving state provision is just one part of the picture. As highlighted earlier, a key thrust of pension policy throughout the last decade has been a strengthened partnership between public and private provision and a balance between pension income from tax and from private savings. Here, much depends on the success of Personal Accounts. It is too early to say much about this as Personal Accounts have yet to be legislated. Nevertheless, the reforms are expected to generate a substantial increase in the number of people saving in a workplace pension scheme, many for the first time (DWP, 2008e). Many of these will be women and individuals from black and minority ethnic groups, reflecting the fact that women and black and minority ethnic groups are overrepresented in the target group for auto-enrolment (that is, those earning less than £33,000). Although Personal Accounts will be advantageous for many people, there are some subgroups for whom it will not be due to the interaction of Personal Accounts with taxes and means-tested benefits (PPI, 2006b). In particular, some low-income groups may lose entitlement to means-tested benefits as a consequence of saving into a Personal Account – extending the old 'occupational pensions trap' into a new domain. Given auto-enrolment, in order for Personal Accounts to gain credibility and reduce the risk of 'mis-selling', it will be essential to ensure that sufficient clear and accessible guidance is available to allow people to make informed decisions about whether to stay in or opt out of Personal Accounts. Only time will tell.

Conclusion

Over the decade since 1997, the pensions landscape has been radically transformed. These changes have resulted in positive outcomes for both today's and tomorrow's pensioners, but the picture is not entirely upbeat. Progress in tackling poverty among *today's* pensioners has been achieved through the extension of means testing. But significant numbers of older people continue to fail to claim their entitlements and so live in poverty. Moreover, the large reductions in poverty achieved in the early 2000s have now stalled and there may even have been a reversal in the last year. Many older people continue to live on incomes at or around the poverty line, making them vulnerable to even small changes in income.

In its first two terms of office, New Labour's strategy to ensure that more of *tomorrow's* pensioners retire on a decent income largely focused on extending private pension saving. Contributions to private pensions did not increase to the extent envisaged and the most notable outcome has been the 'seismic shift' from final salary to money purchase schemes. The last two years have seen far-reaching reform. The 2007 Pensions Act has radically revised state pension provision, extending eligibility to both the BSP and the S2P and increasing the future value of the state pension package through a commitment to restore indexation of the BSP to earnings. These reforms will significantly increase the base on which people can build their own private entitlement, while reducing the proportion of pensioners who would have become dependent on means-tested benefits. The reform package goes a long way towards closing the gap between men and women's state pension entitlement. However, fundamental differences remain between men and women – and rich and poor – in third-tier provision. Moreover, the shift to money purchase schemes and the growing individualisation of risk means that incomes in later life are likely to become more unequal in the future. Much rests on the success of Personal Accounts to close that gap and to ensure a secure retirement for all.

Notes

[1] Defined here as living in a household with below 60% of the contemporary median net disposable household income after housing costs.

[2] Unless otherwise stated, the figures reported here are period life expectancies: the number of years a person aged 60 could expect to live if they were exposed to the probability of dying at each age according to the age-specific mortality rates prevailing in that year.

[3] The authors gratefully acknowledge Curry and O'Connell (2003) for the inspiration for visual representation of the pensions system used here. Any errors are the authors' own.

[4] For a useful depiction of the evolution of the different tiers of the pension system over time, see Pemberton (2006, p 54, figure 3.1).

[5] The 2004 Pensions Act falls in the second term but largely affected private sector pension savings.

NINE

Ethnic inequalities: another 10 years of the same?

Coretta Phillips

Introduction

New Labour signalled its commitment to responding to racism in society early in its first term. By launching a public inquiry into the Metropolitan Police Service's investigation of Stephen Lawrence's racist murder and accepting its controversial findings (Macpherson, 1999), it appeared to send a powerful message after the 'racism-blind' years of the Conservative government. At the end of the 20th century, New Labour had recognised that 'institutional racism' was endemic to public institutions, such as the police, schools and government departments.

The government's policy response, outlined in the *Home Secretary's Action Plan* (Home Office, 1999), proposed a rigorous reform programme expressed through the language of racial equality *of opportunity*. At the centrepiece was the 2000 Race Relations (Amendment) Act, which places a statutory duty on all public authorities to promote equality of opportunity and good relations between different racial groups. Public authorities must audit, consult on, and monitor existing policies and services to assess whether these adversely impact different ethnic groups and publish a race equality scheme.

Aside from New Labour's legislative framework to produce racial equality, the prevention of social exclusion has been pivotal, with a focus on reducing multiple disadvantage for *all groups* (SEU, 2000c). This chapter will assess the effects of such policies – and those specifically targeted at *minority ethnic groups* – on longstanding ethnic inequalities in education, employment and income, and policing. It will conclude with an overall appraisal of New Labour strategies and consider where further policy developments are required. First, however, it is necessary to outline some relevant conceptual and methodological issues.

Conceptual and methodological issues

In reviewing various statistical and empirical material, this chapter relies wholly on the ethnic categorisations used by government, policy researchers and academics. Yet the ways in which *ethnic group/origin* is operationalised varies considerably across different datasets, and may often be remote from the self-identifications of those categorised or conceptualisations of *ethnicity* as understood by sociologists and anthropologists (see, for example, Fenton, 2003).

This has important ramifications when considering that the study of ethnic inequalities essentially involves examining *between-group* differences at an aggregate level, which largely assumes that there is little variation *within groups*. However, there has long been evidence that the *Asian* categorisation, for example, masks significant demographic, socioeconomic, religious and cultural differences among the main ethnic groups of Indian, Pakistani and Bangladeshi origin. Such diversity is also inherently present in the Mixed Race category, as well as other ethnic categorisations. Immigration by new migrant groups, particularly from Eastern European states, has additionally created an internally varied white ethnic group. At the time of writing, this diversity has yet to fully filter through to published statistics and research data, but where possible in this chapter white ethnic experience is disaggregated.

The chapter is also dependent on positivist analyses that attempt to predict which factors are statistically related to particular outcomes in an effort to quantitatively assess the role of ethnic origin in producing, say, relatively high or low levels of unemployment. Such analyses must be viewed cautiously as it is rarely possible to fully isolate any one factor when individuals occupy intersecting social positions (Rattansi, 2005). Disaggregating the effects of class, ethnicity, and racial discrimination may be misleading as the social processes that situate individuals within or outside of a class position are themselves racialised. Young men of Pakistani origin may experience unemployment because of their low educational attainment, but this may be linked to their attendance at a poorly performing school or experiences of racial discrimination. It is rarely possible to meaningfully disentangle these interacting processes.

Bearing these caveats in mind, it is still possible to come to some general conclusions about the differential experiences of the main ethnic groups in British society, and to trace changes in outcomes during the 10 years after New Labour came to power in 1997, beginning first with education.

Education

With New Labour's pre-election mantra of *Education, Education, Education* it is axiomatic that raising educational attainment has been central to the reform agenda. Traditionally, education has been viewed as a mechanism for assisting the integration of minority ethnic groups into the social fabric of society, and for reducing prejudice and discrimination.

Educational attainment

New Labour inherited a legacy of unequal educational attainment among ethnic groups in British society. Using the standard measure of five or more passes at

GCSE (General Certificate of Secondary Education), Gillborn and Mirza's (2000) secondary analysis of Youth Cohort Study data found that, by the mid-1990s, the highest-attaining pupil group were of Indian origin, followed by the white majority ethnic group, then Bangladeshi, Pakistani and Black pupils.

Government policies

Broadly speaking, during New Labour's first term in office its strategy to improve educational attainment was to target disadvantaged areas. The Excellence in Cities (EiC) initiative, for example, covered 60% of minority ethnic children of secondary school age, because of their residential concentration in areas experiencing multiple disadvantage.[1] It involved providing additional resources and guidance, through Gifted and Talented programmes, learning mentors, units working with those at risk of exclusion, enhanced information and communication technology (ICT) facilities, and the sharing of good practice through partnership efforts. Evaluative evidence indicated that at the end of Key Stage 4, minority ethnic educational attainment in EiC schools was higher than in non-EiC schools, although this varied somewhat depending on the measure of attainment used (Kendall et al, 2005).

Additionally, since September 2002, the National Curriculum has incorporated a statutory citizenship element in secondary schools. While research has indicated implementation difficulties, there are signs that citizenship education is slowly becoming more embedded in educational practice, although a review of diversity and citizenship in the curriculum has suggested that it may not be prioritised highly enough in schools or be undertaken by enough trained and engaged teachers (Ajegbo et al, 2007).

New Labour also introduced initiatives specifically targeted at minority ethnic pupils. The Ethnic Minority Achievement Grant (EMAG), introduced in 1998-99, has funded language development training, peer mentoring and mediation schemes, targeted literacy and numeracy sessions, behaviour management programmes, and summer schools for areas with high concentrations of minority ethnic pupils. Evaluated alongside EiC, findings indicate a positive return with an appreciation of project work by pupils, particularly in learning African and Asian history, raising self-esteem and motivation, and increased parental support (Cunningham et al, 2004). Improved initial teacher training has occurred alongside the setting of incremental targets for increased minority ethnic teacher employment. These have been met, and by 2006, 12% of entrants were from minority ethnic groups, mainly in London and the South East (Training and Development Agency for Schools, 2006).

In March 2003, the government consulted on raising minority ethnic, particularly African Caribbean, pupils' educational achievement, in *Aiming High* (DfES, 2003d). This resulted in the piloting of the African Caribbean Achievement Project in 30 schools from November 2003. Each school received consultant expertise and a funded senior manager to lead on engaging more fully with the needs of African Caribbean pupils. The Black Pupils Achievement Programme was launched in October 2005 to further target interventions in 100 schools across 25 local authorities. Activities including lesson observations, focus groups with parents and children, mentoring and curriculum review were used.

An evaluation of the African Caribbean Achievement Project by Tikly et al (2006) found that, between 2003 and 2005, the proportion of Black Caribbean boys achieving Level 5+ in English and mathematics at the end of Key Stage 3 increased by 12-13 percentage points. There was also an increase in attainment of five or more GCSEs at grades A★-C for Black Caribbean boys (5%) and girls (7%), but this was lower than the national average, suggesting a limited project effect. Moreover, Black Caribbean boys remained the lowest-achieving group in *Aiming High* schools at Key Stages 3 and 4, with little change in their value-added score between Key Stages 2 and 3.

Various other developments have targeted other minority ethnic groups – including the Gypsy/Traveller Achievement Project, which ran from November 2003 to August 2004 for schools to increase attainment and attendance levels, the publication of a management guide on improving attainment among secondary school pupils of Pakistani, Bangladeshi, Somali and Turkish origin (DfES, 2007a), and the establishment of a New Arrivals Excellence Programme in July 2007.

Outcomes

Figure 9.1 sets out the attainment levels for the main ethnic groups[2] during New Labour's first two-and-a-half terms. Immediately evident is the overall improvement in achievement with the proportion of those achieving five or more GCSEs at grades A★-C in 2007 higher than in 1997, with the largest increases from 2002 onwards, and this pattern holds for all ethnic groups. The increase in the percentage of pupils achieving the standard measure of educational attainment was most marked for those of minority ethnic origin (16-24 percentage points) compared with the white school population (13 percentage points). It is also noteworthy that the highest-achieving groups in 2007 were of minority ethnic origin: 83% of Chinese pupils achieved five or more GCSEs at grades A★-C in England, followed by 74% of Indian pupils (DfES, 2007b). This is a significant accomplishment that shows that New Labour's efforts to tackle educational disadvantage are having a definite impact (see Chapter Four for a fuller discussion of this improvement).

However, it remains the case that ethnic inequalities in educational attainment are still observable, although the gap appears to be closing. In 1997, the gap in attainment levels between the highest-achieving ethnic group (Chinese) and the lowest-achieving groups (Black and Pakistani) was 38 percentage points, which had reduced to 30 by 2007.[3] Using the comparator of the white majority ethnic group indicates a more dramatic narrowing of the gap. As Table 9.1 shows, this was one percentage point in 2007 for Bangladeshi and White pupils, compared

Figure 9.1: Proportion of pupils obtaining five or more GCSE A*-C passes, by main ethnic groups, 1997-2007

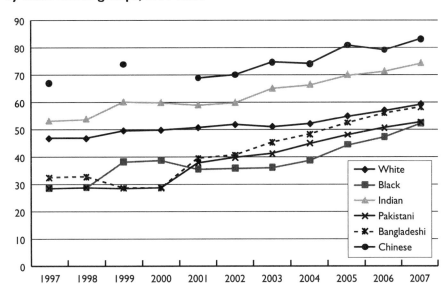

Sources:

(1) Data for 1997, 1999 and 2001 were taken from Connolly (2006). Data for pupils of Chinese origin were only periodically available from 1997 to 2001

(2) Data for 1998, 2000 and 2002 were taken from DfES (2003c). Both used sweeps of the Youth Cohort Study

(3) Data for 2003-07 were taken from DfES (2007b) and earlier equivalents drawing on the Pupil Level Annual School Census

with 14 percentage points in 1998, a remarkable achievement, which appears to indicate the positive impact of interventions. Likewise, pupils of Black and Pakistani origin had more similar attainment levels to the white majority ethnic group in 2007 than in earlier years.

A more comprehensive categorisation of pupils by ethnic origin since 2003 reveals a high-attaining cluster with 70% or more achieving five GCSEs at grades A*-C comprising those of Chinese, Indian and Mixed-White and Asian origin in

Table 9.1: Attainment level gaps for the lowest-achieving groups compared with the white majority ethnic group, selected years

	Size of the gap (% points)			
Minority ethnic groups	**1998**	**2001**	**2004**	**2007**
Black	18	15	13	7
Pakistani	18	13	7	7
Bangladeshi	14	11	4	1

Source: See Figure 9.1

2007. The mid-range cluster with 55-65% was the largest cluster, including those of Irish, White British, Bangladeshi, Mixed–White and Black African, and Black African origin. The performance of the lowest-attaining cluster (Pakistani, Black Caribbean, Mixed–White and Black Caribbean, Irish Travellers and Gypsy/Roma) was 14-54% (DfES, 2007b). The last two of these groups had only 14 and 16% respectively obtaining five or more GCSEs at grades A*-C in 2007. For these groups, attainment levels were lower in 2007 than in 2003 whereas all other ethnic groups performed better in 2007 (see Figure 9.2). This gap increase is the subject of current research being conducted by the Department for Children, Schools and Families.

The explanatory frameworks proposed to explicate these differential outcomes have included socioeconomic/class disadvantage and teacher/school racism. Variants of these two themes highlight the role of poor family–school links and parental support, large concentrations of minority ethnic pupils in unpopular and poorly resourced schools as a result of the corrupting effects of parental choice policies, positive and negative teacher stereotyping of minority ethnic pupils, and ethnocentric bias in the curriculum (Gillborn, 1998; Tomlinson, 1998; Abbas, 2002; Archer and Francis, 2005). Sewell's (1997) work has also pointed to anti-school black masculinities leading to educational disaffection and low attainment.

In exploring the role of socioeconomic/class disadvantage further, Figure 9.3 uses the proxy of free school meals (FSM) to examine the performance of selected ethnic groups[4] and it reveals a complex picture. Looking first at those eligible for FSM, it is evident that the poorest performers are those of White British and

Figure 9.2: Proportion of pupils obtaining five or more GCSE A*-C passes, by selected ethnic origins, 2003-07

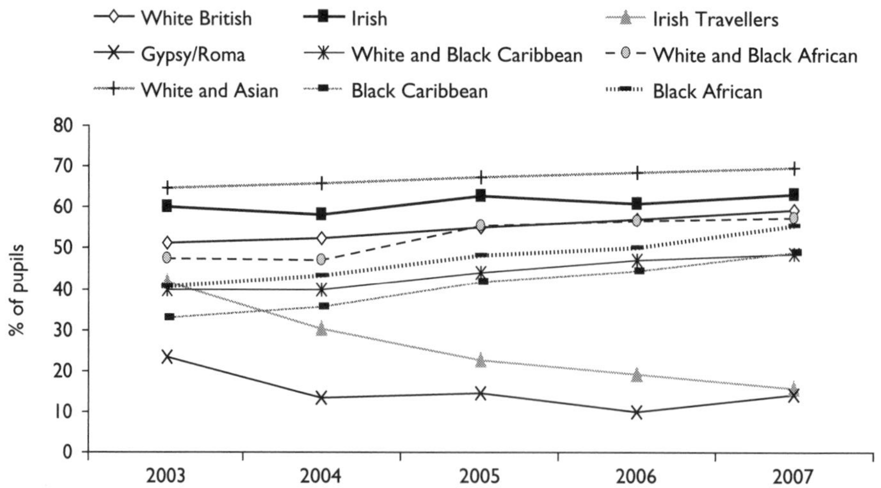

Source: DfES (2007b) and earlier equivalents drawing on the Pupil Level Annual School Census

Figure 9.3: Proportion of pupils obtaining five or more GCSE A*-C passes, by eligibility for FSM, 2007

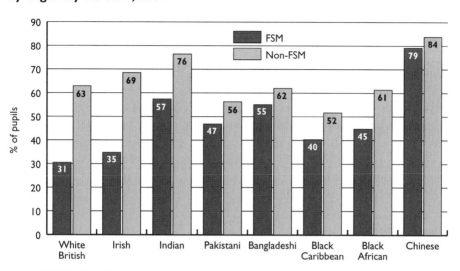

Source: DfES (2007b). Selected ethnic groups only (see Note 5 at the end of the chapter)

Irish origin, followed by those of Black Caribbean, Black African and Pakistani origin. It is also striking that those of Chinese origin have very high levels of attainment (79%). Among those not eligible for FSM, it is still those of Black Caribbean and Pakistani origin who fare worst. Taken together, these findings suggest multi-causal explanations for educational disadvantage, which may vary for different ethnic groups.

Acknowledging the limitations of the FSM measure, which undoubtedly obscures significant advantage and disadvantage within the broader categories (see Hobbs and Vignoles, 2007), Strand's (2008) study provides a more sensitive measure of socioeconomic status using head of household occupation, mother's highest education qualification, FSM, housing tenure, family structure, and neighbourhood disadvantage. Using data from the Longitudinal Study of Young People in England for 2006, Strand suggests that the social class gap in education attainment is larger – and therefore a more significant cause of concern – compared with the ethnicity gap.[5] In particular, Strand found that low socioeconomic status impacted hardest on the White British ethnic group, leading to very low levels of attainment for boys and girls. This was mediated through lower parental and pupil aspirations for educational success and a low academic self–concept (see also Evans, 2007). In contrast, Black Caribbean and Black African pupils from high socioeconomic status homes had high aspirations and academic self-concepts, but they underachieved in relation to White British pupils. Indian, Pakistani, Bangladeshi and Black African pupils from low socioeconomic status homes had relatively elevated attainment levels, seemingly because of their higher aspirations and academic self-concepts. Strand (2008, p 46) concluded that there is 'a need to move from a monolithic conception of White British as an homogeneous group to explicitly recognise this high degree of polarisation around socioeconomic status for White British pupils', whereby they are represented in both the highest- and lowest-attaining groups.

This leaves the question of Black Caribbean pupils' experiences, particularly those from higher socioeconomic status homes. In Tikly et al's (2006) evaluation of the African Caribbean Achievement Project, the research highlighted the perception among African Caribbean pupils and parents of unfair and inconsistent behaviour management within schools, which contributed to low teacher expectations, with some indication that pupils were sometimes moved to lower ability sets because of their behaviour rather than their academic ability. Central to low educational attainment among Black Caribbean pupils then, is behaviour management, which is considered next in relation to school exclusions.

School exclusions

Figure 9.4 shows an impressive reduction in permanent school exclusions between 1997-98 and 1999-2000, which was most marked for Black Caribbean and Black African pupils, although it predated the introduction of the government target of reducing school exclusions by one-third by 2002 (SEU, 2000c).

Sustained attention to the problem of disproportionate *black exclusions* is evident in various government strategy documents in the education field, particularly since

Figure 9.4: Rate of school exclusions, by ethnicity, 1997-98 to 2005-06

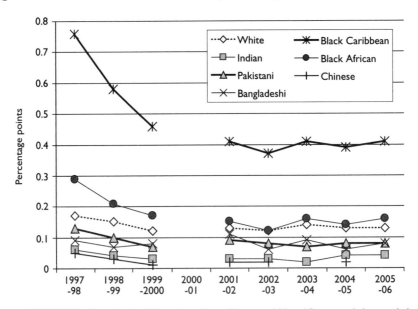

Source: DCSF (2007b). Data for Irish Travellers, Gypsy/Roma, and Mixed Race pupils have only been available since 2002-03 so these have been excluded from the graph but are discussed in the text

2002. Funding to reduce black exclusions has been made available under various national programmes including EiC, EMAG, the Standards Fund and the Street Crime Initiative. Local education authorities have mounted projects using social skills and anger management training, mentoring, counselling, assertive discipline, and minority ethnic-run support groups drawing on community expertise (see Parsons et al, 2005).

While there was a reduction in the number of school exclusions throughout the late 1990s for all ethnic groups, the most recent data (2005-06) on permanent exclusions is rather discouraging, showing that Black Caribbean, Irish Traveller, Gypsy/Roma and Mixed White/Black Caribbean pupils are still over three times as likely as White pupils to be permanently excluded, with only slightly lower exclusion rates for those of Black Other origin (DCSF, 2007b). Indian, Pakistani, Bangladeshi and Chinese pupils are either proportionately or underrepresented among those excluded.

A *Priority Review* by the Department for Education and Skills (DfES, 2006c) re-emphasised the importance of a school-wide commitment to race equality, effective monitoring, restorative approaches, the involvement of parents, and exclusion as a last resort. Targeting one hundred schools, teachers and senior managers would receive training on the impact of judgement and discretion on pupil outcomes, and the need to be 'race aware' in behaviour management strategies. It is too early to measure the effect of these proposals.

Summarising New Labour's interventions in education, it cannot be denied that its policies have had a considerable positive effect on attainment levels. However, ethnic inequalities are stubbornly enduring, particularly when considering the gap between the highest- and lowest-achieving groups. Renewed efforts must concentrate on low pupil and parental aspirations among the white working class and improving the extremely low levels of attainment among Traveller and Gypsy/Roma children. As the section on exclusions suggests, there is also a need to fundamentally change teacher perceptions about poor behaviour among black pupils as this is implicitly linked to educational attainment.

Employment and income

Like education, employment influences social status, quality of housing, health and leisure. As New Labour entered government, the Fourth National Survey of Ethnic Minorities (1997) demonstrated that at each qualification level, unemployment rates for Black Caribbean and Pakistani/Bangladeshi men and women were higher than for white men and women (Modood et al, 1997). This differential was reduced but did not wholly disappear for those of Indian and African Asian origin. A similar pattern was observed for male and female occupational attainment and men's average earnings[6] (see also EOC, 2007).

Analytical research commissioned by the Cabinet Office (2001) highlighted the complex explanations for labour market underachievement, relating to, on the demand side, fewer business opportunities in areas with high minority ethnic concentrations, with cultural and religious factors seeming to play a part (see also Clark and Drinkwater, 2007). On the supply side, lower skills and qualifications among some minority ethnic groups, poorer language fluency, poorer health, and the quality and location of childcare and transport facilities may all contribute to less advantageous outcomes. Racial discrimination also undoubtedly affects labour market experiences. Heath and Cheung's (2006, p 63) analysis of managers and employers' self-reported prejudice led them to conclude that 'there is a fairly clear parallel between the patterns of racial prejudice across broad industrial groupings and the patterns of sectoral choice and ethnic penalties in these groupings'.

Government policies

Increased minority ethnic participation in the labour market has been regarded by New Labour as a central plank in the strategy to reduce social exclusion and is outlined in Public Service Agreements for 2001-04 and 2005-08. The cost of the employment gap has been estimated at £8.6 billion for the cost of benefit payments, lost tax revenue and lost output (NAO and DWP, 2008).

Mainstream strategies to improve employment were critically assessed in Chapter Five. The early evidence on the impact of the New Deal for Young People from minority ethnic groups in Oldham found higher dropout rates at the Gateway stage compared with young white people. Moreover, disappointingly, fewer individuals from minority ethnic groups entered subsidised or unsubsidised employment, with more going into education and training or the voluntary sector options. It was unclear whether this reflected a greater degree of commitment to training, lack of choice or lower expectations by clients or advisers (Fieldhouse et al, 2002). Nationally, however, since 1998, 144,000 minority ethnic individuals have found work through the New Deals (EMETF, 2006).

In 2003, a 10-year vision for eliminating disproportionate barriers to minority ethnic employment was outlined by the Prime Minister's Strategy Unit, recognising that minority ethnic disadvantage had continued unabated for two decades (Cabinet Office, 2003). The agenda has been carried forward by the Ethnic Minority Employment Task Force (EMETF) with a three-pronged strategy embedded across Whitehall to enhance human capital through education, connect people to work by removing barriers, and promote equal opportunities in the workplace by reducing employer discrimination.

In the Taskforce's second annual report (EMETF, 2006), it reviewed progress up to 2006. Looking first to measures specifically targeted at minority ethnic groups, it found that the Ethnic Minority Outreach Programme, which ran from 2002 to 2006, using local minority ethnic providers of employment training and support, exceeded its original target of getting 32% of 'starters' into work with over 13,000 job entries. The programme appeared less effective in working with adult immigrants who often had some English for Speakers of Other Languages

(ESOL) needs, and some UK-born participants without work experience (Barnes et al, 2005). A further 2,500 people found jobs through projects funded under the Ethnic Minority Flexible Fund. The Fair Cities Programme, which ran in 2005-08, attempted to increase employer engagement and create 'pipelines' to jobs with major employers, and had 80% minority ethnic programme entrants. However, interim evaluations of pilot projects revealed that 47% of jobseekers had not secured a job offer, in large part because of implementation failures. The number placed in jobs was 248, around 10% of the target for the first year. Specialist Employment Advisers also operated in seven pilot areas (with higher minority ethnic unemployment) in 2004-06 in an attempt to build strategic relationships between Jobcentre Plus and employers, but an evaluation indicated that these were beleaguered by a lack of focus and trust (Pettigrew et al, 2005). Partners Outreach for Ethnic Minorities ran from January 2007 to March 2008 to engage non-working partners from low-income families who were not in contact with Jobcentre Plus, providing job search support, assistance finding culturally sensitive childcare, ESOL, soft skills and mentoring services. It has not yet been formally evaluated.

In New Labour's third term, a range of projects centred on disadvantaged areas have been initiated,[7] moving away from minority ethnic targeted provision. These have yet to bed down or be evaluated.

Outcomes

The data presented in Table 9.2 show that all minority ethnic groups, with the exception of men of Indian origin, had unemployment rates two to three times higher than the white majority in 1997. For both men and women, this pattern of employment inequality has persisted to the same degree in 2007. Notwithstanding, minority ethnic groups, particularly Black African and Pakistani men, and all minority ethnic women, have benefited from the significant drop in unemployment seen throughout the 1990s and early 2000s. Indeed, the absolute improvement was greatest for minority ethnic groups compared with the white majority ethnic group. The exceptions to this general trend appear to be men of Indian and Mixed Race origin and Pakistani women, the latter experiencing *increased* unemployment during New Labour's terms in office.

While men of Indian (and Chinese origin) perform better than other minority ethnic groups in terms of unemployment, earnings and occupational attainment, multivariate analyses reveal an ethnic penalty for all minority ethnic groups (Heath and Cheung, 2006). Controlling for educational qualifications, age, generation, marital status, year of survey, and region,[8] for example, still leaves minority ethnic men and women disadvantaged compared with their white counterparts. This goes some way to explaining why minority ethnic groups' position in the income distribution is generally lower than the white group and this too is a longstanding pattern. As Table 9.3 illustrates, even those of Chinese/other, and

Table 9.2: Unemployment rates (1997 and 2007) and % change

Ethnic origin	Unemployment rate, 1997	Unemployment rate, 2007	% point change, 1997-2007	% change, 1997-2007
Men				
White	4.7	3.3	1.4	−29.8
Indian	5.2	3.8	1.4	−26.9
Black Caribbean	14.4	10.6	3.8	−26.4
Black African	18.2	11.2	7.0	−38.5
Pakistani	10.2	6.5	3.7	−36.3
Bangladeshi	–	10.1*	–	–
Mixed	11.9	10.2*	1.7	−14.3
Women				
White	2.7	2.4	0.3	−11.0
Indian	5.8	4.6	1.2	−20.7
Black Caribbean	7.4	4.8	2.6	−35.1
Black African	11.4	7.0	4.4	−38.6
Pakistani	5.7	7.2	+1.5	+26.3
Mixed	–	7.3*	–	–

Notes: Labour Force Surveys do not include a Chinese subsample. Because of small sample sizes for Bangladeshi women they have been excluded from the table. *Data for 2006.

Source: ONS (2008e) using Labour Force Surveys

to a lesser degree Indian, origin experience poorer incomes, particularly after housing costs (AHC). Over one-half of those of Pakistani/Bangladeshi origin were in the bottom income quintile before housing costs (BHC) or AHC, according to the most recent figures available (DWP, 2006c, 2008b). New Labour policies have had only a limited impact in reducing income disparities or reducing the proportion in the bottom income quintile overall.

The EMETF's policy measures to increase employability, connect people with work and promote equal opportunities among employers are clearly important elements of increasing labour market participation among minority ethnic groups. The National Audit Office (NAO and DWP, 2008), however, has been critical of the lack of continuity in funding and resources for increasing minority ethnic employment. Still missing, moreover, is concerted action to reduce employer prejudice as illustrated in the study by Heath and Cheung (2006), which linked such prejudice to ethnic penalties.

The West Midlands model of contract compliance demonstrates the possibilities of reducing ethnic inequalities with contractors establishing and monitoring their equal opportunities policies and formalising recruitment practices so that

Table 9.3: Share of each ethnic group in the bottom income quintile

Ethnic group	1996-97 to 1998-99	2006-07
BHC		
White	19	19
Indian	28	23
Black	31	31
Pakistani/Bangladeshi	63	54
Mixed	–	27
Chinese/other	32	27
AHC		
White	19	18
Indian	26	25
Black	40	39
Pakistani/Bangladeshi	60	55
Mixed	–	34
Chinese/other	41	33

Source: DWP (2006c, 2008b) using Family Resources Survey data. Includes those in full-time self-employment

they are eligible for public contracts (Orton and Ratcliffe, 2005). In their review, Clark and Drinkwater (2007) point to the need for a more nuanced strategy that targets Pakistani, Bangladeshi and black men only. It is also worth considering that there may be a time lag on improved labour market performance among minority ethnic groups as higher educational attainment levels filter through a new cohort of employees in the coming years. However, given the considerable ethnic penalties in the labour market that remain despite educational performance, this may be overly optimistic.

Policing

While the Lawrence Inquiry (Macpherson, 1999) began with a specific focus on the police investigation of Stephen Lawrence's racist murder, its brief was widened to look at other problematic dimensions of police–minority ethnic community relations. Perhaps inevitably, given the historical significance of claims of oppressive policing by minority ethnic communities, stop and search practices also came under considerable scrutiny during the Inquiry. The *Home Secretary's Action Plan* (Home Office, 1999, p 3) established a Ministerial Priority 'to increase trust and confidence in policing amongst minority ethnic communities' and this led to an extensive reform programme within the police service. In this section, consideration is given to, first, the policing of racist incidents, and second, stop and search policing practices, given their centrality to the reform agenda.

Racist incidents and offences

Even before the Lawrence Inquiry reported its findings, New Labour's first flagship criminal justice legislation, the 1998 Crime and Disorder Act, introduced 'penalty enhancements' for *racially aggravated offences* of assault, harassment, public disorder and criminal damage. In so doing, New Labour recognised the fear and vulnerability generated by such crimes, which can spread to whole communities. Undoubtedly, this has had some effect in communicating that such victimisation is considered by the government as abhorrent.

The Macpherson Report (1999, pp 312-14) also acknowledged the devastating impact of non-criminal *racist incidents*, defined as 'any incident which is perceived to be racist by the victim or any other person'. Following the Inquiry, the Home Office produced a *Code of Practice on Reporting and Recording Racist Incidents* in April 2000 (Home Office, 2000), which applied to all statutory, voluntary and community organisations, and the Association of Chief Police Officers drafted its own guidance *Identifying and Combating Hate Crime* (Association of Chief Police Officers, 2000), which is now used by all police forces. Additionally, many police forces have created specialist units with officers specially trained to investigate racist and other hate crimes.

Such initiatives appear to have increased victims' willingness to report racist incidents to the police and have contributed to improved police recording practices, as can be seen in Figure 9.5, with more than a doubling (243%) of recorded incidents between 1997-98 and 1999-2000 (Home Office, 2003; see also Docking and Tuffin, 2005). Looking to the most recent figures for 2005-06 reveals an increase of 333% since 1997-98. British Crime Survey (BCS) estimates of racially motivated incidents, which are unaffected by the vagaries of victim reporting and police recording practices, appear to indicate that the rise in police-recorded incidents is the result of an increase in reporting and recording, and not an overall increase in victimisation. The BCS estimated that there were 139,000 racist incidents in 2005-06, which represented a marked fall on estimates of 206,000 recorded in 2002-04 (Jansson, 2006; Ministry of Justice, 2007a).

Evaluations of criminal justice practice post-Lawrence have been broadly encouraging. Docking and Tuffin's (2005) examination of police practice found well-developed systems for supervising police investigations of racist incidents, with somewhat higher levels of victim satisfaction, although this varied by police force, and was more common among victims dealt with by specialist rather than operational officers. This has now been matched by a higher clear-up rate for these offences, despite the difficulties involved in proving racial aggravation in court (Burney and Rose, 2002). In 2005-06, clear-up rates were higher for racially aggravated offences compared with non-racially aggravated equivalent offences (Ministry of Justice, 2007a). The Crown Prosecution Service proceeded to prosecute 84% of defendants charged with racially aggravated offences in

Figure 9.5: Police-recorded racist incidents and racially aggravated offences, 1995-96 to 2005-06

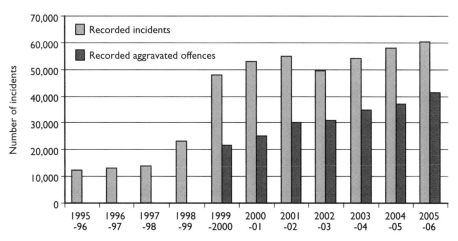

Source: Home Office (various) *Statistics on Race and the Criminal Justice System*

2006-07 (CPS, 2007), indicative of the seriousness with which racist victimisation has come to be viewed under New Labour. Following a pilot in West Yorkshire, there are plans to establish Hate Crime Scrutiny Panels across Crown Prosecution Service areas to increase prosecutions and reduce attrition.

Stop and search

More than 15 years before New Labour was elected, police use of stop and search[9] powers had been investigated by the Scarman Inquiry into the Brixton disorders (Scarman, 1981). Regarded then as a flashpoint in police–minority ethnic community relations, now too it remains a dominant theme because of the persistent ethnic disparities in the use of these powers and the attendant claims of racial discrimination.

As can be seen in Figure 9.6, in 1997-98 the rates of stop and search were 19 per 1,000 for the white population, but seven times higher at 139 per 1,000 for black people and two times higher for Asians at 45 per 1,000 (Home Office, 1998a). Criminologists have proposed a range of explanations for ethnic disproportionality in stop and search rates. These have included the legitimate possibilities that it is the younger age structure of the minority ethnic population, their greater 'availability' on the streets because of higher levels of school exclusions and unemployment, their residential concentration in higher crime areas where more stops and searches take place, and their elevated rates of offending particularly for 'street crime' (according to victim reports) that account for these higher rates (Bowling and Phillips, 2007).

Figure 9.6: Stops and searches per 1,000 population, by ethnic appearance (ascribed by police officers)

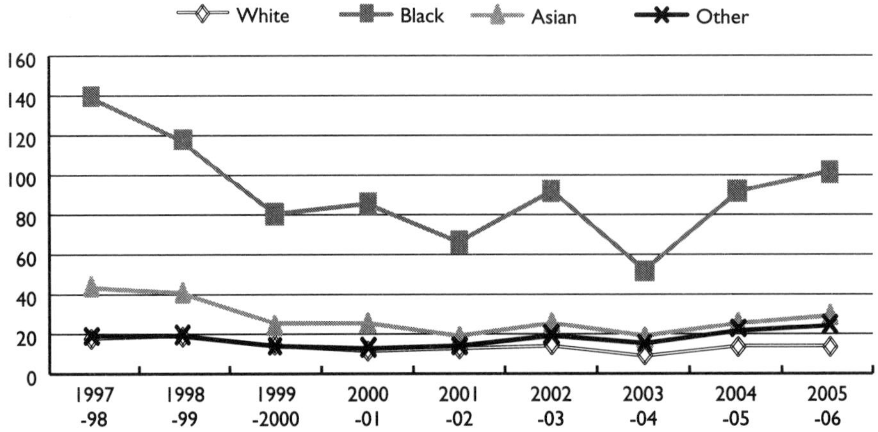

Source: Home Office (various) Section 95 Criminal Justice Act 1991 publications. Excludes stops only, and those conducted under road traffic legislation

However, even the Macpherson Report (1999, para 45.10) acknowledged that 'the majority of police officers who testified before us accepted that an element of the disparity was the result of discrimination'. Such discrimination has been informed by perceptions of black people as criminally disposed, drug-abusing and violent, with Asian men increasingly being perceived as disorderly, militant, culturally separatist and inclined towards Islamic terrorism (see Phillips and Bowling, 2007). While 'racial profiling' is not officially practised, some sources, such as minority ethnic police officers interviewed by Cashmore (2001, p 652), suggest that it occurs. They reported being advised to stop 'black kids with baseball caps, wearing all the jewellery', in order to enhance their performance levels: 'if you see four black youths in a car, it's worth giving them a pull, as at least one of them is going to be guilty of something or other'.

Stop and search has an extremely limited impact on crime disruption and detection (see Miller et al, 2000) and in 2004-05 only 11% resulted in an arrest, but the government has continued to support full use of these powers (Home Office, 2006). However, it has recognised the danger of reduced police legitimacy in minority ethnic communities and has tightened the regulation of police powers and attempted to increase accountability at the force and individual officer level. In August 2004, a revised 1984 Police and Criminal Evidence Act *Code of Practice A* was adopted, implementing Recommendation 61 of the Lawrence Inquiry that those stopped and searched should receive a written record containing legally credible reasons for their encounter with the police.[10] Force monitoring, it was envisaged, would 'flush out' individual officers, stations or forces that had unjustifiably high levels of ethnic disproportionality (Home Office, 2004). The revised Code[11] also more clearly specified the grounds for 'reasonable suspicion', which must exist before the power is used, requiring objective and specific intelligence rather than stereotypical generalisations about particular groups in society. Alongside the Home Office's Stop and Search Manual launched in 2005, in many police forces, independent scrutiny panels comprising community representatives have been established to critically assess local data on ethnic disproportionality.

Despite these developments in policy and practice, Figure 9.6 shows that the pattern of ethnic disproportionality in stop and search continues. In 2005-06, the rates of stop and search were 15 per 1,000 for the white population, but still seven times higher at 102 per 1,000 for black people and two times higher for Asians at 31 per 1,000 (Ministry of Justice, 2007a).[12] There was a decline in stop and search around the time of the Lawrence Inquiry as police officers became less confident in using stop and search legitimately. Foster et al's (2005) evaluation of the Lawrence Inquiry reforms reported that fears of being accused of racism had generated much anxiety and anger among operational police officers. It similarly underlined some officers' uncertainty about the legality of their stop and search practices. However, by 2005-06, the total numbers of stops and searches had returned to their 1996-97 levels (Ministry of Justice, 2007a). Central government-assisted efforts[13] to reduce violent crime (including robbery and crime involving weapons) and terrorism may explain the continued reliance on stop and search as a crime control tactic despite its low yield in terms of resultant arrests. The black:white ratio for stop and search has fluctuated somewhat (from 5:1 to 8:1) since New Labour has been in government; but not enough to dispel concerns about the unfair targeting of black people by the police service.

The publicity regularly given to ethnic disparities in stop and search most likely fuels broader concerns about discriminatory treatment by the agencies of the criminal justice system, illustrated in Figure 9.7. In 2005, minority ethnic groups still had more negative perceptions of, and lower confidence in, the system, particularly the police and prison service, than the majority white population. Ultimately, minimal progress towards the aim of increasing trust and confidence among minority ethnic groups appears to have been achieved.

Community cohesion

In the spring/summer of 2001, violent racialised confrontations between young Pakistani/Bangladeshi and white men and the police occurred in several Northern English towns. The official reports into the disturbances focused on communities experiencing 'parallel lives', inhabiting segregated residential, educational, occupational and leisure spaces, with much negative stereotyping of the 'other'. Fuelled by socioeconomic deprivation, problematic political leadership, disengagement, weak policing and the presence of extremist groups,

Figure 9.7: Minority ethnic and white people expecting to be treated worse than other races by criminal justice system in 2005 (%)

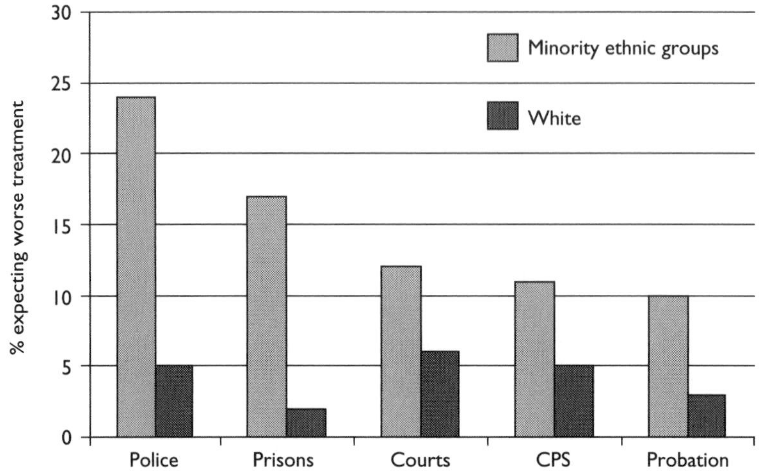

Source: Home Office (2006)

the disturbances were also linked to an absence of 'community cohesion' (Cantle, 2001; Denham, 2001).

Drawing on the original conceptualisation by Forest and Kearns (cited in Cantle, 2001, p 13), New Labour adopted the concept as a means for addressing broader concerns about ethnic identification, diversity, multiculturalism and integration. Definitions of community cohesion have emphasised a common vision and sense of belonging for all groups in a community, the positive valuation of diversity, similar life opportunities, and strong relationships between individuals from different backgrounds (see LGA, 2002). Initially, academic commentators were highly critical of what was regarded as an undue emphasis on self-segregation among Asian communities in the government's discourse on community cohesion (Amin, 2002; McGhee, 2003; Alexander, 2004). It was argued that this minimised the impact of socioeconomic disadvantage, racial discrimination, and segregation resulting from external constraints on settlement rather than choice decisions.

In April 2003, the government's Community Cohesion Unit established 14 Community Cohesion Pathfinder projects to assist in the development and dissemination of best practice. Local programmes included initiatives such as funding a voluntary sector worker to establish an inter-faith council, including a political champion in strategy groups and producing a video and feedback event to illustrate the perspectives of young people, parents and professionals. The progress report for the first six months emphasised the need for community cohesion to be well understood locally and for all government initiatives to be joined up at a local level (Home Office and Vantage Point, 2003). Further work, initially spearheaded by the independent Community Cohesion Panel, has included the provision of guidance on defining community cohesion, implementing local projects, particularly aimed at cross-cultural interaction, a practitioner toolkit and developing a performance management framework in local authorities and schools (see www.coventry.ac.uk/researchnet/icoco/a/2471#2001).

Academic criticism of the government's community cohesion discourse has been more muted since the government's strategies on race equality and community cohesion were brought together in *Improving Opportunity, Strengthening Society*, published in 2005 (Home Office, 2005). In this there is a greater balance between the expressed need for a common British identity and sense of belonging *and* the eradication of social and economic inequality between ethnic groups. The strategy document also makes explicit the need for white social participation and cultural appreciation to prevent alienation and resentment, as well as legislative protection against discrimination on the grounds of religious belief, which was introduced in 2003. Funding has also been made available to help faith-based groups develop better working strategies with government agencies.

In 2006 the advisory Commission on Integration and Cohesion's first report described internally complex communities, arguing for greater shared experiences expressed through the common language of English amid concerns about 'home-grown' Muslim terrorism (COIC, 2007a). Its final report recognised changing migration patterns and population dynamics (COIC, 2007b). Research in six case study sites highlighted that stakeholders often prioritised the need for social and economic well-being in proximate communities and were less persuaded that residential mixing automatically led to community cohesion. More important was meaningful interaction, participation and engagement, and recognising the need to include disparate groups in targeted and mainstream initiatives (Ipsos-MORI, 2007a). Promoting community cohesion is a developing area of social policy and as such it cannot yet be formally evaluated. Current thinking appears to be moving in the right direction, in that New Labour has somewhat belatedly acknowledged the need to address inequality as a prerequisite for enabling cohesive communities.

Assessing the impact of New Labour policies on ethnic inequalities

Since New Labour has been in government it has introduced policies to ameliorate the material and social disadvantage experienced by marginalised groups in society. Mainstream initiatives have produced impressive gains that have improved opportunities for both minority ethnic and white groups. With few exceptions, educational attainment levels have risen and unemployment rates have declined during New Labour's tenure.

However, this has not eradicated *ethnic inequalities*, which appear more resistant to changes in policy and practice, and this is particularly the case in the labour market. Despite targeted and tailored initiatives in New Labour's second and third terms, unemployment rates remain much higher for the minority ethnic population than for their white counterparts. The education gap has been more receptive to policy change and has narrowed considerably (but not closed) over the period 1997-07. The exceptions to this general pattern include children of Traveller and Gypsy/Roma heritage, white children from lower-socioeconomic status homes and black children from higher-socioeconomic status homes. Such entrenched disadvantage clearly requires more concerted policy action sustained through longer-term funding.

A similar mixed picture can be observed in the policing arena. Improved reporting and recording practices have been well documented alongside a welcome decline in racist victimisation. Such success is not evidenced in stop and search practices where black overrepresentation has barely altered during New Labour's time in office. This has undoubtedly affected perceptions of trust and confidence in criminal justice agencies, which have shown little sign of improvement since monitoring began. Promoting community cohesion has been a key aim of the New Labour government in its second and third terms, but there is little development work on the ground that has yet been critically evaluated.

In reflecting on this assortment of findings, it is not possible to definitively highlight successes and failures of government policy – either mainstream or targeted. Where initiatives appear to have had an impact (for example, EiC and the EMAG), a range of measures has been introduced to tackle the problem and their individual effects cannot usually be discerned. That said, four key issues emerge that have implications for future attempts to reduce ethnic inequalities.

First, the elimination of individual (direct and indirect) and institutional forms of racism and discrimination have tended not to be explicit elements of New Labour policy, with the exception of policing. While efforts have been made to improve service provision through the employment of minority ethnic officers and providers (for example, teachers, police officers, and in employment outreach work), less attention has been paid to discriminatory behaviour by teachers, employers, managers and police officers from the white majority ethnic group. The former efforts will not escape accusations of 'window dressing' (Cashmore, 2002) until the latter is more comprehensively addressed.

Second, there remain significant tensions in New Labour intentions and policies. 'Racially informed' choosing of schools by white parents is a mechanism through which quasi-market reforms in education militate against community cohesion and limit progress in disadvantaged and under-resourced schools with large Pakistani and black populations (Tomlinson, 1998). Likewise, disproportionality in the use of stop and search powers is unlikely to diminish when proactive policing initiatives to reduce street crime and terrorism target minority ethnic groups. Given the limited disruptive impact of stop and search on crime, this contradiction is hard to sustain in policy terms, despite pressures to reduce these very high-profile crimes. There may also be a clash between neoliberal approaches that privilege devolved decision making and budgets and the promotion of racial equality. Thus, school-based admissions policies that covertly select pupils on aptitude or ability can adversely affect disadvantaged groups, including those of minority ethnic origin (Pennell et al, 2006). Similarly, local recruitment of health staff can lead to biased employment practices that disadvantage minority ethnic employees (Carter, 2000). Such policy tensions are likely to play out to the detriment of minority ethnic groups, particularly those that experience social and economic disadvantage.

Third, managerialist tendencies that promote the auditing of race equality can obscure more deep-seated inequalities through bureaucratic obfuscation. Ahmed's (2007) study of the production of race equality documents in higher education described them as having fetish-like qualities concerned only with managing images of diverse organisations. Moreover, Ahmed (2007, p 597) described how 'having a "good" race equality policy was quickly translated into being good at race equality' without real engagement with the presence of racism in institutional practices. The empirical evidence reviewed in this chapter highlights the need for such documents to be action-oriented and not simply ends in themselves.

Fourth, and this is a general point, while pilot projects are likely to remain a pecuniary imperative, reversing long-term inequalities is likely to require funding commitments that last five years or more in order to allow for them to be fully implemented and embedded in practice. The difficulty lies in balancing the need for tailored programmes that aim to meet the specific needs of minority ethnic groups and avoiding claims of preferential treatment that are likely to exacerbate community tensions. Such challenges are likely to become even more diffuse in the coming years as politicians, policy makers and service providers respond to the increasingly diverse composition of British society, particularly with regard to ethnicity and faith, an issue more fully explored in Chapter Ten on migration, migrants and inequality.

Notes
[1] In EiC Phase 1 areas (September 1999), almost 40% of pupils were from minority ethnic backgrounds compared with 15% in Phase 2 (September 2000) and 25% in Phase 3 (September 2001). This compares with non-EiC areas where over 90% of pupils were from White British backgrounds (Kendall et al, 2005).

[2] This includes those for whom attainment data have been available since 1997.

[3] This uses Youth Cohort Study data for Chinese pupils in 1997 (Connolly, 2006) rather than national-level data.

[4] This is based on those groups for whom comparative attainment data have been available since 2003 and where additional empirical research has been undertaken to explain attainment patterns.

[5] The social class gap is estimated at 1.34 SD (higher managerial and professional versus long-term unemployed) and the ethnic gap is estimated at 0.65 SD (Indian versus Black Caribbean).

[6] Analysis of the Family Resources Survey by Berthoud (1998) also found lower average earnings for Chinese and African households.

[7] These include the Deprived Areas Fund and the City Strategy.

[8] The models for access to the salariat and hourly earnings additionally controlled for sector, part-time work and size of establishment.

[9] The police have extensive powers to stop and search individuals under a variety of legislation (see Bowling and Phillips, 2007, pp 937-8).

[10] This was a phased implementation beginning in seven police areas in April/May 2003 and completed in April 2005.

[11] Excludes later revisions that are not relevant to the current discussion.

[12] Ethnic disproportionality can also be seen in Section 60 of the 1994 Criminal Justice and Public Order Act in relation to stop/searches in anticipation of violence, where reasonable suspicion is not required by police officers, and under Section 44 of the 2000 Terrorism Act (see Phillips and Bowling, 2007).

[13] For example, funding was made available to the five metropolitan police forces with significant robbery problems in 2000, followed by the Street Crime Initiative in 2002, and local Crime and Disorder Reduction Partnerships have included targets to reduce robbery since 1999.

TEN

Migration, migrants and inequality

Jill Rutter and Maria Latorre

Introduction

Although international migration has always been a feature of national life, this aspect of population change has increased substantially since the 1990s, mostly as a result of asylum arrivals to the UK between 1990 and 2002, sustained work visa flows and large-scale migration from the new European Union (EU) member states after 2004. This substantial population change presents two challenges to those concerned with equality and poverty reduction. First, how are migrant communities faring in terms of their labour market experiences, educational outcomes and progress towards equality. Second, how, if at all, does migration impact on the employment prospects, wages and employment conditions of non-migrants?

This chapter focuses on these two questions. It examines who has migrated to the UK in the period 1997-2007 and analyses the changing socioeconomic profiles of migrant communities. The chapter then examines the impact of migration on broader progress towards greater equality in the UK.

Definitions and data sources

The United Nations (UN) definition of migrants is persons who are resident outside their country of birth. In the UK, many migrants have British citizenship and have been resident in the UK for many years and might also be described as members of minority ethnic communities (see Chapter Nine). This chapter uses the term 'foreign-born' to describe those living outside their country of birth, and uses the term 'new migrants' in a qualitative sense to describe those new to the UK.

The chapter primarily draws on Census 2001 and Labour Force Survey (LFS) data for its analysis of both migrant communities and the impacts of migration on the UK-born population. The LFS is a quarterly survey, which, like the Census, includes questions about country of birth that can be analysed alongside other variables such as total income and occupation. Country-of-birth data are used to define migrant groups in this chapter, rather than ethnicity or nationality variables. As noted in Chapter Nine, ethnicity categories in both the Census and the LFS are very broad and aggregate diverse groups. Somalis and Nigerians, for example, are grouped together as Black Africans. Nationality data are also imprecise, as migrants may retain the citizenship of their country of birth, take up British citizenship, possess the citizenship of a third country or be stateless.

There are a number of inherent problems with the LFS. First, the LFS is a quarterly survey based on a sample of about 100,000 people and is therefore prone to sampling errors (ONS, 2003). These errors get proportionally larger the smaller the country-of-birth group. For this reason, data on smaller country-of-birth groups are not presented. Second, the LFS does not sample business addresses, and there have been criticisms that it undercounts migrants living in tied accommodation on farms or in hotels. Third, irregular migrants may be unwilling to take part in the LFS. Fourth, the qualification levels of immigrants may be underestimated in the LFS as it classifies overseas qualifications, including those at a higher level as 'other qualifications' (Manacorda et al, 2006). For this reason, the 2001 Census is used in the analysis of qualifications.

Despite these weaknesses, the LFS represents the best and most up-to-date picture of migrants in the UK and enables researchers to map differences between and within country-of-birth groups.

Who are migrants?

The foreign-born population of the UK increased from 4.2% of the population in 1951 to an estimated 6.2% at the end of 1997. In 2007, the foreign-born population was estimated to be 10.7% of the total population, of whom just under 45% had arrived since 1997. This foreign-born population of the UK is increasingly diverse, in terms of their national origin and residency (immigration) status. Table 10.1 presents LFS data on the largest 25 foreign-born groups resident in the UK, and on the proportions of the population who have arrived since 1997.

While Table 10.1 gives population data on the largest foreign-born communities resident in the UK, it does not represent the national diversity of the UK's foreign-born population. There are nationals of almost every country in the world living in the UK. Population 'super-diversity' is an increasing feature of British cities. In the past, UK migrant and minority populations comprised a small number of large communities, predominately from the UK's former colonies. Today, many parts of the UK manifest super-diversity where many different communities live side by side. These communities are diverse not only in their national origin, but also in terms of their residency status, ethnicity, language, household composition, employment experiences, educational qualifications as well as factors such as religious and political affiliations. This super-diversity presents challenges to those concerned with equality as much existing quantitative data on issues such as educational achievement, post-16 education and training use very broad ethnicity codes and, as noted above, these aggregate very diverse groups.

Table 10.1: Numbers of foreign-born residents in the UK, by country of birth, for 25 largest groups, 1997-2007

Country	LFS population estimate		% of country-of-birth group who have arrived since quarter four 1997[1]
	quarter four 1997	quarter four 2007	
India	404,100	591,500	43
Poland	67,800	457,600	91
Ireland	534,600	410,400	10
Pakistan	222,400	393,000	33
Germany	251,600	268,100	23
South Africa	93,400	204,800	60
China and Hong Kong	86,500	192,700	74
Bangladesh	140,200	177,100	28
US	126,800	176,800	59
Jamaica	139,900	175,000	20
Nigeria	59,400	146,000	50
Kenya	122,300	141,700	11
Australia	85,900	124,800	56
Sri Lanka	51,200	119,700	47
Italy	91,800	98,600	36
France	66,400	97,100	61
Zimbabwe	<40,000	96,000	75
Somalia	46,100	93,300	72
Philippines	<40,000	90,300	74
Ghana	41,300	80,600	49
Turkey	64,600	71,300	50
Cyprus	57,200	69,800	15
Malaysia	48,100	64,500	45
Portugal	<40,000	63,300	59
Iran	<40,000	62,900	48

Note: [1] Because migrants come and go from the UK, many of them staying a short period of time, these figures do not equal the difference between 1997 and 2007 population estimates.

Source: LFS and ippr calculations

Migrants from EU states comprise the largest foreign-born population resident in the UK. They include migrants from pre-2004 EU states such as Ireland, France and Portugal, as well as those from the new accession states. European Union law gives them freedom of movement within Europe and the right of residence as European Economic Area (EEA) workers.[1] European Union migrants who have secured EEA worker status also qualify for social housing and in-work benefits in the UK.

Those born in Ireland and France are the largest migrant groups from the 'old' EU. Portuguese migrant workers are also a substantial group, with one wave of migration occurring in the mid-1970s and a more recent movement since 2000, with many of the latter employed in the agricultural and food processing sectors. By far the largest national groups from new accession states of the EU are the Poles, of whom an estimated 457,600 were resident in the UK at the end of 2007.[2] Unlike most previous migrations to the UK, where most new arrivals tended to settle in urban areas, significant proportions of migrants from the EU's new accession states have settled in the countryside, which in the past has received very few new migrants (CRC, 2007).

In the last five years there has also been a significant onward migration of migrant communities from other EU countries to the UK. One of the largest of this type of migratory movement is that of Somalis from the Netherlands, Germany and Scandinavia. Other large onward migratory movements to the UK include Nigerians and Ghanaians from Germany and Austria, Sri Lankan Tamils from France and Germany and Latin Americans from Spain and Portugal. (There is very little movement of groups such as the Somalis out of the UK.) While many of these onward migrants have secured EU citizenship or refugee status elsewhere in the EU, some are irregular migrants (Koser, 2005). Most will have received their education outside the EU and may have different qualifications and prior employment profiles to other EU-born groups who have moved to the UK. For example, a Somali onward migrant may well have a similar background to a refugee from that country.

Labour migrants also come from outside the EU. In 2006, some 96,600 work permit and other work visa holders came to the UK from outside the EU. In 2006, the main countries of origin of work permit holders were South Africa, India, Pakistan, Bangladesh, China, Japan, the Philippines and Australia (Home Office, 2007). The work visa scheme is undergoing simplification and change and will be a five-tier system by 2009:

- Tier 1 – a points-based scheme for highly skilled migrants;
- Tier 2 – a points-based scheme for skilled workers with a job offer who will be employed to fill gaps in the UK labour market;
- Tier 3 – low-skilled temporary workers;
- Tier 4 – students;
- Tier 5 – a points-based youth mobility scheme, where the aim of working in the UK is not primarily economic. Au pairs will be admitted through this route, for example.

For the new points-based work visas, points are awarded for qualifications. English language fluency is also a prerequisite for Tier 1 and Tier 2 migrants.

Asylum seekers and refugees comprise another migratory movement. Although the numbers of asylum applications has decreased since a peak in 2002, some 23,430 asylum applications were lodged in the UK in 2007 (Home Office, 2008). Since 2002, the main countries of origin of asylum seekers have been the Democratic Republic of Congo, Eritrea, Somalia, Zimbabwe, Turkey, Afghanistan, China, Iran, Iraq and Sri Lanka.

Of those who received an initial decision on their asylum applications in 2007, some 16% were granted refugee status, another 11% were granted humanitarian protection or discretionary leave to remain in the UK. In 2007, some 73% of asylum applicants were refused asylum after an initial decision (Home Office, 2008). While some of those refused asylum leave the UK or are removed, the vast majority remain and make up a significant component of the UK's irregular migrant population.

Small numbers of refugees have also come to the UK through the Gateway Protection Programme and other programmes for vulnerable refugees (Home Office, 2008).[3]

Some 47,100 *spouses, fiancé(e)s* and *civil partners* were admitted to the UK in 2006 (Home Office, 2007). In 2006, the top five countries of origin of spouses were Pakistan, India, Bangladesh, the US and Thailand. The numbers of *overseas students* from outside the EU have gradually increased in the last 15 years, with some 309,000 admitted to the UK in 2006. Overseas students generally have the right to part-time employment in the UK. Many overseas students return home after completing their studies although there have been a number of initiatives to retain overseas university graduates in the UK labour market, for example, the Fresh Talent: Working in Scotland scheme and its English equivalents.

A further group of international migrants are *British nationals 'returning' to the UK.* Research suggests that in 2005 there were 5.5 million British nationals living abroad (Sriskandarajah and Drew, 2006). British nationals who live abroad are a diverse population and returnees are equally diverse. They include those returning to the UK after short periods working abroad, and long-term migrants who have maintained their British passports and are now faced with changed circumstances necessitating a 'return' to a country with which they may have few connections.

There are also an unknown number of *irregular migrants* in the UK. This group of people mostly comprises visa and asylum overstayers, as well as a smaller number of clandestine entrants (ippr, 2006). Research commissioned by the Home Office estimated that in 2001 the irregular migrant population was between 310,000 and 530,000 people (Pinkerton et al, 2004). This figure is likely to be higher now as a result of the 2002 peak in asylum migration and the larger numbers of work and visitor visas that have been granted in the last five years (Home Office, 2007).

Research that has examined the survival strategies of irregular migrants highlights low-income levels and reliance on the informal sector for employment. Many irregular migrants are working at rates near to or below the National

Minimum Wage, and fear of officialdom makes it difficult for them to seek redress for this. Yet, informal sector working and the hidden nature of irregular migration may mean that datasets that are meant to capture patterns of inequality may not enumerate irregular migrants. However, increased irregular migration has been a major facet of increased migrant inequality since 1997.

Residency status and benefit entitlement

Since the establishment of the post-1945 welfare state, government has relied on a safety net to prevent people falling into destitution and to ameliorate the worst effects of inequality. However, many migrants have no entitlement to claim benefits – at present only those who have secured British citizenship, or possess EEA worker status or settled status (indefinite leave to remain), and those who have received a positive decision on their asylum case can access the UK benefit system.

Among migrants who are entitled to benefits, their take-up is at a lower rate than the UK-born population (Roney and Cook, 2008). This is a consequence of a lack of awareness of entitlements among migrants, an inability to understand the application process, often as a result of limited English language fluency, and an inability to produce documentation to support a benefit claim. There are obvious consequences of low take-up of these benefits in relation to household income and poverty levels. Failure by migrants to register for benefits such as free school meals also distorts some measures of inequality.

Since the mid-1980s, increasing proportions of migrants have had their welfare safety net removed, and a proportion has been rendered entirely destitute. This is a process that continues, with new immigration legislation, proposed for 2009, likely to restrict further the rights to benefits of migrants (BIA, 2008).

In 1995 and 1996, the-then government attempted to remove benefits from asylum seekers who had lodged their claims 'in country' rather than at the port of entry, as well as those appealing against a negative initial decision. The 1999 Immigration and Asylum Act profoundly changed the way in which asylum seekers were housed and supported in the UK. Removing existing rights to housing and all types of benefits, the Act set up a new housing and welfare scheme for asylum seekers, administered by the UK Border Agency. Homeless asylum seekers were housed in specially commissioned emergency accommodation when they first arrived in the UK. With legislation preventing them from working in the UK, they had the option to apply for a 'subsistence only' package, or for subsistence and accommodation. Until April 2002, subsistence entailed a cash allowance of £10 per person per week, plus vouchers exchangeable at designated retail outlets. Vouchers were abolished in April 2002, and replaced by a cash allowance, although adult asylum seekers are still supported at levels below Income Support that is offered to mainstream claimants (Burchardt, 2005). An account of the poverty faced by many asylum seekers is given in *Poverty and Asylum in the UK* (Penrose, 2002).

For most asylum seekers, housing and support cease after the asylum and appeal process is exhausted. However, the government's own estimates suggest that about 300,000 former asylum seekers remain in the UK at the end of this process, unable or unwilling to return to their home country, joining a larger population of irregular migrants. Some of them find work, but some live a hand-to-mouth existence, reliant on the charity of compatriots and non-governmental organisations (Lewis, 2007). Many pro-migrant organisations would argue that the undoubted increase in destitution among irregular migrants since 1997 is a fundamental inconsistency for a country that desires to move to greater equality. The response of many governments across Europe has been to argue that equality policies apply only to citizens and those who have a legal residence status.

What qualifications and skills do migrants bring to the UK?

Among migrants who are legally allowed to work in the UK, many factors influence their labour market experiences. Much research has suggested that among the most important factors that determine whether a migrant will find work are fluent spoken English and a UK qualification (Bloch, 2004). Arrival in the UK with an overseas qualification also confers an advantage in jobseeking, but less so than a UK qualification.

An analysis of Census and LFS data suggests that the qualifications profile of the foreign-born population is much more polarised than the UK-born population (see Table 10.2). The foreign-born population is much more likely to possess a higher-level qualification than the UK-born population. But higher proportions of foreign-born groups possess no qualifications at all. For example, 31% of those born in the Democratic Republic of Congo possess higher-level qualifications, but 29% possess no qualifications and research suggests that about 30% of Congolese women resident in the UK have received little or no schooling (Haringey Council, 1997; Rutter, 2003).

There are a number of country-of-birth groups where high proportions of population have no qualifications, including India, Ireland, Pakistan, Bangladesh, Jamaica, Italy, Somalia, Turkey, Portugal, Cyprus and Afghanistan-born populations. These are all groups who experience higher levels of unemployment and lower average earnings than the UK-born population.

There are also migrant groups whose educational participation, as well as ability to find work or find work appropriate to their skills, is impeded by poor levels of English: those born in Poland, Bangladesh, Sri Lanka, Somalia, Turkey, Iraq and Slovakia. Poor English does not mean that migrants will be unable to find any work, rather that their employment options may be more restricted than the overall population.

Table 10.2: Qualifications and basic skills profiles of 15 largest country-of-birth groups, 2007

Country of birth	% aged 16-74 with higher level of qualifications	% aged 16-74 with lower level of qualifications	% aged 16-74 with no qualifications or qualifications unknown	% aged more than 16 with difficulties in language, literacy or keeping/finding job
UK	18	46	36	2
India	31	24	45	11
Poland	35	31	35	24
Ireland	21	26	53	31
Pakistan	18	24	59	18
Germany	29	49	22	3
South Africa	45	41	14	3
China and Hong Kong	44	22	34	14
Bangladesh	13	28	59	21
US	59	29	12	0
Jamaica	17	29	54	0
Nigeria	54	36	11	0
Kenya	30	46	24	4
Australia	52	36	13	0
Sri Lanka	33	55	12	21
Italy	25	26	49	10

Sources: ippr calculations, Census 2001 and LFS

The government has responded to these challenges mostly by increasing the budget for English for Speakers of Other Languages (ESOL) and targeted and non-targeted interventions to improve the skills and job-readiness of migrants. Between 2001 and 2004, the government tripled the total budget for adult ESOL, which in England is delivered through the Skills for Life Programme. New ESOL for Work qualifications were introduced in 2007 to meet the needs of migrants who are already in employment. Despite the increase in total funding, there remain some long-term problems in the delivery of adult ESOL that do not seem to have improved since 1997. Too much teaching is of poor quality and many students do not progress beyond the most basic levels (NIACE, 2006). There is also little evidence of colleges and adult education services developing alternative models of provision to meet the needs of a rural working population (Rutter and Latorre, 2008a).

Generation 1.5

Many foreign-born populations have spent most or all of their educational career in UK institutions, having migrated as children, a group sometimes called Generation 1.5 (Rumbaut and Portes, 2001). Their qualifications profile is different from those who have migrated as adults. The polarised educational profile of some adult migrant groups, encompassing the illiterate and those holding PhDs, does not apply to Generation 1.5. Nevertheless, patterns of educational achievement are diverse among child migrants.

Education departments in all parts of the UK do not collect country-of-birth data. In England, data on school achievement tends to be analysed using broad ethnicity categories, although local authorities can collect more nuanced data by using extended ethnicity codes. This system allows broad ethnicity categories – for example, White UK, Black African – to be refined using extended categories, such as extended ethnicity codes for Nigerians and Somalis. Any analysis of migrant children's educational achievement has to use extended ethnicity codes as a proxy for migrant groups and is further hampered by incomplete national data, as not all local authorities use extended codes.

Table 10.3 shows GCSE performance, as measured by the proportion securing five GCSEs at grades A★-C, by ethnic group in 2003, for the local authorities that collected data on a particular ethnic group. It should be noted that the numbers of local authorities collecting data on Portuguese and Italian children was (and still remains) very small.

Achievement at GCSE level has improved for all ethnic groups since 2003. In 2003, just 22.8% of Somali students of their age cohort secured five GCSEs at grades A★-C, compared with a national average of 51% of the age cohort of all ethnicities (DfES, 2005c). In 2005, this figure was 29%, compared with 55% of their age cohort (DCSF, 2007d). While there have been recent improvements, there is still significant educational underachievement in some migrant and minority communities. This gap will impact on the labour market participation and earnings potential of some of Generation 1.5.

A more detailed analysis of local authority data highlights some worrying trends. There are big differences in male and female school achievement among some communities – girls do better than boys – but much less so among others. The gender differential is high among Turkish-speaking pupils. Among Somali pupils, there was little or no gender gap in the mid-1990s, but now girls are achieving much higher results than boys in most, although not all, local authorities (Rutter, J., 2006). In some local authorities the proportion of some migrant children leaving school with no qualifications appears to be increasing (Rutter and Newman, 2008).

There are multiple causes of these differential levels of achievement, some of which relate to the specific pre-migration and migratory experiences of these groups. Among the Portuguese, for example, negative parental educational

Table 10.3: 2003 GCSE performance by ethnic group, mean % difference from England mean

Ethnic group	Mean % difference in proportion achieving five A*-C grades relative to mean for England, 2003
Chinese	+11.0
Sri Lankan	+8.0
Indian	+7.0
Iranian	+5.0
Irish	+4.5
Filipino	+4.5
French	+3.0
Nigerian	+1.5
White British	+1.0
Ghanaian	−0.8
Italian	−1
Cypriot	−5.5
Bangladeshi	−9.3
Pakistani	−11.3
Jamaican	−15.3
Somali	−22.8
Turkish	−23.6
Portuguese	−32.3

Sources: DfES and ippr calculations

experiences, a culture of leaving school early, in-work poverty, poor and overcrowded housing, a lack of English language support in schools and parental absences from the home due to shift work appear to be significant causes of underachievement. Among Somalis, an interrupted or non-existent education prior to migration to the UK is a significant cause of underachievement (Rutter, J., 2006).

In England and Wales, there is some targeted funding for children who have English language learning needs. The Ethnic Minority Achievement Grant (EMAG) funds language support for this group in England (see Chapter Nine). It also targets funding for 'nationally under-achieving minority ethnic groups', who it defines as children of Bangladeshi, Pakistani, Black Caribbean and Black African origin. However, the size of grant has not kept pace with numbers of migrant children entering schools needing to learn English. A lack of English language support, and thus a lack of academic literacy, appears to be a major cause of underachievement among some migrant groups. The prevailing anti-migration climate may make the government reticent to increase funding for migrants.

Labour market participation among migrants

The labour market experiences of migrants are as diverse as their qualifications profile (see also Chapter Nine). As can be seen from Table 10.4 and Figure 10.1 some country-of-birth groups have higher levels of employment than the UK-born population and some have lower levels of employment.

Broadly, the employment status of different migrant groups relates to their mode of entry into the UK. Newly arrived EU migrants and work visa holders, who

Table 10.4 Employment status, by country of birth, for 25 largest groups

Country of birth	% working-age population who were employed 1997	% working-age population who were employed 2007	% working-age population who were unemployed 2007	% working-age population who were economically inactive 2007
UK	76	79	4	18
India	65	70	5	26
Poland	56	86	4	10
Ireland	67	73	4	23
Pakistan	40	48	5	47
Germany	77	79	4	17
South Africa	82	85	2	12
China and Hong Kong	78	72	6	21
Bangladesh	35	46	6	48
US	75	80	3	17
Jamaica	59	71	8	21
Nigeria	69	83	6	11
Kenya	75	77	2	20
Australia	79	88	2	9
Sri Lanka	69	74	6	20
Italy	73	79	8	13
France	78	85	5	10
Zimbabwe	n/a	82	7	11
Somalia	11	29	11	60
Philippines	n/a	88	2	10
Ghana	67	84	6	10
Turkey	49	52	8	41
Cyprus	59	66	5	29
Malaysia	74	84	1	15
Portugal	63	74	5	21
Iran	64	54	7	39

Sources: LFS and ippr calculations

Figure 10.1: Employment rate for UK-born, Somalia-born and Bangladesh-born people, 1997-2007*

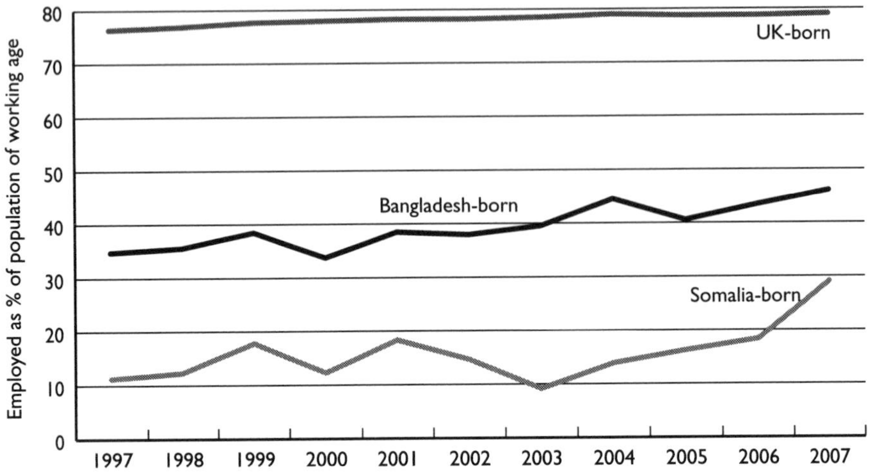

Note: *Excludes full-time students.
Sources: LFS and ippr calculations

have essentially come to the UK to work, have high levels of employment. Those populations who have come to the UK as refugees tend to have much lower levels of employment – for example, just 29% of Somalia-born adults and 35% of Afghanistan-born adults of working age were employed in 2007.[4] Research on barriers to labour market participation among refugees suggests that poor levels of fluency in English, employer prejudice, the absence of qualifications, childcare obligations and the fear of loss of benefits and social housing contribute to high levels of unemployment (Bloch, 2004). Poor health, reluctance among highly skilled refugees to seek unskilled work and reluctance to invest time in retraining have also been identified as barriers to work (Rutter and Newman, 2008).

Longer-settled populations from Bangladesh and Pakistan also experience low levels of employment: just over 46% of the Bangladesh-born population were in work in 2007.[5] Many of this group are older and reside in northern cities. Their barriers to work include the absence of qualifications needed in a changed industrial landscape.

Table 10.4 also shows that the employment rate for most country-of-birth groups has increased since 1997, as it has for UK-born persons. This increase is probably largely due to a healthier economy, a factor that has benefited migrants and non-migrants alike. But there are three exceptions to this overall trend: the employment rate of those born in Canada, China and Iran has decreased. The arrival of much greater numbers of Chinese students during the last five years may account for a decrease in working Chinese migrants, as many Chinese students have sufficient means not to work while studying in the UK. (Some 38,280

Chinese nationals were admitted as students in 2006, making them the second largest overseas student group in the UK; Home Office, 2007.) For Iran-born populations, their falling employment rate has been caused by marked changes in the background of migrants. In 1997, many Iranians were refugees who had migrated to the UK around the time of the 1979 Revolution. Many had been students in the UK and were consequently well-educated English speakers who hailed from more prosperous families. Later arrivals have tended to be less well qualified and from less prosperous areas, particularly those from Iranian Kurdistan. Census data suggest that 66% of the Iran-born population possessed higher-level qualifications in 1991, whereas in 2001 this figure was just 12%.

There have been a number of welfare-to-work interventions targeted at specific communities or groups such as refugees. These include training funded by the Learning and Skills Council, the European Social Fund, the New Deal for Communities and the Neighbourhood Renewal Fund (now the Working Neighbourhood Fund) and mostly delivered by colleges and migrant groups. Non-targeted interventions include Jobcentre Plus welfare-to-work programmes.

As already noted, employment levels for most migrants have increased since 1997. But it may create a false sense of success to claim that this increased employment is a direct result of interventions. Among the Bangladesh-born population, increased employment may be a result of a more healthy economy and the entry into the labour market of more qualified members of Generation 1.5 (Rutter and Newman, 2008). Indeed, there have been many criticisms of the effectiveness of Jobcentre Plus welfare-to-work programmes for unemployed migrants, in particular their inflexibility and failure to meet the requirements of those with multiple social needs (Harker and Oppenheim, 2007). Most jobseekers – regardless of their particular needs – are treated in the same way. Those who have multiple or complex needs – for example a refugee with little literacy or English – are offered the same kind of support as other jobseekers. Some programmes require people to work through a specified set of activities, such as filling in a set number of job application forms. Present welfare-to-work programmes are based on a 'work first' approach, informed by strong evidence that gaining a job offers better long-term prospects than attending training while on benefit. This assumption may not be appropriate to migrant communities who lack fluency in English and may not be able to enter the labour market because of this.

The earnings of migrants

The patterns of earnings of migrants are also diverse, between and within groups. Some country-of-birth groups such as those born in Australia and the US earn more than the UK-born population. Others, particularly those from the EU's new member states, earn far less, with those born in Poland earning an average of £7.30 per hour in 2007 (see Figure 10.2). The overrepresentation of new member state migrants in elementary occupations and in sectors such as agriculture and hospitality, where wage rates are low, accounts for this. Research on the earnings of previous migrant groups suggests that, over time, migrants' earnings may converge with the UK-born population, so it remains to be seen whether the low earnings of workers from the EU's new member states will persist over time (Dickens and McKnight, 2008c).

Earnings have increased at a rate above the rate of inflation since 1997 for all country-of-birth groups, with the exception of those born in Poland. The UK-born population has seen an increase in the average gross hourly pay of 18% in real terms since 1997, and the Somalia-born population an increase of 80%, although their earnings are still far below the UK average. Income inequalities *within* country-of-birth groups persist and these inequalities are most stark among refugee communities. Some 27% of the Somalia-born population in work had a weekly income from all sources of under £100 per week in 2007, compared with 10% of the UK-born population.

Many migrants have an additional demand on their income – remittance payments. It was been estimated that £1.5 billion was sent from the UK as remittance payments in 2005 (Datta et al, 2006). Migrants who are newly arrived in the UK are more likely to send home more remittances than longer-established migrant groups. Research with low-paid migrant workers in London indicated that they were sending home between 20 and 30% of their net income and engaged in many different money-saving strategies to do this. Having more than

Figure 10.2: Average gross hourly pay of selected country-of-birth groups, 2007 (£)

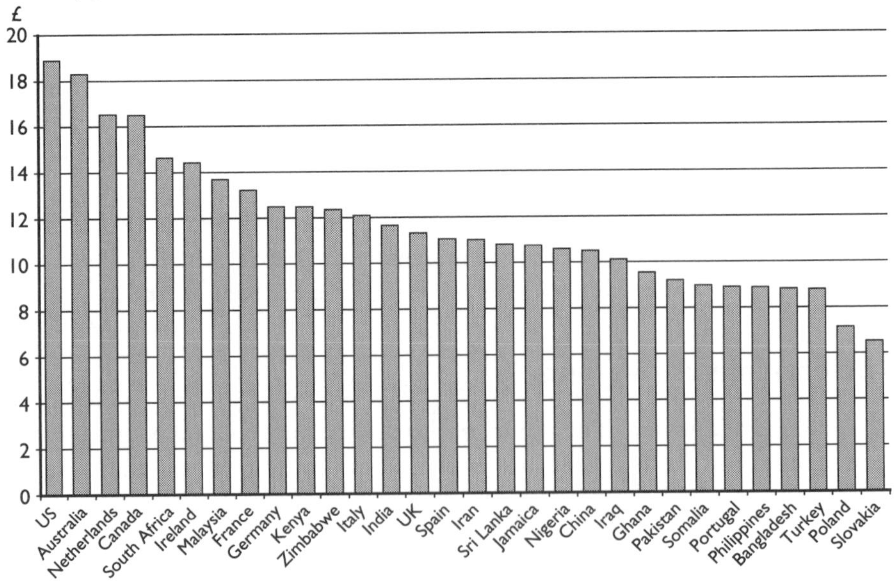

Sources: LFS and ippr calculations

one job, 'hot-bedding' and eating the cheapest food were common approaches (Datta et al, 2006). Remittance payments also impact on the children of migrants who are resident in the UK (Rutter, J., 2006). Income inequalities, coupled with a lower take-up of in-work benefits and the demands of remittance payments, contribute to the persistence of poverty among migrants.

Housing and health inequalities

Much writing of the last 30 years has also highlighted major housing and health inequalities among some migrant groups. Analysis appears to show that some of these inequalities have widened since 1997 (Sellen et al, 2002; Robinson et al, 2007; Taylor and Newall, 2008).

Figure 10.3 shows that patterns of housing tenure among migrant communities are very different from those of the UK-born population. New migrants to the UK are overwhelmingly housed in the private rental sector. Of those who have arrived in the UK during the last five years, some 63% were private tenants in 2007. Just over a tenth of this group were social tenants, but they make up less than 2% of all social tenants. A number of factors account for this differential pattern of housing tenure, of which immigration status and income are the most important. Most new migrants are not entitled to social housing on arrival – only migrants who have EEA worker status, have settled status in the UK or have received a positive decision on their asylum application have an entitlement to social housing (Rutter and Latorre, 2008b). Lower income and savings mean that migrants are unable to purchase property.

The proportion of migrants who rent privately or are housed by social landlords has not changed significantly since 1997. Housing overcrowding has increased in London, with migrants affected disproportionately by this trend (LHF, 2004).

Figure 10.3: Housing tenure distribution, by country of birth, 2006-07

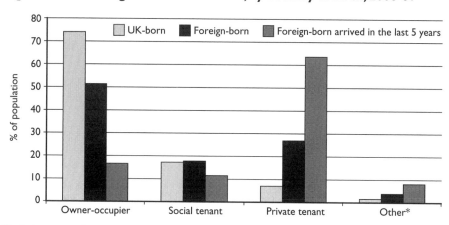

*Includes renting from relative of household member or related to work
Source: LFS 2006Q4-2007Q3

Much qualitative research on migrant housing has highlighted issues such as substandard tied accommodation and the inability of migrant populations to seek redress for poor housing (Roney and Cook, 2008; Rutter and Latorre, 2008b). These concerns are so widespread that the government has commissioned a review of migrant housing as part of a larger review of the private rental sector (DCLG, 2008d).

Over time, migrants leave the private rental sector and become owner-occupiers or social tenants. But only the Kenya-born population has a higher rate of owner-occupancy (80%) than the UK-born population (74%). Among communities that are largely newly established in the UK, for example Ghanaians and Somalis, rates of owner-occupancy are much lower (30.5% and 2.5% respectively).

Larger families with lower incomes may be unable to afford to purchase suitable property and will be more reliant, if entitled to it, on social housing. Family size among some foreign-born populations is higher than the UK-born population. The Afghanistan, Bangladesh, Pakistan and Somalia-born populations have the highest proportion of families with five or more children. These groups are overwhelmingly housed in the rental sector.

Where housing is of high cost, greater proportions of migrants remain in social housing. This factor partly accounts for the high proportions of foreign-born populations in social housing in Inner London in comparison with other parts of the UK. Greater London has the highest proportion of those living in temporary accommodation of any government region. Partly as a result of their location in London, migrant communities are overrepresented in temporary accommodation and spend longer in such accommodation than do UK-born households.

In the UK, there are also significant health inequalities by country of birth, although epidemiological data are under-analysed from the perspective of international migration. Stillbirth at term and infant mortality are significantly higher among African, Asian and Caribbean-born populations than for those born in the UK. They are highest for Pakistan-born populations, a trend partly attributed to cousin marriage, although there are marked class and region-of-origin differences in this practice among Pakistanis (Shaw, 2008). Infant mortality is also almost as high among mothers born in the Caribbean and West Africa, where consanguinity is uncommon. A child born to a mother born in the Caribbean is twice as likely to die before the age of five than a child born to a UK-born mother.[6] Poverty and absence of contact with health professionals are factors that may contribute to increased mortality (Taylor and Newall, 2008).

Almost all migrant groups have a lower life expectancy than the UK-born population, although there are significant differences in the causes of death among different country-of-birth groups. Analysis of the ONS Longitudinal Study suggests that there is significantly higher mortality among young adult men born in the Caribbean and Eastern Europe and among young adult women born in Africa and the Caribbean than the UK-born population (Griffiths and Brock, 2004).

The absence of health data on migrant populations and the newness of migrant populations in the UK make it difficult to examine migrant epidemiological trends over time. Clearly, these health inequalities need to be monitored and the government needs to respond at a national level to them, as at present, targeted interventions for migrant communities have been left to primary care trusts.

The impacts of migration on the UK-born population

Much media coverage of the economic impacts of migration has focused on the perception that migration has had a negative impact on the employment prospects, as well as the earnings, of the UK workforce. It is thus argued that recent large-scale migration has contributed towards increased inequality in the UK. However, academic studies on the UK labour market impacts of migration are inconclusive (Manacorda et al, 2006; Reed and Latorre, 2008). Moreover, much research on this issue is limited by imperfect data and conceptual difficulties. Research on the labour market impacts of migration attempts to construct 'the counterfactual' – what the labour market outcomes for workers in the UK would have been *in the absence of migration*. This is usually done by dividing the national labour market into smaller geographical areas that experience different amounts of immigration and comparing wages or employment levels across these different areas. But a fundamental problem that arises when doing this is that immigration is not an exogenous variable. Immigrants are likely to 'self-select' into areas that are doing well economically (Reed and Latorre, 2008).

If there were a fixed number of jobs in the UK, then increased net immigration would increase the level of competition for these jobs and could lead to some of the existing workforce being displaced by migrants. However, the number of jobs available in the UK is a function of the demand for labour. Micro-economic evidence for the UK shows very limited job displacement as a result of immigration (Dustmann and Fabbri, 2005; Manacorda et al, 2006). Studies that have been based on macro-economic modelling generally show that in the short term (the first two to three years) there is some increase in unemployment among UK-born populations, but in the long term there is unlikely to be a discernable effect (Barrell et al, 2006).

Despite net immigration, employment rates have been steady in the last few years. But there has been an increase in youth unemployment at a time when students' qualifications have increased, and the UK-born workforce has contracted (see Figure 10.4).

Moreover, young unqualified workers fare far worse than those with qualifications. The unemployment rate of unqualified 16- to 25-year-olds is more than 20%, compared with around 6% for those with Level 3 qualifications and above. Many young unqualified workers have multiple social needs and like some migrant groups have not benefited from current welfare-to-work approaches. This growth in youth unemployment has taken place concurrently with increasing migration, giving rise to the supposition that rising migration has caused rising youth unemployment, particularly among the unskilled. However, there is considerable disagreement about the impact of immigration on even unskilled 16- to 25-year-olds (Lemos and Portes, 2008). Clearly, this is an area that requires further research.

The idea that migrants will 'undercut' UK workers' wages arises from the perception that they are prepared to do certain types of work for a lower hourly wage than the prevailing UK rate. Dustmann and Fabbri (2005) show a positive impact of immigration on the wages of the *overall* UK-born population, but a negative impact for low-paid workers. This research suggests that at the fifth percentile of the wage distribution (those who earn at the cut-off for the 5% least well paid) the impact on wages of a 1% increase in total population size arising from immigration is a *decrease* of 0.6% in wages. At the tenth percentile it is a decrease of 0.4%. To the extent that there is a negative impact of immigration on wages, it is small and felt at the bottom of the wage distribution.

Overall, the best UK research on the impact of immigration on wages suggests that there are, at worst, no large negative impacts of the increased migration we have seen in the last decade on *average* wages for workers in the UK. It also fits with the findings of research into why companies hire migrant workers, which consistently suggests that lower wage demands are a relatively insignificant factor in the recruitment of migrant workers. Insufficient applications from UK-born workers and a more skilled foreign-born workforce are much more common reasons than lower wage demands (CIPD, 2005).

Figure 10.4: Unemployment rate for UK-born populations, by age range, 2001-2007

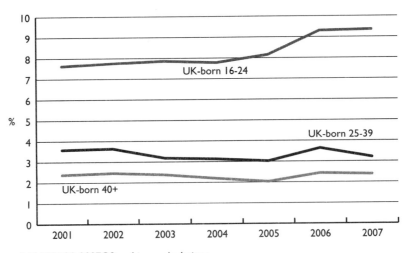

Sources: LFS 2001Q2-2007Q2 and ippr calculations

The equalities picture: 1997 to 2007

The proportion of the UK population who are migrants has increased substantially from 6.2% at the end of 1997 to 10.7% in 2007. Studies undertaken outside the UK suggest that international migration has the potential to make societies less equal. Migration may impact on the employment prospects, wages and employment conditions of non-migrants. Migrants themselves may be less qualified than the non-migrant population or may experience labour market segregation into low-paid work.

There is little conclusive evidence that increased immigration has worsened the employment prospects of the overall UK-born population, although more research is needed in relation to job displacement among UK-born people under the age of 25. There is also some evidence that the least well paid may have experienced a small decrease in wage levels.

Migrant communities are very diverse in relation to their qualifications profiles and labour market experiences, both between and within communities. Some migrant groups are broadly prosperous, enjoying employment levels and earnings above that of the UK-born population. Other migrant groups, particularly those from the EU's new member states, are more likely to be in work than the UK-born population, but have far lower earnings. Other migrant groups, particularly refugees, have far lower earnings and employment levels than the UK-born population. In the period 1997 to 2007, there was some increase in the employment rate and wage levels of most foreign-born populations. It is, therefore, difficult to draw conclusions about the equalities picture in relation to migrant communities. There remain a number of issues of concern in relation to inequalities among migrant communities.

First, there are around half a million irregular migrants in the UK and most qualitative research points to an increase in destitution among this group since 1997. This is a fundamental inconsistency for a country that desires to move to greater equality and an issue to which the government has not effectively responded.

Second, although there have been some improvements in school performance among underachieving groups, there remains a huge 'equalities gap' between groups such as the Somalis and the UK-born population in relation to qualifications. It will take many, many years for some groups to catch up with the UK-born population, as well as more successful migrant and minority groups.

Finally, present welfare-to-work interventions for migrants with multiple social needs seem ineffective in getting them into work and keeping them in this employment. These are the equalities challenges that the government must strive to meet.

Notes

[1] Article Six and Seven of EC Directive 2004/38/EC.

[2] 2007 LFS data, Q3.

[3] Three programmes are in operation: the Gateway Protection Programme, the Mandate Refugee Programme and the Ten or More Plan.

[4] LFS data.

[5] LFS data.

[6] ONS tables, Live Births, Still Births and Infant Mortality by Mothers' Country of Birth, 2005.

Part Two
Cross-cutting issues

Moving in the right direction? Public attitudes to poverty, inequality and redistribution

Tom Sefton

Introduction

New Labour committed itself to eliminating child poverty mid-way through its first term and made significant progress towards this goal during its first two terms (see Chapters Two and Three). However, there is a growing body of opinion that more radical measures will be needed to make further progress in reducing poverty and that this in turn will require much stronger public support (Bamfield, 2005; Fabian Society, 2006a; Rutherford and Shah, 2006). According to Piachaud (2001, p 448), for example, 'there are limits to redistribution by stealth, and a clear, explicit recognition of the need for more redistribution, as well as public explanation and defence of it, are necessary if child poverty is to be further reduced'. This has been accompanied by a growing interest in understanding public attitudes to poverty, inequality and redistribution (Castell and Thompson, 2007; Orton and Rowlingson, 2007).

In this chapter, we attempt to pull together the evidence on attitudes to social justice and the beliefs and values that underpin them. How has public opinion changed since New Labour came to power and, in particular, is the British public more or less progressive in its views now than in 1997? Our analysis is based on a combination of quantitative and qualitative sources, including national surveys, opinion polls and focus groups. Any conclusions must be qualified by the recognition that public attitudes towards these issues are complex, often ambiguous and sometimes contradictory (Orton and Rowlingson, 2007).

Changing perceptions of the Labour Party

Consciously or not, the way government talks about social problems and presents its policies can over time shape the way people think about these issues. Before investigating people's own attitudes to social justice, we look briefly at how their perceptions of the Labour Party have altered over the last decade or more as this sets the context for the discussion that follows.

Even before it came to power, New Labour was keen to drop the Labour Party's traditional commitment to explicit redistribution and to shed its image as the 'big tax and spend party', which many felt was responsible for the party losing the 1992 election. There is little doubt that New Labour has been very successful in changing people's perceptions of the party. The British Election Survey (BES), which is administered after each General Election, includes a series of questions about what people think the Labour Party's view is on certain key issues. The proportion of respondents who thought that the Labour Party is strongly in favour of putting up taxes and spending more on health and social services fell from 59% in 1992 to 35% in 1997, 7% in 2001 and 5% in 2005 (see Table 11.1). People's perceptions of the Labour Party were already beginning to change even before New Labour was elected, but people's views also altered substantially during its first term. The same survey reveals a similar transformation in perceptions of the Labour Party's view on making people's incomes more equal.

Separately, the BES asks people how well they think the Labour Party looks after the interests of different groups in society. This shows that New Labour's image as the party of the working class and anti-business has radically altered. Shortly after the General Election in 2005, as many people thought that the Labour Party looked (fairly or very) closely after the interests of business (60%) as felt this was true of the working class (62%) or trades unions (57%). This is a significant change from 1997 when there was a 20-25 percentage point gap in favour of the last two of these three groups. A similar set of questions was asked in a YouGov poll in September 2007, shortly after Gordon Brown took over as Prime Minister. Over half of respondents (55%) saw the Labour Party as being close to 'the rich', whereas only a third (34%) thought it was close to 'the poor'.

Table 11.1: Perceptions of Labour Party's views on the balance between cutting taxes and spending more on health and social services, 1992-2005 (%)

Labour Party's view is that government should ...	1992	1997	2001	2005
cut taxes a lot and spend much less	3	2	2	1
cut taxes and spend less	3	3	7	4
neither cut taxes nor spend more	11	26	56	54
increase taxes and spend more	24	34	29	35
increase taxes a lot and spend much more	59	35	7	5

Notes:

(1) Respondents are asked to record their views on an 11-point scale (0 to 10) with the extremes labelled as in the table. These five categories are classified as follows: 0 or 1; 2 or 3; 4, 5 or 6; 7 or 8; and 9 or 10.

(2) Responses are weighted using the appropriate GB weights provided in each dataset.

Source: Own analysis using British Election Study, face-to-face post-election questionnaires

The next section examines people's attitudes to different aspects of social justice and considers the interaction between government policies and rhetoric, on the one hand, and public opinion, on the other. Is there evidence that New Labour's attempts to 'modernise' the party and to define a new approach to welfare provision have influenced the way people think about these issues?

Public attitudes to poverty

Tony Blair's unexpected announcement in 1999 that Labour would seek to abolish child poverty by 2020 was genuinely historic – 'by far the toughest social pledge any British politician has ever made', according to Polly Toynbee, the Guardian columnist (*The Guardian*, 7 July 2006). It is difficult to question Gordon Brown's commitment to reducing child poverty as Chancellor, particularly in New Labour's first two terms; yet, the child poverty target has never been given a high profile, even when the government was making good progress early on. But, do people share New Labour's concern about poverty?

Overall, poverty in Britain is low down the general public's list of policy priorities. In a long-running monthly poll by MORI, only 3-6% of respondents in 2007 said that 'poverty and inequality' was among the three most important issues facing Britain today, compared with 7-10% in 1998. A separate ICM poll in June 2007 asked people what two or three things they thought should be Gordon Brown's main priorities when he becomes Prime Minister. Issues connected to poverty or inequality were all towards the bottom of the list (only 1% mentioned poverty and 1% mentioned equality in society). Jim Murphy, Minister for Welfare Reform, summed up the public mood when he said that he 'gets more letters from his constituents about Spanish donkeys and circus elephants than on child poverty' (quoted in *The Guardian*, 30 March 2007). On a more positive note, when people are asked directly, things look different: over 80% of those interviewed in a YouGov poll in 2007 thought that it was a 'very good idea' for Britain to aim for a society in which 'no child grows up in poverty' or 'no pensioner lives in poverty'. So, while tackling child and pensioner poverty is currently seen as a low priority by comparison with other policy issues, these are still seen as worthy objectives.

According to qualitative research by the Fabian Society and others, most people have very little awareness of domestic poverty or are dubious about its seriousness (Castell and Thompson, 2007; McKendrick et al, 2008). Furthermore, there is virtually no knowledge of the government's ambition to address this issue or the progress that has already been made (Fabian Society, 2006b). In an omnibus survey commissioned by the Department for Work and Pensions (DWP) in 2007, only 19% of respondents thought that child poverty in Britain had decreased over the previous 10 years, 38% thought that it had stayed at about the same level and 34% thought that it had increased, even though it fell significantly over this period (see Figure 3.1, this volume). People's responses were very similar when asked about trends in overall poverty in the 2006 British Social Attitudes (BSA) survey, suggesting that most people are unaware of the special priority accorded to tackling *child* poverty (Kelly, 2008). However, the proportion saying that poverty has increased in the last decade is considerably lower than it was in 1994, so there appears to be some recognition that the rise in relative poverty in the preceding decade has been stemmed, even if most people do not think that this trend has been reversed (see Table 11.2).

One of the fundamental assumptions underlying the government's social justice agenda is that poverty is a relative concept. Implicit in the government's main headline measure of child poverty is the notion that whether someone is poor must be assessed in relation to the prevailing norms of the society in which they are living. Does this reflect a public consensus on what poverty means in a modern economy like Britain? Responses to the 2006 BSA survey indicate that only around one in five (22%) subscribes to what is unambiguously a relative definition of poverty – that someone in Britain is in poverty 'if they have enough to buy the things they really need, but not enough to buy the things that most people take for granted'. And only one in two believes that someone is poor if 'they have enough to eat, but not enough to buy other things they need', which incorporates a weaker notion of relativity, assuming people's concept of need changes over time with general living standards. So, people appear to be quite strict in their understanding of poverty and have become slightly stricter over the past decade (see Table 11.3).

The DWP survey referred to above also included several questions about the adequacy of benefits. When asked about a low-earner couple with two children

Table 11.2: Views on recent trends in poverty in Britain (%)

	1994	2000	2006/2007
Over the last ten years, do you think that child poverty in Britain has been increasing, decreasing, or staying at about the same level:			
... decreasing	–	–	19
... staying at same level	–	–	38
... increasing	–	–	34
Over the last ten years, do you think that poverty in Britain has been increasing, decreasing, or staying at about the same level:			
... decreasing	6	20	23
... staying at same level	24	38	39
... increasing	68	36	32

Source: Kelly (2008) for the first question (asked in 2007) and own analysis using the BSA survey for the second question (asked in 1994, 2000 and 2006)

Table 11.3: Explicit views on the definition of poverty in Britain, 1994-2006 (%)

Proportion of respondents who would say that someone in Britain is in poverty if ...	1994	2000	2006
they had enough to buy the things they really needed, but not enough to buy the things that most people take for granted	28	27	22
they had enough to eat and live, but not enough to buy other things they needed	60	60	50
they had not got enough to eat and live without getting into debt	90	93	90

Source: Own analysis using the BSA survey

on £241 per week (after rent and Council Tax), 51% felt that this was enough to live on and 49% that they would be hard up or really poor, so this might be considered an implicit poverty line, below which about half the population would say that this family did not have enough to live on. This level of income is substantially below the government's relative poverty threshold for a couple with two young children (£312 per week in 2006-07, after housing costs [AHC]) and much closer to its absolute poverty standard based on median incomes in 1998–99 (£253 per week in 2006-07 prices). Similarly, when asked about a single mother with a young child living on £123 per week, respondents were evenly split on whether or not this was enough to live on (48% versus 52%). Again, this implied poverty line is considerably lower than the official relative poverty threshold for a lone parent with one child (£150 per week in 2006-07) and almost identical to the absolute poverty threshold. These responses are consistent with either an absolute conception of poverty or else a relative one that is substantially below 60% of median income. On this evidence, the main poverty standard used by the government is more generous than a majority of the population would consider appropriate.

However, people's views on what constitutes a minimum acceptable standard of living are very different when judgements are reached by informed negotiation and consensus. Recent work carried out for the Joseph Rowntree Foundation used such an approach to define, itemise and cost a minimum income standard for different family types (Bradshaw et al, 2008). The agreed budgets for lone parents and for couples with children were greater than 70% of median income, in sharp contrast to the poverty line implied by responses to quantitative surveys (see above). Deliberative research carried out for the Fabian Society also shows that people's attitudes to poverty can change quite dramatically when given more information about people's experiences of poverty: participants moved quite quickly from being sceptical about the existence of poverty in the UK to recognising it as an important issue. And, when told about what the government was already doing, they expressed surprise at, and approval of, the government's vision to eradicate child poverty (Fabian Society, 2006b).

These findings highlight the need for a more open debate in order to build a public consensus about what level of income no one should have to live below (JRF, 2008). In addition, people need to be informed about the action that can be taken to tackle poverty or else the problem will seem intractable and they will disengage (Castell and Thompson, 2007). To make this case to the public at large would require clear, consistent messages over many years. More than 10 years into this Labour government, this process has barely got underway.

Public attitudes to inequality

New Labour's social justice agenda has focused on reducing relative poverty and improving the life chances of the poorest children with little apparent concern about the rapid growth in very high incomes (see Chapter Two). New Labour leadership's stance on the super-rich is perhaps best described as one of conscious indifference. When questioned repeatedly by Jeremy Paxman before the 2001 General Election about whether it was acceptable for the gap between rich and poor to widen, Tony Blair responded by saying that 'it's not a burning ambition of mine to make sure that David Beckham earns less money' (quoted in Bromley, 2003, p 74). More recently, John Hutton, the business and enterprise secretary, went a step further when he said that 'rather than questioning whether huge salaries are morally justified, we should celebrate the fact that people can be enormously successful in this country' (quoted in *The Guardian*, 11 March 2008). The deputy leadership contest in 2007 exposed sharp differences of opinion within the Labour Party when, for example, Harriet Harman complained of 'a society where some struggle and others spend £10,000 on a handbag'. But, Gordon Brown remained silent on this issue in his first year as Prime Minister.

Opinion polls show that people are not oblivious to rising inequality. A Harris/FT poll in July 2007 found that 78% of respondents felt that the gap between rich and poor was getting larger in Britain. But, do people care about what is going on at the top of the income distribution? The BSA series shows that three-quarters or more of the population have consistently said that the gap between those on high and those on low incomes is too large and there is widespread agreement on this across socioeconomic groups and supporters of different political parties (Bromley, 2003). While most people accept that some occupations should be paid more than others, pay differentials are significantly greater than most people think is appropriate (Hills, 2004). However, the BSA survey suggests that concerns about inequality have started to decline somewhat in recent years. The proportion saying that the gap is too large, while still high, declined from 85% in 1997 to 76% in 2006 – and to 75% in 2008 (in an ICM poll in February 2008, using exactly the same question). Having peaked in the mid-1990s, the proportion agreeing with this statement is back to its level in the early 1980s prior to the sharp rise in income inequality, suggesting perhaps that people are now more accepting of much higher levels of inequality. Other related BSA questions show a similar or larger decline in public concern about inequality. Those agreeing that 'income differences in Britain are too large' fell from 80% in 1999 to 63% in 2004 and the proportion agreeing that ordinary working people do *not* get their fair share of the nation's wealth fell from 66% in 1996 to 55% in 2006. Furthermore, there was a disproportionate fall in those agreeing strongly with the last two statements, so even among respondents who think that inequality is too high, these feelings do not appear to be as strongly felt as in the recent past. Contrary to Bromley (2003), using data up to 2002, it does now appear that Britain is becoming more immune to inequality.

Sociologists and media commentators have long noted the widespread acceptance by the majority of the population of considerable levels of inequality (for example, Toynbee, 2003; Runciman, 2006). Qualitative research finds little evidence of serious resentment of the rich when people are making social comparisons provided they have worked hard, in contrast to the considerable resentment felt towards those who are perceived as scroungers living off the state (Pahl et al, 2007).

It is possible that New Labour's apparent indifference to inequality has legitimised the public's quiescence. It is notable that attitudes to inequality have changed most among Labour supporters, who we might expect to be more strongly influenced by their own party. But, most explanations for this phenomenon point to longer-term social and economic trends. People may be less concerned about inequality because, due to rising living standards, they can now afford most of the things they want. While aware that some people are much wealthier than them, these lifestyles are seen as so far removed from their own that there is no point in making comparisons; indeed, the lifestyles of the super-rich have become a 'fabulous spectator sport' (*The Guardian*, 25 June 2007). Secular shifts in the occupational structure, in particular the emergence of a much larger and more diverse middle class, have also contributed to a decline in collective ('them' and 'us') solidarities. The latter is consistent with the observed decline in the proportion of BSA respondents agreeing with statements such as 'there is one law for the rich and one for the poor' (from 71% in 1996 to 55% in 2006) and 'management will always try to get the better of employees if it gets the chance' (from 62% to 52%).

Although the public may be more accepting of large income differentials, most people oppose what they perceive to be unmerited income or wealth, as epitomised by huge City bonuses. In an ICM opinion poll in February 2007, 73% of respondents thought that City bonuses had become excessive and that something should be done about it and only 19% thought they were deserved. These concerns are aggravated by the perceived knock-on effects on house prices, which, according to some commentators, is leading to a powerful sense of grievance among Middle England (for example, *The Guardian*, 25 June 2007).

On this issue, it seems that Harriet Harman is more in tune with public attitudes than John Hutton.

Figure 11.1, which charts the number of references in national newspapers to 'fat cats' and the 'super-rich', shows three peaks in press coverage over the last decade: in 1997-98, the focus was on managerial salaries in the recently privatised utilities and Camelot; the second peak, in 2003-04, was linked to large executive pay rises in a bear market; and, in 2007-08, the main concern was the huge profits reported by private equity firms and hedge fund managers. While specific cases of 'excessive' pay periodically arouse media outrage, the Labour leadership has yet to take a clear position around which public opposition can coalesce.

Figure 11.1: Press coverage of top-end inequality, 1997-98 to 2007-08

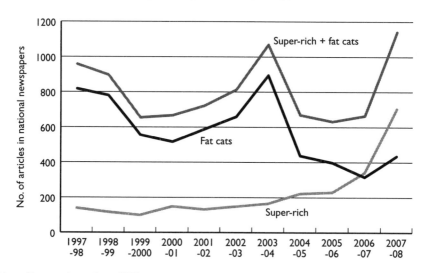

Notes: Key word searches of UK national newspapers (including the *Financial Times*) were conducted using the Nexis UK system for the period 1 May 1997–30 April 2008. The search terms used were as follows: (1) fat cats: fat cats and (Government or Minister or Blair or Brown); and (2) super rich: (super rich or super wealthy or mega wealthy or mega rich) and (Government or Blair or Brown or Minister) and not (Russia or Russian or Ireland or Irish) and not (fat cats). The latter search was restricted to minimise press coverage relating to other countries and avoid duplication with the first search term.

Source: Analysis by Paulina Terrazas (LSE) using Nexis UK system

Public attitudes to redistribution

Selective increases in benefits and tax credits have led to a substantial redistribution of incomes to lower-income groups since 1997. But, the redistributive components of Brown's Budgets were never trumpeted, to the growing frustration of many on the Left. As one commentator put it: 'It has been an odd failing that Labour has redistributed more to the poor than any government since the war, but has done it in radar silence, never seeking to persuade, never using it as a flagship boast in elections' (*The Guardian*, 31 March 2006).

Was the government's cautious approach justified, given public attitudes to redistribution or could it have made a stronger case for an overtly redistributive agenda? Analysis of the BSA survey data suggests that there is much less support for redistribution than we might expect given stated levels of concern about inequality – and that the level of support for government intervention falls as the degree of explicit intervention increases (Taylor-Gooby and Martin, 2008). In 2004, 73% of respondents said that the gap between high and low incomes was too large, 43% agreed that it was the government's responsibility to reduce income differences, and only 32% agreed that 'Government should redistribute income from the better-off to those who are less well-off' (see Figure 11.2).

Furthermore, explicit support for redistribution has been steadily declining since 1994 (when around 50% agreed with the last of the above statements). Compared with the rest of Europe, Britain is less inclined to think that it is the government's responsibility to reduce income inequality, despite being the most unequal of the major European economies (see Figure 11.3).

One possible explanation is that most people do not feel sufficiently strongly about inequality to want action to be taken, especially if they have concerns about how

Figure 11.2: Attitudes towards inequality and redistribution, 2004

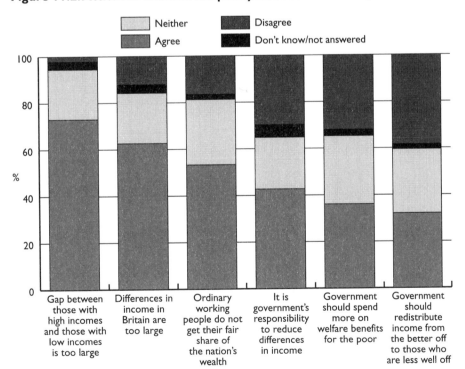

Source: Own analysis using the BSA survey 2004

Figure 11.3: Relationship between income inequality and concerns about inequality among European countries, 2006

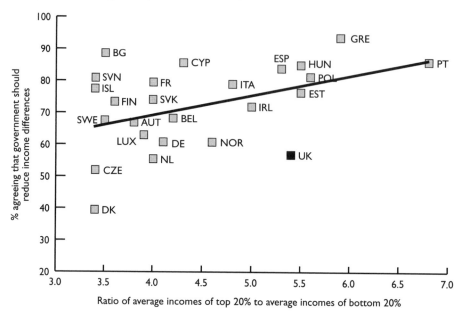

Ratio of average incomes of top 20% to average incomes of bottom 20%

Notes:

(1) X-axis: ratio of total income received by the top 20% to that received by the bottom 20%. Data is from Eurostat (for 2006 or latest available year corresponding to attitudinal data).

(2) Y-axis: proportion of respondents who agree or agree strongly that 'Government should take measures to reduce differences in income levels'. Data is from the 2006 European Social Survey (or latest available year – either 2002 or 2004).

(3) BG: Bulgaria; SVN: Slovenia; ISL: Iceland; FIN: Finland; SWE: Sweden; CZE: Czech Republic; DK: Denmark; CYP: Cyprus; FR: France; SVK: Slovakia; BEL: Belgium; AUT: Austria; LUX: Luxembourg; DE: Germany; NL: Netherlands; ITA: Italy; IRL: Ireland; NOR: Norway; ESP: Spain; HUN: Hungary; POL: Poland; EST: Estonia; UK: United Kingdom; GRE: Greece; PT: Portugal.

Source: Own analysis using European Social Survey and Eurostat database

such policies might affect their own household or the economy. Among the small minority who *strongly* agreed that income differences in Britain are too large, explicit support for redistribution is much higher than among those who 'agreed' with this statement (57% versus 33% in 2004). Another possible explanation is that people are put off by the language of redistribution (Orton and Rowlingson, 2007), although there has also been a decline in support for equivalent statements that do not use the R-word (for example, that 'greater efforts should be made to make incomes more equal'). Lastly, people may favour alternative policies to reduce inequality other than direct income transfers and may have been encouraged in this view by the government's repeated emphasis on work as the best route out of poverty, even though a large part of the reduction in child poverty has in fact been due to changes in the tax-benefit system (see Chapter Two).

Having said this, implicit support for redistribution seems to be much higher than explicit support for redistribution. The most common idea is that the welfare state should ensure that people have their basic needs met and that the amount everyone contributes should reflect what they can afford. This is redistributive in *effect*, but not necessarily in *intention* (Hedges, 2005). Sefton (2005) found that nine in ten BSA respondents favoured tax and benefit policies whose overall effect is clearly redistributive – either proportional or progressive taxation in combination with either flat-rate or means-tested benefits; this includes most of those who, when asked directly, did not agree that the government should redistribute income from rich to poor. This suggests that an explicitly redistributive agenda, while it would attract the support of a significant minority, might put off many others who would otherwise support these kinds of policies. If so, this provides some vindication for New Labour's policy of 'redistribution by stealth'.

People's views on redistribution also depend on the perceived fairness of the specific measures being proposed. Some of the government's redistributive policies command widespread support, the best example of this being the National Minimum Wage (NMW), which is both popular and the most visible of the government's anti-poverty measures. In a special YouGov survey for the Fabian Society in August 2007, 75% thought it was a very good idea that 'every full-time worker should be entitled to a basic living wage' and 43% recognised that 'some' or 'a lot' of progress had been made towards achieving this objective over the last 10 years, compared with around 20% who said this about reducing child or pensioner poverty. The NMW also came top in a YouGov poll in April 2007 of the greatest successes of Blair's time as Prime Minister. Other government policies that command broad public support include earnings top-ups for working parents and higher spending on benefits for retired people and children. In this respect, New Labour could be said to have gone with the progressive grain of public opinion, implementing policies that are quite strongly redistributive while recognising that people are selective in the kinds of measures they support (Hills, 2002).

Public attitudes to public spending

Although less directly redistributive than the tax-benefit system, spending on public services plays a critical role in tackling the root causes of poverty. Margaret Hodge, the first Children's Minister, put it this way:

> As poverty is linked to other disadvantages, some redistribution is required but this should not only be from the tax and benefit system, but also through public service programmes.... *We need to win the argument for tax and spend* – but taxing fairly and spending efficiently. (quoted in Powell, 2002, p 24; emphasis added)

The 2002 Budget set out an explicit policy of raising taxes (an extra 1% on National Insurance contributions) to finance higher spending on public services. Six years on, and following a period of rapid growth in public spending, has New Labour won the argument for tax and spend? What does the public's reaction to recent increases in public spending indicate about their willingness to support further increases? And was the government's case helped or hindered by Blair's insistence that additional investment in public services be matched by reforms to extend competition and choice in the National Health Service (NHS) and schools (Seldon, 2007)?

The New Labour government promised to stick to the Conservative's spending plans for its first two years in office, but most voters expected and indeed wanted greater investment in public services. Given the choice between reducing taxes and spending less on 'health, education and social benefits', keeping taxes and spending at about the same level, or increasing taxes and spending, 63% of respondents in the 1998 BSA survey selected the last option (and only 3% selected the first option).[1] In the 2006 BSA survey, however, the percentage of respondents in support of higher taxes and spending had fallen to 46%. Support for higher spending started to decline after 2002, coinciding with the period of rapid growth in public expenditure.

The BES includes a similar question, asking respondents to rate their own views on an 11-point scale ranging from 'cutting taxes a lot and spending much less on health and social services' to 'increasing taxes a lot and spending much more on health and social services'. This series shows a substantial drop in support for higher (or much higher) taxes and spending from 65% in 1997 to 38% in 2005. Unlike the BSA survey, this survey suggests that support for higher public spending and taxes was already starting to drop during New Labour's first term and so was not necessarily a reaction to spending increases during its second term. The same survey reveals an even more dramatic change in people's perceptions of the Labour Party's position on taxation and spending from being seen as very much to the Left of the average voter to being in the centre-ground of politics (see Table 11.4). In the process of shedding its image with voters as a 'big tax and spend party', New Labour may have pulled public opinion further to the Right, inadvertently dampening people's enthusiasm for more public spending.

Subsequent opinion polls, although not directly comparable with either the BES or BSA surveys, suggest that support for public spending has declined even further in the two years since 2006 – and that a substantial and growing minority are now in favour of lower taxes and spending. An ICM poll in March 2007 asked people if they would be most likely to support a party that offered tax cuts (or tax rises) even it meant spending less (or more) on public services: 21% opted for tax cuts, 21% for tax rises and 51% for the status quo. The last of these is the most popular option among supporters of all the major political parties. When asked a similar question in February 2008, but given the choice between current *or* higher levels of public spending, on the one hand, and lower spending on public

Table 11.4: Respondents' views on the balance between cutting taxes and spending more on health and social services, 1992-2005 (%)

	1992	1997	2001	2005
Government should...[1]				
cut taxes a lot and spend much less	4	3	2	2
cut taxes and spend less	5	3	4	4
neither cut taxes nor spend more	34	30	43	56
increase taxes and spend more	28	31	35	30
increase taxes a lot and spend much more	28	34	17	8
Difference between own views and perceptions of Labour Party's views:[2]				
Much more in favour of cutting taxes than Labour	23	7	5	5
More in favour of cutting taxes than Labour	22	15	12	15
Similar views to Labour	43	58	49	59
More in favour of higher spending than Labour	7	13	23	16
Much more in favour of higher spending than Labour	5	6	12	5

Notes: [1] Respondents are asked to place their own views on a scale an 11-point scale (0 to 10) with the extremes labelled as in the table. These five categories are classified as follows: 0 or 1; 2 or 3; 4, 5 or 6; 7 or 8; and 9 or 10. [2] Respondents are also asked to assess the Labour Party's views on the same scale (see Table 11.1). In the bottom panel of this table, we deduct their own score (from 0-10) from their scoring of Labour Party's views (both on a scale of 0-10) and then group the responses as follows: –4 or less; –2 to –3; –1 to +1; +2 to +3; +4 or more.

Source: Own analysis using British Election Study, face-to-face post-election questionnaires

services and tax cuts, on the other, 51% of respondents chose the former option and 36% the latter option. (By contrast, only 6% of BSA respondents said that they favoured lower taxes and spending in the 2006 survey.) Increased support for lower taxes could well be linked to the slow growth in living standards since 2002 and, more recently, growing fears of a recession (for example, *The Guardian*, 22 July 2008), affecting people's willingness to pay taxes.

Previous studies have argued that people are quite selective about the kinds of public spending they favour – health, old age pensions and education being the most popular (for example, Hills and Lelkes, 1999; Sefton, 2003). However, the evidence suggests that enthusiasm for higher spending is waning even in relation to these flagship services. In 1996 and 2006, BSA respondents were asked if they would like to see more spending on each of eight services. The proportion who said they wanted 'more' or 'much more' public spending fell over this period for all the major services, including health, education, old age pensions and law enforcement, which together comprise the vast majority of government expenditure (see Table 11.5).

Prior to the big spending increases announced in the 2001 and 2002 Budgets, around two-thirds of BSA respondents believed that higher spending would

Table 11.5: Support for higher government spending by spending area, 1996-2006

% who would like more or much more spending in each area...	'Spend much more'[1] (%)		'Spend more' or 'spend much more' (%)	
	1996	**2006**	**1996**	**2006**
Health	42	26	90	78
Education	31	21	82	68
Old age pensions	26	23	76	70
Police and law enforcement	20	15	70	58
The environment	8	12	41	53
Unemployment benefits	7	3	33	13
Military and defence	3	9	17	28
Culture and the arts	1	2	6	10

Note: [1] Respondents are told that if they say '*much more*', this might require a tax increase to pay for it.
Source: Own analysis of the BSA survey

improve public services 'a great deal' or 'quite a bit' and that managerial reform alone was unlikely to achieve real improvements in the NHS (Taylor-Gooby and Hastie, 2002). But, cynicism appears to have set in soon after; according to a YouGov poll in September 2003, two-thirds of respondents thought that the extra money spent on the NHS and education 'will mostly be wasted' (as opposed to 'being used to improve services'). Opinion polls suggest that, in retrospect, most people think that the additional money was spent badly and made little difference. An ICM poll in October 2006 found that 72% of all respondents (and 58% of Labour supporters) agreed that a lot of the extra money put into the NHS had been wasted (with 56% agreeing strongly with this statement), indicating widespread disillusionment with New Labour's big spending plans.

At the same time, there is evidence that people's appetite for higher spending was quite small to start with. An ICM poll in February 1997 asked people how much they would be willing to pay in extra tax in order to provide more money for public services: 51% of respondents specified an amount of less than £10 per month, 18% specified an amount between £10 and £20 per month (roughly equivalent to a 1-2 pence increase in the basic rate of Income Tax for someone on average earnings at that time) and only 8% were willing to contribute more than £20 per month. And, given the choice between spending *more* or *much more* on public services, most respondents opted for the former (see Table 11.5). When around two-thirds of the population in 1997 said that they wanted the government to spend more on public services, it seems that most people only meant a bit more.

If Tony Blair was hoping that radical reforms to public services would persuade people that the extra investment would be spent efficiently and that further increases in spending and taxation were justified, then he appears to have failed. But, this was always going to be difficult, given most people's unwillingness to pay much more in taxes. In the end, combining spending increases with public service reforms may have had precisely the opposite effect, providing ample opportunity for critics to argue that the additional expenditure was being wasted. The government tried to be more upfront about its public spending plans, but this does not appear to have been any more successful in building public support for more radical measures than its quietly redistributive tax and benefit policies. This is problematic for future governments as demographic and other pressures will mean that higher levels of spending are needed in the long term just to maintain current levels of provision (see Chapter Fifteen).

Underlying attitudes and beliefs

In the same speech in which he made his child poverty pledge, Tony Blair warned that:

> For if people lose their faith in welfare's ability to deliver, then politicians have an impossible job persuading hard-pressed taxpayers that their money should go to a system that is not working.... *I want to make all of the welfare state as popular as the NHS* because it is providing real security and opportunity, because we have rooted out fraud and because we are giving greatest help to those with the greatest needs. (Blair, 1999, p 12; emphasis added)

New Labour's 'rights and responsibilities' agenda emphasises the government's role in helping people overcome structural barriers that hinder them from escaping poverty, but also the duty of individuals to take advantage of opportunities offered to them (HM Treasury, 2008a). In substantive policy terms, the emphasis on personal responsibility and on linking state entitlements to behaviour has strengthened under New Labour, particularly since Gordon Brown became Prime Minister (for example, *The Guardian*, 27 February 2008). At the same time, Labour ministers have aggressively tackled benefit fraud. But, has this increased people's confidence in the welfare system, as Tony Blair hoped it would? And, how has people's understanding of the causes of poverty altered after more than a decade of a Labour government that has simultaneously sought to tackle the structural causes of poverty and promote personal responsibility? This matters, because support for redistributive policies is closely associated with people's underlying beliefs about the causes of poverty and the perceived integrity of the benefits system (Fong, 2001; Georgiadis and Manning, 2007).

According to the BSA survey, more people are now inclined to attribute poverty to personal rather than structural causes. When asked why some people live in need, fewer people say this is because of 'injustice in society' (down from 29%

in 1994 to 21% in 2006) and more people say it is because of 'laziness or lack of willpower' (up from 15% to 27%). Eurobarometer surveys indicate that this latter view has become more prevalent in the UK over the last 15 years than in almost any Western European country (see Figure 11.4). Qualitative studies find little evidence of empathy for the poor and an overwhelming tendency to attribute poverty to deficiencies of personal behaviour, such as poor parenting or financial mismanagement, rather than structural explanations (Fabian Society, 2006b; McKendrick et al, 2008). In a recent survey commissioned by the DWP, parental addiction was most commonly identified as one of the reasons why children are in poverty,[2] even though evidence suggests that only a small minority of parents are in fact dependent on alcohol or drugs (Kelly, 2008).

Successive BSA surveys indicate that attitudes to benefit claimants have hardened substantially since the mid-1990s, linked to growing concerns about the disincentive effects of the benefits system (Hills, 2001; Sefton, 2003; Taylor-Gooby, 2005). In a long-running BSA question, respondents are asked to choose between two statements about the level of benefits for unemployed people: that they are 'too low and cause hardship' or 'too high and discourage them from finding work'. From the mid-1980s to the mid-1990s, the predominant view was that benefits were too low, selected by around half of all respondents, while less than a third

Figure 11.4: Views on the causes of poverty: evidence from Eurobarometer, 1993-2007

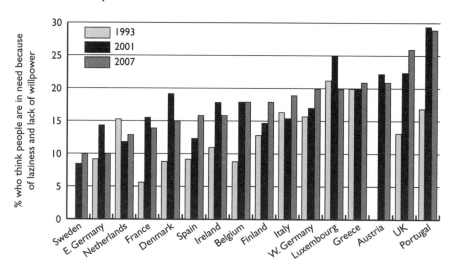

Notes:
(1) Survey respondents were asked why they think there are people who live in need and asked to select one of four options: 'because they have been unlucky'; 'because of laziness and lack of willpower'; 'because there is much injustice in society'; or 'it's an inevitable part of progress'. We report the percentage of all respondents selecting the second option.
(2) The results shown here are for the subset of countries that took part in at least two out of these three surveys.
Source: Eurobarometer 40 (1993), Eurobarometer 56.1 (2001), and Eurobarometer 67.1 (2007)

said that they were too high. Since then, there has been a complete reversal of opinion with less than a quarter now saying that benefits are too low and over half saying that they are too high (see Figure 11.5), even though unemployment benefits have not risen in real terms for many claimants (see Chapter Two). The same trend is evident in a number of related indicators; more people now agree that 'if welfare benefits weren't so generous, people would learn to stand on their own two feet' (33% in 1996, rising to 47% in 2006) and more people agree that 'around here, most unemployed people could find a job if they really wanted one' (39% to 67%).

Longer-term trends in the BSA data show that these changes in attitudes mostly occurred after Tony Blair became Leader of the Labour Party in 1994 and may have been unwittingly encouraged by New Labour rhetoric on 'rights and responsibilities'. As Table 11.6 shows, the biggest swing in opinion was among Labour's own supporters, perhaps because statements about the deficiencies of the system have been coming from Labour ministers (Hills, 2001). The irony is that Mr Blair's tenure as Prime Minister was marked by a shift in opinion towards views more similar to those held by Mrs Thatcher (Curtice and Fisher, 2003).

These trends in survey data are consistent with findings from qualitative research. A common view of the welfare state is as a kind of national 'club' into which people pay their dues and are then entitled to seek support when they need

Figure 11.5: Changing attitudes towards benefits for the unemployed, 1987-2006

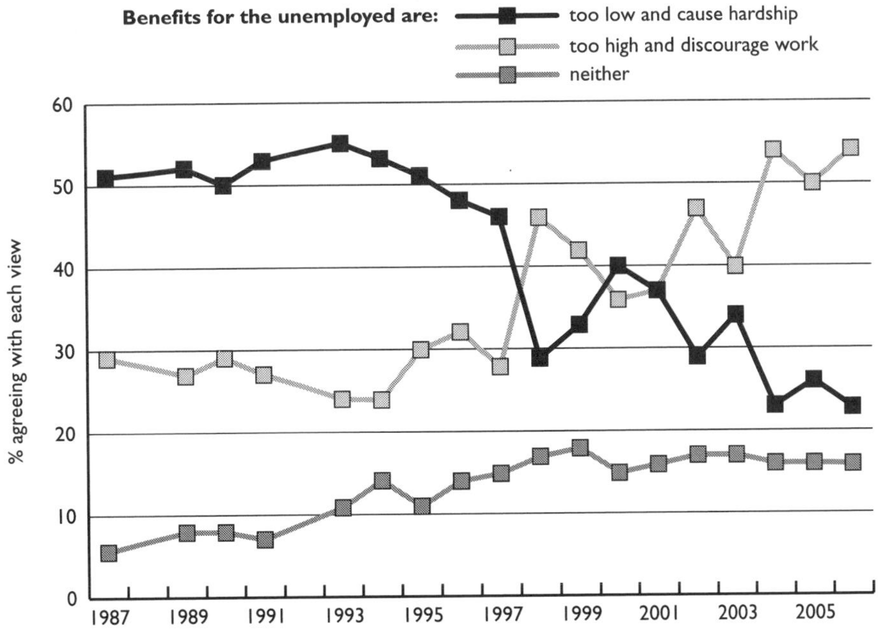

Source: Own analysis using the BSA survey

Table 11.6: Changes in underlying attitudes to welfare among Labour and Conservative supporters, 1987-2006 (%)

	1987	1996	2006	Change: 1987-96	Change: 1996-2006
... benefits for unemployed are too low and cause hardship	**49**	**48**	**23**	**–1**	**–25**
Conservative	30	29	13	–1	–16
Labour	68	62	30	–6	–32
... if welfare benefits weren't so generous, people would learn to stand on own two feet	**29**	**33**	**47**	**+4**	**+14**
Conservative	41	52	58	+9	+6
Labour	18	21	39	+3	+18
... around here, most unemployed people could find a job if they really wanted one	**45**	**39**	**67**	**–6**	**+28**
Conservative	59	54	75	–5	+21
Labour	32	28	60	–4	+32
... why do you think there are people who live in need?[1]					
... because of injustice in our society	**27**	**29**	**21**	**+2**	**–8**
Conservative	11	15	15	+4	0
Labour	43	41	22	–2	–19
... there is one law for the rich and one for poor	**65**	**71**	**55**	**+6**	**–16**
Conservative	45	53	44	+8	–9
Labour	83	83	61	0	–22

Note: [1] For this question, the responses are for 1987, 1994 and 2006 and the changes in the last two columns are for 1987-94 and 1994-2006.

Source: Own analysis of the BSA survey

it. The important qualifier is that people should have fulfilled their part of the bargain by contributing what they reasonably can (Hedges, 2005). According to Castell and Thompson (2007), this 'club view' of the welfare state appears to be in the ascendancy, with rising concerns about 'outsiders' and 'free-riders' taking advantage of the system. Media commentators, too, have noticed a difference: when, for example, a government minister declared that the state will never pay benefits high enough to lift people out of poverty and that he did not think it should, a piece in the *Financial Times* (2 May 2007) noted that: 'a decade ago, such remarks from a Labour MP would have caused a riot. Today, they are a measure of how far public attitudes to welfare have hardened'.

Looking at the welfare state more broadly, there also appears to have been a narrowing in public perceptions of the role of government. The proportion of BSA respondents agreeing that it should definitely be the government's responsibility to meet a whole range of needs is considerably lower than it was 10 years ago or than at any time since these questions were first asked in 1985 (see Table 11.7). This extends to services that are traditionally seen as pillars of the British welfare state – healthcare and support for older people – and seems to point to a generalised loss of confidence in government, following an initial burst of optimism during New Labour's first term.

Welfare, it would appear, has become *less* popular than it was when New Labour came to power – and even those aspects of the welfare state that were popular are being called into question. In hindsight, attempts by Tony Blair and his ministerial colleagues to shore up confidence in the welfare system by 'talking tough' may have reinforced the very concerns that they were seeking to address. For example, the recent suggestion by the Housing Minister, Caroline Flint, that social sector tenants should be compelled to undertake additional employment-search activities serves to legitimise the prejudices of those suspicious towards benefit claimants (Sinclair, 2008). Similarly, the heavily publicised clampdown on 'benefit cheats' may have given people the impression that benefit abuse was widespread, instead

Table 11.7: Public attitudes to the role of government, 1985-2006 (%)

Proportion of respondents who agree that it should definitely be the government's responsibility to ...	1985	1990	1996	2000	2006
provide a job for everyone who wants one	36	23	26	39	16
keep prices under control	59	47	40	64	31
provide healthcare for the sick	85	84	81	87	68
provide a decent living standard for the old	77	77	69	80	58
provide industry with the help it needs to grow	52	41	38	–	27
provide a decent standard of living for the unemployed	42	30	26	–	10
reduce income differences between rich and poor	45	40	32	–	25
give financial help to students from poor families	–	48	35	–	32
provide decent housing to those who can't afford it	–	45	34	–	24
impose strict laws to make industry do less damage to the environment	–	–	58	–	45

Source: Own analysis of the BSA survey

of reassuring them that it was under control. New Labour could and should have done more to challenge negative preconceptions about the poor.

It would, however, be misleading to hold the government wholly responsible for these changes in underlying attitudes. When the economy was doing well, people were perhaps more likely to think that people should be responsible for meeting their own needs. Longer-term trends in society towards a more individualistic and meritocratic outlook (Marshall et al, 2007) may also be contributing factors. Last, but not least, the media has been largely silent on the issue of domestic poverty, rarely exploiting its capacity to inform the public or to challenge existing images and beliefs (McKendrick et al, 2008).

Conclusions

The two questions we posed at the beginning of this chapter were whether the British public have become more 'progressive' in their attitudes to social justice since 1997 and whether New Labour's attempts to redefine the party have influenced the way people think about these issues.

On the first question, it is hard to escape the conclusion that public attitudes are now less progressive than 10 years ago:

- UK poverty is a low priority and seems to attract little public sympathy. Most people are unaware of the child poverty target or what the government is doing to tackle it.
- People seem to be more accepting of high levels of income inequality, although specific cases of perceived excess periodically arouse public and media outrage.
- Support for explicit redistribution has declined substantially since the mid-1990s, although certain redistributive policies, such as the NMW, are popular.
- Initial enthusiasm for higher levels of public spending appears to be waning even in relation to flagship services, because most people's appetite for higher expenditure was easily satisfied and many believe the additional money has been spent badly.
- Attitudes to the benefits system and its beneficiaries have hardened substantially, especially among Labour's own supporters.

It is too soon, at the time of writing, to say how the financial crisis of 2007-08 and its knock-on effects on the rest of the economy will affect public attitudes to these issues. Will it make people even more resistant to redistribution, because the resources available for this are so constrained? Or will it make people more sympathetic to those dependent on benefits as the structural causes of unemployment are now so evident?

The verdict on New Labour depends on how far you think it is responsible for these changes in public attitudes. A critical perspective would be that the government should have done more to challenge people's preconceptions about poverty and its underlying causes. It could also have made a more explicit case for its social justice agenda, perhaps using its initial success in reducing child poverty to build a consensus for the more radical measures that are needed to make further progress. Yet, this process of informing and persuading the general public has barely got under way. In seeking to shed its image with voters as a 'big tax and spend/pro-redistribution party', New Labour has neglected to foster broader support for the values with which the party has traditionally been associated (Curtice, 2007; Moon, 2007), perhaps inadvertently weakening public support for redistribution and public spending. The government's emphasis on rooting out fraud and on the responsibilities of benefit claimants seems to have backfired, undermining people's confidence in the welfare system and reinforcing negative stereotypes of its beneficiaries. Linking spending increases to public service reform made it easy for its opponents to create the impression that the extra investment in public services was being wasted. And, when public and media concerns about the super-rich have flared up, the Labour leadership has failed to take a clear position around which public opposition could coalesce.

A less critical interpretation is that the government should be applauded for pressing ahead with a social justice agenda that has gone largely unrecognised. It could be argued that the government's understated anti-poverty strategy made it more palatable to voters who might have resisted more overtly redistributive policies. The NMW, more generous in-work benefits, and additional spending on public services, have gone with the progressive grain of public opinion, being quite strongly redistributive in effect, while recognising that people are particular about the kinds of measures they support. Those who criticise the government for pursuing this agenda too quietly are vague about what exactly 'noisy' redistribution would look like (Kenway, 2006) and possibly underestimate the challenges of 'selling' a more progressive agenda. The government tried to be more upfront about its public spending plans, but this was no more effective in generating public support for more radical action than its more quietly redistributive tax and benefit policies. Can the government really be blamed if its messages about personal responsibility seem to have been received more clearly than its messages about the structural causes of poverty?

Last but not least, the nature of the political debate around poverty and social exclusion has been transformed in the last decade. An editorial in the *Financial Times* in 1999 noted that: 'Poverty and inequality and what to do about them – words banned from the political lexicon by the Conservatives – are now openly discussed … at the heart of government....' (*Financial Times*, 27 September 1999).

More recently, the Conservative Party, under David Cameron, formally recognised poverty as relative: 'I want this message to go out loud and clear: the

Conservative Party recognises, will measure, and will act on relative poverty' (Cameron, 2006). This is a major turnaround for a party that previously questioned the very existence of poverty in contemporary Britain (see Clark and Hunt, 2007). That the Conservative Party has now joined in the debate around social justice, even though there is no political consensus about how to tackle poverty, is a very significant development and may turn out to be one of New Labour's key legacies. In the short term, it will help to keep the government accountable for its child poverty target, and in the longer term, it increases the chances that poverty will not drop off the political agenda with a change of government.

Notes

[1] In a separate BSA question, only 43% agreed that the government should spend more on welfare benefits for the poor, implying greater support for spending on benefits in kind than on cash benefits.

[2] Respondents were shown a list of 13 possible causes of child poverty and asked which three might best explain why children are in poverty. The most common responses were parental addiction (45%), family break-up (38%) and low pay (37%).

TWELVE

Inequality and the devolved administrations: Scotland, Wales and Northern Ireland

Tania Burchardt and Holly Holder

Introduction

A great deal has been written about devolution since 1997, mostly in relation to the institutional and constitutional complexities produced by multiple layers of government. Rather less attention has been paid to the social policy innovations that devolution may have generated, and still less to the actual consequences of those changes in terms of poverty and inequality. This chapter takes up that challenge, with a particular focus on income and educational inequalities.

The remainder of this introductory section briefly reviews the degree of devolution that Scotland, Wales and Northern Ireland have each enjoyed since 1997 and examines the reasons why we might or might not expect devolution to reduce inequality within and between the nations. The review suggests that the scope for policy divergence has been limited.

The second section describes the policies pursued in practice in Scotland, Wales and Northern Ireland since devolution and explores the extent to which they represent a divergence from the past and/or a divergence from policy as it has evolved in England and the UK.

The third section reports changes over the period 1998-99 to the present in some key outcomes: poverty (including child poverty), income inequality and educational attainment, overall and by social class.

The final section draws on the evidence of policies and outcomes to offer an assessment of whether devolution has so far produced more effective strategies for reducing inequality and poverty than would have occurred in its absence and reflects on the prospects for the future.

Does devolution tend in principle to increase or decrease inequality?

In thinking about inequality, we can consider:

(a) inequality among the population of the UK as a whole;

(b) inequality within the populations of each constituent country; or

(c) inequality between the nations themselves.

The different measures may not move in the same direction. This chapter is concerned primarily with individuals as the unit of analysis rather than countries (since it is individuals who experience the effects of inequality), so will concentrate on inequality within each country and within the UK population as a whole (a and b), rather than on inequality between England, Scotland, Wales and Northern Ireland.[1]

There are a number of reasons for thinking that devolution could produce more effective strategies for reducing the gap between rich and poor within each country (Keating, 2005; Andrews and Martin, 2007; Morelli and Seaman, 2007; North et al, 2007). One account of a virtuous circle goes something like this:

(i) There is greater scope for creativity and experimental policies in smaller populations.

(ii) This, together with a stronger information base and freedom from the requirements of national (UK) uniformity, enables policies to be devised that reflect the specific socioeconomic context, rather than being based on a broad-brush national picture.

(iii) Country-specific solutions may among other things act as a spur to economic development.

(iv) More efficient use of resources and economic growth generate a surplus in public finances that can be used for spending on social programmes.

(v) Policy makers are more directly accountable to the electorate in a devolved administration, improving governance and incentives to tackle disadvantage.

(vi) The nationalism that tends to be associated with devolution enhances feelings of solidarity and prioritises social cohesion.

There is evidence to support some links in this chain in the UK context. Scotland was used as a policy laboratory for the rest of the UK even before devolution and a number of the post-devolution policies described in this chapter show signs of innovation and creativity. Andrews and Martin (2007) observe that the Welsh approach to public service delivery was intended to be tailored to the needs of a largely rural population. Economic development has been comparatively strong in Northern Ireland in the wake of the Northern Ireland Assembly being established, although the trend was already upwards (see Figure 12.2). North et al (2007) argue that there has been greater attention to the needs of deprived areas and populations in the devolved administrations, and Mooney et al (2006, p 488) describe the rhetoric of the Scottish Executive and early commentators as making Scotland out to be a 'Scandinavian welfare regime writ small', with a strong emphasis on social inclusion.

In the UK case, given that Scotland, Wales and Northern Ireland are among the poorest regions, improving the circumstances of the worst off in those countries without making comparable changes in England would be likely to reduce inequality in the UK overall. However, other considerations might lead one to expect devolution to have a negative impact on inequality within the devolved administrations and across the UK:

- A bid for economic competitiveness in a global market leads to cutting social expenditures and reducing employment regulation – a 'race to the bottom' (Keating, 2005). This may be particularly acute in countries or regions starting from a low economic base.
- The additional layers of bureaucracy and constitutional complexity created by devolution make policy *less* responsive and resources are sucked away from social programmes into supporting the governance structures themselves.
- A focus on national identity militates against attention to within-country differences, such as social class (Law and Mooney, 2006).

Interestingly, these considerations suggesting a tendency towards increasing inequality mirror the arguments (iii) to (vi) put forward above to support the idea of devolution *reducing* inequality. The effects of increased economic competitiveness, more localised governance, and nationalism can cut either way – an issue to which we return in the conclusions to this chapter.

Finally, for completeness, there are good reasons to believe that devolution will have little effect on inequality within nations either way. Constraints on divergence operate within each administration, at nation state level, and globally:

- Path dependencies in social policy are strong (Mooney et al, 2006).
- Countries learn from each other, so that successful innovations are quickly copied in other parts of the UK.
- Many relevant powers are reserved to the UK government (for example, social security, except in Northern Ireland).
- Many drivers of inequality operate at supranational level, such as skill-based technological change and migration. Devolution is 'a transmission belt for global pressures to the local economy' (Morelli and Seaman, 2007, p 524), and globalisation is likely to lead in the long run to the erosion of differences between states and welfare systems (Mooney et al, 2006).

Of course, all of these arguments only come into play if a significant degree of devolution has actually occurred. But has it? The next subsection investigates.

Scope and extent of devolution in the UK: 1997-2008

Figure 12.1 gives a timeline of devolution to Scotland, Wales and Northern Ireland. Devolution is a process, rather than an event: historically, Scotland and Northern Ireland have had significant, although varying, degrees of administrative independence (Wales less so). For example, the Scottish Office received an annual block grant from 1979-80 to 1998-99 to run many aspects of Scottish affairs (Parry, 2004). The devolved administrations created in 1999 did not begin with a blank sheet.

The Labour Party has been the dominant party for much of the period in Scotland and Wales, albeit as part of coalitions, but the nationalist parties made significant gains in 2007, with the Scottish National Party taking power as a minority government and Plaid Cymru entering a governing coalition in Wales for the first time. Many commentators have noted that it is only now that different parties are in power in Westminster, Edinburgh and Cardiff that devolution will be put to the test (for example, Schmuecker, 2008).

The differences in the evolution of devolution across the countries are marked. In Scotland, devolution was electorally popular, while in Wales, the 1997 referendum was won by the slimmest of majorities. In Northern Ireland, devolution was part and parcel of the peace process and hence fraught with difficulties. This variety reflects the different roles of the devolved administrations. The Scottish Parliament was granted wide-ranging powers by the 1998 Government of Scotland Act, including primary legislative powers in health, social care, education and housing (among other areas), and the ability to alter the basic rate of Income Tax by up to three percentage points. The Welsh Assembly had no primary legislative powers until the 2006 Government of Wales Act came into force, so for the majority of the period under consideration it acted like a Secretary of State of the UK government – proposing but not having final say over policy and legislation. The Northern Ireland Assembly has similar powers to Scotland, with the exceptions of criminal justice and Income Tax-varying powers (although it does have discretion over matters of local taxation), and with the addition of social security as a devolved matter. However, in the eight years between the Assembly being inaugurated in 1999 and the elections in 2007, devolution was in effect in Northern Ireland for less than three (December 1999 to October 2002), and the Assembly was suspended and restored several times even within that brief period.

The departmental 'comparability factors' used by the Treasury to calculate the block grants to the devolved administrations are one way to understand which policy areas are and are not devolved (Table 12.1). The comparability factor is the Treasury's assessment of the (expenditure-weighted) proportion of a UK, GB or English department's functions that are being carried out by the devolved administration rather than centrally.

Table 12.1 shows that education (including higher education), housing and regeneration, health, culture and agriculture are entirely or almost entirely

Figure 12.1: Devolution timeline

		UK	Scotland	Wales	Northern Ireland
1997	Spring	General Election			
	Summer				
	Autumn		Referendum	Referendum	
	Winter				
1998	Spring				Good Friday Agreement and referendum
	Summer			Govt of Wales Act	Elections (UUP, SDLP, DUP, SF)
	Autumn		Scotland Act		N. Ireland Act
	Winter				
1999	Spring		Elections (Lab/LD)	Elections (Lab min)	
	Summer				
	Autumn				
	Winter				Assembly inaugurated
2000	Spring				Suspended and restored
	Summer	General Election			
	Autumn			Lab/LD coalition	
	Winter				
2001	Spring				
	Summer				Suspended and restored
	Autumn				Suspended and restored
	Winter				
2002	Spring				
	Summer				
	Autumn				Suspended
	Winter				
2003	Spring		Elections (Lab/LD)	Elections (Lab)	
	Summer				
	Autumn				Elections (UUP, SF, UUP, SDLP)
	Winter				
2004	Spring				
	Summer				
	Autumn				
	Winter				
2005	Spring	General Election			
	Summer				
	Autumn				
	Winter				
2006	Spring				
	Summer			Govt of Wales Act	
	Autumn				St Andrews agreement
	Winter				
2007	Spring		Elections (SNP min)	Elections (Lab/Plaid)	Elections (DUP, SF, UUP, SDLP) and Assembly restored
	Summer	Brown becomes PM			
	Autumn				
	Winter				
2008	Spring				
	Summer				
	Autumn				
	Winter				

Table 12.1: 'Comparability factors', 2007(%)

	Scotland	Wales	Northern Ireland
Children, Schools and Families	100	100	100
Communities and Local Government	100	100	100
Local Government	19	100	17
Home Office	100	0	0
Legal Departments (courts, etc)	99	0	1
Health	99	99	99
Culture, Media and Sport	96	91	99
Environment, Food and Rural Affairs	95	94	95
Transport	92	68	94
Innovation, Universities and Skills	79	79	79
Business, Enterprise and Regulatory Reform	32	29	33
Cabinet Office	7	7	18
Work and Pensions	1	1	100
Chancellors' Departments (HMRC, Bank, etc)	1	1	5

Source: HM Treasury (2007a, p 12)

devolved to each of Scotland, Wales and Northern Ireland. Scotland additionally has responsibility for the courts and criminal justice. Scotland and Northern Ireland are responsible for the majority of their own public transport systems, Wales less so. Thus, the traditional pillars of the welfare state – health (including social services), education and housing – are all substantially devolved, the significant exception being social security, which is devolved only to Northern Ireland (and does not include tax policy or tax credits).

However, devolution of responsibility is not necessarily the same as devolution of power. In the first place, there is limited room for manoeuvre on issues that lie adjacent to a boundary between a devolved and a reserved matter. For example, although regional economic development is devolved, international relations and trade are not, which limits the range of development strategies the devolved administrations can independently adopt. In the welfare field, because the social security system interacts with so many other aspects of welfare, its reservation (except in Northern Ireland) creates numerous constraints in other policy areas: on welfare-to-work programmes, on housing and on social care, for example. The Scottish Executive initiative in 2002 to make personal care for older people free at the point of use provided a test case of one of these boundary issues, as Parry (2004) explains. The initiative was expected to produce savings on disability extra-costs benefits (Attendance Allowance and Disability Living Allowance) that would offset the cost of providing free care, but in the event these savings were retained by the non-devolved Department for Work and Pensions (DWP), leaving the Scottish administration to bear the gross cost of the reform.

Even Northern Ireland's control over social security may be more apparent than real. As with other devolved areas, the funding through the block grant from the Treasury is calculated on the assumption of British benefit levels and eligibility criteria. Without revenue-raising powers, this effectively means that any proposed benefit reform would have to take the form of 'robbing Peter to pay Paul', and in the event Northern Irish social security has moved in lockstep with the British system (Parry, 2004).

The second reason for thinking that devolved responsibility is not the same as devolved power is the way in which the funding available to the devolved administrations is determined more generally. Scotland, Wales and Northern Ireland have historically enjoyed higher per-capita funding of welfare and public services than the average for the UK. In part this is a reflection of their higher social needs, but only in part: although there are difficult methodological issues in adjusting for needs, the per-capita rates are probably high even after making such an adjustment. Midwinter (2007) reports that total identifiable public spending per capita in Northern Ireland was 29% above the UK average in 1999, and 23% above after adjusting for needs. The differentials for Scotland are lower (about 19% per capita higher than the UK average in the late 1990s, without adjusting for needs), but still significant.

The residual has been explained by some commentators as a sop to fend off devolution (Keating, 2005). The incentive for Westminster to maintain these higher levels of per capita spending clearly decreases as devolution becomes a reality, and to the extent that electoral accountability for welfare outcomes shifts to the devolved Parliaments and Assemblies. The so-called Barnett formula, used to determine the block grants to the devolved administrations, will in fact deliver these decreases over time, relative to the UK average. The formula takes the baseline budget for each country as given and allocates cash increases in UK expenditure proportionally to the nominal population shares of each country.[2] Given the comparatively high baseline expenditures in the devolved administrations, the allocated increases in expenditure represent smaller *percentage* increases than is the case for England. Shrinking populations in Scotland and Wales in recent years have offset the 'Barnett squeeze' to a certain extent, and will continue to do so until the population weights are revised, but Northern Ireland has experienced a growing population and consequently a double squeeze on funding.

The combination of budgetary border skirmishes between Westminster and the devolved administrations, the lack of flexibility inherent in a block grant based on the structure of England-dominated policies and programmes and the long-term relative squeeze on funding means that the scope for policy divergence in practice is considerably less than it is on paper.

Policies of the devolved administrations

Policy divergence in general

Welsh First Minister Rhodri Morgan claimed to be creating 'clear red water' between Cardiff and Westminster (quoted in Andrews and Martin, 2007, p 150), while Donald Dewar set out to find 'Scottish solutions for Scottish problems' (3 November 1998; quoted in Scott et al, 2008). In Northern Ireland, devolution, and the peace process of which it was part, was widely believed to herald a new era of policy making, including in welfare policy. But to what extent have policies in fact diverged?

Before turning to detailed consideration of policies and outcomes in relation to poverty and educational inequality, it is worth noting where other welfare policies have diverged from those pursued elsewhere in the UK. As Table 12.2 shows, Scotland and Wales have signalled a more universalist approach to provision with the introduction and expansion of a range of benefits in kind: in transport, leisure, schools and healthcare. These are high-profile and relatively inexpensive innovations, whose impact is unlikely to be progressive in a strict sense, since many of these services were already free to those on low incomes, but which may well have wider benefits in terms of promoting access and participation, and reducing means testing. The devolved administrations also led the rest of the UK in a range of measures to protect individuals and groups at risk of discrimination.

One aspect of divergence in policy that caught the public and media attention was Scotland's decision in 2002 to make personal care for older people free at the point of use, in line with the recommendations of the Sutherland Commission on Long-Term Care in 1999 (Royal CSSN, 1999; recommendations that were not followed elsewhere in the UK). As discussed above, the anticipated savings from social security benefits were retained by the UK's DWP, raising some concerns about the long-run fiscal sustainability of this policy, costing around £22 million per year (Parry, 2004).

Scotland's homelessness legislation widened the eligibility criteria for receiving assistance (Kintrea, 2006; Pawson and Davidson, 2008), and although land reform fell short of the most radical demands, it has made it easier for rural communities to buy land (Laible, 2008).

Finally, Wales rejected the Best Value framework adopted elsewhere in the UK for local authorities to assess their performance. The Welsh approach is said to emphasise cooperation rather than competition between service providers, to rely on trust and professionalism rather than targets and inspection to regulate quality of services and to use the mechanism of 'voice' (particularly collective voice) rather than 'choice' of service users to ensure that services are responsive to need (Drakeford, 2007).

However, Andrews and Martin (2007) failed to detect an overall improvement in public service performance in Wales relative to England over the period 2000-01

Table 12.2: Main areas of welfare policy divergence

	Scotland	Wales	Northern Ireland
Benefits in kind	• National concessionary fares on public transport (2005) • Free fruit in schools (2007) • Free breakfasts in schools in deprived areas (2007)	• Free bus travel for older and disabled people (2002) • Free breakfasts in schools (2003) • Free swimming for children and older people (2004)	• Free breakfasts in schools in deprived areas (2006)
Welfare to work	• New Futures Fund (1999) • Working for Families Fund (2004)	• Want to Work (2005)	
Anti-discrimination	• Repeal of 'Section 28' inhibiting teaching about homosexuality in schools (2000) • Protection for breast-feeding in public (2004)	• Creation of Children's Commissioner (2000) (rest of UK followed)	• Equality Commission (1998) (rest of UK followed)
Education	• Graduate endowment (introduced 2001, abolished 2008) • New Community Schools (1999) • Comprehensive education (2000) • Reduction of testing and modification of school league tables (2003) • Parental participation in schools (2006)	• Abolition of school league tables (2001) • Making the Connections strategy (2004)	• Abolition of school league tables (2001) • Abolition of 11-plus examination; creation of integrated schools; state funding for all schools (announced 2002)
Health and social services	• Free personal care for older people (2002) • Health service delivery reform (2004) • Expansion of NHS dentistry; free eye tests (2005)	• Extension of free eye tests and free prescriptions (1999) • Retention of community health councils (2004)	
Housing	• Land reform (2003) • Homelessness provisions (2003)		
Local government		• Self-assessment replaces Best Value regime (2001)	• Local taxation reform (2007)

Notes: Year in parentheses refers to the date the relevant Act or measure was passed; titles are descriptive rather than the formal title of the Acts.

Sources: Hazell (2000); Andrews and Martin (2007); Birrell (2007); Laible (2008); Schmuecker (2008); Scottish Parliament, National Assembly for Wales, and Northern Ireland Assembly websites;

to 2004-05, on the basis of statutory performance indicators. The only service in which an unambiguous improvement relative to the English comparator authorities could be detected was policing, which is not a devolved function. If the distinctive Welsh approach to public services is especially well suited to the Welsh context, either it has yet to make itself felt, or these are the wrong performance indicators with which to measure its success.

Policies on poverty and income inequality

One can certainly identify differences in the rhetoric used in the four countries post devolution with respect to poverty and income inequality. In Scotland, great play was made of the social *inclusion* agenda, in contrast to Westminster's Social Exclusion Unit. The agenda was outlined initially in *Social Justice ... A Scotland where Everyone Matters* (Scottish Executive, 1999), although no definition of social justice or social inclusion was offered, and indeed the goals were not dissimilar from those being monitored in the DSS's (1999) *Opportunity for All* publication: for example, ending child poverty, tackling young people not in education, employment or training (NEETs), full employment, and reducing inequality between the most deprived communities and the rest. A review of the strategy produced *Closing the Opportunity Gap* (Scottish Executive, 2002), downplaying social justice and focusing more explicitly on poverty prevention and routes out of poverty. The analysis of the causes of poverty and the corresponding solutions were once again parallel to those identified south of the border – welfare-to-work schemes, targets for raising educational attainment among underachievers and area regeneration through 'Social Inclusion Partnerships'.

The arrival of the Scottish National Party (SNP) in government in 2007 heralded a further change in terminology and a more concerted attempt to join up the economic strategy with social objectives, identified under five headings: Wealthier and Fairer, Healthier, Safer and Stronger, Smarter, and Greener (Scottish Government, 2007). However, although the connection between them is made, the social objectives are clearly subservient to the overall aim of economic growth, as First Minister Alex Salmond states in the Foreword to the economic strategy: 'Sustainable economic growth is the one central Purpose to which all else in government is directed and contributes' (Scottish Government, 2007, p v; capitalisation in original). Scott et al (2008) detect a more 'old Labour' note in the social aspirations of the SNP but argue that this is in tension with its neoliberal assumptions about how to secure and enhance economic competitiveness.

The Welsh Assembly Government's *Plan for Wales 2001* (WAG, 2001) sets out its commitments to social inclusion, equality and sustainable development. Drakeford (2007) argues that the interpretation given to equality has more in common with equality of outcome than the English/UK emphasis on equality of opportunity. Following the 2003 elections, a Minister for Social Justice was created, although as in Scotland it remains unclear how the relationship between social inclusion, equality and social justice is to be understood.

In Northern Ireland, Wilson (2007, p 151) observes that there is no shortage of discussion of equality: 'The e-word is frequently employed, including by ministers and officials as well as non-governmental organisations', but this is often in relation to non-discrimination (equal treatment) between Catholics and Protestants rather than social and economic inequalities more generally. Indeed, Section 75 of the 1998 Northern Ireland Act requires the Northern Ireland Assembly and all public bodies to have due regard to promoting equality of opportunity, but this is specified exclusively in terms of horizontal equality (characteristics such as gender, disability and religion) rather than vertical equality (the gap between rich and poor). Wilson (2007) argues that the requirement for equal treatment between the two communities has in fact obscured and obstructed efforts to tackle economic inequality, with the politics of recognition taking precedence over the politics of redistribution.

A programme to direct government expenditure towards deprived areas and groups, known as Targeting Social Need, predated the Labour government and devolution, and was simply rebranded as *New* Targeting Social Need thereafter. Its social inclusion strand closely followed Social Exclusion Unit initiatives in Westminster. An anti-poverty strategy was produced while the Assembly was still suspended in 2006 (OFMDFM, 2006), again explicitly mirroring UK government programmes, and it remains to be seen to what extent the strategy will be pursued by the restored Office of the First Minister and Deputy First Minister.

So much for the differences in the rhetoric of the devolved administrations. How different have the policy agendas turned out to be in practice? One approach is to examine the extent to which public spending priorities have changed. This is far from straightforward, given the lack of comparability between the Finance Acts (budgets) in the different countries, but Adams and Schmuecker's (2006) analysis of the Treasury's 'Public Expenditure Statistical Analyses' provides some insight. They find that growth rates in public spending on health and education – generally pro-poor categories of expenditure – were faster in England over the period 1999-2000 to 2004-05 than in Scotland, Wales or Northern Ireland. This could be simply the effect of the Barnett formula, discussed above, which delivers smaller *percentage* increases in funding to the devolved administrations as a result of their historically high baselines. What is more revealing is the fact that in other categories of expenditure – recreation, culture and religion, and agriculture, fisheries and forestry – spending in the devolved administrations has grown faster than in England over the same period, which tends to support the interpretation that there has been a shift in priorities rather than simply an overall squeeze. The final expenditure category analysed by Adams and Schmuecker – housing and community amenities – presents a mixed picture, with expenditure rising fastest in Scotland, followed by England, then Wales and finally Northern Ireland.

In terms of specific anti-poverty initiatives, both Scotland and Wales have supplemented the DWP's welfare-to-work programmes with their own programmes. In Scotland, this has taken the form of the New Futures Fund to help ex-offenders and substance abusers, and the Working for Families Fund for lone parents with complex needs who need assistance to move towards participation in the New Deal for Lone Parents, never mind participation in paid work. Both of these programmes have received positive evaluations (GEN consulting, 2004 and McGregor et al, 2005, quoted in Scott, 2006). In Wales, the DWP and the Welsh Assembly have joined forces in a programme called Want 2 Work, designed to help Incapacity Benefit claimants return to work. Wales has high concentrations of Incapacity Benefit claimants especially in the ex-mining and other ex-industrial areas (North et al, 2007).

These welfare-to-work initiatives are complementary to, rather than divergent from, UK-wide policies. The same can be said of the area regeneration programmes, Communities First in Wales, and the Community Regeneration Fund in Scotland, both of which are targeted at deprived areas and are designed to involve a significant element of community participation (Adams and Schmuecker, 2006).

In Northern Ireland, the reform of local taxation, although still being implemented and already subject to review, has the potential to have significant impacts on poverty in the long run (Birrell, 2007). Northern Ireland escaped the Poll Tax debacle and the Council Tax that followed it. The changes that came into force in Northern Ireland in April 2007 included moving from rates based on banded capital values to a continuous scale. The progressive potential of this move in terms of wealth redistribution has been limited by the imposition of a cap set at £500,000, and the progressive effect will be further eroded if this cap is not increased in line with property price inflation. Nevertheless, there are likely to be more low-income gainers than losers, and the package also includes increases in targeted relief for pensioners, disabled people and low-income households (DFPNI, 2007).

Education policies

The most high-profile divergence in education policy has been with respect to the funding of higher education, with Scotland taking the decision in January 2000 to abolish tuition fees (Parry, 2002). In its place, a 'graduate endowment' was payable after completing the degree, with bursaries to support students from low-income backgrounds. Although this was hailed as an endorsement of the principle of free education, in contrast with the pay-as-you-go English system, it was in reality a delayed payment. England followed suit in 2006-07, replacing upfront fees in England with fees payable on graduation (albeit higher and variable fees). The latest development in February 2008 was the SNP's abolition of the graduate endowment for current and new students. How the funding gap for Scottish higher education institutions is to be met has yet to be determined.

Each of the devolved administrations has also introduced reforms to the schooling system. In Northern Ireland, the abolition of the 11–plus examination was announced in 2002, although it will not be implemented until 2009-10. Support for academic selection and school specialisation remains strong, so the demise of the 11–plus does not signal a move to comprehensive education (Osborne, 2006). Instead, the reforms have been accompanied by support for parental choice, funding for Irish language schools, integrated Catholic–Protestant schools and a common curriculum (Donnelly and Osborne, 2005).

Wales and Scotland have taken a different route, reducing the emphasis on school league tables, decreasing the amount of national testing and reiterating the comprehensive principle. The Welsh Assembly has taken the view that its largely rural population is too dispersed to be able to make effective use of a choice-based system, and that institutions such as schools and colleges should be encouraged to cooperate to produce a full curriculum within reach of every child and young person (WAG, 2004). In Scotland, New Community Schools, piloted prior to devolution but continued and extended thereafter, aim to offer a wide range of services beyond simply education, including health and social services, in order to address the barriers to learning that children especially in deprived areas can experience (Stewart, J., 2004).

Changes in key outcomes since 1998/99

Significant structural differences between the four countries of the UK predate devolution and need to be taken into account when assessing the impact of specific policies. This section begins by summarising some of those differences.

Population, economy and labour market

Over the period 1991 to 2006, England's share of the UK population rose very slightly from 83.3% to 83.8% and the shares of Wales and Scotland each fell, from 5.0% to 4.9% in the case of Wales and from 8.8% to 8.4% in the case of Scotland (ONS, 2008c). The population share of Northern Ireland increased slightly, from 2.8% to 2.9%. These relative changes mask much more significant absolute rates of population change in each country. Northern Ireland has enjoyed particularly strong population growth since 1981, while Scotland experienced falls in population between 1981 and 2001.

Figure 12.2 shows that according to one measure of regional economic activity – the Gross Value Added (GVA) per head of resident population – all four countries enjoyed significant absolute growth both before and after devolution. England has the highest per capita GVA and it has gained on each of the other three countries from the mid-1990s onwards.

Figure 12.2: Index of gross value added per head, by country, 1989-2006

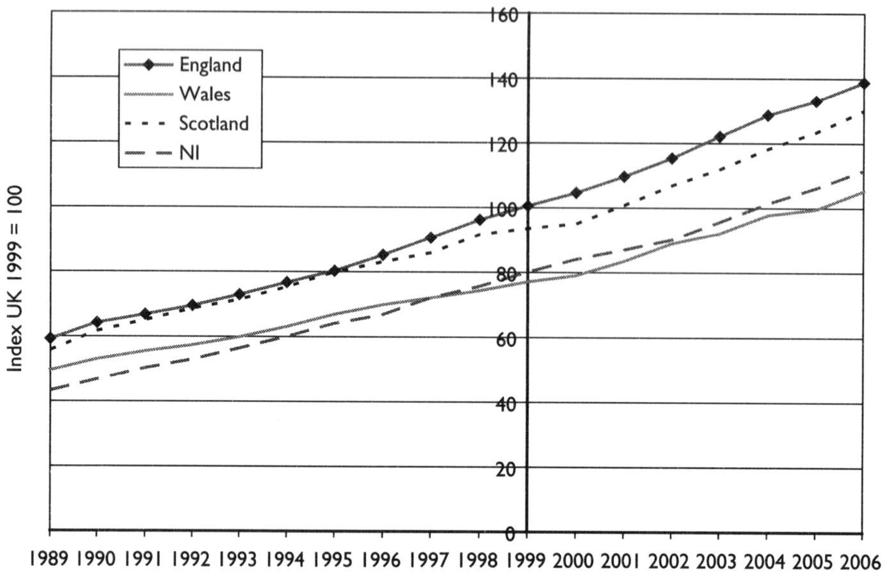

Source: Author's calculations based on ONS (2007b); not deflated

All four countries have slower growth rates in the 2000s compared with the previous decade (ONS, 2007b). The drop is particularly marked in Northern Ireland, although it started with the strongest annual growth rates of the four countries.

Employment rates since 1995 have generally been higher in England than in Scotland (with the exception of the most recent observation) followed by Wales and finally Northern Ireland (Figure 12.3).

All of the devolved administrations have a comparatively high proportion of the workforce in public sector employment, especially Northern Ireland: in 1999, the percentages were 28.8 for Northern Ireland, 24.2 for Wales, 23.2 for Scotland and 18.3 for England, and these were virtually unchanged by 2007 (Barnard, 2007).

Education

Inheritance

School pupils in England, Wales and Northern Ireland all take General Certificates of Secondary Education (GCSEs) at around the age of 16, but while the structure of schools was similar in England and Wales at the time of devolution (Daugherty et al, 2000), Northern Ireland was unique among the four countries of the UK in having retained the 11-plus examination and academically selective grammar schools.

Figure 12.3: Employment rates, by country, 1995-2007

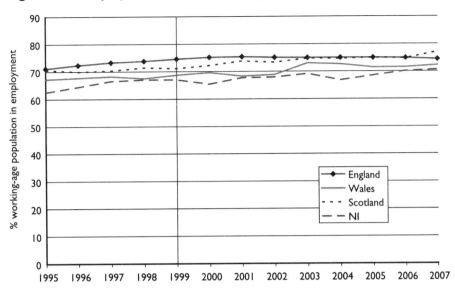

Source: ONS (2008c) and previous editions

The conventional view is that the comprehensive principle was more thoroughly implemented in Scotland than in England (Stewart, J., 2004; Arnott and Ozga, 2008). A smaller proportion of Scotland's school pupils are educated privately than in England (3.8% compared with 6.0%; Keating, 2005), and the very small number of schools that had chosen to opt out under the Conservative education reforms of the 1980s were brought back into the fold in 2000. The principal school qualifications, known as Highers and usually taken at the age of 17, were reformed in the 1990s in response to criticism that they were outdated (they were created in 1888!). The Scottish Qualifications Certificate is now available to take at the age of 16, and a reformed Highers programme is available for 17- and 18-year-olds.

In terms of higher education, for centuries, Scotland had four universities while the whole of England managed only two (Keating, 2005); honours degree courses last four years; and there is greater integration between further and higher education institutions than in England, with many further education colleges offering diplomas that are the equivalent to the first or second years of an honours degree.

Changes in outcomes

The middle panel of Table 12.3 shows the baseline of educational attainment and educational inequality in 1999-2000, comparing across countries, while the right-hand panel shows the outcomes in 2005-06. Not all measures are available for all countries or years.

What impact has the divergence in funding of higher education, such as it is, had on participation, particularly by students from lower social class backgrounds? Scotland began with a higher proportion of the age cohort overall participating in higher education than did England, and this has been maintained, although there has been some convergence. England has not yet met its target of 50% participation, and the trend is unclear (the latest figures, for 2006-07, are lower than those shown in Table 12.3 for 2005-06: see Chapter Four); Scotland exceeded this level in 2001 and 2002, before falling back slightly (OECD, 2007a).

Scotland also had a high proportion of children from working-class backgrounds achieving higher education entry-level qualifications, compared with England, in 1999-2000. These baseline figures refer to the proportion of working-class 18- to 19-year-olds achieving the potential for higher education entry, while the more recent figures refer to the proportion of higher education entrants who are from a lower social class background, so they are not directly comparable. Nevertheless, we can see that Scotland's advantage relative to England seems to have been attenuated by 2005-06.

Evidence here is still emerging. Dearden et al (2008) argue that comparing 2006-07 to 2003-04, the new system of financing in England is more favourable to students from less well-off backgrounds but this is on the basis of modelling rather than observation. J. Stewart (2004) finds that the proportion from partly skilled and unskilled backgrounds has remained steady in Scotland. According to data from the Higher Education Statistics Authority (HESA, 2008), a higher proportion of English-domiciled students are now from a lower social class background than the proportion of Scottish-domiciled students. These figures need to be interpreted carefully, however, since Scotland continues to have higher rates of participation overall: levels may be more important than trends (Scottish working-class young people are still more likely to participate in higher education than working-class young people in the rest of Britain) and, depending on whether one is more interested in fulfilment of potential or in labour market advantage, the absolute chance of getting to university may be more important than opportunities relative to others (Iannelli, 2008).

Further down the educational ladder, the proportion of pupils achieving five or more good GCSE passes has increased across the board. Wales and England started with similarly low rates of achievement, but the improvement has been less marked in Wales, with the result that it now lags behind the other countries of the UK on this measure. Meanwhile, Scotland started with the highest level of achievement but has barely improved at all; England and Northern Ireland have leapfrogged over it.

There have also been improvements in all four countries at the other end of the spectrum of educational attainment, with a smaller proportion of pupils than

Table 12.3: Educational achievements and educational inequality, by country, 1999-2000 and 2005-06

	1999-2000				2005-06			
	E	W	S	NI	E	W	S	NI
Initial participation rate (%) in HE[1] (17- to 30-year-olds)	39		49		42		47	
% of HE entrants from NS-SEC[2] 4-7					29	33	27	38
% of age 18/19 achieving HE entry qualifications	25		37					
% of working-class age 18/19 achieving HE entry qualifications[3]	13		20					
% achieving 5+ GCSE grades A*-C or Scottish National Qualification equivalent	49.2	49.1	58.3	56.9	59.2	53.8	58.6	63.0
% no graded qualification at school-leaving age	5.6	7.7	[5.6]	3.6	2.2	6.8	[4.6]	3.1
Mean PISA[4] reading score	523		526	519	496	481	499	495
(standard error)	(3.0)		(3.8)	(3.1)	(2.7)	(3.7)	(4.0)	(3.5)
Reading score 95th minus 5th percentile	328			354	337	323	316	348
Mean PISA mathematics score	529		533	524	{495}	{484}	{506}	{494}
(standard error)	(2.9)		(3.7)	(3.4)	(2.5)	(2.9)	(3.6)	(2.8)
Mathematics score 95th minus 5th percentile	303			321	{293}	{270}	{280}	{306}

Notes:
1 HE = higher education.
2 NS-SEC = National Statistics Socio-Economic Classification.
3 Classification used in this source is 'service' (highest social class), intermediate and working class, with a residual unclassified category (Iannelli, 2007).
4 PISA = Programme for International Student Assessment. PISA results are from PISA 2000 and PISA 2006 respectively. PISA 2000 had a low response rate in England, Scotland and Northern Ireland: see Chapter Thirteen and Ruddock (2006) for a discussion of the implications.

Cells are blank where no figures are available.
[] not comparable to other countries.
{} not comparable to base year.

Sources: PISA 2000, 2006; DCSF (2007c); DIUS (2007); Iannelli (2007) HESA (2008); New Policy Institute (2007); OECD (2007a); ONS (2008c) and earlier editions

previously now leaving school with no qualifications. England, starting from a relatively poor base, appears to have performed particularly well in this respect, and Northern Ireland continues to do well. Wales has two to three times more pupils leaving school with no qualifications than other parts of the UK.

The 2006 Programme for International Student Assessment (PISA)[3] results confirm this difference in levels of attainment – Welsh reading and mathematics scores are lower than the other countries – although they also suggest that the distribution of Welsh results is less wide than in England, or, especially, Northern Ireland.

Comparing 2006 with the 2000 PISA reading results (the mathematics results are not computed on the same basis), standards appear to have deteriorated in England, Scotland and Northern Ireland, but rather less in Northern Ireland than elsewhere – a levelling-down effect. Scotland retains a slight advantage.

Income

At the time of devolution, rates of poverty in the UK population as a whole and especially among children were lower in England than in the rest of the UK (Table 12.4). Wales and Northern Ireland were similarly poor (although the figures for Northern Ireland are for a slightly later period), and Scotland was not far behind. Even on a before housing costs (BHC) measure, nearly one in three children were below the threshold of 60% of median income, compared with one in four in England. It is not surprising then, that all four countries made high-profile commitments to tackling child poverty.

However, although England had the lowest poverty rate, its income distribution was among the most unequal, together with Northern Ireland. Scotland and Wales were slightly less unequal.

By the most recent period for which figures are available – 2004-05 to 2006-07 – overall rates of poverty had fallen slightly in all the countries except Northern Ireland. Scotland improved marginally more than the other countries, although the difference is unlikely to be statistically significant. Child poverty rates fell more substantially in all four countries, with an especially large drop in Scotland. Northern Irish and Welsh children fared less well: they began and ended the period with the highest poverty rates, despite five and four percentage point falls respectively.

Tracking income inequality in the four countries historically is challenging because of the absence of a consistent time series. There may have been slight falls in income inequality as indicated by the whole-population Gini coefficient in Wales, Scotland and England. However, the overall UK Gini coefficient stands at the same level in 2006-07 as it did in 1998-99.

A larger fall in overall income inequality appears to have occurred in Northern Ireland, although again caution must be exercised in making this comparison. However, other forms of inequality have been increasing. By the most recent data,

Table 12.4: Poverty and income inequality, by country, and over time

	1998-99 to 2000-01 (3-year average)				2004-05 to 2006-07 (3-year average)			
	E	**W**	**S**	**NI**	**E**	**W**	**S**	**NI**
% below 60% median income	18	21	19	20†	17	20	17	20
% children below 60% median income	24	29	28	29	22	25	21	24

	1998-99				2005-06			
	E	**W**	**S**	**NI**	**E**	**W**	**S**	**NI**
Whole distribution Gini coefficient	0.35	0.32	0.33	0.35	{0.34}	{0.29}	{0.31}	{0.30}

Notes:
Income is equivalised household income BHC in all cases. The median is defined on the UK distribution for the later years and for GB for the earlier period.
{ } not comparable to base year.
† NI whole population poverty rate is for 2002/03 to 2004/05, the first years NI was part of HBAI. (The time series for children has been calculated retrospectively from the FES.)

Sources: For poverty rates, Households Below Average Income (HBAI) publication for various years including 2000-01 chapter 4; 2004-05 appendix 5; 2006-07 chapters 3 and 4; and author's calculations, and, for NI whole population poverty rate, Kenway et al (2006). For Gini coefficients, 1998-99 figures author's calculations from FES; 2005-06 author's calculations from HBAI (based on FRS), so may not be precisely comparable. For the years 1998-2000, Morelli and Seaman (2007) give Gini coefficients of 0.38 for England, 0.37 for Wales and 0.38 for Scotland, based on BHPS. The discrepancy is probably due to differences in the way income is reported in the surveys. Since the Gini coefficient for inequality in the UK has changed little over the period (0.35 in 1998-99 and the same in 2006-07, according to HBAI), the large changes that would be implied by taking Morelli and Seaman's figures as the baseline are implausible.

Catholics are at considerably greater risk of poverty than Protestants (Table 12.5). The difference is especially pronounced among children (the classification is based on the religion of all adult members of the household), and horizontal inequality of this kind appears to have worsened since 2002-03, with poverty rates among Protestant adults and children falling consistently and rapidly while they rose significantly among Catholic adults and children (DSD, 2007). Although a longer time series is not available on a consistent basis, other evidence suggests that the relative social and economic advantage of Protestants over Catholics fell between the 1970s and the 1990s and this was arguably an important facilitator of the peace process (Breen, 2000; Stewart and Langer, 2008). The most recent trends are therefore particularly worrying.

Table 12.5: Poverty rates by religion, Northern Ireland, 2005-06[1]

	Whole population	% of population	Children	% of population
Protestant	18	47	19	42
Catholic	24	43	31	48
Other	21	3	28	2
No religion	22	1	14	1
Unwilling to answer	18	1	n/a	n/a
Mixed	17	6	25	7
All	21	100	25	100

Note: [1] % below 60% UK median equivalised household income, BHC.

Source: HBAI, Northern Ireland report, 2005-06

Assessment

The chapter began by outlining reasons to think that devolution would intensify or mitigate inequality within and across nations. We have now reviewed the policies that have been implemented, particularly with respect to poverty and education, and the change in various indicators of poverty and inequality over the period. But to what extent have the observed changes been brought about by the policies of the devolved administrations? And what does this tell us about the impact of devolution on inequality in general?

In education, at secondary school level, there has been a deterioration in reading score results in all three countries that took part in the PISA survey in both 2000 and 2006, and inequality in this measure has grown in England (it has fallen in Northern Ireland). On the other hand, top GCSE (or equivalent) results have improved in all four countries, but especially strongly in England, while the proportion achieving no graded qualification at the end of compulsory schooling has fallen, again, particularly quickly in England. There have been changes to the curricula in all four countries, and to the structures within which primary and secondary education are delivered, but these results do not look like a devolution success story, in terms of either levels of achievement or narrowing gaps within each country. The most charitable explanation for the devolved administrations is that changes in education may have a long lead-in time before positively affecting final examination results.

We saw earlier that the importance of differences in higher education funding between Scotland and England until 2008 has probably been overstated. Nevertheless, in so far as there are differences, their impact has probably been to narrow inequalities overall and within England, but not within Scotland (although Scotland was less unequal at the outset). Continuing to monitor these trends will be important.

With respect to poverty and income inequality, the outcomes are mildly encouraging – poverty rates have fallen slightly among the population as a whole in Scotland, Wales and England and have fallen to a greater extent among children in all four countries. Measures of inequality across the distribution are more difficult to track over time, but these too if anything show an improvement. However, the likelihood that these changes are related to devolved policies is remote: welcome as measures such as free breakfasts for children in deprived areas and free bus travel for low-income groups may be, they are not likely to result in a detectable shift in the income distribution. Scotland has had some success in raising its employment rate relative to England, and that may have contributed to a reduction in poverty, but again the relationship with specific policies of the devolved administration is difficult to identify. The principal tools of redistribution – taxation and social security – are not, in the main, devolved powers.

Meanwhile in Northern Ireland, a fairer deal for the two communities, Catholic and Protestant – one of the great hopes of the peace process and devolution – has yet to become apparent in the poverty statistics, with Catholics and especially Catholic children being at greater, and *increasing*, risk of poverty.

So what does this mean for the impact of devolution on inequality in general and in the future? There is some evidence here of creative, regionally specific policies, with the potential to narrow inequalities within each country. The reform of local taxation in Northern Ireland, the attempts to join up services for a dispersed rural population in Wales and the add-ons to welfare-to-work programmes in Scotland are all examples of policies that have been tailored to local circumstances and demographics, which have the potential to be progressive, and which would have been more constrained in the absence of devolution. On the other hand, there is no evidence that the rhetorics of social justice and inclusion that have accompanied devolution and the rise of nationalist parties in Scotland and Wales have been translated into a significant shift of resources to the worst off or even towards the categories of public spending (like health and education) that tend to be pro-poor.

There are many possible reasons for this failure to translate words into action. One is that most welfare policies take many years to implement and yet more years to take effect. Another is that devolution of responsibility has not been accompanied by devolution of real power: the devolved administrations' hands are tied internally (by their political inability to pursue radically redistributive agendas or to raise tax revenue, even where they have the formal authority); by Westminster (which retains the purse strings and many reserved matters); and internationally (by global economic pressures).

But devolution is gathering momentum – the Wales Assembly Government has gained legislative powers, the Northern Ireland Assembly is restored and the Scottish Government is becoming more confident and gaining in experience. Greater devolution will tend to increase inequality between the four countries, but whether or not this translates into a positive or a negative impact on inequality within countries, between people, depends on the particular policies adopted. In the present political climate, despite some important gestures towards universalism by the Scottish and Welsh administrations and bold but empty rhetoric in every country, there are few signs of a radically progressive agenda being pursued anywhere in the UK. Contemporary capitalism, left to its own devices, threatens to drive inequalities ever wider – between rich and poor and between the skilled and unskilled – so that standing still, in policy terms, means worsening outcomes. As far as equality is concerned, there is nothing intrinsically good or bad about devolution: it is the balance of forces arguing for the interests of the ordinary man and woman and against the privilege of the few that will determine the outcome, in each and every corner of the nation.

Notes

[1] Much of the literature on the effects of devolution on inequality concerns itself with differences between countries, states or regions (Rodriguez-Pose and Gill, 2004; Mooney et al, 2006; Schmuecker, 2008). The consensus is that devolution tends to increase inequality between the administrative units to which policy is devolved – an unsurprising conclusion, given that creating the potential for diversification of policy is one of the reasons for devolution in the first place. Even if this does not necessarily translate into an increase in inequality among the population as a whole, it could still be a matter of concern. For example, if entitlements that we are accustomed to regarding as universal, such as social security benefits or access to free healthcare, become significantly dependent on the part of the UK in which you live, this could lead to a postcode lottery on a large scale (Walker, 2002; Piachaud, 2008).

[2] Currently, as percentages of England's population: 10.08% for Scotland, 5.84% for Wales and 3.43% for Northern Ireland (HM Treasury, 2007a).

[3] PISA is an international study of educational attainment; see Chapter Thirteen for more details.

THIRTEEN

Poverty, inequality and child well-being in international context: still bottom of the pack?

Kitty Stewart[1]

Background

In 1997, the UK compared badly with other Organisation for Economic Co-operation and Development (OECD) countries on poverty and inequality indicators. Indeed, the country's relative position on child poverty in particular formed part of the impetus for taking action to improve living standards for children. The strategy was wide-ranging, as has been detailed earlier in this book – it included increased funding for childcare and early years policies; policies to promote parental employment; a National Minimum Wage (NMW) and additional support for low earners through the tax credit system; more generous out-of-work benefits for families with younger children; and investment in compulsory education.

Despite these efforts, in 2007 the United Nations Children's Fund (UNICEF) published a report that placed the UK bottom of a child well-being league (UNICEF, 2007). Indicators were persistently poor across the six domains of well-being examined in the report, with the UK ranking bottom or near bottom on material well-being, education, family and peer relationships, risk-taking behaviour and subjective well-being; and middle-ranking on health and safety. The report was greeted as a blow to the New Labour government after a decade of investment in children's welfare (see, for example, *The Guardian*, 14 February 2007). In reality, however, much of the data represented Labour's starting point more fairly than its achievements: 18 out of 40 indicators came from a 2001-02 survey of 11- to 15-year-olds (Currie et al, 2004).

Given the impact and prominence of the UNICEF study, this chapter aims to provide a more up-to-date assessment of the comparative standing of UK children, and one that more accurately reflects changes in policy since New Labour came to power. It covers in some part all of the UNICEF areas except (for space reasons) infant health and child mortality, where the UK's performance stood out less at the outset. At the same time, it broadens the picture in two ways: it includes measures of overall inequality and poverty for working-age adults and pensioners, and it discusses some of the factors behind the lead indicators. The first half of the chapter is dedicated to the material well-being domain. The second half examines relative progress in education, risks and behaviours (including health behaviour), peer relationships and subjective well-being. At times, discussion is restricted to European Union (EU) member states because of the data available, but where possible information for other OECD countries is included.

Material well-being

Poverty and inequality

The UNICEF report uses the year 2000 for its comparison of child poverty rates – unfortunate for the UK given that child poverty peaked in 1998-99 and fell in every subsequent year until 2004-05, since when it has increased slightly. However, as detailed in Chapter Three, progress was less rapid than had been hoped. Figure 13.1 shows child poverty in the EU15 in 1998 (reflecting the peak), 2001 and 2006. Rapid reductions in poverty between 1999 and 2001 brought the UK up from bottom of the table to fifth from bottom, but while the UK rate continued to fall slowly for several years after this, the subsequent upturn combined with rapid improvement in Portugal and Ireland left the UK ranked joint bottom with Italy and Spain in 2006.

We should be wary of placing too much emphasis on small changes in poverty rates, particularly as the dataset used by Eurostat to calculate these figures has itself changed since 2001: the European Community Household Panel (ECHP) was collected until 2001, and a new panel survey, the European Union Survey of Income and Living Conditions (EU-SILC), began in most countries in 2005, with national sources used to assess progress in the meantime. However, it seems clear that despite substantial progress in New Labour's early period, in 2006 child poverty in the UK remained firmly ranked alongside high-poverty Southern European countries, although closer to the best-performing countries.

To place the change in child poverty in wider context, Table 13.1 gives poverty rates for children alongside those for the population aged 25-49, the population of older people and the total population, as well as the income inequality measure adopted by the EU, which is the ratio of the income share of the top and bottom quintiles. For the population of older people and the total population, only 2006 data are included as changes in methodology and income definition mean that comparisons with earlier years are misleading. For the other two measures, both the UK figure and the UK ranking have remained the same or worsened slightly. Working-age poverty has been stable or rising in every country except Spain and Ireland, but the Irish performance – poverty fell from just above to just below the UK rate – was enough to shift the UK ranking from tenth to joint tenth. The income quintile share ratio shows convergence across the EU15 between 1998 and 2006: inequality has risen in the eight most equal countries,

Figure 13.1: Child poverty rates in the EU15

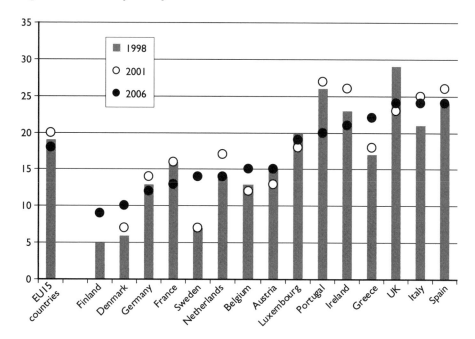

Notes:
(1) Figure shows children under 16 living in households with equivalised income below 60% of the median, on a before housing costs (BHC) basis.
(2) Data for 1998 and 2001 are from the European Community Household Panel (ECHP); data for 2006 are from the new EU Survey of Income and Living Conditions (EU-SILC). Data have been harmonised and are presented as a series by Eurostat.
(3) Income is collected in the year reported but refers to the previous year, with the exception of the UK (the reported year) and Ireland (rolling year).
(4) Rates for the UK differ from those presented earlier in the book because of the different datasets used, and because in other chapters the definition of children includes all those under 18 if in full-time education.

Source: Eurostat (2008) *Social Inclusion, Monetary Poverty and Living Conditions,* http://epp.eurostat.ec. europa.eu/tgm/table.do?tab=table&init=1&plugin=0&language=en&pcode=tsdsc230

and fallen or remained steady in five of the seven most unequal (with falls in France, Greece, Spain and Ireland and no change in Portugal). The UK and Italy are the two high-inequality countries that have seen inequality rise further. Not all inequality measures have risen significantly in the UK, as discussed in Chapter Two: Figure 2.1 shows that the 90:10 ratio has remained broadly stable, while the Gini coefficient has risen. The income quintile share ratio is similar to the Gini coefficient and different from the 90:10 ratio in including the effect of incomes at the very top and bottom.[2]

Overall, of the four countries in Figure 13.1 where child poverty fell substantially over the period, only the UK has a mixed story for other indicators. In Portugal, Ireland and France, all indicators have been steady or improving. There are two

Table 13.1: Poverty and inequality in the EU 15 (ranked by child poverty 2006)

	Poverty among children under 16 (%)		Poverty among people aged 25-49 (%)		Poverty among the population 65 plus (%)	Poverty among the total population (%)	Income quintile share ratio	
	1998	2006	1998	2006	2006	2006	1998	2006
Finland	5	9	7	9	22	13	3.1	3.6
Denmark	6	10	7	10	17	12	2.9	3.4
Germany	13	12	9	12	13	13	3.6	4.1
France	16	13	11	11	16	13	4.2	4.0
Sweden	7	14	7	11	12	12	3.0	3.5
Netherlands	14	14	9	9	6	10	3.6	3.8
Belgium	13	15	10	11	23	15	4.0	4.2
Austria	15	15	10	11	16	13	3.5	3.7
Luxembourg	20	19	11	14	8	14	3.7	4.2
Portugal	26	20	15	15	26	18	6.8	6.8
Ireland	23	21	15	13	27	18	5.2	4.9
Greece	17	22	15	17	26	21	6.5	6.1
Italy	21	24	16	18	22	20	5.1	5.5
Spain	24	24	17	15	31	20	5.9	5.3
UK	29	24	14	14	28	19	5.2	5.4
EU15	19	18	13	13	20	16	4.6	4.7
UK rank	**15**	**Joint 12**	**10**	**Joint 10**	**14**	**12**	**Joint 11**	**12**

Notes:

(1) Poverty is defined as living in a household with income below 60% of the equivalised median, BHC. The modified OECD scale is used for equivalisation.

(2) The different dataset and differences in definitions explain the differences from poverty rates reported earlier in the book, which are calculated from national data sources: for instance, in the UK child poverty estimates include children up to age 18 if in full-time education. Pensioner poverty estimates are particularly sensitive to small changes in definition as pensioners tend to be bunched closely around the poverty line.

(3) The income quintile share ratio is the ratio of the income received by the top 20% of the distribution to that received by the bottom 20%.

Source: Eurostat (2008). 1998 data are from the ECHP and 2006 data from the EU-SILC

ways of looking at this. On the one hand, it points to the success of the UK policy effort put into tackling child poverty in particular. On the other hand, it underlines the limits placed on the anti-poverty agenda in the UK, which may themselves have made the task harder. This is highlighted by Figure 13.2, which plots the child poverty rate against the income quintile share ratio for 2006, and for 1998 for the UK and other countries that have seen significant change in the relationship. The Figure shows a broad positive association between the child poverty rate and the inequality measure. Child poverty in the UK in 1998 was higher than might have been expected given the level of income inequality, but as child poverty has fallen the relationship has moved into line with that in other countries. However, to make further progress without affecting the income share ratio between top and bottom – that is, to continue to reduce child poverty without touching the top end of the income distribution – looks from Figure 13.2 to be extremely difficult, and there is logic behind this: ruling out a significant share of national income requires a tighter squeeze in the middle. The UK strategy so far has succeeded in part through significant 'horizontal' redistribution, from households without children towards those with children, but there are both equity and practical reasons why this cannot continue indefinitely (see discussion in Chapter Two).

Figure 13.2: Child poverty plotted against the income quintile share ratio, 2006

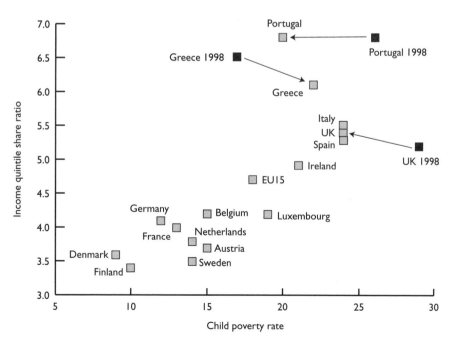

Source: Eurostat (2008) using EU-SILC data (1998 from ECHP)

Worklessness

The high share of households without a member in work is a key factor driving high poverty in the UK, and worklessness among households with children is treated as a well-being indicator in its own right in UNICEF's (2007) report. In that report, which uses data for 2000, the UK comes fifth from bottom among OECD countries, with a worklessness rate of 8% among households with children, just below that in Germany, Poland, Australia and Hungary. Figure 13.3 shows a slightly different measure (the focus is on children, not households) from a different source (the EU Labour Force Survey [LFS], a more consistent source than OECD Income Distribution questionnaires, although covering fewer countries). Germany fares far better in this dataset, and the UK ranks bottom of the EU15 throughout the period, despite the improvements of the first few years. Since 2000, as earlier chapters have outlined, worklessness has proved stubbornly difficult to budge. This is despite a steady decline in unemployment from 1993 to 2005, down from 6.8% in 1997 to 5.3% in 2006, against an OECD average that fell from 6.9% to 6.1% (OECD, 2007b).

One of the challenges for the UK in trying to reduce worklessness is the high – and growing – prevalence of lone parenthood. At nearly one in four households with children, the lone-parent rate is among the lowest in the Anglophone countries but still higher than anywhere else in the EU apart from Sweden, as illustrated in the first column of Table 13.2. The middle column shows the lone parent employment rate: this increased by 11 percentage points in the UK between 1996 and 2005, but this has been enough to overtake just two countries in the table.

Figure 13.3: Share of children aged 0-17 living in a household where nobody works (%)

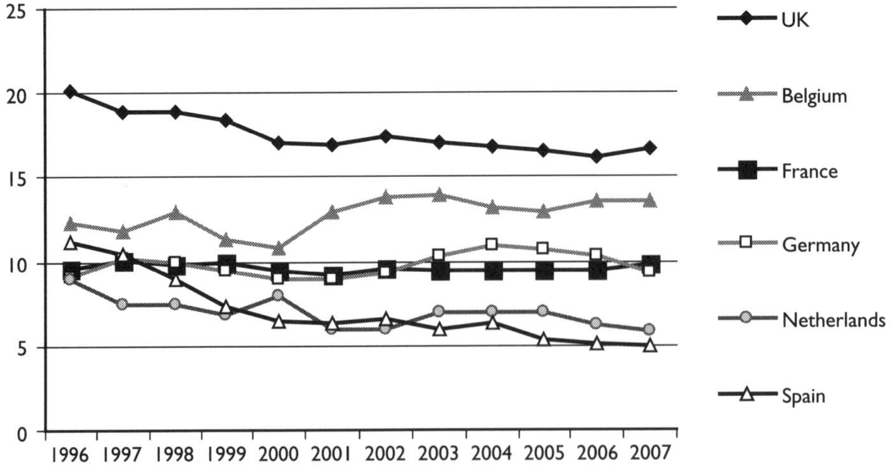

Source: Eurostat, 2008 using EU LFS

Table 13.2: Lone parenthood and employment 2005-06 (ranked by lone parent employment rate)

	Lone parents as share of all households with children 2005 (%)	Share of lone parents employed 2005 (%)	Non-working lone-parent households as share of all households with children (%)
Ireland	22	45	12.1
(UK 1996)	*(22)*	*(45)*	*(11.9)*
Australia	22	50	11.0
New Zealand	28	53	13.1
UK 2005	**24**	**56**	**10.5**
Netherlands	13	57	5.6
Belgium	18	62	6.8
Germany	16	62	6.1
Canada	25	68	8.1
Norway	17	69	5.3
Finland	10	70	3.0
France	14	70	4.2
US	33	74	8.6
Austria	12	75	3.0
Portugal	7	78	1.5
Italy	6	78	1.3
Sweden	24	82	4.3
Denmark	16	82	2.9
Greece	5	82	0.9
Spain	6	84	1.0
Luxembourg	9	94	0.5

Notes:

(1) Lone parent rate is spring 2006 from EU LFS (children less than 24 and still dependent) except for Denmark and Finland 2004 and the following from national sources: Australia 2003, Canada 2001, Iceland 2004, Ireland 2002, New Zealand 2006 (children not in full-time employment, Norway 2001, Sweden 2002 (children 15 or under), the US 2005 (children aged less than 18 and still dependent).

(2) Lone-parent employment is 2005 (children less than 24 and still dependent) except Denmark (1999), Belgium, Canada, Germany, Greece, Italy, Japan, Spain (2001), Finland and Portugal, (2002), Iceland and Norway (2003), the Netherlands (2004), and Switzerland (2006 2nd quarter).

(3) Third column calculated by author from previous two columns.

Source: OECD (2007d, tables 1.1 and 2.1); except UK 1996 from Chambaz (2001) using ECHP and Sweden lone parent rate from OECD (2005, table 2.3)

The UK is currently set to miss its target of 70% of lone parents in employment by 2010, as discussed in Chapter Five, and even this goal is only midway up the table. The final column shows that the combination of widespread lone parenthood and low employment results in more than one in ten UK children living with a lone parent not in work, compared with well below one in 20 in much of the rest of Europe. Of course, the impact of the higher employment rate on this statistic for the UK has been partly offset by the simultaneous rise in lone parenthood.

The share of children living with a lone parent is itself one of UNICEF's well-being indicators, on the grounds that growing up in a single-parent family (or step-family) is associated with greater risk to educational, health and employment outcomes, even after controlling for family income. This factor therefore contributed in more ways than one to the UK's poor ranking. But reversing a long-run demographic trend with complex causes is quite a challenge for government policy. Increasing the employment rate among lone parents – as New Labour policy sought to do – seems the more obvious place to intervene, especially when international evidence suggests that much higher rates are possible, in regimes ranging from the US to Sweden.

So why has progress not been faster despite the policy emphasis given to this area? First, it should be noted that there is evidence that the characteristics of lone parents in the UK differ from those in other countries in ways that present greater barriers to work: Bradshaw et al (1996) found that the education gap between single and married mothers was particularly large in the UK, while UK lone mothers were also younger and likely to have more children, including more children under the age of five. A second factor that has been underlined, for instance by David Freud's (2007) report for the Department for Work and Pensions, is much greater conditionality of benefit payments in other countries. The much harsher regime in the US is well documented, with strict time limits on welfare payments – although the combination of high maternal employment with high poverty rates in the US makes it unattractive as a role model. (Child poverty was 29% in the US in 2004 on a measure comparable to that presented in Table 13.1.[3])Perhaps less well known is that the European countries with a reputation for having the most supportive welfare states also have strong work requirements: Sweden, Denmark, Norway and Finland all require lone-parent benefit recipients to be available for work well before the youngest child reaches school age. Lewis (1998) points to the UK and the Netherlands as unusual in treating lone mothers as mothers, not workers, and not requiring them to register for work (although benefits are far more generous in the Netherlands, historically sufficient to replace a male breadwinner's earnings).

Increased compulsion for lone parents has risen up the agenda recently in the UK, with moves to much greater conditionality from October 2008. Even by 2010, when lone parents will be required to work once their youngest child reaches seven, the regime will be less stringent than that in most other industrialised countries (including the Netherlands, where job search is now required when the youngest is five). However, the new approach has still generated concern (see, for example, House of Commons Work and Pensions Committee, 2008). Critics maintain that the countries where conditionality works well do much more to make work an attractive proposition. In particular, they tend to have universal childcare systems that are accepted as high quality and which are low cost at the point of delivery. The cost aspect is illustrated in Figure 13.4, which shows the price at the point of delivery of having two children in a day nursery, and the share of disposable income that would be paid by a lone parent on average earnings and by one on two-thirds of average earnings. The UK, which has fostered a market-led childcare system, has also targeted subsidies to lower-income households, bringing the effective costs down sharply from half of the average wage to around 14% of earnings for a low-waged lone parent. The contrast with Ireland is clear, and shows the achievement of the Labour government; until the late 1990s, childcare was considered to be a private responsibility. But it is also clear that costs remain relatively high compared with other countries, even assuming that a parent applies for the subsidy (evidence cited in Chapter Three shows that only half of potentially eligible lone parents with a child under five receive the benefit). A system of demand-side as opposed to supply-side subsidies may also discourage participation because it makes it harder for parents to see clearly how much better off they will be in work, and because of the uncertainty about how a

Figure 13.4: Gross childcare fees and net costs to working lone parents with two children aged 2 and 3, as a share of average pay/net household income, 2004

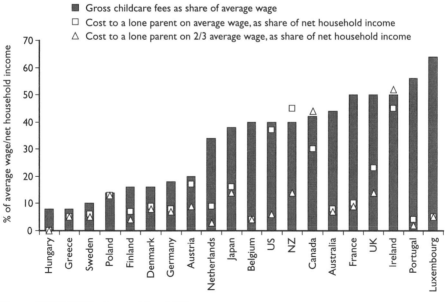

Source: OECD (2007e, figures 4.1 and 4.3)

child will cope with the change. As the subsidy is linked to employment, a parent is forced to take two leaps at once.[4]

Cost is not the only issue, and as discussed in Chapter Three, there are questions about how effective the government has been in persuading parents that leaving children in formal childcare constitutes good parenting. Lewis (2001) points to evidence of 'alternative moral rationalities' underlining the approach of mothers in the UK and the Netherlands compared with mothers elsewhere in Europe. Changing deeply held beliefs about what is best for young children is neither easy nor uncontroversial. But it is difficult to believe that the high acceptance of formal childcare in the Scandinavian countries has no link to the fact that formal childcare in those countries is of a quality on a par with the education system, with workers educated to the same level as workers in primary education and enjoying equal pay and conditions. Moreover, while the childcare debate most often focuses on preschool children, the new conditionality rules will affect children who are already school age. Big gaps remain in holiday and after-school provision, as outlined in Chapter Three, and there are large differences with other Northern European countries in quantity, cost and quality (for example, Gerhard et al, 2005; Bennett, 2006). The importance of improving all these aspects of childcare to make it more attractive to parents and children is clear from Table 13.2. The cost to government of acting as sole provider for one in ten households with children would be exceedingly high if it were to keep the children clear of the poverty line, and even higher if it were to do this without creating a deep poverty trap.

Poverty in work

While worklessness is an important driver of poverty, another key factor is the wage people command when they enter employment. Is a job enough to lift a family out of poverty? Eurostat data suggest that the in-work poverty rate for the UK population as a whole has actually risen since 1997 (as was the case for only Ireland and Luxembourg of the rest of the EU15), and at 8% in 2006 fell below the rate in only the Southern European states and Luxembourg. We know from Chapter Three (Table 3.3) that poverty was the same as or higher than 1997 for children in households where at least one adult works full time, but fell where only part-time workers are present (albeit from a higher level). Table 13.3 shows that only two countries – Luxembourg and Greece – had higher poverty rates among households with children with full work intensity (W = 1, meaning all adults in the household work full time). Only three countries – Spain, Greece and Italy – had higher poverty rates for households with some work activity (0 < WI < 1, meaning one of two adults work full time, or adults work part-time only). In contrast, only 5% of full-time working households with no children lived below the poverty line in the UK, the same share as in Denmark, France and Germany, and lower than the share in Sweden.

Table 13.3: Poverty rates in the EU15 by level of work intensity in the household, 2006 (%)

	Child poverty rate (%)	Share of children 0-17 living in jobless households (%)	Households with children			Households without children	
			WI = 0	0 < WI < 1	WI = 1	WI = 0	WI = 1
Finland	9	5	51	10	4	30	4
Denmark	10	5	65	11	5	24	5
Germany	12	10	49	10	5	30	5
France	13	10	70	18	5	21	5
Netherlands	14	6	51	15	4	16	3
Sweden	14	n/a	56	16	7	16	6
Belgium	15	14	72	13	4	33	2
Austria	15	7	55	14	4	22	5
Luxembourg	19	4	53	23	10	20	6
Portugal	20	5	74	26	8	33	9
Ireland	21	11	73	16	7	50	3
Greece	22	4	53	28	12	27	11
UK	24	16	61	26	9	41	5
Spain	24	5	70	27	9	45	4
Italy	24	5	68	30	5	32	5

Notes:

(1) Only households with working-age adults are included.

(2) WI = 0 means no employed adult in the household. WI = 1 means all adults are employed full time. 0 < WI < 1 covers all intermediate options, including a lone parent working part time and two parents with at least one not in work or working part time.

(3) Shading represents country ranking: the worst-performing third of countries are shaded dark grey for each indicator, the middle third are light grey and the top third are unshaded.

Source: Eurostat, from EU-SILC and EU LFS

Is relatively high in-work poverty for parents due to lower returns from work or to less support from the state? Bradshaw and Finch (2002) found the package of support for low-income working families with children in the UK comparatively generous, and Bradshaw (2006a) points to improvement in the position between 2001 and 2004 – although the results are better when judged in Euro Purchasing Power Parities (with the UK coming second only to Austria) than as a share of average earnings (with the UK middle-ranked). That transfers are working relatively well for poor families with children was also acknowledged by the 2008 EU *Joint Report on Social Protection and Social Inclusion*, which placed the UK in the third best of four groups for child poverty outcomes, not ranked with the Southern European countries (which fell into the fourth group) but alongside Hungary and Slovakia (EC, 2008). The report argued that while the UK suffers from high levels of both joblessness and in-work poverty, the situation is partially alleviated by relatively efficient transfers.

This suggests a bigger problem than elsewhere with respect to low labour market returns. Figure 13.5 shows child poverty before taxes and transfers plotted against the post-transfer child poverty rate for 2006, while the single dark square shows the same data for the UK for 1998 – a year in which the UK poverty rate was the highest in the EU both before and after transfers. The horizontal distance from the 45° line shows the impact of taxes and transfers in reducing the poverty rate. We know from Figure 13.1 that the post-transfer child poverty rate came down in the UK over this time, but Figure 13.5 shows that it did this despite a slight *increase* in pre-transfer poverty, which in 2006 was still the highest in the EU. Thus, taxes and transfers appear not only to be responsible for all of the improvement in UK child poverty, but even to have compensated for a worsening in the pre-transfer situation. That pre-transfer poverty has not fallen is surprising and discouraging

Figure 13.5: Child poverty before and after taxes and transfers, 2006

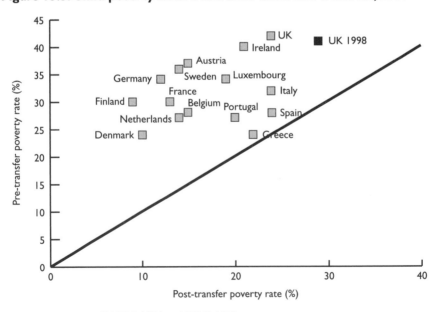

Source: Eurostat, using EU-SILC 2006 and ECHP 1998

Figure 13.6: Impact of taxes and transfers on child poverty rate, 1998 and 2006: % reduction in the poverty rate achieved by taxes and transfers

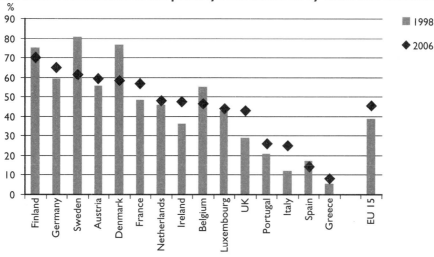

Source: Eurostat (2008)

given improvements in worklessness and increases in parents' working hours, and suggests that wages for those who have recently entered employment have not kept pace with rising average earnings. Before further considering low pay, it is worth noting that – while UK transfers are clearly having a significant impact – high pre-transfer poverty can be consistent with much better post-transfer outcomes. Sweden, for example, has the fourth highest pre-transfer rate of child poverty in 2006, but is ranked tenth highest on post-transfer rates. The key difference is a much greater use of Income Tax to iron out differences in labour market earnings, rather than the more targeted approach adopted in the UK, where the overall tax burden is lower and benefits are directed at low-income families with children. Figure 13.6, which shows the impact of the tax and transfer system on the child poverty rate, illustrates the comparative position more clearly: while the UK government has succeeded in pushing the country from a low-ranking to a middle-ranking group on this measure, the impact of redistribution is still considerably smaller than in the six highest ranking countries.

Low pay and wage inequality

Table 13.4 presents OECD data on wage dispersion and low pay for the most recent year available. The proportion of men earning below two-thirds of the male median has risen across many OECD countries over the last two decades, but most consistently in the UK, the US and Korea as well as the former communist bloc. By 2006, 16% of men in the UK were low paid under this definition – twice the rate of Denmark or Japan and over three times that of Sweden or

Table 13.4: Low pay and earnings inequality, 2006

	Earnings inequality		Low pay incidence (% earning below 2/3 male median)	
	50:10 ratio	90:50 ratio	Men	Women
Sweden	1.38	1.67	5	9
Finland	1.43	1.69	5	10
France	1.49	1.96		
Denmark	1.53	1.73	8	16
Japan	1.67	1.86	8	34
Australia	1.69	1.85	16	20
Austria	1.70	1.92		
Czech Republic	1.73	1.80	7	24
Ireland	1.75	2.07	14	24
UK	1.83	1.98	16	29
Germany	1.89	1.73	9	31
Hungary	1.94	2.34	25	22
Poland	1.95	2.16	21	26
Canada	2.00	1.87	15	28
Korea	2.05	2.22	17	42
US	2.10	2.30	20	29

Notes: Latest available year, 2004-06. Gross earnings for full-time employees. Earnings calculated hourly for Denmark; weekly for Australia, Ireland, the UK, Canada, and the US; monthly for Japan, the Czech Republic, Germany, Hungary, Poland and Korea; annually for Sweden, Finland, France and Austria.

Source: OECD Statistics, downloaded from www.oecd.org/dataoecd/9/59/39606921.xls

Finland. Among women, trends in low pay have been rather different: a number of countries show considerable improvements reflecting greater gender equality in pay, although figures here include only full-time employees, and as such are likely to underestimate the true incidence of low pay for the UK and the US in particular (Harkness and Waldfogel, 1999). In the UK, the proportion of full-time women who were low paid fell steadily from 58% in the 1970s to 30% in 1997, but has stabilised since then. In 2006, 29% of women were still low paid in the UK, compared with 20% in Australia, 16% in Denmark and 10% or less in Sweden and Finland. In part, the high incidence of low pay reflects lack of qualifications: in 2005, the UK ranked 22nd out of 30 OECD countries for the share of 25- to 34-year-olds (men and women) who had completed upper secondary education – compared with 14th position for 55- to 64-year-olds (OECD, 2007a, table A1.2a). But even among those who had not completed upper secondary education, employment rates in the UK were below the OECD average for this group (despite being above the average for school and university graduates), and low pay was more common, with 35% earning half or less of the national median, compared with an OECD average of 26%; only Canada and the US had higher rates (OECD, 2007a, tables A8.1a, A8.3a, A9.4a). As well as explaining high pre-transfer poverty rates, these facts point to another reason why work appears less attractive to UK lone parents – not only are they less likely to have qualifications than their counterparts in other parts of Europe, but for their qualification levels the options available are less enticing.

Table 13.4 also shows the 50:10 ratio for men and women together (the ratio of earnings at the median to earnings at the bottom decile). This ratio rose steadily for both men and women in the UK during the 1980s and 1990s, stabilising from the late 1990s (see Figure 5.3). In 2006, it was higher than anywhere else in the EU15 except Germany. The 90:50 ratio (the ratio of the top decile to the median) is also given, although this will affect measures of inequality but not poverty. Country rankings look a little different for this indicator, and the spread is narrower, but the UK remains in the same position: of the EU15 countries, only Ireland has a higher ratio.

Support for those out of work

Low levels of employment, short working hours and a high incidence of low pay all appear to be factors contributing to the UK's high level of child poverty. Stewart (2005b) also pointed to particularly high rates of poverty among non-working households. Analysis by Behrendt (2002) showed that in the mid-1990s, benefit levels were not sufficient to lift non-working households of any composition above the poverty line in Britain. In contrast, in both Germany and Sweden, most family types would have been able to live on benefits but not be in poverty. Stewart (2005b) updated Behrendt's results for the UK and showed that despite substantial above-inflation increases in benefits for households with children and pensioners, benefits for most groups (all except a single parent with a child under the age of one) were even lower as a share of average earnings in 2004-05 than they had been in 1994-95. Since then (between 2004-05 and 2008-09), as Table 2.4 in Chapter Two shows, out-of-work benefits for nearly all groups have been stable or falling slightly as a share of the poverty line.

Despite this, however, poverty has fallen since 1996/97 for children in non-working households in the UK, especially in lone-parent households (see Chapter Three, Table 3.3). This has led to an improvement in the country's EU ranking on this measure. Bradshaw (2006b) notes that children in workless households in the UK had the third highest poverty risk in the EU15 in 2001, behind only Portugal and Italy, but the 2006 EU-SILC data ranks the UK in the middle, as shown in Table 13.3. Using EU-SILC data, 61% of children in UK workless households lived on incomes below 60% of the equivalised median in 2006 – still a clear majority, but lower than the share in France, Denmark and Belgium as well as in Portugal, Spain, Italy and Ireland.[5] Indeed, among households with children, non-working households are the only UK group that does not have a poverty risk among the bottom third of EU countries, as indicated by the lighter shading of cells in Table 13.3. Among non-working households with *no* children, the UK's relative position is much worse, reflecting the much harsher approach to uprating the adult elements of Income Support, which have increased only in line with prices.

Education

The first half of this chapter focused on UNICEF's material well-being domain, allowing us to unpack some of the policy and structural differences lying behind continuing high rates of poverty and inequality. Despite lower formal unemployment rates and successful efforts to target increased financial support to households with children in and out of work, parental employment rates remain relatively low, and low pay and wage inequality appear to be bigger problems than almost anywhere else in Europe, while the tax system remains less redistributive than in many other EU countries.

Low employment and low pay are strongly associated with low qualification levels. UNICEF's (2007) report placed the UK fifth from bottom out of 24 countries for educational well-being, with the low ranking driven not by low scores in international comparative studies but by low aspirations at age 15, low participation among 15- to 19-year-olds and a high share of this age group in neither education nor employment. The government has been explicit that investment in education is crucial to widening opportunity and to tackling child poverty in the long term (see Chapter Four). Government education spending increased from 4.6% of gross domestic product (GDP) in 1997 to 5.3% in 2004 (the last year for which we have comparative OECD data) and has continued rising since. However, while Ruth Lupton et al point out in Chapter Four that spending is now at its highest level for 30 years, the increase to 2004 represents only a slight gain on the OECD average, which rose from 4.8% to 5.4% over this period (OECD, 2000, 2007a). Nevertheless, this small relative improvement alongside the focus on basic skills and reducing educational inequalities may still be expected to pay off in improved international standing, and this section looks for early signs that this is happening.

Educational attainment in international surveys

A number of international studies seek to assess and compare achievement across countries. Three studies have been repeated during Labour's time in office, in principle allowing us to track progress over time. The first – the Progress in International Reading Literacy Study (PIRLS) – assessed reading achievement among 9- to 10-year-olds in England and Scotland in 2001 and 2006. The second – the Programme for International Student Assessment (PISA) – assessed reading, mathematics and science among 15- to 16-year-olds in the UK in 2000, 2003 and 2006, although only the reading scores are fully comparable between 2000 and 2006. The third study – the Third International Maths and Science Study – was carried out among 9- to 10-year-olds and 13- to 14-year-olds in England and Scotland in 1995, 1999 (13- to 14-year-olds only), 2003 and 2007, although England's participation rates in 2003 were too low for full inclusion in the study tables.

The 2001 PIRLS results, which gave England the third highest average score, were hailed by then Education Secretary Charles Clarke as evidence that 'the National Literacy Strategy we set up five years ago to raise standards in primary schools is working' (BBC, 2003). Critics raised questions about possible cultural and linguistic bias in the tests, and also pointed out that children in England, Scotland and New Zealand had had a year more formal schooling by the age of 10 than children elsewhere (Hilton, 2006). Whatever the validity of these concerns, the results told a much less positive story about inequality, with the gap in performance between the best and worst readers (the 95th and 5th percentiles) greater in England and Scotland than in any other OECD country except New Zealand.

In 2006, PIRLS surveyed a new cohort of 9- to 10-year-olds, who were babies when Labour took office (Twist et al, 2008). Average results for England were significantly worse in absolute as well as relative terms, with the level of dispersion very similar. Results had also significantly worsened for the other two top-performing countries – Sweden and the Netherlands – leading to an investigation into the methods used to link the two surveys (Twist et al, 2008, appendix 5). The investigation tested different methods and found results to be sensitive to the method chosen: results for England have either declined significantly or fallen slightly but not significantly. None of the methods suggests that results may have improved.

For 15- to 16-year-olds, the 2000 PISA study showed a respectable performance on the overall literacy score (the UK ranked 7 out of 24) but also a poor performance on inequality (rank 18). The report by UNICEF (2007) used overall scores from the 2003 PISA study (with the UK ranked tenth out of 25), but with the caveat that UK data should be treated with caution, as the country failed to satisfy minimum participation rates in that year. Prais (2003, p 139) pointed to similar concerns regarding sampling methodology and response rates for the 2000 study, arguing that 'it is difficult to draw valid conclusions for Britain from this survey'. But in an investigation into response bias in the 2000 and 2003 PISA studies, Micklewright and Schnepf (2006) argue that the direction and magnitude of the biases can be reliably estimated: they conclude that mean scores are biased upwards by about six points in both years and standard deviations biased downwards by three to four points, with only a slight impact on the UK's international ranking.

The 2006 results show a 28-point drop in performance from 523 to 495, taking the UK below the 2001 OECD average of 500 points (OECD, 2007c).

Dispersion increased slightly between the two surveys, but because it is likely to have been underestimated in the 2000 PISA study this may be consistent with an improvement. The drop in average scores is far higher than could be explained by response bias in the 2000 survey, but the choice of linking methodology is likely to be as influential in PISA as it is in PIRLS (see Gebhardt and Adams, 2007) and may also explain part of the fall.

The 2007 TIMSS results, published just as this book was going to press, tell a much more positive story for England, although not for Scotland (Mullis et al, 2008a, 2008b). No more than five countries out of at least 35 in the study significantly outscored England on mathematics or science at Year 5 or Year 9, all of them in the Asian Pacific rim. Scores in all four assessments represented a significant improvement on the 1995 and 1999 surveys. Analysis of inequality in scores, as measured by the ratio in performance of the 95th to the 5th percentile or the 75th to the 25th percentile, also points to improvement in all four assessments, although England remains one of the OECD countries with the highest level of inequality in performance, especially among Year 9 pupils. Of OECD countries in the study, the 95th/5th percentile ratio in England was the highest in the OECD for Year 9 mathematics, and second only to Scotland in science. For Scotland, the TIMSS results are a cause for concern: scores in the four 2007 assessments were similar to or lower than scores in 1995, with only one or two OECD countries doing less well. The gap between the 75th and 25th percentiles was narrower in 2007 than in 1995 for both science assessments and for mathematics for the younger age group, but in science this appears largely due to a deterioration in the scores of high performers rather than to improvement at the bottom (Horne et al, 2008).

The TIMSS results for England provide welcome reassurance about the reality of some of the improvements in national standards reported in Chapter Four, but the lack of improvement in scores in PIRLS and PISA raises questions about changes in literacy standards, and leaves open the possibility that at least some of the improvement in national test results can be explained by easier examinations and/or by increasing success in 'teaching to the test'. The distinction between 'high stakes' and 'low stakes' assessment is probably important here: schools and pupils have much more reason to worry about achieving well in Key Stage tests and General Certificates of Secondary Education (GCSEs) than in anonymised international surveys. But there is no reason to believe that this makes the international surveys less reliable or informative indicators of educational standards.

Participation and aspirations among 15- to 19-year-olds

In 1998, only 70% of young people aged 15-19 were enrolled in education in the UK: among OECD countries only Mexico and Turkey had a lower proportion. By 2005, six countries had lower proportions and the UK rate of 79% had moved closer to the OECD average of 82%. Improvement was particularly impressive among 17-year-olds, with a jump from 66% to 81% between 1998 and 2004. Some of the increase was due to the inclusion in the statistics for the first time of young people taking part in apprenticeship programmes, which the OECD argues now have a strong formal education component (OECD, 2007a).

The measure of employment aspirations included in the UNICEF (2007) report has also improved, with a drop in the percentage of 15-year-olds listing a low-skilled job as their expected occupation at age 30, down from 22% in 2000 to 16% in 2006.[6] This translates to a single place change in ranking, but only three other countries recorded larger percentage changes, and as the data are from PISA, the 2000 figure is likely to be biased downwards, suggesting that the true improvement is larger.

However, the share of 15- to 19-year-olds not in education, employment or training (NEET) has not improved, reflecting a similar finding for 16- 18-year-olds in Chapter Four as well as evidence in Chapter Five of high unemployment among those not in education. Just over 10% of young people were NEET in 2004, the fifth highest rate in the OECD.

Risks and behaviours, peer relationships and subjective well-being

For three of its six domains (family and peer relationships, risk-taking behaviour and subjective well-being), the UNICEF study relied heavily on indicators from an international study of young people aged 11, 13 and 15 carried out in 2001–02 – the Health Behaviour of School Aged Children (HBSC) Study (Currie et al, 2004). Eighteen out of the 40 indicators in the report were from this single source, including 15 in these three domains.[7] Britain emerged badly from this study, strongly affecting its overall ranking in UNICEF's league table. British teenagers recorded:

- relatively poor health behaviour (other than for physical exercise);
- high-risk behaviours (smoking, drinking and sex, especially without a condom);
- high levels of bullying and fighting;
- the lowest share of any country of teenagers finding their peers 'kind and helpful'; and
- low scores for subjective well-being measures.

The data in the 2001-02 HBSC survey were really a fairer representation of New Labour's starting point than its achievements. In 2005-06, the same data were collected again: more than 15,000 young people in England, Scotland and Wales completed the questionnaires (Currie et al, 2008).[8] The results, presented in Table 13.5, are little short of astonishing. One of the 15 measures (physical exercise) is not comparable across the two surveys. Of the rest, 12 show improved performance for Britain, while two show no change. Some of the changes translate to a modest two- or three-place change in ranking, but others are more dramatic. The share of young people agreeing that their peers are kind and helpful increased from 47% to 72%, resulting in a 10-place rise in ranking. The share who 'like school a lot' went up from 20% to 37%, leading to a 12-place ranking improvement. Ten indicators have data for the 21 OECD countries included in the study and on these the UK's average rank moved up from 17 to 12.

Can we believe the story presented here? There is nothing in the study's methodology that would explain away the change (although if this were a factor it would at least cast doubt on the UK's low ranking in the 2007 UNICEF report). The size of the study, the consistency of the improvement across indicators and the relative stability in wider international rankings (as reflected in the correlation coefficients presented in the final column of Table 13.5) all suggest that the survey is picking up a real phenomenon. Furthermore, available national sources support the HBSC survey findings: the 2006 Health Survey for England also shows considerable falls in smoking and alcohol use among 15-year-olds since 2001-02, increased fruit intake and a sharp decline in obesity between 2004 and 2006, which has taken levels back to or below those of 2001 (Craig and Mindell, 2008). It appears that falling child poverty, increased investment in schools and perhaps smaller initiatives such as healthier school meals and the '5 a day' campaign have paid off with a measurable impact on well-being among 11- to 15-year-olds.

It is interesting, however, that while British children are now much more positive about their peers, the indicators of bullying and fighting show no sign of improvement. The extent to which these are still problems is illustrated in Figure 13.7, which shows an index of perceived safety at school for nine- and ten-year-olds who have grown up under Labour. Only New Zealand has a lower share of children scoring a high value than England, with Scotland, too, ranked in the bottom half. The Figure also shows the views of headteachers in the same schools on a range of related issues, including intimidation and fighting. Headteachers in England and Scotland are more likely than those in any other country to give their schools a high score (that is, to respond that these issues are not a problem or are only a minor problem), revealing a shocking contrast with the perceptions of children.

One additional measure used by UNICEF as an indicator of risk behaviour is the teenage fertility rate. The incidence of early motherhood can be seen as a measure of young women's perceptions about the alternative prospects available to them, while early motherhood also carries a strong association with ongoing disadvantage in education and employment (for example Hobcraft and Kiernan, 2001). UNICEF used data for 2003, with the UK third bottom to the US and New Zealand at 28 births per 1,000 women aged 15-19. Reducing teenage pregnancy was an early government goal, with a target of halving conceptions to those aged under 18 in England between 1998 and 2010, to be achieved through better access to information and advice. In practice, conceptions fell by

Table 13.5: Peer relationships, health behaviour, risk taking and subjective well-being: latest evidence from the HBSC survey

	GB score (% of 11-, 13- and 15-year-olds)		GB rank (1 = best)		Total countries included for ranking	Direction of change (GB score)	Direction of change (GB rank)	Correlation coefficient 2001-02 and 2005-06 (excl. GB)
	2001-02	2005-06	2001-02	2005-06				
Peer relations								
Agree that their peers are kind and helpful	47	72	20	10	21	Up	Up	0.89
Risk behaviour and experience of violence								
Smoke at least once a week	13	8	16	13	21	Up	Up	0.69
Have been drunk at least twice	30	24	21	21	21	Up	Stable	0.85
Have ever used cannabis (15-year-olds only)	40	25	19	15	20	Up	Up	0.94
Have had sexual intercourse (15-year-olds only)	37	29	16	15	16	Up	Up	0.31
Used a condom last time (15-year-olds who have had sex)	70	82	11	5	14	Up	Up	0.79
Have been in at least 3 fights in last 12 months	14	14	16	13	21	Stable	Up	0.81
Have been bullied at least twice in the last 2 months	10	10	12	12	21	Stable	Stable	0.97
Health behaviour								
Eat fruit every day	27	43	18	3	21	Up	Up	0.32
Eat breakfast every school day	56	64	16	15	21	Up	Up	0.93
Are overweight according to BMI (13- + 15-year-olds only)	15	13	17	14	21	Up	Up	0.98
Subjective well-being								
Rank their own health as fair or poor	23	19	20	18	20	Up	Up	0.75
Rank themselves above middle of life satisfaction scale	84	85	16	13	21	Up	Up	0.83
Like school a lot	20	37	16	4	21	Up	Up	0.89

Note: Results are an unweighted average of results for 11-, 13- and 15-year-olds. Results for Great Britain are a weighted average of results for England, Scotland and Wales and results for Belgium a weighted average of French and Flemmish Belgium. The 21 OECD countries covered by the HSBC Survey are included, as long as data were available for both years.

Sources: Currie et al (2004, 2008)

Figure 13.7: Index of student safety in schools as perceived by children aged 9/10 and their headteachers, 2006

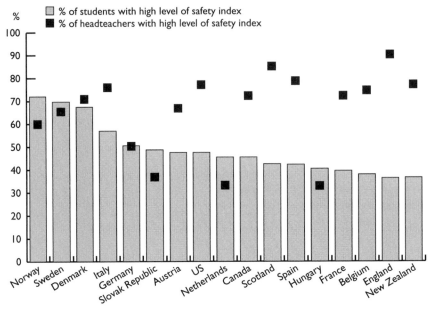

Notes: Results for Canada are unweighted average of results for five provinces; results for Belgium are unweighted average of results for French-speaking and Flemmish-speaking Belgium. To achieve a high value of the index a student has to agree with the statement 'I feel safe when I am at school', and report one or fewer incidents of stealing, bullying and injury involving themselves or a classmate in the last month. The headteachers' index is based on headteachers' responses about the degree to which each of the following was a school problem: classroom disturbances, cheating, profanity, vandalism, theft, intimidation, verbal abuse and fighting among students.

Source: PIRLS 2006 (tables 7.15 and 7.16)

12% between 1998 and 2005, while the teenage birth rate fell 16% from 29 to 24 births per 1,000 between 1997 and 2006 (almost all of this achieved between 2002 and 2006). While this is not insignificant, three other OECD countries (France, Canada and Australia) achieved higher falls in percentage-point terms in the same time, from lower starting points; and the drop was far from enough to change the UK's ranking.

Conclusions

The indicators discussed in this chapter can be divided into three categories. First, there are those that show evidence of a UK improvement in performance, which has been sufficient to push the country up the international rankings. This, the happiest sort of story, applies to participation in education between the ages of 15 and 19, to TIMSS mathematics and science results for England and to 12 out of the 14 indicators in the HBSC survey of 11- to 15-year-olds, including measures of health behaviour and subjective well-being, with big gains between 2001-02 and 2006. The UK's child poverty rate in non-working households has also improved both in absolute and comparative terms, as has the effectiveness of the benefit system in preventing child poverty.

The second category includes indicators that have improved for the UK, but not by enough to climb the rankings. This is true of child poverty after taxes and transfers, of worklessness, of job aspirations at age 15 and of the teenage birth rate. For the last of these, 2002-06 were the important years; for the first two, we know that most progress was made in New Labour's first term, after which change slowed and then went into reverse.

Finally, there are indicators that have seen no change (wider working-age poverty, inequality in literacy scores, and NEETs) or have worsened (income inequality and literacy as measured in PIRLS and PISA). Of the underlying factors, measures of low pay and wage inequality between the middle and the bottom of the earnings distribution have not changed while pre-transfer rates of poverty for children have worsened very slightly.

Summarised like this, the overall picture looks very positive: the bulk of indicators has improved, often by enough to affect the rankings, with just one or two moving in the wrong direction. If UNICEF were to recalculate its index of child well-being using the latest available data it is likely that the UK would be lifted several places from the bottom, largely on the basis of the 2005-06 HBSC survey.

However, the indicators that have not moved much, have worsened or stalled in recent years are rather important ones, with probable medium-term consequences for other areas – for instance, health and risk behaviours are unlikely to keep improving if the upturn in child poverty is permanent.

While the literacy findings may come as a surprise, failure to deliver sustained progress on poverty, worklessness and income inequality does not. The evidence points to three areas in particular where UK policy still falls well short of that in other countries. First, while the Labour government has increased childcare expenditure substantially, spending still lags well behind that in many other EU countries, leaving a childcare system that has improved but is still both high cost and relatively poor quality, with inevitable consequences for worklessness and child poverty.

Second, the government has sought to address high levels of pre-transfer poverty without touching higher incomes. This has complicated its task both by ruling out additional resources raised in countries with more progressive Income Tax regimes, and because high levels of income inequality have an impact on living standards for all – for example through the knock-on effect on all house prices of the ability to pay ever higher prices at the top – as well as a subtle but insidious impact on social cohesion.

Third, despite the NMW, Labour has not succeeded in addressing the inherited problem of low pay. Its long-term strategy in this area relies on investment in education to deliver a higher-skilled workforce in the future. Results from Chapter Four are fairly positive in this regard but some of the international surveys present a different picture; either way, it will be a long time before change makes itself felt in the labour market. Without further action on these three areas, Secretary of State Ed Balls' (2008) goal of making the UK 'the best place in the world for children and young people to grow up' will remain a fantasy.

Notes

[1] I am grateful to Paulina Terrazas for very helpful research assistance throughout.

[2] An OECD report released in late 2008 showed a fall in the Gini for the United Kingdom between 2000 and 2004 (OECD, 2008). The period chosen was favourable for the UK as the Gini peaked in 2000-01 and started rising again from 2003-04. The OECD ranking is very similar to that shown in Table 13.1, with the UK third highest in Europe after Portugal and Italy.

[3] Luxembourg Income Study Key Figures, accessed at www.lisproject.org/keyfigures.htm

[4] Part-time places for three- and four-year-olds are not linked to employment, but at 2.5 hours per day they are not effective childcare. If taken in the form of a reduction in day nursery fees, the concerns described in the text apply to the fee balance.

[5] This is lower than the share implied by Table 3.3, which can be explained by the use of a different dataset and methodology. The cross-national comparison using EU-SILC should still be valid.

[6] Calculated from PISA data by Paulina Terrazas. Numbers differ from those in UNICEF (2007), because those answering 'don't know' or giving a vague answer were excluded from our calculations, but counted in as low-skilled occupations in the UNICEF figures. In general, this difference affects the level but not the rank.

[7] The other three indicators measured family affluence and the incidence of step-families and lone parenthood.

[8] All data for Britain were collected in 2006.

Part Three
Where do we go from here?

FOURTEEN

The Equality and Human Rights Commission: a new point of departure in the battle against discrimination and disadvantage

Polly Vizard

Introduction

This chapter examines the programme of equality and human rights reform undertaken by New Labour. The reform programme is evaluated against two benchmarks: (1) Labour's 1997 election manifesto commitments to 'end unfair discrimination wherever it exists' and to incorporate the European Convention on Human Rights (ECHR) into domestic law; (2) more far-reaching reform models that view equality and human rights standards as elements of a broader social justice agenda. As well as providing a retrospective analysis of Labour's equality and human rights programme, the chapter has a forward-looking aspect. Increased momentum in the reform programme since 2005 has resulted in a new equality and human rights landscape that provides a distinct point of departure for tackling horizontal inequality and disadvantage. The chapter considers the importance of the arrangements and their potential role in tackling horizontal inequalities during New Labour's third term and beyond.

Overview: New Labour's equality and human rights reform programme, 1997-2008

Equalities and human rights champion Lord Lester recalls that in 1997, when New Labour came to power, there was talk of the need for a Single Equality Act that would provide a comprehensive, integrated and overarching legislative framework for combating discrimination and disadvantage in Britain. There was also talk of the need for a single equality institution – a permanent, independent body with overarching responsibilities for addressing inequality in Britain, with investigative and enforcement powers, that would function as a watchdog and spearhead a process of long-term change – and a similar independent body providing institutional support for human rights. However, while there was *talk* in 1997, there was an absence of *political momentum* – either for a Single Equality

Act or for an independent single equality and/or human rights institution (Lester, 2003a, 2003b).

Eleven years on, the machinery of equality and human rights regulation in Britain is in the process of being transformed. A Single Equality Act has been included in the government's draft legislative programme for 2008-09, while an independent equality and human rights institution – the Equality and Human Rights Commission (EHRC) – became operational in October 2007. The EHRC replaces the pre-existing strand-based equality bodies and has an overarching mandate to combat inequalities and disadvantage based on a broad range of characteristics (gender, ethnicity, disability, gender, age, religion and belief, transgender and sexual orientation) as well as for protecting and promoting human rights.

In 2008, then, the vision is of a new era in equality and human rights regulation – with a comprehensive and coherent legislative framework that can provide an effective tool in combating horizontal discrimination and disadvantage, and an effective independent institutional framework that can spearhead and regulate the process of change. What prompted this change in approach? What were the initial policy directions when New Labour came to power in 1997, and why did momentum increase after 2005? And have there been additional policy directions during New Labour's third term?

The inheritance

Before 1997, the equality landscape was dominated by three legislative instruments that predated the Thatcher era. The 1970 Equal Pay Act, the 1975 Sex Discrimination Act and the 1976 Race Relations Act were introduced under the Wilson and Callaghan administrations. Two statutory equality institutions – the Commission for Racial Equality (CRE) and the Equal Opportunities Commission (EOC) – were also created (Box 14.1). There was one significant piece of additional legislation under subsequent Conservative administrations: the 1995 Disability Discrimination Act (DDA), which also set up the National Disability Council. There was little or no legislative protection or institutional support against discrimination on additional grounds such as age, religion and belief, transgender and sexual orientation.

On the human rights side, the legislative landscape prior to 1997 was characterised by the absence of codified human rights in domestic law; and the absence of an independent statutory body with responsibilities for protecting and promoting human rights.

New Labour's response: key priorities in 1997

Equality and human rights reform were important elements of New Labour's agenda in 1997. On the equality front, the 1997 election manifesto included

---

Box 14.1: The inheritance

Legislation:

1970 Equal Pay Act Prohibition of discrimination between men and women in their terms of employment.

1975 Sex Discrimination Act Prohibition of discrimination on the grounds of sex in employment, training, education, the provision of goods, facilities, services and premises, and by public authorities.

1976 Race Relations Act (incorporating the 1965/1968 Race Relations Acts) Prohibition of discrimination on the grounds of race, colour, nationality and national and ethnic origin in employment, the provision of goods, facilities, services and premises, in education and by public authorities.

1995 Disability Discrimination Act Prohibition of discrimination on the grounds of disability in employment, the provision of goods, facilities and services, and the disposal and management of premises; also includes provisions covering education and transport. Includes a duty of 'reasonable adjustment' covering goods, facilities and services and employment.

Institutional monitoring and enforcement:

Equal Opportunities Commission (created by the 1975 Sex Discrimination Act)

Commission for Racial Equality (created by the 1976 Race Relations Act)

National Disability Council (created by the 1995 Disability Discrimination Act)

---

commitments to 'end unjustifiable discrimination wherever it exists'. A specific commitment was included to support comprehensive, enforceable civil rights for disabled people; and age discrimination in the workplace was flagged up as a particular concern. However, the package did not reflect more radical proposals for prohibiting unjustifiable discrimination per se (covering additional grounds such as religion and belief, sexual orientation, transgender and age, as well as race and ethnicity, gender and disability) in all relevant domains (that is, covering goods, facilities and services as well as the workplace). Policy options such as proposals for a Single Equality Act, a single equality commission and the creation of positive duties on public authorities to promote equality were not, for example, included.

On the human rights front, the 1997 election manifesto included a flagship commitment to incorporate the European Convention on Human Rights (ECHR) into domestic law. The UK ratified the ECHR in 1951, providing protection for key civil and political rights; and prior to 1997, the UK was bound in international law to observe the Convention and was accountable for violations. Generally, however, there was no means of having the application of the Convention rights tested in domestic courts. The 1997 election manifesto commitment built on the opposition document *Bringing Rights Home* (Straw and Boateng, 1996) and the final report of the Labour/Liberal Democratic Joint Consultative Committee on Constitutional Reform (the 'Cook–Maclennan agreement'; Cook and Maclennan, 1997) and represented a major constitutional initiative that would bring the UK more into line with European models and the international human rights framework by making it possible for people to invoke Convention rights in normal domestic court proceedings (Home Office, 1998b).

Domestically, the 1997 manifesto commitment on human rights represented a radical departure from constitutional models emphasising 'residual liberties' rather than codified fundamental rights. The argument that pre-existing constitutional conventions provide adequate safeguards for liberties such as freedom of association, assembly and speech in the form of 'residual liberties' (liberties that by convention have not been 'taken away' by the state) rather than in the form of fundamental positive rights (fundamental rights that are codified in written Constitutions and Bills of Rights) had been invoked to block previous attempts to incorporate the ECHR during the 1980s. Support for this argument was not limited to the libertarian Right but was an important factor across the political spectrum. Within the Labour Party, the 'Bennite tradition' also emphasises traditional constitutional safeguards rather than written Bills of Rights; and the 1997 election manifesto commitment represented an important departure from the Left-Labour sceptical position of the early 1980s, which maintained that binding human rights are fundamentally undemocratic because they limit parliamentary sovereignty and shift power to an unelected and unrepresentative judiciary.

For others within the Labour Party, who viewed human rights as elements of a broader social justice agenda, the 1997 election manifesto commitment was overly restrictive. Whereas the Cook–Maclennan agreement envisaged two new bodies for monitoring and enforcement (a Joint Parliamentary Select Committee and a Human Rights Commission or Commissioner), there was no specific commitment on institutional reform. Central tenets of the broader human rights reform agenda – such as children's rights and key economic and social rights (including the human right to health) – were also notably absent. The 1997 election manifesto hinted at the possibility of a broader reform programme with no firm or explicit commitment: 'The incorporation of the European Convention on Human Rights will establish a floor, not a ceiling, for human rights. Parliament will remain free to enhance these rights….' (Labour Party, 1997, p 35).

The 1997 election manifesto commitments were viewed by key players within the Labour Party and beyond as representing the first stage of a broader model of human rights reform. Stage one would focus on the domestic incorporation of Convention rights; stage two would involve a more far-reaching reform package (including the possibility of a British Bill of Rights). The possibility of a broader reform model had been discussed in key policy documents (for example, Straw and Boateng, 1996, p 14; Cook-McClennan, 1997, p 23; Lester, 2003a, p 15) and underpins the recent proposals to introduce a British Bill of Rights under Gordon Brown (see later in this chapter).

The overall reform programme, 1997-2008

The remainder of this chapter analyses the programme of equality and human rights reform (1997-2008) in terms of three discrete waves or policy clusters (see Box 14.2). The next section covers the first wave of the equality and human rights reform programme – the gradual strengthening and broadening of anti-discrimination and equality law, and the 1998 Human Rights Act. This is followed by a section on the 2005 election manifesto and the second wave of the reform programme – Equality and Human Rights Commission (EHRC) and the proposed Single Equality Act. Then there is a discussion of the additional new policy directions under Gordon Brown, including the possibility of a British Bill of Rights, and an assessment of the extent to which, in 2008, equality and human rights standards provide an overarching framework for public policy. Finally, the chapter concludes with a summary of main achievements in, and limitations of, the equality and human rights programme thus far and looks to the future.

The first wave of equality and human rights reforms: the gradual broadening and strengthening of anti-discrimination and equality law

The programme of anti-discrimination law reform

The period after 1997 was characterised by a gradual broadening and strengthening of anti-discrimination law to provide protection for previously uncovered grounds (for example, age, sexual orientation, transgender, and religion and belief) and additional domains (that is, in the provision of goods, facilities and services as well as the workplace) (Box 14.3). As well as the election manifesto commitments, European Union (EU) Equality Directives were an important reform imperative. The 2000 Employment Framework, providing a common basis for tackling unfair discrimination on six grounds (sex, race, disability, sexual orientation, religion and belief, and age) was particularly influential; and the need for legislative and institutional provision to be in line with these standards underpinned the reform programme.

Box 14.2: New Labour's programme of equality and human rights reform, 1997-2008

The *first* wave of New Labour's equality and human rights reform programme: the gradual broadening and strengthening of anti-discrimination and equality law, and the 1998 Human Rights Act.

- Gradual extension of protection of anti-discrimination law, 1997-2008.
- New positive duties on public authorities to promote equality – race equality duty (2000), disability equality duty (2005), gender equality duty (2006).
- 1998 Human Rights Act.
- Disability Rights Commission (2000).

The *second* wave of New Labour's equality and human rights reform programme: the 2005 election manifesto, modernisation and the single equality agenda.

- Equality and Human Rights Commission (established as a result of the 2006 Equality Act) operational 2007, replaces the Commission for Racial Equality, the Equal Opportunities Commission and the Disability Rights Commission.
- Single Equality Act included in 2008-09 draft legislative programme.

The *third* wave of New Labour's equality and human rights reform programme: additional new policy directions under Gordon Brown – a British Bill of Rights?

- British Bill of Rights (consultations announced July 2007 and in draft legislative programme 2008-09), Green Paper due by Christmas 2008.
- New models of public services governance (NHS Constitution).

Equality campaigners criticised the anti-discrimination reform programme on the grounds that it constituted a piecemeal and minimalist response to European Directives through statutory instruments, rather than a radical forward-looking reform programme based on a single equality model. According to Lester (2003b, p 6), the consequence of this approach was that by the mid-2000s, the legal regime was 'complex, incoherent and ineffective' – with a multiplicity of definitions of discrimination and a varying degree of protection for different groups. The solution in Lester's view was a single, transparent and user-friendly legal instrument covering all protected grounds and all domains in which unjustifiable discrimination arises.

Box 14.3: The extension and strengthening of anti-discrimination and equality law, 1997-2008

- Prohibition of discrimination on the grounds of transgender status in employment and vocational training (1999 Sex Discrimination [Gender Reassignment] Regulations).

- Established Disability Rights Commission (1999 Disability Rights Commission Act).

- Extension of the prohibition against direct and indirect racial discrimination to public service providers that were previously exempt (2000 Race Relations [Amendment] Act).

- Race equality duty: duty on public authorities to promote equality of opportunity and good relations between racial groups (2000 Race Relations [Amendment] Act).

- Equalisation of the age of consent at 16 (2000 Sexual Offences [Amendment] Act).

- Further protection against discrimination on grounds of disability in schools and other educational establishments (2001 Special Educational Needs and Disability Act).

- Enabled unmarried couples, including same-sex couples, to adopt jointly in the context of an 'enduring family relationship' (2002 Adoption and Children Act).

- Repeal of Section 28 of the 1988 Local Government Act (in 2003) (and the Scottish equivalent in 2000), which prohibited the 'promotion' of homosexuality by local authorities.

- Implementation of the UK's anti-discrimination obligations under European Directives 2000/78/EC and 2000/43/EC by providing harmonised criteria relating to direct and indirect discrimination and harassment, and thereby strengthening protection against discrimination:
  - on the grounds of religion and belief in employment and training (Employment Equality [Religion or Belief] Regulations [Statutory Instrument 2003]).
  - on the grounds of sexual orientation in employment and training (Employment Equality [Sexual Orientations] Regulations [Statutory Instrument 2003]).
  - on the grounds of disability by broadening the coverage of the 1995 Disability Discrimination Act (Disability Discrimination Act 1995 [Amendment] Regulations [Statutory Instrument, 2003]).
  - on the grounds of racial or ethnic origin (Race Relations Act 1976 [Amendment] Regulations [Statutory Instrument, 2003]).

- Established civil partnerships to provide legal status for same-sex couples (2004 Civic Partnerships Act).

- Enabled transsexual people to obtain legal recognition in the gender in which they wish to live (2004 Gender Recognition Act).

- Strengthened protection against discrimination on the grounds of gender (2005 Employment Equality [Sex Discrimination] Regulations, implementing European Gender Directive 2004/113/EC, equal treatment between men and women in the access to and supply of goods and services).

- Broadening the scope of the Disability Discrimination Act, including a new definition of disability (strengthening protection for people with HIV, cancer and multiple sclerosis), the strengthening of the anti-discrimination provisions (for example in relation to public authorities when carrying out public functions, and in relation to transport) and the strengthening of the duty of reasonable adjustment in relation to the provision of premises (for example rental accommodation) (2005 Disability Discrimination Act).

- Disability equality duty: duty on public authorities to promote equality of opportunity between disabled and non-disabled people (2005 Disability Discrimination Act).

- Implementation of the UK's obligations under European Council Framework Directive 2000/78/EC by protecting against age discrimination in employment and training (Employment Equality [Age] Regulations [Statutory Instrument, 2006]).

- Prohibition of discrimination on the grounds of religion or belief in the provision of goods and services and permission to issue regulations prohibiting discrimination in the provision of goods, facilities and services on the grounds of sexual orientation (2006 Equality Act).

- Gender equality duty: duty on public authorities to promote equality of opportunity between men and women (2006 Equality Act).

- Established Equality and Human Rights Commission (2006 Equality Act).

- Prohibition of discrimination on the grounds of sexual orientation in the provision of goods, facilities and services (Equality Act [Sexual Orientation] Regulations [Statutory Instrument 2007]).

- Extension of protection against direct discrimination and harassment on the grounds of gender reassignment and explicit prohibition of discrimination in the provision of goods and services on the grounds of maternity or pregnancy and the regulation of discrimination on the grounds of sex by the insurance industry (Sex Discrimination Act 1975 [Amendment] Regulations [Statutory Instrument 2008], implementing European Gender Directive 2004/113/EC: equal treatment between men and women in the access to and supply of goods and services).

The government established a Disability Rights Task Force in 1997. Following the Task Force's first recommendations, the Disability Rights Commission (DRC) was created. The DRC was modelled on the CRE and the EOC, and replaced the National Disability Council, which had been criticised for having weak enforcement powers. A key achievement of the DRC was to promote consensus around the Social Model of Disability (SMD) – the view that disadvantage results from barriers to opportunity that impact on people with disabilities; and that in order to create a level playing field, positive steps may be required to tackle the underlying constraints. The 1995 DDA reflected this model in that it created a duty to make 'reasonable adjustments' to ensure equality in practice, for example by ensuring that the physical environment of a shop does not put wheelchair users at a disadvantage. The law was strengthened by the 2001 Special Educational Needs and Disability Act. In 2005, the DDA was extended and refined, including a strengthening of the duty of 'reasonable adjustment'. Within the government, the Office for Disability Issues was set up to support the objective of equality for disabled people by 2025 (see later in this chapter).

Early moves to equalise the age of consent and to repeal Section 28 of the 1988 Local Government Act were opposed and delayed in the House of Lords but were ultimately successful. Measures to prohibit discrimination on the grounds of sexual orientation in employment (the 2003 Employment Regulations) and in the provision of goods, facilities and services such as hotel, bed and breakfast and adoption services (the 2006 Equality Act and the 2007 Sexual Orientation Regulations) were opposed by certain religious groups on the grounds of a perceived conflict with religious freedom. The government itself was divided at times and policy was modified and diluted on occasions (including by introducing a religious exemption into the 2003 Employment Regulations).

Public duties to promote race, disability and gender equality

Positive duties on public authorities to promote equality by race (2000), disability (2005) and gender (2006) have also been established under New Labour. The public equality duties were not a 1997 election manifesto commitment. The CRE had recommended repeatedly and unsuccessfully that the 1976 Race Relations Act should be amended to require public authorities to promote equality and a model for a single equality duty had been set out in the Hepple Report (Hepple et al, 2000). Following the murder of Stephen Lawrence and subsequent Macpherson Inquiry (1999), addressing institutional racism became a political priority. The 2000 Race Relations (Amendment) Act extended the prohibition against racial discrimination to public service providers, and imposed a positive duty on public authorities to have due regard to the need to eliminate unlawful racial discrimination, and to promote equality of opportunity and good relations between persons of different racial groups (Lester, 2006).

A similar legislative change created a public duty to promote disability equality. The 2005 DDA established a general duty on public authorities to eliminate disability discrimination and to promote equality of opportunity between disabled and non-disabled people, and provided explicit recognition that this can involve treating disabled persons differently in order to facilitiate their different needs (Section 49A [d]). In 2006, the public duties legislation was again extended with the introduction of a positive duty on public authorities to promote equality of opportunity between men and women (2006 Equality Act).

The public duties legislation represents an important new point of departure for tackling inequality and disadvantage in British society. Anti-discrimination law has historically recognised that treating everyone identically can result in inequality in practice. For example, the prohibition of indirect as well as direct discrimination under the 1975 Sex Discrimination Act and the 1976 Race Relations Act provides recognition that practices and rules (for example relating to full-time work requirements, or blanket bans on headgear) can be discriminatory; while the 1995 DDA included a duty of 'reasonable adjustment'. The public duties legislation takes forward these ideas and provides a platform for a reform agenda that recognises that negative principles of non-discrimination are an insufficient basis for tackling entrenched inequality and disadvantage. Structural changes in institutions may be required and a range of proactive policies and programmes may be necessary to ensure that the organisation, structure and delivery of public services are non-discriminatory and recognise and accommodate the different needs and situations of individuals and groups (DfES et al, 2007; Fredman, 2008).

It is early days to evaluate the implementation of the public equality duties. A recent audit of public authorities suggested that the race equality duty has had an important impact on local authorities and in a range of public services ranging from the criminal justice system to hospitals (Schneider-Ross, 2007). However, early reports of low rates of compliance with the race equality duty in the health sector (for example CRE, 2002) were confirmed in a recent audit (HC, 2007a). Compliance with disability equality duties appears to be higher, with 81% of National Health Service (NHS) trusts, and 72% of a sample of 1,484 public authorities, publishing Disability Equality Schemes (Ipsos-Mori, 2007b).

The new powers of the EHRC should help to address this picture of piecemeal and patchy implementation; and the government's recent decision to extend the public duties legislation to cover new grounds should further increase the momentum (as discussed below). Concern that the emphasis has been on *process* (for example the publication of equality plans and schemes) rather than on *results* has led to calls for a reformulation of the public duties in terms of outcomes or goals (DfES et al, 2007; GEO, 2008, paras 2.1-2.40). In 2008, there is a more positive picture of change on the ground, with new forms of statistical monitoring and target setting, and evidence of good practice and policy shifts in some areas (see later in this chapter).

The 1998 Human Rights Act

The 1998 Human Rights Act (HRA), which came into force in Britain in 2000, was a watershed in British legislative history. Casting aside the traditional scepticism on the Left regarding human rights, and building on the opposition document *Bringing Rights Home* (Straw and Boateng, 1996), human rights reform was a flagship 1997 election manifesto commitment and established an innovative constitutional model for governing the balance between parliamentary sovereignty on the one hand, and judicial enforcement of fundamental rights on the other. Under this model, the courts are not empowered to strike down legislation but can make judicial declarations of 'incompatibility'. The HRA enables the civil and political rights guaranteed in the ECHR to be enforced in domestic courts and includes a general prohibition of discrimination (Article 12) and one socioeconomic right under Protocol 1 (Box 14.4). Whereas prior to 1997 public authorities were not explicitly required to comply with the ECHR under domestic law, Section 6 of the HRA establishes that it is unlawful for a public authority to act in a way that is 'incompatible with a Convention right'. The HRA is therefore relevant to a broad range of public services including the police, the immigration and prison services, local authorities, housing, education, health services, social services and care homes.

The introduction of the HRA was preceded by a White Paper entitled *Rights Brought Home: The Human Rights Bill* (Home Office, 1998b). The government's position focused on the reduction of the delays and costs associated with the previous Strasbourg-based arrangements. Against this benchmark, the HRA has been a great success. Human rights cases are regularly heard before domestic courts and a significant body of case law has emerged. This now extends across domestic law including in areas such as criminal justice, anti-terrorism, refugees and asylum, privacy and the media, assisted suicide, the withdrawal of medical care, mental health, and the functions of public authorities (for reviews, see Wadham et al, 2003; DCA, 2006). The courts have exercised their power to declare legislation to be incompatible with the HRA while emphasising 'an area of judgment within which the judiciary will defer, on democratic grounds, to the considered opinion of the elected body' (Fredman, 2008, p 94). This has resulted in judicial caution in areas of policy sensitivity and where there are significant resource implications. However, the deferential approach has not always prevailed – for example, in the *Limbuela* case, when it was ruled that withdrawing support from destitute asylum seekers can constitute a violation of the prohibition against torture and inhuman and degrading treatment or punishment under Article 3 (Wadham et al, 2003, pp xiv-xvi1, 23-128; Fredman, 2008, pp 94-9).

Box 14.4: The Human Rights Act: incorporation of ECHR provisions

Article 2	Life
Article 3	Torture/inhuman/degrading treatment or punishment
Article 4	Slavery and forced labour
Article 5	Liberty and security
Article 6	Fair trial
Article 7	Punishment under the law
Article 8	Private and family life
Article 9	Freedom of thought, conscience and religion
Article 10	Freedom of expression
Article 11	Freedom of assembly and association
Article 12	Right to marry
Article 14	Non-discrimination

First Protocol

Article 1	Property
Article 2	Education
Article 3	Free elections

Thirteenth Protocol

Article 1	Death penalty

Human rights as an overarching framework for public policy

For many human rights campaigners, there were high hopes in 1997 that as well as providing for enforceable human rights under domestic law, the enactment of the HRA would result in the establishment of a human rights *culture* in Britain. By this, it was meant that human rights would have a leading role in shaping the general framework of social norms and values, and would become a central focus for public policy, *without* recourse to legislation. For example, the Joint Committee on Human Rights regards a culture of human rights as having institutional and ethical dimensions, with human rights shaping the goals, structures and practices of public bodies, and with the legislature, executive and judiciary sharing responsibility for protection and promotion (Lester and Clapinska, 2005, p 172). According to this broader view, human rights standards are not about a narrow legalistic agenda, but provide a platform for a new approach to social justice

– with values such as freedom, equality, dignity, respect and autonomy playing a major role in specifying the ground rules of a good society and providing an overarching framework for public policy.

Could the reform package of 1997 ever have achieved this broader purpose? Arguably, the general duties of public authorities under Section 6 imply not only a minimal obligation of compliance but also a duty to give due regard to the protection of human rights by adopting positive, proactive measures (Klug and Wildbore, 2005; Fredman, 2008). To this extent, the HRA not only incorporates the ECHR but also has its own provisions for moving beyond a legalistic rights model. For example, human rights can play an important role in ensuring that the different needs of individuals and groups are facilitated in public policy; in challenging poor treatment of vulnerable groups such as children, older people, disabled people (including people with learning disabilities) and users of mental health services; and as a policy framework for longer-term transformation and improvement in public services.

In practice, progress was limited. In 2003, the introduction of human rights standards into public service planning, commission and evaluation was officially recognised as patchy and slow (Audit Commission, 2003). The Joint Committee on Human Rights concluded that the HRA had not 'given birth to a culture of respect for human rights or made human rights a core activity of public authorities' (JCHR, 2003, p 2). In the courts, the potential impact of the HRA on public services was limited not only by 'democratic objections' to positive duties posited by the courts (discussed above) but also by restrictive judicial interpretations of the term 'public authority'. The HRA covers private or voluntary sector bodies performing functions 'of a public nature' and ECHR jurisprudence specifies that state responsibility is not absolved when public functions are delegated to private bodies or individuals (Fredman, 2008, pp 59-61). However, a landmark judgment in the House of Lords resulted in gaps in key areas, such as in relation to care homes.[1]

The limits of the 1997 reform agenda

A number of policy options that might have established human rights as a basis for a broader social justice agenda were rejected as policy options in 1997. Whereas *Bringing Rights Home* (Straw and Boateng, 1996) and the Cook–Maclennan agreement (Cook and Maclennan, 1997) had envisaged an independent human rights commission as well as a Joint Parliamentary Committee on Human Rights, the former was ruled out as an immediate policy option (Home Office, 1998b, chapter 3). The introduction of human rights in countries such as Canada, New Zealand and South Africa was preceded by a process of broad-based public consultation and debate; but there was no equivalent process in the British context (Klug, 2007a; Wildbore, 2008).

The government's approach to the further extension of human rights protection – over and above the limited set of civil and political rights included in the HRA (1998) - has been cautious. An Inter-departmental Review of International Human Rights Instruments reported in 2004. This followed on from a Home Office Review in 1998/99 which concluded that a further review should be undertaken when the HRA had been implemented and embedded. The 2004 Review resulted in additional protocols to the ECHR being ratified (e.g. Protocol 13, abolishing the death penalty in all circumstances) and protection under international treaties being strengthened (e.g. allowing for independent inspection of places of detention under the UN Convention Against Torture, and a right of individual petition under the UN Convention on the Elimination of all forms of Discrimination against Women) (DCA 2004). More recently, the government has indicated that it will ratify the new UN Convention on the Rights of Persons with Disabilities (CRPD) by the end of 2008.

Important gaps remained following the 2004 Review, for example, the failure to ratify protocol 12 of the ECHR, a free-standing equality provision; and the failure to allow individuals to complain to additional international human rights bodies. The almost exclusive focus of the HRA on civil and political rights is also out of line with the international human rights framework, which establishes economic and social rights as a core element of human rights protection. The government's failure to incorporate the UN International Covenant on Economic, Social and Cultural Rights has been criticized by UN Human Rights Committees (UNCESCR, 2002, para. 11) and the Joint Committee on Human Rights (JCHR, 2004).

At the European level, the UK is a party to the 1961 European Social Charter, the Council of Europe treaty that protects economic and social rights; but not the revised European Social Charter, which has been signed but not ratified, and the status of which remains under review. Maintaining a distinction between the classic civil and political rights set out in the ECHR – which have been viewed as justiciable and enforceable – and additional economic and social rights – which have been viewed as constituting principles or policy guides – has in fact been a central element of the government's negotiating strategy with the European Union. One of the final moves of Blair's premiership was to secure an opt-out from the European Charter of Fundamental Rights. This sets out economic and social rights such as access to health care, as well as the classic civil and political rights, and will become legally binding in other member states if the Lisbon Treaty comes into force.

The failure to incorporate the UN Convention on the Rights of the Child (CRC) into domestic law is another area where the UK falls short of internationally recognised human rights standards. The CRC was ratified by the UK in 1991, giving children a comprehensive set of civil, political, economic, social and cultural rights, but has not been directly incorporated. This situation was most recently highlighted by the UN Committee on the Rights of the Child in

October 2008, which recommended incorporating the principles and provisions of the CRC in a special section of a future British Bill of Rights (UNCRC 2008: para 11). On a more positive note, a decision to lift two reservations to the CRC (covering immigration and the treatment of children in custody with adults) was announced in September 2008.

Human rights and the anti-terrorist agenda

The government's commitment to the HRA itself began to be questioned in the wake of the 11 September 2001 terrorist attacks. The UK's derogation from Article 5 of the ECHR (liberty and security of the person) and the 2001 Anti-Terrorism, Crime and Security Act set the stage for a series of controversial legal judgments (such as the 2004 ruling that anti-terrorist measures allowing foreign terrorist suspects to be detained indefinitely without charge were incompatible with the ECHR) (DCA, 2006).

Further protracted debates concerning control orders and pre-charge detention periods have ensued following subsequent anti-terrorism legislation. Amnesty International (2006) has alleged that the government's domestic anti-terrorism measures, combined with other practices abroad (including deportation with inadequate safeguards to prevent torture and prohibited treatment), constitute a breach of New Labour's 1997 election manifesto promise to 'bring rights home'. Detention of foreign terrorist suspects without trial, the control order regime, deportation practices and other counter-terrorist measures have also been criticised by the UN Committee Against Torture and the UN Human Rights Committee (for example, most recently, UNHRC, 2008). Ministerial statements made in the context of these events have often been interpreted as raising the possibility of the government weakening or repealing the HRA. Public opinion has also seemed increasingly hostile, with sections of the media associating the HRA with the interests of terrorists, criminals and 'bogus' asylum seekers (for details, see Lester, 2003a).

In 2006, an official review of the impact of the HRA on anti-terrorism policy rejected the case for a repeal of the HRA or withdrawal from the ECHR. An alternative reform model – which highlights the possibility of 'rebalancing' rights and public safety objectives within the scope of the HRA by 'clarifying' what is 'proportionate' as an anti-terror measure – was proposed. The review found that in other areas (for example criminal law) the HRA posed no difficulties. In relation to human rights mainstreaming, the HRA was found to have had a significant beneficial impact on public policy outcomes by strengthening personalisation and helping to ensure that diverse needs are appropriately considered in the policy process (DCA, 2006).

The second wave: the 2005 election manifesto, the modernisation agenda and the single equality model

New Labour's 2005 election manifesto announced major policy initiatives to establish an Equality and Human Rights Commission (EHRC) and to introduce a Single Equality Act within its third term. The initiatives signalled a significant increase in the momentum of New Labour's programme of equality and human rights reform, driven by the modernisation agenda and a new commitment to a single equality model.

The EHRC

The 2005 election manifesto commitment to create a single independent equality and human rights commission was the culmination of a protracted process of consultation. The creation of a human rights commission was only rejected in the short term in 1997. The argument for moving towards a single equality institution was recognised in 2001, and plans to create a single commission bringing together the pre-existing equality institutions and with new responsibilities covering additional equality strands and human rights were announced in 2002 (DTI, 2002). A White Paper was issued in 2004 (DTI, 2004) and the EHRC became operational in 2007. The new institution brings together and integrates the mandates of the pre-existing equality bodies (covering ethnicity, gender and disability) – namely the Equal Opportunities Commission, the Commission for Racial Equality and the Disability Rights Commission – and has expanded responsibilities covering additional equality strands (age, sexual orientation, transgender, and religion and belief) and human rights.

The government justified the new policy stance in terms of the need for a modern, rationalised and effective framework for equality and human rights regulation. However, the proposals were received by many as a smokescreen for cost-cutting and deregulation, and a bitter and protracted battle with key stakeholders ensued. Yet not all equality campaigners were opposed to change. Lester notes that notwithstanding the importance of the work of the pre-existing equalities agencies, the CRE and to a certain extent the EOC had important limitations that meant they were no longer fit for purpose. Limitations included weak strategic law enforcement and inadequate capacity in relation to multiple deprivation and the public equality duties (Lester and Clapinska, 2005, pp 177-81; Lester, 2006).

The statutory framework of the EHRC is set out in the 2006 Equality Act. The Commission has as a general duty to encourage and support the development of a society based on equality and human rights. Specific duties include the duty to monitor the law from the equality and human rights perspective; and the duty to monitor results (or social outcomes) by developing indicators and assessing progress in a triennial report. General powers include the provision of information, the agreement of codes of conduct and the initiation of investigations; while enforcement powers include investigations, legal proceedings and the assessment of compliance with the public equality duties. The Commission also has a specific duty to encourage public authorities to comply with Section 6 of the HRA.

An early challenge has been to develop an independent monitoring system that will enable the Commission's legal duty to monitor social outcomes to be discharged. Work to date has built on the recommendation in the Equalities Review (2007, pp 12-28, 125-32) that an Equality Measurement Framework (EMF) with theoretical roots in the capability approach developed by Amartya Sen should be used by public bodies to agree priorities, set targets and evaluate progress on equality; and by the EHRC as a basis for its triennial report. The underlying objective in developing the Equality Measurement Framework is to reposition the British equality debate by providing a multidimensional equality framework that focuses directly on the substantive freedoms (central and valuable things in life that people can actually *do and be*), rather than on other informational focuses, such as formal freedom, resources and subjective well-being. Three irreducible elements of inequality will be monitored: inequality in *outcomes* (for example, living standards, education, health and physical security); inequality in *autonomy* (that is, differentials in empowerment and the independence, choice and control that people experience in their day-to-day lives); and inequality in *process* (that is, discrimination and other forms of unequal treatment, such as a lack of dignity and respect) (Box 14.5).[2]

Proposals for a Single Equality Act

The 2005 election manifesto also announced the government's intention to introduce a Single Equality Act. Since 1997, campaigners had called for the government to adopt a single equality model and to create a single, overarching legislative framework for tackling discrimination and disadvantage. The 2005 manifesto indicated acceptance of this argument. A consultation paper (DfES et al, 2007) outlined proposals for a Single Equality Bill. A Single Equality Act was included in the government's draft legislative programme for 2008-09 and solid proposals were set out (GEO, 2008). The reform package will achieve legislative simplification and rationalisation; require public bodies to tackle discrimination and promote equality through their purchasing functions; establish powers to prohibit age discrimination in goods and services; and extend the public duties regime to cover additional grounds. Controversially, while public authorities will be required to publish information on gender pay differentials, large companies will be encouraged, rather than required, to publish information on the gender gap (Box 14.6).

Box 14.5: Equality Measurement Framework: core building blocks

Inequality *of* substantive freedom

3 aspects of inequality

(i)   outcomes;

(ii)   autonomy (independence, or choice and control);

(iii) processes (discrimination and other aspects of unequal treatment, such as lack of dignity and respect)

Inequality *in 10 domains*

* Life
* Physical security
* Health
* Education
* Standard of living
* Productive and valued activities
* Participation, influence and voice
* Individual, family and social life
* Identity, expression and self-respect
* Legal security

Inequality *by* at least 7 characteristics

(gender, ethnicity, disability, sexual orientation, transgender, age, religion/belief ...)

A third phase of reform? Additional policy directions under Gordon Brown and the picture of equality and human rights mainstreaming in 2008

In the summer of 2007, there seemed little doubt that the ongoing efforts to modernise equality and human rights regulation would dovetail with, and be underpinned by, the broader promises of the Brown administration. The explicit duty to monitor social outcomes under the 2006 Equality Act resonated with the prospect of increased concern with *inequality of outcome* in New Labour's third term. To underpin the change of emphasis, one of Gordon Brown's first moves as Prime Minster was to establish the self-standing Government Equalities Office with responsibilities for overall equality strategy.

Box 14.6: The Single Equality Bill

- Reduction of complexity by bringing together nine major pieces of legislation and around 100 other laws in a single Bill.
- Extension of duties on public authorities to promote equality by bringing together the three pre-existing equality duties and extending the scope of such duties to cover gender reassignment, age, sexual orientation and religion or belief.
- Introduction of new powers to outlaw unjustifiable age discrimination in the provision of goods, facilities and services (including arbitrary exclusion from health insurance products).
- Introduction of requirement for public bodies to give due regard to tackling discrimination and promote equality through their purchasing functions.
- Increase in the transparency of public bodies in relation to statistical monitoring of employment practices (gender pay, minority ethnic employment and disability employment).
- Extension of scope of positive action in employment by enabling employers to take into account underrepresentation of disadvantaged groups when selecting between two equally qualified candidates.
- Extension of permission to use women-only shortlists in selecting parliamentary candidates to 2030.
- Strengthening of enforcement by allowing tribunals to make wider recommendations in discrimination cases (benefiting the wider workforce rather than individuals).
- Under consideration: allowing cases to be brought on combined multiple grounds (for example discrimination on the grounds of being a black woman)/allowing for representative actions.

Source: GEO (2008)

A British Bill of Rights?

Another of Brown's early moves was to deliver a flagship statement to the House of Commons on constitutional reform, including a major policy initiative to consult on the introduction of a British Statement of Values and a Bill of Rights. Reform models were outlined in a consultation paper *The Governance of Britain* (Ministry of Justice, 2007b). This noted that proposals for a Bill of Rights had been considered but ultimately rejected as a reform model in 1997. Further reform would represent the 'second stage' of a broader process of human rights reform envisaged by many in 1997-98.

The prospect of a Bill of Rights raises the possibility of a new approach to social justice in Britain, with the extension of existing equality and human rights standards by codifying economic and social rights and children's rights;

by incorporating a statement of values and purposes focusing on goals such as freedom, autonomy, equality, dignity and respect; and through entrenchment, putting equality and human rights on a secure constitutional footing and making these standards more difficult to overturn. For example, recognition of the human right to health as a codified fundamental right in domestic law could help to secure health protection and promotion as a core area of government responsibility. This could help to establish a new model of public service governance that ultimately focuses on the expansion of the capability to achieve good health rather than on particular delivery mechanisms (for further discussion, see below).

In practice, *The Governance of Britain* expresses caution in the field of economic and social rights. Internationally, new legal models are emerging for judicial enforcement of economic and social rights based on the 'minimum core obligations approach' (developed by the UN Committee on Economic, Social and Cultural Rights) and judicial scrutiny of the notion of 'reasonableness' (developed in South African jurisprudence).[3] However, *The Governance of Britain* fails to address the importance of normative standard-setting in this area and highlights the 'democratic objections' to economic and social rights – with codification viewed as limiting the power of the elected Parliament and government, resulting in an unreasonable shift in power to an unelected and unaccountable judiciary on resource allocation matters (Ministry of Justice, 2007b, para 209).

More recently, there appears to have been a shift in the government's position, with an acknowledgement of the possibility of including economic and social rights in a Bill of Rights as aspirational goals, without moving towards full justiciability. In its most recent report, the Joint Committee on Human Rights (JCHR, 2008, pp 170-81) rejects the view that economic and social rights are inherently non-justiciable and recommends the inclusion of education, health, adequate standard of living and housing as well as children's rights in a British Bill of Rights. The proposed reform model is based on a judicial review of a duty of progressive realisation of economic and social rights by reasonable legislative and other measures, within available resources, based on the South African model.

Human rights campaigners are nevertheless concerned that a Bill of Rights might be used by the government not to strengthen and extend human rights, but to dilute and reduce the minimum protections afforded by the HRA and the ECHR (Klug, 2007a, 2007b; Liberty, 2007) and/or to link human rights to the 'responsibilities agenda'. While repeal and withdrawal have apparently been rejected as policy options, the government explicitly acknowledges that a Bill of Rights could provide a vehicle for *clarifying* and *legislating for* the 're-balancing' of rights and other objectives (Ministry of Justice, 2007b, p 210).

Solid proposals were absent from the 2008 Constitutional Renewal White Paper (Ministry of Justice, 2008). Following the consultative process, debates within Cabinet – including on the vexed issue of economic and social rights – are ongoing and heated. Lord Lester, who resigned as an adviser to Gordon Brown in November 2008, summarised the situation as follows:

In spite of its achievement in introducing the Human Rights Act, the government has a deeply disappointing record in giving effect to the values inderpinning the Human Rights Act in its policies and practices. Through a lack of political leadership, it has also failed to match the expectations raised by the Governance of Britain green paper for much-needed constitutional reform (*The Guardian*, 11 December 2008).

The Equality Public Service Agreement

Under Gordon Brown, equality standards are becoming increasingly embedded as high-level government performance targets. The 2008-11 Public Service Agreements (PSAs) included, for the first time, a cross-cutting public service agreement on equality. PSA 15 commits the government to address the horizontal inequalities and disadvantage associated with gender, race, disability, age, sexual orientation, religion or belief by reducing the gender pay gap; tackling barriers that limit people's choice and control in their lives; increasing participation in public life; reducing discrimination in employment; and reducing unfair treatment by public services in areas such as education, health and transport (HM Treasury, 2008c). The PSA suggests that momentum will increase in these areas in the coming period. In relation to gender, while anti-discrimination and equality legislation has been supplemented by new maternity and paternity arrangements, as well as by provisions for flexible working and childcare, pay gaps remain a key concern (see Chapter Three).

In relation to disability, the latest statistics on the implementation of the 1995 DDA paint a reasonably optimistic picture of progress since 1995. Anti-discrimination legislation seems to have been partially successful in reducing the discrimination experienced by disabled people in accessing goods and services, with a fall in reported difficulties from 43% to 34% between 1996 and 2006 (ODI, 2008, table 3.1). However, the reform of anti-discrimination law underpins a broader policy strategy aimed at eliminating underlying barriers and constraints and achieving equality in the independence, choice and control of disabled people by 2025 (PMSU, 2005). The Office for Disability Issues is developing new indicators of autonomy and independent living that will be used to track progress under the PSA and in relation to the broader 2025 strategy.

Inequality in treatment in public services, including discrimination and lack of dignity and respect, has moved up the government's agenda; and this priority is also reflected in PSA 15. The headline statistics suggest that organisational discrimination is a particular factor in the police and criminal justice system, rather than in public services such as education and health (Table 14.1). However, the issue of dignity and respect of older people in areas such as health and social care is currently a key issue on the equality and human rights agenda, with a series of recent qualitative studies raising the profile and establishing the importance

Table 14.1: % of people who expect different organisations to treat them worse than other races, by ethnicity

| | England and Wales, 2001, 2003, 2005 and 2007-08 | | | | | | | |
| | 2001 | | 2003 | | 2005 | | 2007-08 | |
	Minority ethnic groups	White	Minority ethnic groups	White	Minority ethnic groups	White	Minority ethnic groups	White
(1) Police	27	6	23	5	24	5	22	6
(2) Prison service	21	4	17	2	17	2	14	2
(3) Courts	14	5	13	6	12	6	11	6
(4) Crown Prosecution Service	14	5	12	5	11	5	11	5
(5) Probation service	11	4	10	3	10	3	10	2
(6) Council housing department or housing association	13	15	12	21	13	21	11	25
(7) Local general practitioner	4	2	4	2	3	1	4	2
(8) Local school	7	3	4	2	6	2	6	3
Any of the five criminal justice service organisations (1)-(5)	33	11	31	11	31	11	28	10
Any of the eight organisations (1)-(8)	38	20	36	27	37	26	34	29

Source: DCLG (2008c, table 10)

of process inequalities of this type (HC, 2007b; HC et al, 2006; JCHR, 2007). National data on variations in patient experience support suggestions of sharp differentials in older people's experience of privacy and nutritional support, while differentials in reported dignity and respect are significant for disabled people and for certain minority ethnic groups (HC, 2006, pp 32-45).

Equality and human rights mainstreaming: the picture in 2008

In 2008, there is evidence that equality and human rights standards are becoming embedded as an overarching framework for public policy in a number of important ways. In the health context, the implementation of the race equality duty has been associated with new forms of statistical monitoring, official recognition of the need for policy intervention, and good practice on the ground in some areas. A key finding arising from new systems of statistical monitoring has been that rates of inpatient referral to mental health services through the criminal justice system are significantly higher, and rates of inpatient referral by general practitioners significantly lower, for certain black and ethnic minority groups (HC et al, 2007, pp 24-6).

Differentials in the educational achievements of Gypsy and Traveller children were reported in Chapter Nine and similar gaps in the health outcomes of Gypsies and Travellers have now been authoritatively established even when compared with other minority ethnic and disadvantaged groups (Parry et al, 2007). Official recognition of Gypsies and Travellers as an ethnic group, as well as the need to ensure access to public services, is an important breakthrough in many race equality plans being developed for the 2008-10 period (for example, DCLG, 2008b; Denbighshire County Council, 2008; SPCT, 2008). Important new evidence on variations in infant mortality rates by ethnicity are also highlighted in new and emerging data (Hackney Council, 2006, p 59; ONS, 2008d). The race equality duty and local area agreements appear to be helping to drive policy responses forward, with the emergence of specific interventions targeted at women from particular minority ethnic groups (for example Team Hackney LAA, 2007).

Equality and human rights standards have also become embedded in frameworks for public services regulation such as the core standard frameworks adopted by the Healthcare Commission and the Social Care Inspection Commission. In health, core standard 7e ("challenging discrimination, promoting equality and respect for human rights") and core standard 13a ("having systems in place to ensure that staff treat patients, their relatives and carers with dignity and respect") are elements of the Healthcare Commission's Annual Healthcheck. In 2007-08, only 83% of trusts were assessed as being compliant with core standard 7e, compared with compliance rates at 90% or above for 38 of the other 44 standards included in the framework as a whole (HC 2008, pp 44-47). The mainstreaming of equality and human rights objectives is also reflected in many of the supplementary standards developed for health and social care audit, inspection and monitoring (Box 7). At the time of writing, there is evidence that the core standards frameworks are improving outcomes for some groups. This includes a decline in explicit age discrimination since the National Standards Framework For Older People was introduced as a result of NHS trusts auditing policies on access to services and social services reviewing their eligibility criteria (HC et al, 2006).

Recent health policy initiatives may further consolidate this process of equality and human rights mainstreaming. Increasingly, choice-based and voice-based policy instruments, which aim to improve quality in public services by strengthening individual accountability and empowerment, are being supplemented by initiatives that relate more explicitly to equality and human rights standards. In July 2008, the final report of the Darzi Review (DH, 2008a) outlined a new health agenda focusing on the reduction of health inequalities rather than extending capacity as a central goal. The emphasis on information on patient experience reflects many of the core standards set out in Table 14.2.

Table 14.2: Equality and human rights regulation: standards adopted by the Healthcare Commission and the Commission for Social Care Inspection

Healthcare Commission Core Standards Framework	
Core standard C7e	Trusts are required to challenge discrimination, promote equality and respect human rights
Core standard C13abc	Systems are in place to ensure that staff treat patients, relatives and carers with dignity and respect/consent/confidentiality
Core standard C14ab	Complaints
Core standard C15b	Where food is provided, systems are in place to ensure that individual nutritional, personal and clinical dietary requirements are met, including any necessary help with feeding
Core standard C16	Patients are provided with suitable and accessible information on their care and treatment and are informed about what to expect during treatment, care and after-care
Core standard C17	The views of patients, their carers and others are sought and taken into account in designing, planning, delivering and improving healthcare services
Core standard C18	Healthcare organisations are required to enable all members of the population to access services equally and offer choice in access to services/treatment equitably
Core standard C20b	Healthcare services are provided in environments that promote effective care and optimise health outcomes by being supportive of patient privacy/confidentiality
National Service Framework for Older People	
Standard 1: Rooting out age discrimination	NHS services are provided regardless of age, on the basis of clinical need. Social care services should not use age in their criteria for eligibility or policies to restrict access to available services
Standard 2: Person-centred care	NHS/social care services treat older people as individuals and enable them to make choices about their treatment (including single assessment process, integrated commissioning arrangements and integrated provision of services, including community equipment and continence services)

Source: DH (2001a, 2004b)

New models of public services governance, such as the draft NHS Constitution issued with the Darzi Review, may also take equality and human rights mainstreaming forward. The draft Constitution reaffirms the right to NHS services free of charge and with equal access for all, and enshrines patients' rights to choice and to drugs approved by the National Institute for Health and Clinical Excellence (NICE). All NHS organisations will have a legal duty to take account of the Constitution, which will be operative for at least 10 years, making it relatively difficult to overturn. However, while the draft Constitution recognises health as a fundamental moral right, it falls short of the explicit recognition of the human right to health suggested in earlier consultations on core NHS principles.

Conclusion

A major transformation of the equality and human rights landscape has been achieved under New Labour. The main achievements include:

- A programme of anti-discrimination and equality law reform, including strengthened protection against discrimination on the grounds of gender, ethnicity, disability, age, sexual orientation, transgender and religion and belief, new public duties to promote equality and commitment to a single equality act;
- The Human Rights Act, the enforcement of civil and political rights in domestic courts and a duty on public authorities to act in a way that is "compatible" with human rights, and the further extension of human rights protection in some areas (e.g. a right of individual petition under the UN Convention on the Elimination of all forms of Discrimination against Women);
- Creation of an independent institution to spearhead equality and human rights regulation (the Equality and Human Rights Commission);
- Evidence of progress in mainstreaming of equality and human rights standards in public policy (as reflected in high-level performance targets and the regulatory frameworks adopted by audit and inspection in health and social care); and
- Consultation on a Bill of Rights.

However, the reform programme has been a gradual one. Alternative trajectories could have improved outcomes and embedded protection mechanisms for the future. Key limitations, gaps and omissions in the reform programme, at the time of writing, include:

- The long and protracted nature of the anti-discrimination and equality law reform programme, with delays in key areas and late adoption of a single equality model;
- Remaining gaps in anti-discrimination and equality law, some of which the government is committed to addressing in the forthcoming Single Equality Act

(e.g. the introduction of new powers to outlaw unjustifiable age discrimination in goods, facilities and services) and others that may not be covered (e.g. positive equality duties for the private sector, strengthened protection against discrimination on the grounds of marital status);

• Delayed introduction of institutional support for human rights and failure to incorporate the full range of human rights recognised in international law, including children's rights and economic and social rights, or to introduce a Bill of Rights covering these areas; and

• Concerns that government anti-terrorism measures are resulting in an erosion of human rights and that a Bill of Rights might be used to dilute existing human rights standards and/or to link human rights standards to the 'responsibilities agenda'.

Looking to the future, while the incumbent government retains the power to modify and repeal legislation and to alter the institutional environment, the independent and regulatory powers of the EHRC appear, for now, to have secured a key role for equality and human rights standards in combating persistent horizontal inequalities in 21st-century Britain. A Bill of Rights could extend and entrench equality and human rights standards – making them more difficult to overturn. Other policy instruments, such as the constitutional guarantee advocated by the EHRC, could also put equality and human rights standards onto a more secure and permanent footing.

However, the future direction of policy is not certain. The downside risks of a Bill of Rights are policy dilution and reversal. Ongoing political commitment is vital for continued progress during New Labour's third term and beyond.

Notes

[1] For relevant jurisprudence and the closure of the loophole, see JCHR (2006) and the 2008 Health and Social Care Act.

[2] See EHRC (2008). Lester and Clapinska (2005) set out a number of standards for the success of the new Commission, including: (1) being underpinned by an effective, comprehensive and coherent Single Equality Act; (2) being independent and accountable; (3) being sufficiently resourced and empowered; (4) having a broad human rights mandate covering economic and social rights.

[3] An important body of legal thought characterises positive duties as indeterminate, unenforceable and non-judiciable. This position is challenged by the emergence of a new body of legal thinking based on the view that both civil and political rights also involve resource allocations and positive duties and that economic and social rights can be made enforceable and justiciable through normative standard-setting and jurisprudence. See JCHR (2004, 2008) for further discussion.

FIFTEEN

Future pressures: intergenerational links, wealth, demography and sustainability

John Hills

Having surveyed the last decade, it is natural to contemplate how things might change in the future. This is not to forecast inequality. A glance back at Figure 2.1 in Chapter Two shows significant turning points in income inequality that would not necessarily have been foreseen. In 1970, following comparatively little change since the Second World War, the drop in income inequality to an all-time low on the measures shown by the late 1970s would not necessarily have been predicted. When the Royal Commission on the Distribution of Income and Wealth produced its final reports (1979a, 1979b), the data available reflected that all-time low, with no indication of the massive leap that was to come through the 1980s. Equally, the Joseph Rowntree Foundation's *Inquiry into Income and Wealth* reported in 1995 (Barclay, 1995), with data available reflecting the growth to the high point of inequality in the early 1990s, but preceding the fluctuations around a more stable level since.

This warns against simple extrapolation. What happens to income inequality results from a complex mix of factors including labour market structure; returns to different levels and kinds of skill; international trade and technological change; partnership patterns; regional and neighbourhood differences; and – as the rest of the book has shown – policies adopted by governments. Without a crystal ball, we cannot predict whether we are approaching – or have already passed – some new turning point.

However, it is possible to identify some major factors that will affect income distribution, and where the pressures could differ from the past decade. This chapter considers four: intergenerational transmission of advantage; wealth and inheritance; demographic change and pressures on the public finances; and environmental sustainability, specifically the need to reduce carbon emissions in the face of climate change.

Intergenerational transmission of advantage

Whether the objective is equality of opportunity, or more equal outcomes, either is harder to achieve, the more life chances are determined by birth. Policy debate in the last decade has emphasised the former, and has put as a positive achievement, the creation of a more 'meritocratic' society (sometimes oblivious that Michael Young's 1958 book that coined the term – *The Rise of the Meritocracy* – was a satire, by the end of which some of the 'meritocrats' attempted to cement the social position of their children).

However, popular commentary now often suggests that 'social mobility has slowed under New Labour'. This is not necessarily the case, especially as the data are not yet available to give a definitive answer on the links between one generation and another – those who were born since 1997 are not yet teenagers. One also has to take care in what is meant by 'social' mobility. In terms of the links between the *social classes* of children and their parents, as measured by occupational class, through most of the period since the Second World War, there was more *upward* than downward mobility in absolute terms (Heath and Payne, 2000). The expansion of white-collar and professional jobs created 'room at the top' for children from working-class backgrounds. Allowing for the changing sizes of different occupational groups, the *relative* chances of people from different parental social classes moving to another may not have changed: John Goldthorpe and colleagues present evidence suggesting that in relative terms, comparing those aged 25-59 at any date with their parents, social class mobility changed little from the early 1970s to 2005 (Goldthorpe and Jackson, 2007; Goldthorpe and Mills, 2008).

This stability in relative social class mobility does not necessarily mean that the *economic* links between parents and children are unchanged, given that social class only predicts a small part of income differences, and given the widening of the income and earnings distributions. The best-known evidence on economic mobility is of the kind shown in the first panel of Table 15.1. This shows part of Blanden and Machin's (2007) comparison of intergenerational links in incomes within the 1958 and 1970 birth cohort studies. For boys born in 1958, 30% of those with parents in the poorest quarter when they were teenagers ended up in the bottom quarter of the earnings distribution for those aged 33 in 1991. Similarly, 35% of those with parents with the highest quarter of incomes ended up in the highest quarter of earnings. But 37% of poorer boys born in 1970 were themselves low earners in 2004 at age 34, while the proportion of richer boys staying at the top had risen to 45%. Measured this way, intergenerational mobility fell between the two cohorts, and Blanden and Machin find similar falls in income mobility looking more broadly across the distribution, and at women as well as men.

But the childhoods and early adulthoods of the 1970 cohort took place before the change of government in 1997, when they were 27, their education largely complete, and career paths already started. The comparison tells us that tackling inequality in the last 10 years has been much harder in some ways than it would have been a generation before, because the economic position of younger adults is more dependent than in the past on the position of their parents. Blanden

Table 15.1: Indicators of intergenerational mobility, cohorts born 1958 to 2000-01

	Cohort[1]	Born	Parental income group	
			Bottom 25%	**Top 25%**
(a) Son's earnings at 33/34				
Bottom quartile	NCDS	1958	30	18
	BCS	1970	37	13
Top quartile	NCDS	1958	18	35
	BCS	1970	13	45
			Bottom 20%	**Top 20%**
(b) Degree by age 23	NCDS	1958	5	20
	BCS	1970	7	37
	BHPS	1975 (av.)	11	40
	BHPS	1979 (av.)	10	44
(c) Test scores at 10/11 (percentile)	NCDS	1958	43	59
	BCS	1970	38	63
(d) Test scores at 5-7 (percentile)	Children of NCDS	1985 (av.)	38	53
	Children of BCS	1999 (av.)	41	57
	MCS	2000/01	40	58
(e) Externalising behaviour at 5-7 (score)	NCDS	1958	0.06	−0.12
	BCS	1970	0.23	−0.18
	Children of NCDS	1985 (av.)	0.31	−0.19
	Children of BCS	1999 (av.)	0.25	−0.10
	MCS	2000/01	0.27	−0.27

Note: [1] NCDS is National Child Development Study; BCS is the British Cohort Study; and MCS is the Millennium Cohort Study.

Source: Blanden and Machin (2007, tables 1a, 1b, 4 and 6)

and Machin argue that an important driver was the increasing link between the qualifications of children and parental income: the children of better-off parents benefited most over this period from the expansion of tertiary education. The second panel of Table 15.1 shows that the proportion of children with parents from the bottom fifth of incomes who had a degree only rose by two percentage points between the two cohorts (measured at age 23, so in 1981 and 1993 respectively). But the rise for those with the best-off parents – already much more likely to attain a degree – was 17 percentage points.

This was part of New Labour's inheritance, and says little about impacts of policy since 1997 or what has changed since then. To explore this, Blanden and Machin look at indicators of what is happening at younger ages to more recently born cohorts. Their conclusion is that 'the decline in intergenerational mobility between [the 1958 and 1970] cohorts is not ongoing, but neither has there been any significant improvement' (Blanden and Machin, 2007, abstract). In other words, we have plateaued out at a new, lower rate of intergenerational income mobility for those born since 1970.

Given the small sample sizes and tentative nature of some of the links involved in early life stages, this is a fair conclusion, although looking at the lower parts of Table 15.1 some of the associations have grown stronger for those born since 1970. The proportion of better-off children with degrees at age 23 may have risen more slowly than before, but the gap between them and those with poorer parents still widened between those born in 1970 and those born around 1979 (interviewed around 2002). Only in the last few years has the social class gap in *entry* to tertiary education narrowed a little (Chapter Four).

Looking at those born since 1997, the test scores of poorer children born around 1999 and in 2000/01 measured when they were aged five to seven were somewhat closer to the average than for their equivalents born in 1985. However, children of the best-off fifth of parents had moved more quickly up the distribution. Similarly, looking at 'externalising behaviour' at ages five to seven (where a positive score indicates more tantrums, aggressive or disobedient behaviour), there was a deterioration between the poorer children born in 1958 and 1970, but no clear trend since. For the better-off children, however, their already much lower (negative scores) were lower still for the Millennium Cohort children born in 2000/01, which may indicate a further widening of this gap in the early years (although the score for the smaller group of *children* of the better-off members of the 1970 cohort born around 1999 is less good, making the picture unclear).

Even for children born in the late 1950s, the UK was already in some respects less economically mobile than some others in Europe for which there are comparable data. The first two columns of Table 15.2 present information on the links between fathers' and sons' earnings comparable to the first panel of Table 15.1 for the six other countries covered in Jäntii et al's (2006) study. In this case, the figures are for the bottom *fifth* of fathers and sons. In the UK case, the father's 'earnings' measure is net parental *income* as in Table 15.1. The very low mobility

Table 15.2: International comparisons of earnings mobility of sons (born near 1958)

	Sons of fathers from bottom fifth also at bottom (%)	Sons of fathers from top fifth also at top (%)	Father-son earnings elasticity	Father-daughter earnings elasticity
US	42	36	0.52	0.28
UK	30	30	0.31	0.33
Finland	28	35	0.17	0.08
Norway	28	35	0.16	0.11
Sweden	26	37	0.26	0.19
Denmark	25	36	0.07	0.03

Note: UK figures based on parental net income, rather than fathers' earnings.

Source: Jäntii et al (2006, tables 2 and 4)

for US children moving out of the bottom fifth stands out. The UK shows up as less mobile than the Nordic countries in this respect, but for this generation, fewer of the UK sons of better-off fathers stayed at the top than in the other countries. The third and fourth columns of the Table summarise information for the links across the whole of the population, not just the top and bottom: the higher the earnings elasticity shown, the stronger the links between fathers and children. For sons, the US clearly had the strongest intergenerational links; for daughters, it was the UK.

In the mid-1980s, when this generation had embarked on their careers, the Nordic countries in the Table had both low income inequality and lower rates of remaining in the poorest fifth, while the US had both high income inequality and high immobility at the bottom (Hills, 2004, figure 2.10). Overall, income inequality in the UK was between the two for this cohort. If higher income inequality is a factor in reducing economic mobility, it is not clear at which life stage it has its effects. Suggestively, however, by the time of the 1970 cohort, intergenerational links had grown in the UK (Table 15.1), as had overall income inequality in the mid-1990s, measured at the time this cohort was in their mid-twenties.

Implications

It may be harder to change places in a society where the rungs of the ladder are further apart. If so, the slowdown in economic mobility between those born in the late 1950s and the early 1970s is no coincidence: one of the biggest differences between them was that they became adults and entered the labour market on different sides of the great increase in income inequality in the UK shown in Figure 2.1. Looking to later generations, income inequality has grown much more slowly, but has not diminished. Future policy will continue to operate in a world where there are larger differences in the resources available to parents as their children grow up than in the past in the UK or than in many other European countries (see Chapter Thirteen). In this environment, trying to achieve more equality of opportunity will continue to be hard.

Wealth and inheritance

An important part of people's economic position and its transmission between generations is wealth – people's stock of assets. The distribution of wealth between individuals is markedly more unequal than that of annual income flows. For instance, Table 15.3 shows that since 1976, the Gini coefficient summary indicator of marketable wealth inequality[1] has been above 64%, twice the equivalent figure for individual incomes since the early 1990s (Figure 2.1). While the top 10% by income received 28% of individual net income in 2006-07 (DWP, 2008b), the wealthiest 10% own half of all marketable wealth. Within this, the top 1% of adults received 13% of before-tax annual income in 2004-05 (Brewer et al, 2008b), but the top 1% of adults owned more than 20% of marketable wealth. At the other end, the bottom half of the distribution received 27% of net income in 2006-07, but the bottom half of adults owned just 7% of wealth in 2003. For some, debts exceed assets and wealth is negative.

The distribution of wealth has followed a different pattern from that of income. From the 1920s until the mid-1970s, it became less unequal (Hills, 2004, table 2.7). As Table 15.3 shows, this continued, albeit more slowly, until the early 1990s, even as the distribution of income became more unequal. But since then, up until 2002, the official series shown suggests that wealth distribution became

Table 15.3: Distribution of personal marketable wealth, 1976-2003

| | Share of top | | | | | Gini | Marketable |
	1%	5%	10%	25%	50%	coefficient	wealth as % GDP
1976	21	38	50	71	92	66	224
1981	18	36	50	73	92	65	223
1986	18	36	50	73	90	64	250
1991	17	35	47	71	92	64	291
1996	20	40	52	74	93	68	273
2001	22	42	54	72	94	68	349
2002	24	45	57	75	94	71	342
2003[1]	21	40	53	72	93	67	341

Note: [1] 2003 figure is provisional. Publication of later figures has been delayed due to technical difficulties.

Source: HMRC (2006, tables 13.4 and 13.5) and earlier equivalents

more unequal. The most recent published figures – still provisional – suggest that this was reversed in 2003. At this point the value of the stock market had fallen considerably, which will have affected the measured wealth of the very top of the distribution. Unfortunately, there are no published figures for later years reflecting the position after the stock market recovery (or subsequent collapse), so the firmest conclusion is that there is no evidence that wealth has become *more* equally distributed since New Labour came to power.

However, the overall value of personal wealth greatly increased in relation to national income – from around 2.5 times gross domestic product (GDP) in the mid-1980s to more than 3.4 times GDP in the most recent years shown. Much of this is bound up with housing – owner-occupied property (net of mortgages) made up half of all marketable wealth in 2003, and real house prices rose by 80% between 1996 and 2003. As this represents largely a higher nominal price being put on houses that people are already occupying, in itself this may not say so much about the changing distribution of life chances, but it may have a much larger future effect through inheritance. Back in 1981, fewer than half of householders aged over 75 were owner-occupiers; by 2006, nearly 70% were (Hills, 2007, figure 12.7). Many more of those who die over the next two decades are likely to leave a substantial legacy than in the past.

Inheritances have already become larger. Ross et al (2008) show that 5% of those aged over 50 said that they had received an inheritance in each of the two-year periods of 1997-98 and 2003-04, but the average amounts they received doubled in real terms to £60,000. The top 1% of inheritances had reached over £400,000, although most are much more modest, with half being £8,000 or less.

Inheritances tend to go to the next generation – people in their fifties or older. Even within this group, they are not equally spread. The upper panel of Table 15.4 shows the average probabilities given by respondents aged 54-75 with different levels of wealth of receiving different levels of inheritance. Whereas the already wealthiest quarter thought that they had a 10% chance of inheriting £100,000 or more in the next 10 years, the average probability for the least wealthy was only 3%. The chances of the wealthiest quarter receiving *any* inheritance were twice that of the poorest.

Looking across the whole adult population – including the younger groups who are less likely to have received any inheritance yet – the lower panel of the Table shows that 41% thought that they were at least fairly likely to inherit property at some point in future, and 48% money. But fewer than a fifth of social tenants, those with low incomes or from social class E expected to inherit property, and fewer than a third to inherit money. This is already reinforcing tenure patterns: nearly half of young first-time buyers receive help from family and friends, and are therefore able to put in considerably larger deposits to get onto the housing ladder (Hills, 2007). Those able to do so are more likely to come from owner-occupier families.

Table 15.4: Expectations of receiving an inheritance

(a) Mean expectations of receiving an inheritance in next 10 years
(54- to 75-year-olds, 2006, by wealth quartile group)

	Chance of receiving:		
	£100,000 or more	£10,000 or more	Any inheritance
Poorest quarter	3	9	12
Second	4	13	17
Third	6	17	20
Wealthiest	10	22	24

(b) Proportion definitely, very or fairly likely to receive inheritance
(All adults, 2004)

	Property	Money
All	41	48
Lone parents	32	40
Social tenants	19	30
Income £100-199/week	18	23
Social class E	16	27

Sources: upper part: Ross et al (2008), based on ELSA data; lower part: Rowlingson and McKay (2005, table 2.2) based on MORI survey

Implications

Wealth is far more unequally distributed than income, and there is no sign that the trend since the 1990s has been for its distribution to become more equal; if anything else, the reverse. To the extent that this has resulted from the accumulated impact of increased relative incomes at the top – and therefore greater ability to accumulate assets – over the last 20 years, this process could continue as larger proportions of people's working lives are spent in this more unequal environment. At the same time, the value of wealth – particularly owner-occupied property – has become higher in relation to incomes. Inheritance is likely to grow in importance in the next two decades. Already about 1 in 40 of those aged 50 or over receive an inheritance, averaging £60,000, each year. The already wealthiest are most likely to inherit and to expect to inherit in future, tending to entrench their own and their families' economic positions.

Demographic change and pressures on the public finances

Any view of the future involves great uncertainty, but there is consensus that the population is ageing, the uncertainties being around the speed of the process.

Official projections of the future age structure have changed rapidly in recent years as greater future improvements in mortality rates and longevity have been allowed for. The age structure also depends on future fertility rates and migration patterns, each even more uncertain. Bearing in mind the uncertainty around it, Figure 15.1 shows the Government Actuary's Department's most recent (2006-based) central projection for the age structure of Britain in 2046, by comparison with 2006 (ONS, 2007a). The 2046 structure has a more even spread of the population in each age group up to 60, and then a falling proportion in each age group, but with many more in each age band above 70 than now. The proportion of the population aged 65 or over is projected to rise from 16.1% to 23.7%. The proportion over 80 would more than double from 4.5% to 9.7%.

This potentially puts substantial pressure on key elements of social spending, because spending patterns are heavily age related. Figure 15.2 shows average spending on education, social security and healthcare by five-year age group in 2001. While education spending was concentrated on younger age groups, social security spending – dominated by pensions – was concentrated on those aged over 60, and healthcare on those aged over 80 especially. As a result – at 2001 spending levels – those in mid-life received only around £2,000 per year from these three services on average, but those in their seventies £8,000 per year, and those in their eighties up to £10,000 per year.[2]

If the only thing that changed was the population's age structure, and spending per head for each person of given age remained unchanged in relation to incomes, the projected change of age structure shown in Figure 15.1 would, by itself, increase average spending on these items by 16%. In aggregate terms this would mean increased spending from 2006-07 levels of around 3.8% of GDP over the 40 years. This is a fairly simple-minded calculation, not allowing for other things that will change as well. For instance, the state pension rights of today's retirees differ from those of the current oldest cohorts, and will be different again for those retiring in 30 years' time (see Chapter Eight). Equally, there are plans to increase the effective school-leaving age and to raise participation in tertiary education, which would raise education spending for those aged over 16. But in one way the implicit assumption on health spending may be pessimistic. With increased longevity our healthcare needs may stay the same at any given age, but extend over a longer period, as the calculation assumes. Alternatively, if part of increased longevity takes the form of 'healthy life expectancy', some care needs may be postponed, so that the relative needs of those of any particular age would fall. Ageing would then have less of an effect on spending – although other factors, such as technological change and rising preferences for healthcare as affluence grows, may continue to put additional upward pressure on top of this.

Each year, the Treasury carries out a more sophisticated exercise for its *Long-Term Public Finance Report*. Table 15.5 shows some of the results covering the period from 2007-08 to 2047-48[3] (using the same population projections as Figure 15.2). The first five rows show the analysis for 'age-related' spending items. These

Figure 15.1: Population structure, by age, 2006 and 2046, Great Britain (%)

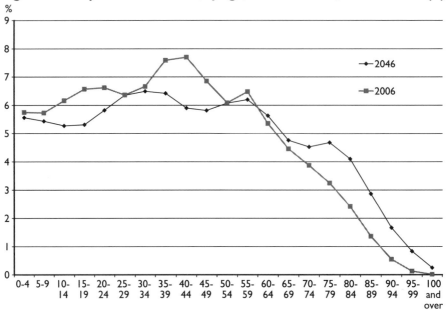

Source: ONS (2007a)

Figure 15.2: Social spending, by age, 2001 (£ per person)

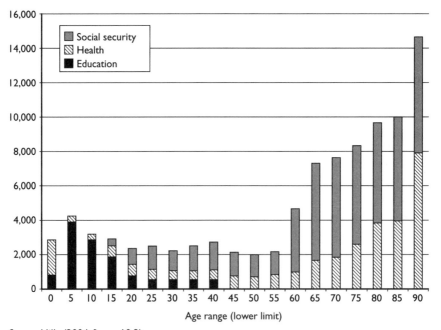

Source: Hills (2004, figure 10.2)

Table 15.5: HM Treasury projections of impact of demographic change on public spending (% of GDP)

	2007-08	2017-18	2027-28	2037-38	2047-48
Education	5.0	5.6	5.8	5.6	5.5
State pensions	4.9	5.1	5.6	6.3	6.3
Health	7.4	7.9	8.6	9.2	9.6
Long-term care	1.2	1.2	1.4	1.7	1.8
Public service pensions	1.5	1.8	2.0	1.9	1.8
Total 'age related'	**20.1**	**21.7**	**23.4**	**24.7**	**25.0**
Other	20.4	19.1	18.9	18.6	18.1
Total	**40.5**	**40.8**	**42.3**	**43.3**	**43.1**

Source: HM Treasury (2008b, table 4.1)

include spending on long-term care and public service pensions, but only the parts of social security specifically related to pensioners. The projections allow for the evolving structure of pension rights, not just the age of the population. As can be seen, the implication is that age-related spending would rise from 20.1% to 25.0% of GDP. For education, state pensions and health, the increase is 4.1% of GDP.[4] With long-term care and public service pensions, the total increase for age-related spending items comes to 4.9% of GDP.

However, partly offsetting this, the Treasury projection for 'other' public spending is a *fall* from 20.4% to 18.1% of GDP. In combination, the rise in total public spending is reduced to 2.6% of GDP. This is not quite so alarming from the government's point of view – although it is already significantly up on earlier projections.[5] But even this depends on a crucial assumption hidden in the calculations for 'other' spending. As the Treasury explains, the fall in non-age-related spending 'is driven by relative falls in non-pension social transfers which are, based on current policies, mainly increased in line with prices' (HM Treasury, 2008b, p 39). If real GDP per capita grew (in line with the Treasury's long-term assumptions) by 2% per year for 40 years, the relative generosity of any given transfer would fall by 55%. Applied to total non-pension transfers of 6.5% of GDP, even allowing for the reduced size of the non-pensioner population, this assumption generates a saving of around 3.3 percentage points of GDP. Without it, the projected increase in aggregate spending by 2046 from the Treasury's projections would be more than twice as large – 5.9 percentage points of GDP.

For those concerned with inequality and relative poverty this is a critical assumption, as witnessed by a recent modelling exercise in which we looked at the effects over just 20 years of continuing to increase benefits, tax credits and tax allowances in line with current practice (Sutherland et al, 2008). In most cases this would mean increases in line with price inflation. For a few, such as the Guarantee Credit for pensioners or the Basic State Pension from 2012, it would mean earnings-linking, but others would remain fixed in nominal terms. First, other things being equal (including demographic composition), the 'benefit erosion' implied by this assumption would mean that public spending would be 2.1% of GDP lower than it would be if all elements of the tax and transfer system were earnings-linked. In addition, direct tax revenues would be 1.5% of GDP higher than they would be if tax thresholds were earnings-linked, as a result of 'fiscal drag'. But the cost of this gain to the public finances would be borne disproportionately by those on lower incomes, as Figure 15.3 shows. The average net incomes of those in the bottom three-tenths of the income distribution would fall 16% behind earnings growth, but those in the top two-tenths only 5% behind. As a result, relative poverty would rise: by five to seven percentage points overall, and by 12 to 15 percentage points for children.

Figure 15.3: Distributional effect of fiscal drag and benefit erosion after 20 years of uprating according to current announced policies

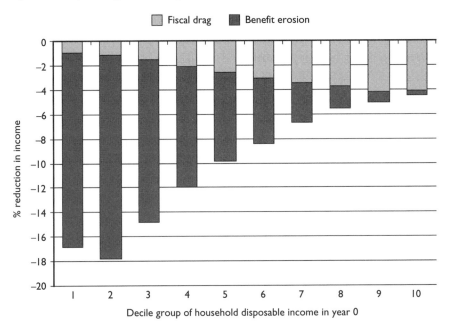

Source: Sutherland et al (2008, figure 18)

Implications

The ageing population will put a significant strain on the public finances, and so something will have to give – higher tax rates, less spending on other items, or reduced expectations of what can be delivered by social spending. But the default assumption built both into current policies for uprating most benefits, tax credits and tax allowances and into the government's long-term public finance projections is that much of the strain will be taken by a fall in the relative generosity of the state to those at the bottom of the income distribution. Other things being equal, poverty rates would rise. This may be one way of meeting the fiscal challenges from an ageing society, but it is one that makes aspirations of creating a more equal society still harder to achieve.

Environmental sustainability and the need to reduce carbon emissions

Beyond the domestic distributional issues with which this book is concerned, the largest challenge facing societies across the world is climate change and the need to limit emissions of carbon dioxide (CO_2) and other greenhouse gases. The Stern Report set out the scale of this challenge, arguing that action to limit greenhouse gases now will have much lower economic cost than unchecked global warming in the longer run (Stern, 2007). In the 2008 Climate Change Act, the government has committed itself to reducing UK carbon emissions by the 80% from 1990 levels by 2050 advised by its Committee on Climate Change, which has now set five-year 'carbon budgets' leading to this outcome.

The mix of instruments available to achieve this includes:

- 'carbon taxes' on those generating greenhouse gases or consumption that leads to them;
- quotas to either producers or consumers setting a limit on how much they can emit, but with trading possible between those who do not use their full quota and those who go over theirs;
- subsidies to allow or encourage people to change their behaviour (for instance, to insulate their homes, or use more energy-efficient transport); and
- regulation (such as phasing out incandescent light bulbs, setting stricter fuel efficiency requirements for cars or compelling power companies to make more use of renewable energy).

If all consumption had an equal impact on greenhouse gases for each pound spent, or if people differed only in the scale of consumption, rather than its composition, there would be no particular distributional impact from carbon taxes or from tradeable quotas distributed in proportion to existing consumption. There would, however, be major distributional consequences if, for instance, everyone in the country was allocated an equal personal carbon quota, as some have suggested. This would leave those with high consumption needing either to make large changes to their lifestyle or to purchase unused quotas from those with lower consumption – usually with lower income – who would gain.

But different forms of consumption have varying carbon contents, and consumption patterns vary widely both between and within income groups. Those with high incomes spend a much greater proportion of income on average on air travel than those with low incomes. Those with low incomes tend to spend a much greater proportion of income on domestic fuel than others. Thumim and White (2008, figure 1) show that average carbon emissions associated with direct spending on domestic fuel, petrol and diesel (excluding aviation and public transport, as well as indirect emissions through other forms of spending) are twice as much per adult for those with the top tenth of incomes as for those in the lowest tenth. However, this increase is not in proportion to income, given that the mean equivalent income of the richest tenth is more than 10 times that of the bottom group. Emissions also vary considerably *within* each income group. By implication, serious attempts to limit carbon emissions will have major distributional effects. Those distributional effects could partly be offset through changes to benefits and tax credits, but as we shall see, it is hard to do this without there still being significant numbers of low-income losers unless other action is taken.

First, the potential scale of this should be noted. Aggregate UK emissions of greenhouse gases, measured as megatonnes of CO_2 equivalent ($MtCO_2E$), were 650 $MtCO_2E$ in 2006, of which 554 Mt were of CO_2 itself (Defra, 2008a). This is equivalent to about 22 tonnes of CO_2 per household, or 12 tonnes per adult. Of this, 42%, or around nine tonnes per household (five tonnes per adult) were accounted for by direct household consumption of domestic fuel and personal transport, including by air (Defra, 2008b). The rest was embodied in other forms of consumption, such as food, services or manufactured goods.

Estimates of the potential size of the 'price of carbon' that would achieve the kinds of change in behaviour required (or would value the damage caused by additional emissions at the margin) vary very widely, and depend heavily on whether or not policy is assumed to be successful in reducing greenhouse gases. In 2008, the government suggested that appraisal of greenhouse gas reduction projects should use a 'shadow price of carbon' rising from £27 per tonne of CO_2 in 2008, to £61 in 2050 at 2008 prices (Defra, 2008c). But this assumes that policy is successful in reducing greenhouse gases, and so the marginal damage of any additional tonne is lower than if policy is less successful. As a rough guide, a figure of £30 per tonne might be seen as a lower bound, but in the long run, figures that are far higher may well be more appropriate.

Putting those two together, the aggregate impact of an average household's total emissions (including indirect) would be equivalent to at least £660 per year, or more than 2% of net household income – but quite possibly much more. Nationally, the amount would be at least £17 billion, or 1.3% of GDP, but again possibly much more. If the way this 'carbon price' was imposed meant revenue accruing to government – for instance through a carbon tax, or through auctioned (as opposed to allocated) quotas – the revenue could be redistributed to households, leaving them in balance on average. Of course, the whole point of the exercise would be behaviour change towards less carbon-intensive consumption, so the ultimate flows would be smaller than this both for government and for households. However, to achieve part of that change would require investments – for instance, in energy efficiency – which would have costs associated with them. While some of these would, in fact, be cost-saving for consumers, others would imply a net cost that households would have to carry, albeit one that would be smaller than the carbon cost avoided. Globally, the Stern Report estimated that the costs associated with prompt action to reduce carbon emissions would be around 1% of GDP (Stern, 2007, p xvi). However one looks at it, serious attempts to reduce greenhouse gas emissions will involve costs that ultimately fall on households – albeit smaller than the long-run costs of climate change and of adaptation to it.

With such large flows involved, the effects on different kinds of household could vary greatly. To put them in perspective, the total cost of the government's flagship Child and Working Tax Credits, crucial to its anti-poverty strategy, was £20 billion in 2006-07. The flows both from and back to households associated with attempts to control greenhouse gas emissions could well be much bigger.

As an example of the scale and distributional consequences, Table 15.6 is derived from analysis by Dresner and Ekins (2006) examining the immediate distributional impact of a carbon tax (or equivalent price change) of £30 per tonne of CO_2 in 2008-09 prices.[6] The first five columns look at a tax imposed on domestic fuel (heating and lighting) in 2008-09. On average, this would, without behaviour change, cost households £150 per year, or 0.5% of net income. However, as the Table shows, such a tax, by itself, would be regressive. On average, the poorest tenth of households would pay 1.1% of net income, but those in the top tenth only 0.26%.

The Table highlights the differences in impact within each income group. Given the revenues that would accrue from the tax, government could afford to make transfers (benefits and tax credits) more generous, or to reduce other taxes. Such adjustments can be structured to offset the distributional effects on any particular income group.[7] Dresner and Ekins experimented with different ways to use improved transfers to protect lower-income groups, looking not just at the average impact, but also at variation within groups. Table 15.6 shows the compensation package that was most effective in minimising the number of low-income losers. This entailed using *all* of the potential revenue to increase both means-tested benefits and tax credits (as well as a lower rate of carbon tax for homes heated by off-peak electricity). On average, this would more than reverse the cost of the carbon tax for the bottom three income groups, and the package would be very progressive, creating a transfer from the top half of the income distribution to the bottom third. But despite this, a third of households in the poorest three-tenths of the distribution would be losers. This is partly because means-tested benefits do not reach everyone for whom they are intended (incomplete take-up), but particularly because domestic fuel consumption varies widely between households, even if they have similar incomes.

Table 15.6: Immediate distributional impact of carbon tax (£30/tonne CO$_2$) on domestic fuel and on road fuels, with compensating measures (2008-09 income levels)

Income group (tenths)	Domestic fuel only				Road fuels only	
	Average impact (£/year)	% income	Change with compensation[1] (£/year)	% losing after compensation	Change with compensation[1] (£/year)	% losing after compensation
1	–111	1.13	+207	35	+120	17
2	–132	0.88	+228	29	+156	17
3	–120	0.68	+165	37	+102	21
4	–129	0.64	+90	45	+60	34
5	–144	0.59	–15	67	–	48
6	–147	0.51	–66	72	–45	62
7	–159	0.49	–117	82	–75	73
8	–171	0.44	–141	87	–90	74
9	–174	0.38	–165	92	–114	77
Top	–201	0.26	–186	95	–120	76
All	**–150**	**0.49**	**0**	**64**	**0**	**50**

Note: [1] Lower carbon tax on night storage electricity (equalising cost/kWh), and Income Support, Pension Credit, Housing and Council Tax Benefits, Child Tax Credits and Working Tax Credit all increased to minimise the number of low-income losers, using revenue generated by tax.

Source: Estimated from Dresner and Ekins (2006, tables 1, 2 and 5), adjusted for income growth between 2000-01 and 2008-09 and for higher carbon tax than originally modelled. Net impacts are approximate as a result of non-linearities in tax-benefit system and use of 2000-01 consumption patterns.

While some of this reflects different preferences (for domestic warmth against other consumption), most of it reflects wide variations in insulation and the thermal efficiency of homes. As a result, one of the authors' conclusions was that it would be unfair – and probably politically impractical – to impose this kind of tax *until* effective measures have been taken – for instance, through subsidised energy efficiency programmes – to bring homes up to much higher minimum standards of thermal efficiency.

The political difficulties can be put in perspective by the controversy around the reforms of Income Tax and tax credits announced in the 2007 Budget, including abolition of the starting 10 pence Income Tax rate from April 2008. Before the additional increase in personal allowances announced in May 2008, the reforms would have added around 0.7% to the incomes of the bottom three-tenths of the income distribution *in aggregate*, but 15% of them would have been losers, and up to a third of the next three-tenths (Sutherland et al, 2008, figures 5 and 6). In other words, the abolition of the 10 pence band initially implied *fewer* low-income losers than a carbon tax on domestic fuel compensated in the way shown in Table 15.6, but still greatly damaged the government's progressive credentials.

The last two columns of Table 15.6 show an equivalent calculation for a carbon tax on road fuels, again with revenues used to compensate lower-income groups. In this case, the tax itself would be broadly proportional, and using all of the revenue available could create an overall package that was significantly redistributive. Nonetheless, a sixth of households in the poorest two income groups would be losers (and half of all households overall). Again, the implication is that other measures would also be needed (such as on public transport), if those with low incomes were to be protected so far as possible. The more this is done, however, the less is available to redistribute to low-income groups in general or to sweeten the pill for middle-income groups and voters.

Finally, Table 15.7 illustrates the immediate distributional consequences of a more radical approach: granting each household a 'domestic tradeable quota' (DTQ) – or personal carbon allowance – of allowed carbon emissions from domestic energy and road fuel (and in the final two columns, from aviation). If households consume more than their quota, they have to purchase the right to create more emissions from those who create less than their quota. In the example shown, the quotas are set to equal average existing consumption, and the Table shows the first-round effects of the net purchases/sales of each income group to support their current level of emissions, before any behavioural change. It again illustrates the position on the assumption that the price of such transactions would be £30 per tonne of CO_2 in 2008-09 prices. Given that generally emissions rise with income, this is broadly redistributive without further compensation. The quotas act as a lump-sum social dividend, financed by the effective additional price put on emissions. Depending on whether quotas are allocated only to adults or to both adults and children, however, between a quarter and a third of the poorest three-tenths of households still end up as losers, even assuming a

Table 15.7: Immediate distributional impact of domestic tradeable quota (DTQ) systems (assumed worth £30/tonne CO2)

Income group (tenths)	Domestic energy and road fuel				With aviation	
	Adult DTQs only		Adult and child DTQs[1]		Adult and child DTQs	
	Change in income (£/year)	% losing	Change in income (£/year)	% losing	Change in income (£/year)	% losing
1	+54	25	+81	21	+108	18
2	+48	29	+48	31	+72	27
3	+48	30	+51	32	+69	27
4	+33	35	+36	38	+42	34
5	+18	43	+21	41	+21	43
6	−6	49	−6	50	−12	47
7	−3	53	−12	50	−21	54
8	−39	61	−45	62	−60	68
9	−30	57	−27	45	−90	75
Top	−99	71	−114	77	−129	78
All	0	45	0	47	0	48

Note: [1] Each child is allocated half a quota.

Source: Derived from Dresner and Ekins (2004, tables 9, 10 and 12)

perfect market in unused quotas. For them, this is clearly an improvement on an uncompensated carbon tax (as in the first columns of Table 15.6), or a carbon tax where revenues are used to reduce general tax rates. But the results again show some of the distributional problems that would remain without other energy efficiency and transport measures.

More recent analysis by Thumim and White (2008) for the Department for Environment, Food and Rural Affairs (Defra) confirms this. They modelled the impact – before behavioural change from 2003-04 to 2005-06 consumption patterns – of a 'Personal Carbon Trading' system applied to domestic fuel and road transport use, with each adult allocated an equal annual carbon allowance of four tonnes of CO_2 emissions. Their analysis showed that 71% of the poorest three-tenths would be 'winners' from such a system, but 29% would be losers, matching the figures in the third column of Table 15.7. Overall, the poorest three-tenths would have surplus quotas averaging 1.3 tonnes – worth £38 per year at Defra's current Shadow Price of Carbon, if they sold the surplus at this price. This is proportionately slightly less progressive than Dresner and Ekins suggested, but nonetheless a gain overall – around a third of one per cent of household income – for this group.

As the final columns of Table 15.7 show, if aviation were included in a quota system – as many would argue for, given its enhanced global-warming impact – the overall distributional effects can be improved and the proportion of low-income losers reduced. In effect, low-income households who never flew would be granted a quota for air travel that they could sell to higher-income frequent fliers.

Increased costs for domestic fuel would – without simultaneous concerted action on insulation and improving the energy efficiency of the least efficient homes – exacerbate fuel poverty. Using the official guideline of needing to spend more than 10% of net income on domestic fuel bills to keep warm, 5.1 million households in England were fuel poor in 1996, falling to only 1.2 million in 2003 (BERR, 2007). However, with gas prices 50% and electricity prices 35% higher in real terms than in 2003, this figure rose to 2.9 million by 2007 and is expected to rise higher still (FPAG, 2008). An uncompensated carbon tax at £30 per tonne of CO_2 would have a smaller effect on fuel bills than these increases, but would still be likely to push substantial extra numbers into fuel poverty. Compensation through adjustment in benefit and tax credit rates could help mitigate this, but it is precisely those low-income households that would be losers even after compensating measures that are the ones most likely to be in fuel poverty, because of the energy inefficiency of their homes. The government's Fuel Poverty Advisory Group argues that 'The choice of climate change policies will significantly impact on fuel poverty ... heavy reliance on prices ... will have a different effect from regulatory intervention (and possibly a much more regressive one)' (FPAG, 2008, p 20).

Implications

The decisions we take on how to control carbon emissions will have significant distributional effects. The difference between average losses from an uncompensated carbon tax at a rate of £30 per tonne of CO_2 (or a tax compensated by reductions in Income Tax rates that they do not benefit from) with the average gains from a personal carbon quota would be equivalent to around 1.5% of the incomes of the poorest three-tenths of the distribution. For the same households, the differences between an uncompensated tax and one with the revenues focused on protecting those with the lowest incomes would be 3% of their incomes. These are significant effects by comparison with those of the reforms to tax and benefit systems introduced in any particular Budget – comparable to more than half of all their distributional gains from tax and transfer reforms since 1996-97 (Figure 2.5[b] in Chapter Two). If the effective cost of carbon was higher, and if indirect carbon emissions were also taken into account, the differences between approaches become larger still.

Further, even the most progressive uses of revenues from carbon taxes to protect the poor or the use of equal carbon quotas for each adult still leaves between a sixth and a third of low-income households losing (and much larger numbers of middle-income households, making the politics harder). The reasons for low-income losses often lie in the poor energy efficiency of their homes, or factors that lead to high reliance on car travel. Dealing directly with these problems would be an essential corollary of the use of these kinds of mechanism for controlling carbon emissions, if difficult distributional effects and increases in fuel poverty are to be avoided. Decisions taken outside the policy areas normally associated with the distribution of incomes will have substantial implications for both inequality and poverty.

Conclusion

Many unpredictable factors will affect whether the distribution of economic resources becomes more or less equal in the future, not least government policies. Indeed, some of the successes of policies towards child poverty, early years education and school achievement of lower-income children described in Chapters Three and Four have the potential to even out the starting points of people's working lives a little. Less acute differences between neighbourhoods (Chapter Six) may help, and while retirement outcomes are the result of complex differences between successive cohorts, some of the pension reforms described in Chapter Eight will lead to less unequal retirements than would otherwise have emerged. But this chapter has suggested four ways in which the environment within which policy will be made in the next decade and years beyond may make it even more difficult to achieve egalitarian objectives:

- It will continue to be dealing with a society where intergenerational economic mobility has been slower than it was for those growing up in the 1960s and 1970s: the position of people's parents appears to matter more than it did when incomes as a whole were less unequal. There is little indication yet that these links are becoming weaker.
- Inheritances in particular will grow in scale, but will be very unequally distributed and will tend to reinforce already large inequalities in wealth (which could themselves continue to grow as longer parts of people's lives are spent with the increased income inequality of the period since the late 1980s).
- Population ageing will put considerable pressures on social spending. Official projections assume that part of these pressures will be contained through linking most cash benefits, tax credits and tax allowances to prices, rather than earnings. This would have strongly regressive effects. Other things equal, without further policy change, relative poverty – particularly for children – would rise substantially.

- Controlling carbon emissions is an environmental imperative, but using tax or price mechanisms alone, compensated for by general tax reductions, would be regressive. By contrast, personal carbon quota systems, or carbon taxes where revenues are used to increase transfers to those with low incomes could have progressive effects overall. However, even in these cases, there would be significant numbers of low-income losers, unless additional action was taken, such as greatly to improve the energy efficiency of people's homes.

Notes

[1] Marketable wealth includes financial assets such as bank accounts or company shares, and property such as houses, but not other assets such as future pension rights.

[2] Spending levels on these services rose by a third in cash terms between 2001 and 2006, although not necessarily equally between age groups.

[3] Results are also given by the Treasury for 2057-58, but this goes beyond the period for which adjustments in State Pension Age have been announced (up to 2048 in the 2007 Pensions Act), and so are arguably misleading as a guide to policy intentions.

[4] This is quite close to the result of the purely age-related calculation that yields a 3.8 percentage point increase, as that figure included the offsetting effect on social security spending of there being a *smaller* proportion of the population below pension age (which might, by itself, reduce spending by around 0.6% of GDP).

[5] The comparable exercise published in 2002, using less optimistic population projections, yielded a rise of only 0.2 percentage points of GDP between 2011-12 and 2051-52 (HM Treasury, 2002, table 6.1).

[6] The figures are derived from Dresner and Ekins' analysis of the impact of £10 per tonne imposed in 2000-01. They are directly scaled up from the earlier results, allowing for income growth since then. The figures are thus approximations as they do not allow for changes in the composition of consumption over the period or for non-linearities in the tax and benefit system, which could affect the distributional impact of the compensating measures used in the original analysis.

[7] Note that the greater the extent to which revenue is used to improve targeted transfers, the less is available to reduce other taxes on economic activity, and so to create the 'double dividend' that is sometimes claimed as an additional benefit from 'green' taxes. Indeed, if means-tested transfers are used, effective marginal tax rates on those with lower incomes would rise, with possible negative effects on work incentives.

SIXTEEN

Conclusions: climbing every mountain or retreating from the foothills?

John Hills, Tom Sefton and Kitty Stewart

Introduction

We started this book with a relatively simple question: had the New Labour government succeeded in making Britain a more equal society than when it took office in 1997? When we carried out a similar exercise four years ago (Hills and Stewart, 2005), one conclusion was that it was too early to tell: much of the evidence then available stopped early in the current decade, while many relevant policies had been introduced too recently to have taken full effect. The tide of rising inequality appeared to have turned, and policy to have contributed to turning that tide. There were, however, gaps in the scope of policy, and doubts about whether the scale of action matched the challenges. In summary, sustained efforts would be needed to make continued progress: policy makers still had mountains to climb.

The evidence now available allows a more considered assessment, but the chapters of this book have not presented a simple picture. What has happened varied between policy areas and over time within the last decade. This chapter attempts to bring these findings together. In carrying out this assessment, we are largely judging policy in its own terms, and often using the government's own criteria for how 'equality' should be measured in different dimensions. It should be recognised, however, that this begs a large number of fundamental questions, about both objectives and measurement (Equalities Review, 2007; Craig et al, 2008).

One striking background feature is that the decade from 1997 was in many ways very favourable to an egalitarian agenda: the economy grew continuously, with low rates of inflation helped by favourable world prices for imports bought by UK consumers, and a government was in power both with large majorities after each of the three General Elections in the period, and with expressed aspirations to creating a 'more equal society', at least in some terms. Writing in the autumn of 2008, none of these looks certain for the immediate future, to say the least, while the previous chapter identified factors that may make egalitarian outcomes harder to achieve over the medium term. The period surveyed may have been 'as good as it gets' for some time to come.

Is Britain 'a more equal society'?

Income inequality

Much of the story of the period since 1997, and its contrast with those preceding it, is told by Figure 16.1. This shows the annual rates of growth in the incomes of each fifth of the income distribution (before housing costs [BHC], measured at the mid–point of each fifth). Looking across the period from 1996-97 to 2006-07 as a whole, growth in real incomes was very even across the distribution, and at around or just below 2% per year, meant a significant rise in living standards for all of the groups. This contrasts starkly with the period when Mrs Thatcher was Prime Minister, when income growth near the bottom was very slow indeed, while incomes for the top fifth grew by nearly 4% per year. Under John Major, average incomes grew much more slowly, but within this, the poorest fifth did much better than under Mrs Thatcher, although less well than in New Labour's first 10 years. Comparing further back, the income growth at the bottom in the New Labour period represents the first sustained rise in living standards since the 1960s and early 1970s.

Figure 16.1: Real income growth, by income quintile group
Average annual income gain (%), before housing costs

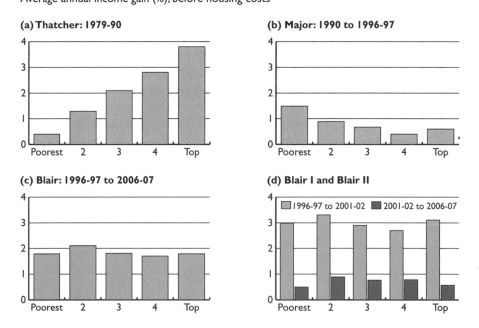

Note: Figures show average annual change in quintile group medians.
Sources: Brewer et al (2004, figure 2.3 for 1979 to 1996-97); DWP (2008b, table 2.1ts) for 1996-97 to 2006-07

However, the fourth panel shows the contrast, explored in more detail in Chapter Two, between the earlier and later parts of the period since 1997. For the first five years, incomes grew impressively – by around 3% each year – for all five groups. But for the second five years, growth was much slower: in the middle of the distribution it was barely faster than during the Major government, and the bottom fifth grew more slowly. This reflects the combination of very slow real earnings growth after 2002 and the lack of any gains (indeed losses lower down the distribution by comparison with an earnings-linked base) from tax and benefit policies after 2004-05, contrasting with the redistributive impact of changes between 2000-01 and 2004-05 in particular (Figure 2.5).

As Chapter Two shows, judgement of how income inequality changes over the period depends on precisely where in the income distribution one is looking. Taking the period as a whole, incomes *near* the bottom grew slightly faster than those *near* the top (Figure 2.2). However, within the bottom tenth, incomes grew more slowly, and within the top tenth they grew more rapidly – particularly for the top 1%. As a result, what happens to summary single index measures depends on how they treat the very top and bottom of the distribution. As the equal rates of growth for the mid-points of bottom and top fifths in Figure 16.1 imply, the '90:10' ratio was the same at the end of the period as at the start. But the Gini coefficient – which is sensitive to the ends of the distribution – grew by two percentage points (Figure 2.1), and other measures that give most weight to the bottom of the distribution grew even faster (Brewer et al, 2008a, figure 3.7), particularly between 2004-05 and 2006-07. Comparison of the *share* of the richest fifth with that of the poorest fifth (which also takes account of incomes at the very top and bottom) put the UK as 11th out of 15 European Union (EU) countries in terms of income equality in 1998. Of the other higher inequality countries, only Italy also experienced an increase in this measure of income inequality between then and 2006, and the UK slipped to 12th out of the 15 (Table 13.1).

These comparisons are for people's (net) cash incomes only. Allowing for the large increases in real spending on services such as healthcare and education equalises things. On the Office for National Statistics' measure of 'final income', including this 'social wage' (and allowing for all indirect taxes), income growth for all of the poorest five-tenths of households between 1996-97 and 2006-07 was faster than for the top half, with the third tenth growing most rapidly (Figure 2.8). On this basis, 'final incomes' were clearly more equally distributed in 2006-07 than nine years before.

Poverty

At the bottom of the distribution, overall poverty rates measured in relative terms fell slightly over the 10 years from 1996-97 to 2006-07. Child and pensioner poverty fell quite rapidly up to 2004-05, but by 2006-07 both had risen, and with them overall poverty rates (Table 2.2). By contrast, relative poverty rates rose over the period as a whole for working-age people *without* children. *Persistent* poverty (being below a relative standard for three out of the four preceding years) fell from 12% to 9% overall, including from 17% to 11% for children, comparing 1994-97 with 2002-05 (DWP, 2008b, table 7.1, BHC).

Wealth

At the other extreme, partly reflecting the accumulated effects of growing income inequality since the early 1980s, as well as asset prices, the distribution of wealth continued to become more unequal between 1997 and 2002, although the latest, still provisional, figures for 2003 (when stock market prices had fallen back) show a partial reversal of this (Table 15.3).

Children

Even though it was not enough to meet the government's target of cutting relative child poverty by a quarter between 1998-99 and 2004-05, the reduction in child poverty over that period was impressive, but since then progress has stalled, even reversed. Measures of the material deprivation of families with children showed impressive gains. For instance, the proportions of lone parents who say they cannot afford a range of items decreased between 1999 and 2006 (or 2005); most of them more than halved (Table 3.2). Affording a particular item measures absolute standards, but indicators of financial difficulties are a more relative measure, and again these improved.

One of the main drivers of child poverty – the proportion of children living in workless families – improved significantly, although most of the improvement was by 2001. The rapid expansion of early years education had its greatest effects on those with low incomes, closing the gaps in use for three- and four-year-olds substantially between 1999 and 2007. At the same time, the most recent evaluation of the government's flagship Sure Start programme was showing (modest) positive effects from the scheme for all groups by the time it had bedded in, as well as strong popularity among parents in disadvantaged areas (Chapters Three and Six).

A high-profile UNICEF (2007) report placed the UK bottom of an international league table of indicators of child well-being, despite all the government's policy attention. However, Kitty Stewart points out in Chapter Thirteen that much of its evidence came from the start of the decade. More recently published data for the position in 2006 shows significant improvements. The improvement in child poverty has only been enough to ensure that the UK now shares its bottom position within the EU15 countries with Italy and Spain (Table 13.1), but improvements in some other respects are 'little short of astonishing' as she puts it (see Table 13.5). If the UNICEF exercise were repeated using these data, the UK would have moved up this particular league table. It may be no coincidence that the improvements in other aspects of well-being between 2001-02 and 2005-06 took place during a period when child poverty was falling.

Schools and education

The government's favoured measures of achievement at ages 11 (Key Stage 2) and 16 (five or more good General Certificate of Secondary Education [GCSE] passes) improved, with more rapid improvement from 2004-05 (Figure 4.2). Ruth Lupton, Natalie Heath and Emma Salter show in Chapter Four that improvements were faster in the poorest schools and areas (Figure 4.3), and looking at individual pupils, the gaps between those receiving free school meals (FSM) and others narrowed slowly across the period (Table 4.2). However, large gaps remain in all these respects, and it may be that the impacts of early improvements in primary schools on secondary school performance have already worked their way through.

After age 16, there has been no reduction in the proportion of all 16- to 18-year-olds who are not in education, employment or training (NEET), which has remained around 10% since 1994, although there has been some rise in the proportion in full-time education. The proportion of young people going into higher education has remained around 40% since 1999-2000, rather than rising towards the government's target of 50%. Up to 2004, the participation rate for those from lower socioeconomic groups also remained flat at about half the national rate, but by 2006-07 the proportion of higher education entrants from lower socioeconomic groups had increased (Table 4.4).

Labour market

Overall measures of inequality in annual earnings rose continuously through the 1980s and early 1990s, but Abigail McKnight shows in Chapter Five that this halted after 1996, and inequality measures were no higher in 2003-04 than they had been in 1995-96 (Figure 5.3). Looking at full-time hourly wages, those at the bottom (helped by the new National Minimum Wage for the very lowest wages) grew faster than those in the middle of the distribution between 1997 and 2002, although those right at the top (the top 5%) grew faster still. After 2002, real wages stagnated across the distribution, although they continued to grow slowly at the fifth percentile, near the bottom (Table 2.1). In summary, earnings stopped becoming more unequal, with some gains right at the bottom, although the very highest wages continued to accelerate away.

Initially, employment and unemployment were the clearest piece of good news after 1997. Total numbers employed grew through the period, although the employment *rate* as a share of the working-age population stopped growing after 2000, with part of the increase in *numbers* employed accounted for by immigration (Chapter Ten). The lone-parent employment rate rose significantly, but not rapidly enough to hit the government's 70% target for 2010. Overall unemployment continued to fall until 2006, to its lowest levels since the mid–1970s. By the third quarter of 2008, it was beginning to rise steeply, as the economy moved into recession. However, unemployment rose for 16- to 17-year-olds from 2000 (Figure 5.7) . For 18- to 24-year-olds it continued to fall for a while after the New Deal was introduced, but then rose and was no lower by the end of 2007 than it was in 1998 (Figure 5.8). Long–term unemployment, also a key initial focus, fell until 2002, but then flattened out, and by the end of 2007 had risen to be only a little lower than it was at the national implementation of the New Deal in 2000.

Neighbourhoods

In Chapter Six, Anne Power presents recent evidence that in several respects – including education, employment, crime and local perceptions – the gaps have narrowed since 1997 between the most disadvantaged areas and other parts of the country, and that this is true looking both at the most deprived 44 local authority areas and at the most deprived 10% of neighbourhoods. Part of this reflects the success of the wave of 'area–based initiatives' introduced in the late 1990s (although now coming to an end in several cases), and the Neighbourhood Renewal agenda following the Social Exclusion Unit's report *Bringing Britain Together* (SEU, 1998). Looking closely at 12 contrasting areas of the country that were all indisputably very poor during the 1990s, four of them consistently improved through the period, another four made progress, but the remaining four – peripheral areas in poorer regions – continued to struggle. Attitudes of families living within four of those 12 areas towards them and towards the prospect of continuing to live within them had markedly improved by 2006.

Health inequalities

By contrast, Franco Sassi finds in Chapter Seven the least evidence of progress towards a 'more equal society' in health inequalities despite the high priority rhetorically attached to tackling this issue and the rapid growth in health spending. Looking across a range of indicators (in England), inequality in many health outcomes increased between 1996 and 2005 in either relative or absolute terms, and often in both, and there were few signs of differences in trend before and after 1997. This included indicators of self-assessed poor health (for women, at least), cardiovascular disease and poor psychosocial health. A common picture was for overall outcomes to be improving, but without gaps narrowing. In contrast to government targets, overall inequality in age at death appears to have widened more rapidly in the most recent five-year period than before 1997 (Figure 7.1), while social class differences in life expectancy at birth continued to widen for women (although they narrowed for men). Differences in life expectancy at birth between local authority areas by level of deprivation widened between 1997 and 2002, although they narrowed slightly from this high point by 2005 (Figure 7.4).

One of the government's own key targets was for a small reduction in relative infant mortality rates between manual social class households and all households (for which a class can be assigned), but by 2004-06 the reverse had happened (DH, 2008b, figure 3.1). Some changes – such as the general reduction in smoking across all social groups, particularly following the public smoking bans in each territory – may in the long run bring the greatest health benefits to those from manual social classes, but the apparent strategy of assuming that increased resources to healthcare in general would bring with it reduction in health inequalities does not appear to have succeeded.

Pensioners and incomes in later life

As Maria Evandrou and Jane Falkingham discuss in Chapter Eight, up to 2005-06, real pensioner incomes rose, and relative pensioner poverty was sharply reduced (Table 8.3). However, the last year for which data are available shows an increased *absolute* pensioner poverty rate, as well as a rise in relative poverty, between 2005-06 and 2006-07 (DWP, 2008b, table 6.5tr). With many pensioners having incomes close to the poverty line, even small changes in income (such as from the size of the annual Winter Fuel Payment and other one-off payments) can have significant effects on the number counted as poor. Much of the progress that has been made in the last 10 years has relied on the increased generosity of means-tested benefits, but a significant group of pensioners fails to claim these.

Looking to the future, the intention of recent reforms is to reduce the extent of means testing in old age, by improving general entitlements to state pensions and opening up low-cost retirement savings through the new system of 'Personal Accounts'. However, these changes will take effect as a new generation reaches retirement, with more unequal (and riskier) private pensions as a result of rapid changes in the pension promises being made by private sector employers since 2000. The implication of the two factors taken together for future inequality of incomes within the pensioner population remains unclear.

Ethnic inequalities

Looking across education, employment and incomes, Coretta Phillips shows in Chapter Nine that there were generally slow reductions in the still large gaps between particular minority ethnic groups and the majority white population. The gap in GCSE attainment between the broad categories of Black, Bangladeshi and Pakistani and the white population narrowed, but the advantage of the Indian and Chinese groups was maintained (Figure 9.1). Looking at narrower groups, the Roma/Gypsy and Irish Traveller groups fell well behind others. Looking at ethnicity and FSM status together, White British and Irish pupils receiving FSM were the worst performing by 2007 (Figure 9.3). There were larger absolute falls in unemployment between 1997 and 2007 for black and minority ethnic groups than for the white population, and generally larger proportionate falls (apart from men of mixed ethnic background, and Bangladeshi women, whose unemployment rates rose). Within the income distribution, there were also falls in the overrepresentation of minority ethnic groups within the bottom fifth of the income distribution, although overrepresentation remained large for most minority groups, as did poverty rates.

Looking ahead, Jill Rutter and Maria Latorre suggest in Chapter Ten that migration patterns over the 10 years have not only led to an increase in the proportion of the UK population that was born abroad, but also to much greater diversity between groups, some of which are very disadvantaged – including significant groups that are not recorded in official figures due to their irregular (illegal) status, with some evidence of destitution among them.

Gender inequalities

This book does not have a specific chapter on gender inequality, but evidence on it recurs in several chapters. Given that women have a greater risk of poverty than men in the first place (even assuming that the benefits of family incomes are shared equally),[1] many of the trends and measures that have reduced poverty overall have affected more women than men. The reductions in poverty among lone-parent families and pensioners have particularly benefited women. In total, while the poverty rate for adult women was four to five percentage points higher for adult women than for adult men in 1996-97, this difference had halved to two percentage points by 2006-07.[2]

Within the labour market, the picture was mixed. The advantage of women in having a lower unemployment rate than men (on the wider International Labour Organisation [ILO] definition) almost disappeared (Figure 5.1), and within broad groups by gender and ethnicity, the only group showing unemployment higher in 2007 than 1997 was Pakistani women (Table 9.2). However, the employment rate for working-age women grew in step with that of men (Figure 5.2).

The median gender pay gap *between* hourly earnings of men and women working full time fell from 17% to 13% between 1997 and 2007 (Figure 5.13). The median gender gap in part-time pay fell by a similar amount, but remained very large – still 39% in 2007. Low pay even for women working full time remained more prevalent in the UK than in most other industrialised countries (Table 13.4). Looking *within* genders, inequality of annual earnings among men rose and had risen to reach the higher, but roughly constant, level of inequality among women by 2005-06 (Figure 5.4).

Within the overall picture of lack of narrowing in health inequalities reported in Chapter Seven, much of the more positive evidence there relates to men, rather than women, with, for instance, widening inequalities for women contrasting with a narrowing for men in life expectancy by social class, self-assessed poor health and incidence of diabetes. Class inequalities widened for women in rates of poor psychosocial health, as a result of the *improvement* for women with a higher social class. The gap widened for men partly as a result of a *deterioration* for men with lower socioeconomic status.

Overall indicators of progress

The previous section shows that there have been clear, if sometimes slow, movements towards greater equality in some important respects, but not in others. The official assessment that attempts to give an overall picture is the government's annual poverty report *Opportunity for All: Tackling Poverty and Social Exclusion*. The-then Secretary of State for Social Security, now Chancellor of the Exchequer, Alistair Darling argued in launching the first report: 'We are prepared to be judged on results. In this, our first Annual Report, we set out a range of indicators against which we can chart our progress' (DSS, 1999, p viii). The indicators have evolved a little since then, sometimes for data reasons, sometimes to better focus on key problems, and sometimes leaving a suspicion that the new measure chosen may give a somewhat more favourable picture. By 2007, the government had decided no longer to publish an annual report on its poverty strategy in the same form, pointing instead to its (rather obscure) report to the EU on social exclusion under the 'Open Method of Coordination'. However, it continues to publish the 'Opportunity for All' indicators each year. These form a useful measure against the government's own original and evolving objectives.

Table 16.1 summarises the set published in 2007. Allowing for the multiple indicators under some headings, there are 59 indicators. For the 55 for which data

Table 16.1: Direction of change of indicators of poverty and social exclusion, 2007

	'Opportunity for All' indicators[1]		'Monitoring Poverty and Social Exclusion' indicators[2]	
	Trend since baseline	Latest year	First 5 years	Latest 5 years
Improving	40	21	30	7
Steady	8	26	19	27
Deteriorating	7[3]	4	7[4]	15[4]
Not available	4	8	–	–
Total	**59**	**59**	**56**	**56**

Notes and sources: [1] DWP (2007d) but using 2006 classification for nine indicators affected by change in measurement basis using Labour Force Survey. 'Baseline' is generally around 1997.
[2] Palmer, MacInnes and Kenway (2008).
[3] Education gap for looked-after children; infant mortality by area; families in temporary accommodation; employment gap for least qualified; numbers contributing to non-state pension; life expectancy at birth by social group.
[4] Five indicators worsened in *both* five year periods: low-income families paying full Council Tax; benefits for out of work adults without children relative to earnings; the gap between the high paid and median earners; pensioner benefit take-up; and over 75s helped to live at home.

are available, an impressive 40 are shown as improved since the 'baseline' chosen for measurement (usually 1997 or 1998, but sometimes when the data series starts). A further eight are recorded as 'steady', and only seven as having deteriorated. Unsurprisingly given the discussion above, two of those that have deteriorated are indicators of health inequalities: the relative gap between areas in infant mortality, and life expectancy at birth by social group. But overall the message is a positive one: by and large – against the government's own benchmarks – things have got better.

There is a natural suspicion that there may be a degree of selection here, so Table 16.1 also shows the indicators produced independently by the New Policy Institute (NPI) each year for its *Monitoring Poverty and Social Exclusion* report for the Joseph Rowntree Foundation. The balance for the most recent five years of the NPI series – incorporating the increases in relative poverty measures between 2004-05 and 2006-07 – is less favourable than for the first five years (up to 2002 or 2003), as the discussion earlier in this chapter has indicated. Looking at both periods, half (28) of the indicators improved in at least one of them and were steady or improved in the other, while 11 deteriorated in at least one of the periods with no improvement in the other (Palmer et al, 2008, table 3). For the 10 years as a whole, the balance is still broadly positive, although less so than the offical series.

However, the meaning of an 'improving trend' varies between indicators. Given the overall increase in national prosperity over a decade, it would be very disappointing if some of the indicators had *not* improved – the numbers with incomes below a fixed real poverty line, for instance. For others – measuring relativities between different groups – an improvement is more impressive. To allow for this, Table 16.2 compares *trends* since 1997 in the official indicators with trends in the same indicator before 1997, where data are available. This represents a more stringent test of 'have things got better?'. If an improving trend has been accelerated, or if a deterioration has been reversed, there is clearer success. The table groups the 31 official indicators for which this is possible according to changes in trend, showing when the pre-1997 trend starts (1990 or the earliest available since then) and when the recent trend finishes.

For nearly half the indicators, the trend appears to have improved since 1997. This includes many of those related to employment, not just levels (such as the overall employment rate), but also some of the gaps in employment between disadvantaged groups and the population as a whole. It also includes all three of the low-income indicators for children, but only persistent low income for pensioners, and only trends against a fixed real poverty line for the working-age population. For nine of the indicators, the previous trend appears to have continued at much the same rate. For five of these, things have got better, but they were doing so already. By contrast, the relative gap in life expectancy between areas has continued to widen at much the same rate as before.

Table 16.2: 'Opportunity for All' indicators, by difference in trend, before and after 1997[1]

Better trends
Was deteriorating, now improving
Children in workless households (1992-2006) Children in relative low-income households (1990/91 to 2006-07)[2] Children smoking (1990-2006) Working-age population in employment (1990-2006) Working-age population in workless households (1990-2007) Pensioners with persistent low income (1991/94 to 2002/05)
Improvement accelerated
Children in absolute low-income households (1990/91 to 2006-07) Children in persistent low-income households (1991/94 to 2002-05) Working-age population in absolute low-income households (1990/91 to 2006-07) Death rates from suicide and undetermined injury (1989/91 to 2004/06)
Was flat, now improving
Conception rates under-18s (1991-2005) Employment gap, over-50s (1992-2006) Employment gap, minority ethnic groups (1992-2006)
Deterioration slowed
Employment gap, people with low qualifications (1992-2006)
Steady trends
Continuing improvement
Smoking rate in pregnancy (1985-2005) Working-age population on long-term out-of-work means-tested benefits (1994-2007) Working-age population with persistent low income (1991/94 to 2002/05) Adult smoking prevalence (1990-2006) Pensioners with absolute low income (1990/91 to 2006-07)
Continuing flat
School attendance (1995-96 to 2005-06) Working-age population with relative low income (1990/91 to 2006-07) Working-age population contributing to non-state pension in three of four years (1992/95 to 2002/05)
Continuing deterioration
Relative life expectancy gap by area (1991/93 to 2004/06)[3]

(continued)

Table 16.2: (continued)

Worse trends
Improvement slowed
11-year-olds achieving Level 4 in mathematics and English (1995-2007) 16- to 18-year-olds in learning (1990-2006) Pensioners with relative low income (1990/91 to 2006-07) Healthy life expectancy at age 65 (1990-2004) Households in fuel poverty (1996-2006)
Was flat, now deteriorating
Families in temporary accommodation (1990-2007)[4]
Accelerated deterioration
Obesity rate for children aged 2-10 (1995-2005)
Was improving, now deteriorating
Gap in infant mortality by social class (1994/96 to 2004/06)[3]

Notes: [1] Trends taken up to and since 1997 or grouped years centred on 1997. Official 'baseline' can be for later year. Comparison of trends allows for breaks in series.
[2] Figures for relative and absolute low-income households taken from DWP (2008b, tables 4.3tr, 4.4tr, 5.3tr, 5.4tr, 6.3tr and 6.4tr), averaging before and after housing costs figures, using thresholds based on 60% of median income.
[3] Figures updated to 2004-06 from DH (2008b).
[4] Trends for *all* families (whether or not with children) from Communities and Local Government live table 624 (www.communities.gov.uk/housing/housingresearch/housingstatistics).

Sources: DWP (2007d) and earlier equivalents; DH (2008b); DWP (2008b)

The last part of the table shows where trends appear to be worse than before 1997. This includes five indicators that have improved, but at a slower rate than before, for instance healthy life expectancy at age 65, and the numbers in fuel poverty (up to 2006, at least, since when fuel poverty has been rising). Most disappointingly, it is not just that the gap in infant mortality by social class widened between 1996-98 and 2004-06, but that this contrasted with the improvement from the preceding two-year period.

On this more stringent basis, the picture, summarised in Table 16.3, remains generally positive: for nearly half (14) of the indicators, trends have improved since 1997. Trends have worsened for a quarter (eight) of the indicators since 1997. This is not quite as shining a picture as the official count in Table 16.1, but it is nonetheless a general improvement on what was happening before.

What would have happened in the absence of policy change?

The extent to which explicit policy shifts can take the credit (or blame) for any improvements since the change of government in 1997 is often an open question.

Table 16.3: Difference between trends in 'Opportunity for All' indicators before and after 1997: summary

Better trends	14
Was deteriorating, now improving	6
Improvement accelerated	4
Was flat, now improving	3
Deterioration slowed	1
Steady trends	9
Continuing improvement	5
Continuing flat	3
Continuing deterioration	1
Worse trends	8
Improvement slowed	5
Was flat, now deteriorating	1
Accelerated deterioration	1
Was improving, now deteriorating	1
Total	**31**

Source: Table 16.2

In the rather limited number of cases where specific evaluations have been carried out, including some kind of control group, many individual initiatives do show positive effects, although often small by comparison with either the scale of the initial problems or the actual changes over the period. Those discussed in Chapters Three to Six include: Sure Start; Excellence in Cities (EiC) (for schools); Education Maintenance Allowances; the New Deals for Young People and Lone Parents; Pathways to Work for disabled people; the New Deal for Communities; and the Neighbourhood Renewal Fund. By implication, in the absence of those initiatives, things would have been correspondingly worse.

Where we can be a little clearer about the counterfactual is in comparing the distributional impact of the tax and benefit system as it had actually emerged by 2008-09 with what it would have been if the 1996-97 system had been preserved. As Chapter Two discusses, to make this comparison requires an assumption about how the system *would have been* adjusted over time under pre-1997 policies. In this case the most plausible assumption is that its parameters would have been increased in line with *price* inflation, given that this was the prevailing policy at the time. If so, the modelling results of the kind shown in Figures 2.5(a) and 2.6(a) indicate the differences in what would have happened from actual outcomes. There are two caveats. First, such modelling assumes that behaviour would have been the same under both systems; in reality, the different patterns of incentives could have changed employment and earnings to some extent. Second, the price-linked version of the 1996-97 tax and benefit system would – assuming unchanged behaviour – have led to the public finances being £14 billion better (from government's point of view) than under the actual system. In that alternative world, this could have led to different policies being pursued in other ways – although if they involved, say, general reductions in rates of all kinds of tax, the distributional balance in the modelled results would be little changed.

Bearing those qualifications in mind, in this alternative world, income inequality and poverty rates would both have been significantly higher. The Gini coefficient for income distribution would have been one percentage point higher than it was – corresponding to a rise of three percentage points since 1996-97, rather than the actual increase of two percentage points by 2006-07 (Figure 2.1). More strikingly, the 90:10 ratio would have increased by nearly a tenth (0.3 percentage points), rather than remaining flat.

Overall, poverty rates would be six to seven percentage points higher than the actual outcome,[3] corresponding to a *rise* in poverty of four to five percentage points over the period, rather than the actual fall of one to three percentage points by 2006-07 shown in Table 2.2. Rather than falling by four percentage points over the period, the child poverty rate would have risen by six to nine points. For pensioners the poverty rate would have risen by seven percentage points, both BHC and after housing costs (AHC), rather than falling by between one and 10 points. By contrast, for childless working-age adults, the policy change makes little difference: an increase in the poverty rate by one to two percentage points under price-linking by comparison with the actual increase of zero to one percentage points.

Future directions and pressures

If a theme running through the book has been that, where action has been taken to address inequalities, there have usually been positive results, the apparent loss of momentum in some areas suggests that ground may be lost and gaps may widen again. Areas where momentum appears to have been lost since our earlier review was written in 2004 identified in earlier chapters include:

- the overall direction of tax and benefit changes since 2004-05 and the slowing of growth in (generally pro-poor) spending on education and health (Chapter Two);
- the plateauing of child-related spending after 2004 (Chapter Three);
- the New Deals for Young People and the Long-Term Unemployed (Chapter Five); and
- the ending of specific area-based initiatives (Chapter Six).

Another area where the initial impetus appears to have been lost is around the ambitions of its policies towards social exclusion. Soon after its launch in 1997, Tony Blair described the Social Exclusion Unit as 'the defining difference between ourselves and the previous government' (*The Observer*, 23 November 1997). The

Unit, originally located in the Cabinet Office but later moved to the Office of the Deputy Prime Minister, had a wide-ranging remit to develop policy that cut across government towards a wide range of disadvantaged groups and across low-income neighbourhoods. When a new Social Exclusion Task Force replaced it, although brought back into the centre in the Cabinet Office, its focus was much narrower, on the 1 in 20 or 1 in 40 that it claimed policy had found it hardest to reach:

> This government has already created the opportunities which have enabled many more people to realise the aspirations they hold for themselves and their families.... Around 2.5% of every generation seem caught in a lifetime of disadvantage and harm. (Cabinet Office, 2006, p 5)

In other areas, there was little momentum to lose. Conspicuously, policy directions after 1997 were little concerned with inequalities at the very top of society, which continued to increase.[4] Franco Sassi argues in Chapter Seven that despite the targets and monitoring, the assumption behind health policy has been that general expansion of services will improve overall standards of care and health outcomes and will also narrow health inequalities, but there is no evidence that this has occurred.

One reason for momentum being lost is the slower economic growth and greater pressures on the public finances in the second half of the New Labour period. Not only have there been fewer resources for new initiatives, but the losses from 'quiet redistribution' of the kind that has marked the last 10 years have become more visible. If incomes in general are rising slowly, policies with a redistributive impact lead to potential falls, rather than slower growth, in living standards for some. The reaction to the low-income losers from the reforms associated with the abolition of the 10 pence starting rate of Income Tax in 2008 reflect this: there was little the government could point to as an offsetting gain – particularly as they were non-pensioners without children, who had systematically been excluded from previous more generous policies, and following several years of very slow growth in real earnings (Chapter Two).

With gloomy economic prospects at the time of writing following the credit crunch and downturn in the housing market that started in 2007, this constraint looks to be much tighter in the short term than it was up to 2006 or 2007, the period for which we have been able to examine outcomes in this book. The previous chapter suggests that in the long run, the fiscal pressures from an ageing society will further constrain the resources available for redistribution and for non-pension transfers, particularly if the political assumption is that the overall share of taxation in national income is fixed or even intended to fall.

To set against these factors, there are areas where policy has been intensified or where the pay-offs to initiatives will be long term, and not yet fully visible. The first of these includes aspects of education policy, recent policies towards economic inactivity, and pensions (Chapters Four, Five and Eight). In current government intentions at least, in the much-reduced set of 30 Public Service Agreements (PSAs) – high-level government objectives – set out with the Comprehensive Spending Review in the autumn of 2007, a third still had a main or subsidiary objective connected in some way with equality (HM Treasury, 2007b). These are generally expressed in terms simply of direction of change (such as 'reducing the gap' between particular groups), rather than an actual target. The commitment to halve child poverty by 2010 was the only quantified target to survive within the headline PSA objectives (despite the difficulties in seeing how it will be achieved given current policies).

Further, as Polly Vizard discusses in Chapter Fourteen, taken at face value, the remit of the new Equality and Human Rights Commission and the intentions of the Equalities Bill proposed for 2009 promise a different and more radical approach to tackling deep-rooted horizontal inequalities between social groups. The potential impact of the new Commission's wider scope and regulatory powers is large, but it is unclear what will happen in practice. Similarly, as Tania Burchardt and Holly Holder describe in Chapter Twelve, there are ways in which more mature devolution between the territories of the UK *could* lead to innovative policies and experiments to tackle disadvantage and inequality, at least within each territory, if not between them. So far, however, it is hard to identify substantial differences, despite the bold rhetoric, in part because many of the key policy instruments are not devolved.

The potential for returns to recent initiatives that are not yet visible is most obvious in terms of early years and other education. If Sure Start's generally positive effects are sustained, it may have benefits that show up much later in the lives of some of the children who have been involved in the programme (Chapter Three). If child poverty does indeed have an independent effect on later outcomes, its reduction since 1998 should help outcomes. Improvement in earlier school attainment described in Chapter Four may help sustain the recent improvement in staying on in school after the age of 16, and with it the gradual narrowing since 2002 in social class gaps in participation in higher education. Pay-offs to changes in pensions policy (Chapter Eight) will have even longer lead times: while some women will be retiring with better state pensions from 2010 as a result of the reforms, it will be 20 or more years' time before we see the results of other changes intended to make it easier for people to build their retirement incomes.

Two kinds of cumulative effect will be in conflict. On the one hand, as discussed in Chapter Fifteen, the effects of people spending more of their lives in the more unequal economic environment of the UK since the 1990s may still not have fed through fully to wealth differences and to the differences that more advantaged parents can make to their children's life chances. On the other hand, simply holding some of the gains made in the last 10 years in narrowing gaps in, for instance, the performance of the most deprived schools or the situation in the most deprived neighbourhoods, will mean that the improvements extend over larger parts of the current generation of young people's lives.

At the same time, Tom Sefton's survey of public attitudes and changes in them in Chapter Eleven suggests that the political constraints on governments implementing progressive policies are probably tighter than they were a decade ago. While large, although declining, majorities continue to agree with general statements about inequalities being too great, attitudes to the benefits system and its beneficiaries appear to have hardened substantially and support for redistributive policies declined, especially among Labour's own supporters. This may in part be the result of 'satiation' – people wanted a *small* degree of redistribution and a *limited* amount of extra 'tax and spend', and that is exactly what New Labour had delivered by the end of its second term. For some, it may be disillusion with the limited results of what has been done after a decade of effort, or lack of awareness of the real progress made in some areas. The government must bear some of the responsibility for not doing more to make the case for its social justice agenda and perhaps for undermining support for some of the progressive values with which the Labour Party has traditionally been associated in endeavouring to alter its own image with voters. However, the nature of the debate around poverty and social exclusion within government and in the broader political arena has been transformed in the last decade, and the knowledge base that helps to inform this debate has been built up considerably from a low starting point.

Conclusions

The findings of this book will come as a disappointment to two groups of readers: those who might have hoped that a Labour government in power for over a decade would decisively reverse the gaps in society that had widened over the previous two decades; and those who – perhaps dominated by the rows over lone-parent benefits and the 10 pence tax abolition that bracket our period – were expecting to see a simple picture showing the betrayal of egalitarian ideals.

The picture is more complex and nuanced. In several key respects, the UK *was* a somewhat more equal society after 10 years of New Labour government. Away from the very top and very bottom of the distribution, income differences narrowed. There were notable reductions in child and pensioner poverty. The relative position of disadvantaged neighbourhoods improved, as did the achievements at ages 11 and 16 of schools with lower-income children and of children from poorer families in general. The large gaps between some minority ethnic groups and the majority white population in employment, education and incomes closed slowly. The significant increases in the 'social wage' delivered through education and healthcare spending had a further substantial equalising effect.

But at the same time, incomes at the very top – especially for the top 1%, and even within it – grew much more rapidly than the average, while incomes of the poorest 10% grew more slowly. Wealth inequality continued to grow, and so did a wide range of measures of inequalities in health outcomes.

The answer to the question posed in this book's title therefore depends on *which* inequalities are being examined, between *whom*, and over *which time period*, some of the more recent trends being less positive than between 1999 and 2004, for instance. Looking across a range of official indicators for which comparison is possible, trends improved after 1997 compared with the period before for nearly half of them, but they deteriorated for a quarter. In international comparisons, particularly with other members of the EU, Kitty Stewart shows in Chapter Thirteen that the UK has improved its position from a very low base. Two international comparisons of school achievement and of inequality in it are less positive than the domestic measures might lead one to expect, but a third is encouraging, while the most recent assessment of a range of indicators of child well-being gives a much less gloomy picture of the state of Britain's children in 2006 than the figures for 2001 that formed much of the evidence for UNICEF's damning 2007 report.

There is one consistent theme running through most of the chapters in this book. Where significant policy initiatives were taken, the outcomes generally moved in the right direction, if not always as rapidly as policy makers and other observers might have hoped. This would include the clearly redistributive tax and transfer changes between 1996-97 and 2004-05 (see Chapter Two), many of the programmes in schools (Chapter Four), employment measures from the original New Deals to the later Pathways to Work pilots (Chapter Five), and the wide range of programmes aimed at poor neighbourhoods (Chapter Six). The experience is far from one where nothing was tried or where nothing worked. Rather, many things were tried, and most worked.

The problem is that the scale of action was often small in relation to the underlying inequalities, and the momentum gained by the middle of the period had often been lost by the end of it. Problems were often harder to tackle than the government appears originally to have assumed, and less amenable to a one-off fix. It is now well known that setting objectives for poverty in relative terms creates the difficulty of a 'moving target', with a threshold that rises with national prosperity (although given the virtual stagnation in average real earnings since 2003, this is a much less convincing excuse for the latter half of the period).[5] But there are other areas where the same applies: better-off parents may be more effective than in the past at understanding what best helps their children's development; the better educated may be most receptive to health education messages; without continual attention and 'renewal', the poorest areas slip backwards rather than stand still. And changes in the social environment made it harder to stand still as well, with for instance the proportion of children living with a lone parent increasing by more than a tenth from 20.1% to 22.5% between 1997 and 2007. The issues surveyed by John Hills in Chapter Fifteen suggest that the environment within which policy operates may become even tougher in the coming decades even beyond the economic down-turn.

There is, however, a contrasting lesson from the distinction between the first part (up to 2003 or 2004) of the period and the second part. That is, that for all the difficulty of keeping up with moving targets at a time of growing prosperity, the government has actually found it harder to do so in the period when overall living standards have grown much more slowly. The government's fiscal position has become much tighter, and the period of rapid increases in some of the relevant parts of public spending came to an end. As has been observed by others, the politics of redistribution *with* growth are far easier than those of redistribution *without* growth.

The UK's experience in the 1980s and 1990s showed that the laissez-faire strategy of hoping that rapid growth in living standards at the top would 'trickle down' to those at the bottom did not work. The last decade has shown that a more interventionist strategy of 'pump up' is hard. The period since 1997 shows that gains are possible, but they require continuous effort to be sustained.

Notes

[1] See Bennett (2008) for a discussion of the realism of this assumption made in drawing up the official income distribution statistics and the implications of relaxing it.

[2] Looking at the proportion of adult women and men living in households with incomes below 60% of the contemporary median both before housing costs (BHC) and after housing costs (AHC) (DWP, 2008b, table 3.7tr).

[3] Before allowing for changes in the actual rate for other reasons between 2006–07 and 2008–09, which are not yet known, and looking at AHC results as well as the BHC results shown in Figure 2.6(a).

[4] Although this may change after the period we survey, following the stock market collapse of the autumn of 2008, and as the recession takes hold. Some of the Income Tax and National Insurance Compensation measures announced in the November 2008 Pre-Budget Report (HM Treasury, 2008d) will also affect some of those within the top 2% of incomes from 2010–11.

[5] And indeed, in the short-term, when living standards are falling in real terms, it is possible that price-linked social security benefits will deliver a temporary fall in relative poverty, as the living standards of those dependent on them are cushioned.

References

Abbas, T. (2002) 'The home and the school in the educational achievements of South Asians', *Race, Ethnicity and Education*, vol 5, no 3, pp 291-316.

ABI (Association of British Insurers) (2003) *Stakeholder Pensions: Time for a Change*, London: ABI.

ACPO (Association of Chief Police Officers) (2000) *Identifying and Combating Hate Crime*, London: ACPO.

Adam, S., Brewer, M. and Shephard, A. (2006) *The Poverty Trade-Off*, York: Joseph Rowntree Foundation.

Adams, J. and Schmuecker, K. (eds) (2006) *Devolution in Practice: Public Policy Differences within the UK*, Newcastle: ippr North.

Ahmed, S. (2007) '"You end up doing the document rather than doing the doing": diversity, race equality and the politics of documentation', *Ethnic and Racial Studies*, vol 30, no 4, pp 590-609.

Ainscow, M., Dyson, A., Goldrick, S., Kerr, K. and Miles, S. (2008) *Equity in Education: Responding to Context*, Manchester: Centre for Equity in Education, University of Manchester.

Aitken, G., Byram, P., Whalley, G. and Moore, D. (2007) *Evaluation of the EMA National Roll-Out: Final Report: Year 1 Evaluation and Measurement of Impact on Participation and Progress Towards LSC Targets*, Preston: RCU.

Ajegbo, K., Kiwan, D. and Sharma, S. (2007) *Diversity and Citizenship*, Curriculum Review, London: DfES.

Alexander, C. (2004) 'Embodying violence: "riots", dis/order and the private lives of the "Asian gang"', in C. Alexander and C. Knowles (eds) *Making Race Matter: Bodies, Space and Identity*, Basingstoke: Palgrave.

Allen, R. and West, A. (2007) 'Religious schools in London: school admissions, religious composition and selectivity', Paper presented at the GLA/LERU/LERN conference 'Social Selection, Social Sorting and Education', 12 October, City Hall, London.

Amin, A. (2002) 'Ethnicity and the multicultural city: living with diversity', *Environment and Planning A*, vol 34, no 6, pp 959-80.

Amnesty International (2006) *Human Rights: A Broken Promise?*, London: Amnesty International, 23 February, accessed at www.amnesty.org/en/library/info/EUR45/004/2006

Andrews, R. and Martin, S. (2007) 'Has devolution improved public services?', *Public Money and Management*, vol 27, no 2, pp 149-56.

Archer, L. and Francis, B. (2005) '"They never go off the rails like other ethnic groups": teachers' constructions of British Chinese pupils' gender identities and approaches to learning', *British Journal of Sociology of Education*, vol 26, no 2, pp 165-82.

Arnott, M. and Ozga, J. (2008) 'Education and nationalism: education policy and the SNP government', Paper at the Social Policy Association Annual Conference, Edinburgh, 23 June, accessed at www.crfr.ac.uk/spa/Conference%20papers%202/Arnott%20M.pdf

Ashworth, M., Seed, P., Armstrong, D., Durbaba, S. and Jones, R. (2007) 'The relationship between social deprivation and the quality of primary care: a national survey using indicators from the UK Quality and Outcomes Framework', *British Journal of General Practice*, vol 57, no 539, pp 441-8.

Audit Commission (2003) *Human Rights: Improving Public Service Delivery*, London: Audit Commission.

Bachmann, M.O., Eachus, J., Hopper, C.D., Davey Smith, G., Propper, C., Pearson, N.J., Williams, S., Tallon, D. and Frankel, S. (2003) 'Socio-economic inequalities in diabetes complications, control, attitudes and health service use: a cross-sectional study', *Diabetic Medicine*, vol 20, no 11, pp 921-9.

Ball, S.J. (2008) *The Education Debate*, Bristol: The Policy Press.

Balls, E. (2008) 'How the government is supporting the 21st-century school', *Education Guardian*, 3 July, www.guardian.co.uk/education/2008/jul/03/schools.education

Bamfield, L. (2005) 'Making the public case for tackling poverty and inequality', *Poverty*, Summer, no 121.

Barclay, P. (1995) *Inquiry into Income and Wealth Volume 1*, York: Joseph Rowntree Foundation.

Barnard, A. (2007) 'Regional analysis of public sector employment', *Economic & Labour Market Review*, vol 2, no 7, pp 31-6.

Barnes, H., Hudson, M., Parry, J., Sahin-Dikmen, M., Taylor, R. and Wilkinson, D. (2005) *Ethnic Minority Outreach: An Evaluation*, DWP Research Report no 229, London: DWP.

Barnes, J., Leach, P., Sylva, K., Stein, A., Malmberg, L. and the FCCC team (2006) 'Infant child care in England: mothers' aspirations, experiences, satisfaction and caregiver relationships', *Early Child Development and Care*, vol 176, no 5, pp 553-73.

Barnes, M., Conolly, A. and Tomaszewski, W. (2008) *The Circumstances of Persistently Poor Families with Children: Evidence from the Families and Children Study*, Research Report no 487, London: DWP.

Barrell, R., Guillemineau, C. and Liadze, I. (2006) 'Migration in Europe', *National Institute Economic Review*, vol 198, no 1, pp 36-9.

Bathmaker, A.M. (2007) 'The impact of skills for life on adult basic skills in England: how should we interpret trends in participation and achievement?', *International Journal of Lifelong Education*, vol 26, no 3, pp 295-313.

Bauld, L., Judge, K. and Platt, S. (2007) 'Assessing the impact of smoking cessation services on reducing health inequalities in England: observational study', *Tobacco Control*, vol 16, no 6, pp 400-4.

BBC (British Broadcasting Corporation) (2003) 'English children excel at reading', 8 April, accessed at http://news.bbc.co.uk/1/hi/education/2928985.stm

BBC (2004) 'Six million receive tax credits', 30 January, accessed at http://news.bbc.co.uk/1/hi/business/3445023.stm

Behrendt, C. (2002) *At the Margins of the Welfare State: Social Assistance and the Alleviation of Poverty in Germany, Sweden and the United Kingdom*, Aldershot: Ashgate.

Bennett, F. (2006) 'Paying for children: current issues and implications of poverty debates', in J. Lewis (ed) *Children, Changing Families and Welfare States*, Cheltenham: Edward Elgar.

Bennett, F. (2008) 'Distribution within the household', in R. Berthoud and F. Zantomio (eds) *Measuring Poverty: Seven Key Issues*, Colchester: Institute for Social and Economic Research, University of Essex.

BERR (Department for Business, Enterprise and Regulatory Reform) (2007) *Fuel Poverty Monitoring: Indicators 2007*, London: BERR.

Berthoud, R. (1998) *The Incomes of Ethnic Minorities*, ISER Report no 98-1, Colchester: Institute for Social and Economic Research, University of Essex.

Beveridge, W.H. (1942) *Social Insurance and Allied Services*, Cmd 6404, London: HMSO.

BIA (Border and Immigration Agency) (2008) *The Path to Citizenship: Next Steps in Reforming the Immigration System*, London: BIA.

Birmingham City Council (2003) *One Size Doesn't Fit All: Community Housing and Flourishing Neighbourhoods*, Birmingham: Birmingham City Council.

Birrell, D. (2007) 'Divergence in policy between Britain and Northern Ireland: the case of taxation', *Public Policy and Management*, November, pp 323-30.

Blair, T. (1994) *Socialism*, Fabian Pamphlet no 565, London: Fabian Society.

Blair, T. (1996) 'My message to the left', *Independent on Sunday*, 28 July.

Blair, T. (1998) *The Third Way: New Politics for the New Century*, Fabian Pamphlet no 588, London: Fabian Society.

Blair, T. (1999) 'Beveridge revisited: a welfare state for the 21st century', in R. Walker (eds) *Ending Child Poverty: Popular Welfare for the 21st Century*, Bristol: The Policy Press.

Blanden, J. and Machin, S. (2004) 'Educational inequality and the expansion of UK higher education', *Scottish Journal of Political Economy, Special Issue on the Economics of Education*, vol 51, no 2, pp 230-49.

Blanden, J. and Machin, S. (2007) *Recent Changes in Intergenerational Mobility in Britain*, London: Sutton Trust/Centre for Economic Performance, London School of Economics and Political Science.

Blanden, J., Gregg, P. and Machin, S. (2005) 'Educational inequality and intergenerational mobility', in S. Machin and A. Vignoles (eds) *What's the Good of Education? The Economics of Education in the UK*, New Jersey, NJ: Princeton University Press.

Bloch, A. (2004) *Making it Work: Refugee Employment in the UK, Asylum and Migration*, Working Paper no 2, London: ippr, accessed at www.ippr.org/members/download.asp?f=%2Fecomm%2Ffiles%2Fmaking%5Fit%5Fwork%2Epdf

Blunkett, D. (1998) Speech announcing the organisations that had successfully bid to run 25 Education Action Zones in England, accessed at http://news.bbc.co.uk/1/hi/education/118374.stm

Bowers-Brown, T., McCaig, C. and Stevens, A. (2006) *National Evaluation of Aimhigher: Survey of Higher Education Institutions, Further Education Colleges and Work-Based Learning Providers: A Report to the Higher Education Funding Council for England by the Centre for Research and Evaluation, Sheffield Hallam University*, London: HEFCE.

Bowling, B. and Phillips, C. (2007) 'Disproportionate and discriminatory: reviewing the evidence on police Stop and Search', *The Modern Law Review*, vol 70, no 6, pp 936-61.

Bradshaw, J. (1999) 'The nature of poverty', in J. Ditch (ed) *Introduction to Social Security: Policies, Benefits and Poverty*, London: Routledge.

Bradshaw, J. (2000) 'Child poverty in comparative perspective', in D. Gordon and P. Townsend (eds) *Breadline Europe: The Measurement of Poverty* (pp 223-50), Bristol: The Policy Press.

Bradshaw, J. (2006a) 'Child benefit packages in 15 countries in 2004', in J. Lewis (ed) *Children, Changing Families and Welfare States*, Cheltenham: Edward Elgar.

Bradshaw, J. (2006b) *A Review of the Comparative Evidence on Child Poverty*, York: Joseph Rowntree Foundation.

Bradshaw, J. and Finch, N. (2002) *A Comparison of Child Benefit Packages in 22 countries*, DWP Research Report no 174, Leeds: Corporate Document Services.

Bradshaw, J., Kennedy, S., Kilkey, M., Hutton, S., Corden, A., Eardley, T., Holmes, H. and Neale, J. (1996) *The Employment of Lone Parents: A Comparison of Policy in 20 Countries*, London: Family Policy Studies Centre.

Bradshaw, J., Middleton, S., Davis, A., Oldfield, N., Smith, N., Cusworth, L. and Williams, J. (2008) *A Minimum Income Standard for Britain: What People Think*, York: Joseph Rowntree Foundation.

Braun, A., Noden, P., Hind, A., McNally, S. and West, A. (2005) *Final Report of the Evaluation of the Pupil Learning Credits Pilot Scheme*, DfES Research Report no 687, London: DfES.

Breen, R. (2000) 'Class inequality and social mobility in Northern Ireland, 1973 to 1996', *American Sociological Review*, vol 65, no 3, pp 392-406.

Brewer, M. and Browne, J. (2006) *The Effect of the Working Families' Tax Credit on Labour Market Participation*, IFS Briefing Note no 69, London: Institute for Fiscal Studies.

Brewer, M., Goodman, A., Myck, M., Shaw, J. and Shephard, A. (2004) *Poverty and Inequality in Britain: 2004*, IFS Commentary no 96, London: IFS.

Brewer, M., Duncan, A., Shephard, A. and Suarez, M.-J. (2006a) 'Did Working Families' Tax Credit work? The impact of in-work support on labour supply in Great Britain', *Labour Economics*, vol 13, pp 699-720.

Brewer, M., Goodman, A. and Leicester, A. (2006b) *Household Spending in Britain: What can it Teach us about Poverty?*, Bristol: The Policy Press.

Brewer, M., Browne, J., Emmerson, C., Goodman, A., Muriel, A. and Tetlow, G. (2007) *Pensioner Poverty over the Next Decade: What Role for Tax and Benefit Reform?*, IFS Commentary no 204, London: Institute for Fiscal Studies.

Brewer, M., Muriel, A., Phillips, D. and Sibieta, L. (2008a) *Poverty and Inequality in the UK: 2008*, IFS Commentary no 105, London: Institute for Fiscal Studies.

Brewer, M., Sibieta, L. and Wren-Lewis, L. (2008b) *Racing Away? Income Inequality and the Evolution of High Incomes*, IFS Briefing Note no 76, London: Institute for Fiscal Studies.

Brewer, M., Saez, E. and Shephard, A. (2008c) *Means-Testing and Tax Rates on Earnings*, A paper prepared for the Mirrlees Review – Reforming the Tax System for the 21st Century, London: Institute for Fiscal Studies.

Bromley, C. (2003) 'Has Britain become immune to inequality?', in A.R. Park, J. Curtice, K. Thomson, L. Jarvis and C. Bromley (eds) *British Social Attitudes: The 20th Report: Continuity and Change over Two Decades*, Aldershot: Ashgate.

Brown, G. (1997) 'Pre-Budget Statement by the Rt Hon Gordon Brown MP, Chancellor of the Exchequer', November 25, accessed at www.hm-treasury. gov.uk/prebud_pbr97_speech.htm

Brown, G. (2007a) Leadership acceptance speech, Manchester, 23 June.

Brown, G. (2007b) Speech at the University of Greenwich, 31 October, Greenwich, accessed at www.number-10.gov.uk/output/Page13675.asp

Brown, R. (2002) 'New Labour and higher education: diversity or hierarchy?', *Perspectives: Policy and Practice in Higher Education*, vol 6, no 3, pp 73-9.

Burchardt, T. (1999) *The Evolution of Disability Benefits in the UK: Reweighting the Basket*, CASEpaper 26, London: London School of Economics and Political Science.

Burchardt, T. (2000) *Enduring Economic Exclusion: Disabled People, Income and Work*, Joseph Rowntree Foundation Report, York: York Publishing Services.

Burchardt, T. (2005) 'Selective inclusion: asylum seekers and other marginalised groups', in J. Hills and K. Stewart (eds) *A More Equal Society: New Labour, Poverty, Inequality and Exclusion*, Bristol: The Policy Press.

Burney, E. and Rose, G. (2002) *Racist Offences – How Is the Law Working? The Implementation of the Legislation on Racially Aggravated Offences in the Crime and Disorder Act 1998*, Home Office Research Study no 244, London: Home Office.

Butt, S., Goddard, K., La Valle, I. and Hill, M. (2007) *Childcare Nation? Progress on the Childcare Strategy and Priorities for the Future*, London: Daycare Trust.

Cabinet Office (2001) *Ethnic Minorities and the Labour Market: Interim Analytical Report*, London: Cabinet Office.

Cabinet Office (2003) *Ethnic Minorities and the Labour Market: Final Report*, London: Cabinet Office.

Cabinet Office (2006) *Reaching Out: An Action Plan on Social Exclusion*, London: Cabinet Office.

Callender, C. and Jackson, J. (2005) 'Does the fear of debt deter students from higher education?', *Journal of Social Policy*, vol 34, no 4, pp 509-40.

Cameron, D. (2006) 'From state welfare to social enterprise', The Scarman Lecture, Institute of Education, London, 24 November.

Cantle, T. (2001) *Community Cohesion: A Report of the Independent Review Team*, London: Home Office.

Carpenter, H. (2006) *Repeat Jobseeker's Allowance Spells*, DWP Research Report no 394, London: DWP.

Carter, J. (2000) 'New public management and equal opportunities in the NHS', *Critical Social Policy*, vol 20, no 1, pp 61-83.

CASE (Centre for Analysis of Social Exclusion) and HM Treasury (1999) *Persistent Poverty and Lifetime Inequality: The Evidence*, CASEpaper 5, London: LSE.

Cashmore, E. (2001) 'The experiences of ethnic minority police officers in Britain: under-recruitment and racial profiling in a performance culture', *Ethnic and Racial Studies*, vol 24, no 4, pp 642-59.

Cashmore, E. (2002) 'Behind the window dressing: ethnic minority police perspectives on cultural diversity', *Journal of Ethnic and Migration Studies*, vol 28, no 2, pp 327-41.

Cassen, R. and Kingdon, G. (2007) *Tackling Low Educational Achievement*, York: Joseph Rowntree Foundation.

Castell, S. and Thompson, J. (2007) *Understanding Attitudes to Poverty in the UK: Getting the Public's Attention*, York: Joseph Rowntree Foundation.

Chambaz, C. (2001) 'Lone-parent families in Europe: a variety of economic and social circumstances', *Social Policy and Administration*, vol 35, no 6, pp 658-71.

Chote, R., Emmerson, C., Miles, D. and Shaw, J. (2008) *The IFS Green Budget: January 2008*, London: Institute for Fiscal Studies.

Chowdry, H., Crawford, C., Dearden, L., Goodman, A. and Vignoles, A. (2008) *Widening Participation in Higher Education: Analysis using Linked Administrative Data*, IFS Report 69, London: Institute for Fiscal Studies.

CIPD (Chartered Institute of Personnel and Development) (2005) *Labour Market Outlook*, Autumn, accessed at www.cipd.co.uk/NR/rdonlyres/149C9564-1AB6-4AED-8F17-A6E71DE60254/0/labmktout1105.pdf

Clark, D. (2002) 'Staying on', *CentrePiece*, London: Centre for Economic Performance, London School of Economics and Political Science.

Clark, G. and Hunt, J. (2007) *Who's progressive now?*, accessed at www.localconservatives.org/pdf/progressive.pdf

Clark, K. and Drinkwater, S. (2007) *Ethnic Minorities in the Labour Market*, York: Joseph Rowntree Foundation.

COIC (Commission on Integration and Cohesion) (2007a) *Our Interim Statement*, London: DCLG.

COIC (2007b) *Our Shared Future*, London: DCLG.

Commission of the European Communities (2008) *Equality between Women and Men*, Report from the Commission to the Council, the European Parliament, the European Economic and Social Committee and the Committee of the Regions, Brussels: Commission of the European Communities.

Connolly, P. (2006) 'The effects of social class and ethnicity on gender differences in GCSE attainment: a secondary analysis of the Youth Cohort Study of England and Wales 1997-2001', *British Educational Research Journal*, vol 32, no 1, pp 3-21.

Conolly, A. and Kerr, J. (2008) *Families with Children in Britain: Findings from the 2006 Families and Children Study (FACS)*, DWP Research Report no 486, London: DWP.

Conservative Party (2008) *Making Poverty History, Report of the Conservative Party*, April, London: Conservative Party.

Cook, R. and Maclennan, R. (1997) *Report of the Joint Consultative Committee on Constitutional Reform*, accessed at www.unlockdemocracy.org.uk/wp-content/uploads/2007/01/4-joint-consultative-committee-report.pdf

CPS (Crown Prosecution Service) (2007) *Racist and Religious Incident Monitoring Annual Report 2006-2007*, London: CPS.

Craig, G., Burchardt, T. and Gordon, D. (eds) (2008) *Social Justice and Public Policy: Seeking Fairness in Diverse Societies*, Bristol: The Policy Press.

Craig, R. and Mindell, J. (eds) (2008) *Health Survey for England 2006, Volume 2: Obesity and Other Risk Factors in Children*, Leeds: The Information Centre.

CRC (Commission for Rural Communities) (2007) *A8 Migrant Workers in Rural Areas: Briefing Paper*, accessed at www.ruralcommunities.gov.uk/files/A8%20m igrant%20workers%20in%20rural%20areas2.pdf

CRE (Commission for Racial Equality) (2002) *Towards Racial Equality: An Evaluation of the Public Duty to Promote Race Equality and Good Relations in England & Wales*, London: CRE.

CRESR (Centre for Regional Economic and Social Research) (2005) *New Deal for Communities 2001-2005: An Interim Evaluation*, Research Report no 17, London: ODPM.

CRESR (2008) *New Deal for Communities: A Synthesis of New Programme Wide Evidence, 2006-07*, Research Report no 39, NDC National Evaluation Phase 2, London: DCLG.

Cunningham, M., Lopes, J. and Rudd, P. (2004) *Evaluation of Excellence in Cities/Ethnic Minority Achievement Grant (EiC/EMAG) Pilot Project*, Research Report no 583, London: DfES.

Currie, C., Roberts, C., Morgan, A., Smith, R., Settertobulte, W., Samdal, O. and Barnekow Rasmussen, V. (2004) *Young People's Health in Context: Health Behaviour in School-Age Children Study*, International Report from the 2001-02 Study, Geneva: WHO Regional Office for Europe.

Currie, C., Levin, K., Todd, J. and Team, H.N. (2008) *Health Behaviour in School-Aged Children: Findings from the 2006 HBSC Survey in Scotland*, WHO Collaborative Cross-National Study, Edinburgh: Child and Adolescent Health Research Unit, University of Edinburgh.

Curry, C. and O'Connell, A. (2003) *The Pensions Landscape*, London: Pensions Policy Institute.

Curtice, J. (2007) 'Elections and public opinion', in A. Seldon (ed) *Blair's Britain 1997-2007*, Cambridge: Cambridge University Press.

Curtice, J. and Fisher, S. (2003) 'The power to persuade? A tale of two Prime Ministers', in A.R. Park, J. Curtice, K. Thomson, L. Jarvis and C. Bromley (eds) *British Social Attitudes: The 20th Report – Continuity and Change over Two Decades*, Aldershot: Ashgate.

Datta, K., McIlwaine, C., Willis, J., Evans, Y., Herbert, J. and May, J. (2006) *Challenging Remittances as the New Development Mantra: Perspectives from Low Paid Migrant Workers in London*, London: Department of Geography, Queen Mary, University of London.

Daugherty, R., Phillips, R. and Rees, G. (2000) *Education Policy-Making in Wales: Explorations in Devolved Governance*, Cardiff: University of Wales Press.

Davey-Smith, G., Dorling, D., Mitchell, R. and Shaw, M. (2002) 'Health inequalities in Britain: continuing increases up to the end of the 20th century', *Journal of Epidemiology and Community Health*, vol 56, no 6, pp 434-5.

DCA (Department for Constitutional Affairs) (2004) *Interdepartmental Review of International Human Rights Instruments*, London: DCA, accessed at www.dca.gov.uk/peoples-rights/human-rights/int-human-rights.htm

DCA (2006) *Review of the Impact of the Human Rights Act*, London: DCA, accessed at www.dca.gov.uk/peoples-rights/human-rights/pdf/full_review.pdf

DCLG (Department for Communities and Local Government) (2007a) *Neighbourhood Management: Empowering Communities, Shaping Places: Review 2006/7*, Research Report no 37, London: DCLG.

DCLG (2007b) *Neighbourhoods, Cities and Regions Analysis (NCRA): Connecting People, Places and Knowledge, Narrative (v 2.1 June 2007)*, London: DCLG.

DCLG (2007c) *New Deal for Communities National Evaluation: An Overview of Change Data: 2006*, London: DCLG.

DCLG (2008a) *Community, Opportunity, Prosperity: Department for Communities and Local Government Annual Report 2008*, London: DCLG.

DCLG (2008b) *Race Equality Scheme: Progress Report and 2008 Forward Look*, London: DCLG, accessed at www.communities.gov.uk/documents/corporate/pdf/705726.pdf

DCLG (2008c) *Citizenship Survey 2007-8 England and Wales: Cohesion Statistical Release*, 4, London: DCLG, accessed at www.communities.gov.uk/publications/communities/citizenshipsurveyaprmar08

DCLG (2008d) *Managing the Impacts of Migration: A Cross Government Approach*, London: DCLG.

DCSF (Department for Children, Schools and Families) (2007a) *The Children's Plan: Building Brighter Futures*, London: DCSF.

DCSF (2007b) *Permanent and Fixed Period Exclusions from Schools and Exclusion Appeals in England 2005/06*, Statistical First Release, London: DCSF.

DCSF (2007c) *Education and Training Statistics for the United Kingdom 2007*, accessed at www.dcsf.gov.uk/rsgateway/DB/VOL/v000761/index.shtml

DCSF (2007d) *Ethnicity and Education: Evidence on Minority Ethnic Pupils Aged 5-16*, London: DCSF, accessed at www.standards.dfes.gov.uk/ethnicminorities/

DCSF (2008a) *UK Education Expenditure as a Proportion of GDP Time Series TS/EXP(UK)06*, accessed at www.dfes.gov.uk/rsgateway/DB/TIM/m002002/index.shtml

DCSF (2008b) *Funding Per Pupil Time Series TS/REV(R)06*, accessed at www.dfes.gov.uk/rsgateway/DB/TIM/m002012/index.shtml

DCSF (2008c) *Trends in Education and Skills*, online statistics, accessed at www.dfes.gov.uk/trends/index.cfm?fuseaction=home.showChart&cid=3&iid=11&chid=42

DCSF (2008d) *Excellence in Cities: What Did it Achieve?*, accessed at www.standards.dfes.gov.uk/sie/documents/abouteic.doc#I

DCSF (2008e) *Raising Expectations: Enabling the System to Deliver*, London: DCSF.

DCSF and DIUS (Department for Innovation, Universities and Skills) (2008) *World Class Apprenticeships: Unlocking Talent, Building Schools for All: The Government's Strategy for the Future of Apprenticeships in England*, London: DIUS.

De Coulon, A. and Vignoles, A. (2008) *An Analysis of the Benefit of NVQ2 Qualifications Acquired at Age 26-34*, DIUS Research Brief CEE-08-02, London: DIUS.

De Giorgi, G. (2005) 'The New Deal for Young People five years on', *Fiscal Studies*, vol 26, no 3, pp 371-83.

Deacon, A. (2003) '"Levelling the playing field, activating the players": New Labour and "the cycle of disadvantage"', *Policy & Politics*, vol 31, no 2, pp 123-37.

Dearden, L., Emmerson, C., Frayne, C. and Meghir, C. (2005) *Education Subsidies and School Drop Out Rates*, London: Centre for the Economics of Education.

Dearden, L., Fitzsimmons, E., Goodman, A. and Kaplan, G. (2008) 'Higher education funding reforms in England: the distributional effects and the shifting balance of costs', *The Economic Journal*, vol 118 (February), pp F100–F125.

Dearing, R. (1997) *Higher Education in the Learning Society, The National Committee of Inquiry into Higher Education*, London: The Stationery Office.

Defra (Department for Environment, Food and Rural Affairs) (2008a) *UK Climate Change Sustainable Development Indicators*, Statistical Release, 31 January, London: Defra.

Defra (2008b) *Synthesis Report on the Findings from Defra's Pre-Feasibility Study into Personal Carbon Trading*, London: Defra.

Defra (2008c) *How to Use the Shadow Price of Carbon in Policy Appraisal*, London: Defra.

Denbighshire County Council (2008) *Denbighshire's Race Equalities Scheme 2008-2011*, Denbighshire: Denbighshire County Council, accessed at www.denbighshire.gov.uk/www/cms/live/content.nsf/lookupattachments/English~DNAP-7DJH9R/$File/RACE%20EQUALITY%20SCHEME%20-%20English.pdf

Denham, J. (2001) *Building Cohesive Communities: A Report of the Ministerial Group on Public Order and Community Cohesion*, London: Home Office.

DfEE (Department for Education and Employment) (1998) *Meeting the Childcare Challenge*, London: DfEE.

DfEE (1999a) *Excellence in Cities*, London: DfEE.

DfEE (1999b) *Improving Literacy and Numeracy: A Fresh Start*, London: DfEE.

DfES (Department for Education and Skills) (2003a) *The Skills for Life Survey*, London: DfES.

DfES (2003b) *Every Child Matters*, Norwich: HMSO.

DfES (2003c) *Youth Cohort Study: Activities and Experiences of 16 Year Olds: England and Wales 2002*, Statistical First Release no 4, London: DfES.

DfES (2003d) *Aiming High: Raising the Achievement of Minority Ethnic Pupils*, London: DfES.

DfES (2004) *14-19 Curriculum and Qualifications Reform: Final Report of the Working Group on 14-19 Reform*, London: DfES.

DfES (2005a) *Higher Standards, Better Schools for All: More Choices for Parents and Pupils*, London: The Stationery Office.

DfES (2005b) *14-19 Education and Skills*, London: The Stationery Office.

DfES (2005c) *Ethnicity and Education: The Evidence on Minority Ethnic Pupils*, London: DfES.

DfES (2006a) *Independent Review of the Teaching of Early Reading*, Nottingham: DfES.

DfES (2006b) *Social Mobility: Narrowing Social Class Attainment Gaps: Supporting Materials to a Speech by the Rt. Hon. Ruth Kelly MP to the ippr*, London: DfES.

DfES (2006c) *Priority Review: Exclusion of Black Pupils: 'Getting It. Getting It Right'*, London: DfES.

DfES (2007a) *Raising the Attainment of Pakistani, Bangladeshi, Somali and Turkish Heritage Pupils: A Management Guide*, London: DfES.

DfES (2007b) *National Curriculum Assessment, GCSE and Equivalent Attainment and Post-16 Attainment by Pupil Characteristics, in England 2006/07*, London: DfES.

DfES, Department of Trade and Industry, Department for Work and Pensions, Ministry of Justice and Department for Communities and Local Government (2007) *Discrimination Law Review: A Framework for Fairness: Proposals for a Single Equality Bill for Great Britain*, London: DCLG, accessed at www.communities.gov.uk/documents/corporate/pdf/325332.pdf

DFPNI (Department of Finance and Personnel Northern Ireland) (2007) *Summary of Domestic Rating Reforms*, accessed at www.ratingreviewni.gov.uk/archive/domestic/domestic-summary.htm

DH (Department of Health) (1998a) *Independent Inquiry into Inequalities in Health Report*, London: The Stationery Office.

DH (1998b) *Our Healthier Nation: A Contract for Health*, London: The Stationery Office.

DH (1999a) *Saving Lives: Our Healthier Nation*, London: The Stationery Office.

DH (1999b) *Reducing Health Inequalities: An Action Report*, London: DH, www.dh.gov.uk/en/Publicationsandstatistics/Publications/PublicationsPolicyAndGuidance/DH_4006054

DH (2000) *The NHS Plan: A Plan for Investment, a Plan for Reform*, Cm 4818-I, London: The Stationery Office.

DH (2001a) *National Service Framework for Older People*, London: DH.

DH (2001b) 'Health Secretary announces new plans to improve health in poorest areas', Press Release 2001/0108, London: DH.

DH (2003) *Tackling Health Inequalities: A Programme for Action*, London: DH.

DH (2004a) *Choosing Health*, London: DH.

DH (2004b) *National Standards, Local Action: Health and Social Care Standards and Planning Framework, 2005/06-2007/08*, London: DH.

DH (2004c) *NHS Improvement Plan*, London: DH.

DH (2005) *Delivering Choosing Health: Making Healthier Choices Easier*, London: DH.

DH (2007) *Tackling Health Inequalities: 2004-06 Data and Policy Update for the National Target*, London: Health Inequalities Unit, DH.

DH (2008a) *High Quality Care for All: NHS Next Stage Review Final Report*, report by Professor Lord Darzi, Cm 7432, London: DH.

DH (2008b) *Tackling Health Inequalities: 2007 Status Report on the Programme for Action*, London: DH.

DH (2008c) *Health Inequalities: Progress and Next Steps*, London: DH.

Diamond, P. and Giddens, A. (2005) 'The new egalitarianism: economic inequality in the UK', in A. Giddens and P. Diamond (eds) *The New Egalitarianism*, London: Policy Network.

Dickens, R. (2000) 'The evolution of individual male earnings in Great Britain: 1975-95', *Economic Journal*, no 110, p 460.

Dickens, R. and McKnight, A. (2008a) *The Impact of Policy Change on Job Retention and Advancement*, CASEpaper 134, London: London School of Economics and Political Science.

Dickens, R. and McKnight, A. (2008b) *Changes in Earnings Inequality and Mobility in Great Britain 1978/9-2005/6*, CASEpaper 132, London: London School of Economics and Political Science.

Dickens, R. and McKnight, A. (2008c) *Assimilation of Migrants into the British Labour Market*, CASEpaper 133, London: London School of Economics and Political Science.

DIUS (Department for Innovation, Universities and Skills) (2007) *Participation Rates in Higher Education: Academic Years 1999/2000-2005/2006*, London: DIUS.

DIUS (2008) *Full-Time Young Participation by Socio-Economic Class, 2008 Update*, accessed at www.dius.gov.uk/research/documents/FYPSECpercent20paper202008.pdf

Docking, M. and Tuffin, R. (2005) *Racist Incidents: Progress since the Lawrence Inquiry*, Online Report no 42/05, London: Home Office.

Donnelly, C. and Osborne, R. (2005) 'Devolution, social policy and education: some observations from Northern Ireland', *Social Policy and Society*, vol 4, no 2, pp 147-56.

Drakeford, M. (2007) 'Social justice in a devolved Wales', *Benefits: The Journal of Poverty and Social Justice*, vol 15, no 2, pp 171-8.

Dresner, S. and Ekins, P. (2004) *Green Taxes and Charges: Reducing their Impact on Low-Income Households*, York: Joseph Rowntree Foundation.

Dresner, S. and Ekins, P. (2006) 'Economic instruments to improve UK home energy efficiency without negative social impacts', *Fiscal Studies*, vol 27, no 1, pp 47-74.

Drever, F. and Whitehead, M. (1997) *Health Inequalities: Decennial Supplement*, London: ONS.

DSD (Department for Social Development) (2007) *Households Below Average Income: Northern Ireland 2005-06*, Belfast: DSD, accessed at www.dsdni.gov.uk/index/stats_and_research/stats-publications/stats-family-resource/households.htm

DSS (Department of Social Security) (1998) *A New Contract for Welfare: Partnership in Pensions*, Cm 4179, London: The Stationery Office.

DSS (1999) *Opportunity for All: Tackling Poverty and Social Exclusion*, First Annual Report, Cm 4445, London: The Stationery Office.

DTI (Department of Trade and Industry) (2002) *Equality and Diversity: Making it Happen*, London: DTI, accessed at www.equalities.gov.uk/equality/project/making_it_happen/cons_doc.htm

DTI (2004) *Fairness for All: A New Commission for Equality and Human Rights*, Cm 6185, London: DTI, accessed at www.wmra.gov.uk/documents/Equalities%20and%20Diversity/Reports%20and%20Publications/Equalities%20cehr_white_paper.pdf

Dustmann, C. and Fabbri, F. (2005) 'Immigrants in the British labour market', *Fiscal Studies*, vol 26, no 4, pp 423-70.

DWP (Department for Work and Pensions) (2002) *Simplicity, Security and Choice: Working and Saving for Retirement*, Cm 5677, London: The Stationery Office.

DWP (2003) *Measuring Child Poverty*, London: DWP.

DWP (2004) *Households Below Average Income 1994/5-2002/03*, Leeds: Corporate Document Services.

DWP (2005) *Principles for Reform: The National Pensions Debate*, London: DWP.

DWP (2006a) *Security in Retirement*, London: DWP.

DWP (2006b) *Personal Accounts: A New Way to Save*, London: DWP.

DWP (2006c) *Households Below Average Income 1994/95-2004/05*, London: DWP.

DWP (2007a) *Low-Income Dynamics 1991-2005 (Great Britain)*, London: ONS/DWP.

DWP (2007b) *Gender Impact of Pension Reform: Pensions Bill 2007*, 5 December, London: DWP.

DWP (2007c) *Income Related Benefits Estimates of Take-Up in 2005/2006*, London: DWP.

DWP (2007d) *Opportunity for All: Indicators Update 2007*, London: DWP.

DWP (2007e) *In Work, Better Off: Next Steps to Full Employment*, Cm 7130, London: The Stationery Office.

DWP (2008a) *Abstract of Statistics: 2007 Edition*, London: DWP.

DWP (2008b) *Households Below Average Income, 1994/95-2006/07*, London: DWP.

DWP (2008c) *Income Related Benefits: Estimates of Take-Up in 2006-07*, London: DWP Analytical Services Division.

DWP (2008d) *Projections of Entitlement to Income Related Benefits to 2050*, London: DWP Analytical Services Division, accessed at www.dwp.gov.uk/pensionsreform/pdfs/Projections-of-entitlement-to-IncomeRelatedBenefitsJune2008.pdf

DWP (2008e) *Pensions Bill: Impact Assessment*, 24 April, London: DWP.

DWP (2008f) *The Pensioner Income Series 2006-07*, London: National Statistics.

DWP (2008g) *No One Written Off: Reforming Welfare to Reward Responsibility*, Cm 7363, London: The Stationery Office.

EC (European Commission) (2008) *Joint Report on Social Protection and Social Inclusion (Accompanying Document)*, SEC 2008, 91, Brussels: Commission of the European Communities.

EHRC (Equality and Human Rights Commission) (2008) *The Equality Measurement Framework: EHRC Briefing Note 2008*, London: EHRC, accessed at http://sticerd.lse.ac.uk/textonly/case/research/equality/Briefing_Equality_Measurement_Framework.pdf

EMETF (Ethnic Minority Employment Task Force) (2006) *Second Annual Report*, London: DWP.

Emmerson, C., Frayne, C. and Love, S. (2004) *A Survey of Public Spending in the UK*, IFS Briefing Note no 43 (updated), London: Institute for Fiscal Studies.

Emmerson, C., Tetlow, G. and Wakefield, M. (2006) 'An initial response to the pensions White Paper', IFS Press Release, London: Institute for Fiscal Studies.

EOC (Equal Opportunities Commission) (2007) *Moving On Up? The Way Forward: Report of the EOC's Investigation into Bangladeshi, Pakistani and Black Caribbean Women and Work*, Manchester: EOC.

Equalities Review (2007) *Fairness and Freedom: The Final Report of the Equalities Review*, London: CLG, accessed at www.theequalitiesreview.org.uk/publications.aspx

Ermisch, J., Francesconi, M. and Pevalin, D.J. (2001) *Outcomes for Children of Poverty*, DWP Research Report no 158, Leeds: Corporate Document Services.

Erturk, I., Froud, J., Johal, S., Leaver, A. and Williams, K. (2006) *Agency, Romance of Management and an Alternative Explanation*, CRESC Working Paper no 23, Manchester: Centre for Research on Socio-Cultural Change, University of Manchester.

Esping-Andersen, G. (2005) 'Inequality of incomes and opportunities', in A. Giddens and P. Diamond (eds) *The New Egalitarianism*, London: Policy Network.

Eurostat (Statistical Office of the European Communities) (2008) *Social Inclusion, Monetary Poverty and Living Conditions*, accessed at http://epp.eurostat.ec.europa.eu/tgm/table.do?tab=table&init=1&plugin=0&language=en&pcode=tsdsc230

Evandrou, M. and Falkingham, J. (2000) 'Looking back to look forward: lessons from four birth cohorts for ageing in the 21st century', *Population Trends*, no 99, pp 21-30.

Evans, G. (2007) *Educational Failure and Working Class White Children in Britain*, Basingstoke: Palgrave Macmillan.

Fabian Society (2006a) *Narrowing the Gap*, Glasgow: Bell & Bain for the Fabian Society.

Fabian Society (2006b) *Life Chances: What Does the Public Really Think about Poverty?*, London: Fabian Society.

Fairclough, N. (2000) *New Labour, New Language?*, London: Routledge.

Falkingham, J. (1989) 'Dependency and ageing in Britain: a re-examination of the evidence', *Journal of Social Policy*, vol 18, no 2, pp 211-33.

Falkingham, J. (1997) 'Financial (in)security in later life', in M. Bernard and J. Phillips (eds) *The Social Policy of Old Age*, London: Centre for Policy on Ageing.

Falkingham, J. and Rake, K. (2003) 'Pensions choices for the 21st century: meeting the challenges of an ageing society', in C. Bochel, N. Ellison and M. Powell (eds) *Social Policy Review 15* (pp 197-216), Bristol: The Policy Press.

Feinstein, L. (1998) *Pre-School Educational Inequality? British Children in the 1970 Cohort*, no 404, London: Centre for Economic Performance, London School of Economics and Political Science.

Fenton, S. (2003) *Ethnicity: Modernity, Racism, Class and Culture*, Cambridge: Polity Press.

Field, F. and Cackett, B. (2007) *Welfare Isn't Working: Child Poverty*, London: Reform.

Fieldhouse, E.A., Kalra, V.S. and Alam, S. (2002) 'A New Deal for Young People from minority ethnic communities in the UK', *Journal of Ethnic and Migration Studies*, vol 28, no 3, pp 499-513.

Fong, C. (2001) 'Social preferences, self-interest, and the demand for redistribution', *Journal of Public Economics*, vol 82, no 2, pp 225-46.

Foster, J. and Hope, T. (1993) *Housing, Community and Crime: The Impact of the Priority Estates Project*, Research Study no 131, Home Office Research and Planning Unit, London: HMSO.

Foster, J., Newburn, T. and Souhami, A. (2005) *Assessing the Impact of the Stephen Lawrence Inquiry*, Home Office Research Study 294, London: Home Office.

FPAG (Fuel Poverty Advisory Group) (2008) *Sixth Annual Report, 2007*, London: BERR.

Frank, R. (2007) *Falling Behind: How Rising Inequality Harms the Middle Class*, Berkeley, CA: University of California Press.

Frank, R. and Cook, P. (1996) *The Winner-Take-All Society: Why the Few at the Top Get So Much More Than the Rest of Us*, London: Penguin.

Fredman, S. (2008) *Human Rights Transformed: Positive Rights and Positive Duties*, Oxford: Oxford University Press.

Freud, D. (2007) *Reducing Dependency, Increasing Opportunity: Options for the Future of Welfare to Work*, Leeds: Corporate Document Services.

GAD (Government Actuary's Department) (2008) *Cohort Life Tables Database, 2006-Based Projections*, accessed at www.gad.gov.uk/Demography_Data/Life_Tables/Eoltable06.asp

Galindo-Rueda, F., Marcenaro-Gutierrez, O. and Vignoles, A. (2004) 'The widening socio-economic gap in UK higher education', *National Institute Economic Review*, vol 190, no 1, pp 75-88.

Gebhardt, E. and Adams, R.J. (2007) 'The influence of equating methodology on reported trends in PISA', *Journal of Applied Measurement*, vol 8, no 3, pp 305-23.

GEO (Government Equalities Office) (2008) *Framework for a Fairer Future: The Equality Bill*, accessed at www.equalities.gov.uk/publications/FRAMEWORK %20FAIRER%20FUTURE.pdf

Georgiadis, A. and Manning, A. (2007) *Spend It Like Beckham? Inequality and Redistribution in the UK, 1983-2004*, CEP Discussion Paper no 816, London: London School of Economics and Political Science.

Gerhard, U., Knijn, T. and Weckwert, A. (2005) *Working Mothers in Europe: A Comparison of Policies and Practices*, Cheltenham: Edward Elgar.

Gewirtz, S., Ball, S. and Bowe, R. (1995) *Markets, Choice and Equity in Education*, Buckingham: Open University Press.

Gillborn, D. (1998) 'Racism, selection, poverty and parents: New Labour, old problems?', *Journal of Education Policy*, vol 13, no 6, pp 717-35.

Gillborn, D. and Mirza, H. (2000) *Educational Inequality: Mapping Race, Class and Gender: A Synthesis of Research Evidence*, London: Ofsted.

Gillborn, D. and Youdell, D. (2000) *Rationing Education: Policy, Practice, Reform and Equity*, Milton Keynes: Open University Press.

Glass, N. (2005) 'Surely some mistake', *The Guardian*, 5 January.

Glennerster, H. (1999) 'Which welfare states are likely to survive?', *International Journal of Social Welfare*, vol 8, no 1, pp 2-13.

Glennerster, H. (2006) 'Why do different? Why so bad a future?', in H. Pemberton, P. Thane and N. Whiteside (eds) *Britain's Pension Crisis: History and Policy*, Oxford: Oxford University Press.

Goldthorpe, J.H. and Jackson, M. (2007) 'Intergenerational class mobility in contemporary Britain: political concerns and empirical findings', *British Journal of Sociology*, vol 58, no 4, pp 525-46.

Goldthorpe, J.H. and Mills, C. (2008) 'Trends in intergenerational class mobility in modern Britain: evidence from national surveys, 1972-2005', Paper presented at the Intergenerational Mobility Conference, London School of Economics and Political Science, 23 June (mimeo).

Gregg, P. and Wadsworth, J. (2001) 'Everything you ever wanted to know about measuring worklessness and polarization at the household level but were afraid to ask', *Oxford Bulletin of Economics and Statistics*, vol 63 (special issue), pp 777-806.

Gregg, P., Hansen, K. and Wadsworth, J. (1999a) 'The rise of the workless household', in P. Gregg and J. Wadsworth (eds) *The State of Working Britain*, Manchester: Manchester University Press.

Gregg, P., Harkness, S. and Machin, S. (1999b) 'Poor kids: trends in child poverty in Britain, 1968-96', *Fiscal Studies*, vol 2, no 2, pp 163-87.

Gregg, P., Jewell, S. and Tonks, I. (2005a) *Executive Pay and Performance in the UK 1994-2002*, Xfi Centre for Performance and Investment Working Paper 05/05, Exeter: University of Exeter.

Gregg, P., Waldfogel, J. and Washbrook, E. (2005b) 'That's the way the money goes: expenditure patterns as real incomes rise for the poorest families with children', in J. Hills and K. Stewart (eds) *A More Equal Society? New Labour, Poverty, Inequality and Exclusion*, Bristol: The Policy Press.

Griffiths, C. and Brock, A. (2004) *Mortality by Country of Birth in England and Wales 2001-2003*, London: ONS.

Hackney Council (2006) *Hackney Borough Profile*, Hackney: Team Hackney, accessed at www.hackney.gov.uk/xp-boroughprofile_chapter3.pdf

Hakim, C., Bradley, K., Price, E. and Mitchell, L. (2008) *Little Britons: Financing Childcare Choice*, London: Policy Exchange.

Haringey Council (1997) *Refugees and Asylum Seekers in Haringey: Research Project Report*, London: Haringey Council.

Harker, L. (2006) *Delivering on Child Poverty: What Would it Take?*, London: The Stationery Office.

Harker, L. and Oppenheim, C. (2007) 'A new deal: citizen centred welfare to work', in J. Bennett and G. Cooke (eds) *It's All About You: Citizen Centred Welfare*, London: ippr.

Harkness, S. and Waldfogel, J. (1999) *The Family Gap in Pay: Evidence from Seven Industrialised Countries*, CASEpaper 30, London: London School of Economics and Political Science.

Harris, A. and Ranson, S. (2005) 'The contradictions of education policy: disadvantage and achievement', *British Educational Research Journal*, vol 31, no 5, pp 571-87.

Hazell, R. (ed) (2000) *The State and the Nations: The First Year of Devolution in the UK*, Thorverton: Imprint Academic.

HC (Healthcare Commission) (2006) *Variations in the Experiences of Patients using the NHS Services in England: Analysis of the Healthcare Commission's 2004/2005 Surveys of Patients*, London: HC, accessed at www.healthcarecommission.org.uk/_db/_documents/Surveys_Variations_Report.pdf

HC (2007a) *Audit of Equalities Publications*, London: HC, accessed at www.healthcarecommission.org.uk/_db/_documents/Equalities_publications_audit_briefing.pdf

HC (2007b) *Caring for Dignity: A National Report on Dignity in Care for Older People while in Hospital*, London: HC, accessed at www.healthcarecommission.org.uk/_db/_documents/Caring_for_dignity.pdf

HC, Commission for Social Care Inspection and Audit Commission (2006) *Living Well in Later Life: A Review of Progress against the National Service Framework for Older People*, London: Commission for Healthcare Audit and Inspection, accessed at www.healthcarecommission.org.uk/_db/_documents/Living_well_in_later_life_-_full_report.pdf

HC, Mental Health Act Commission, the Care Services Improvement Partnership and the National Institute for Mental Health in England (2007) *Count Me In: Results of the 2007 National Census of Inpatients in Mental Health and Learning Disability Services in England and Wales*, London: HC, accessed at www.healthcarecommission.org.uk/_db/_documents/Count_me_in-2007.pdf

Heath, A. and Cheung, S. (2006) *Ethnic Penalties in the Labour Market: Employers and Discrimination*, DWP Research Report no 341, London: DWP.

Heath, A. and Payne, C. (2000) 'Social mobility', in A.H. Halsey with J. Webb (eds) *Twentieth Century British Social Trends*, Basingstoke: Macmillan.

Hedges, A. (2005) *Perceptions of Redistribution: Report on Exploratory Qualitative Research*, CASEpaper 96, London: London School of Economics and Political Science.

HEFCE (Higher Education Funding Council for England) (2005) *Young Participation in Higher Education*, Bristol: HEFCE.

Hepple, B., Coussey, M. and Choudhury, T. (2000) *Equality: A New Framework, Report of the Independent Review of the Enforcement of UK Anti-Discrimination Legislation*, Oxford: Hart Publishing.

HESA (Higher Education Statistics Authority) (2008) *Performance Indicators 2006/07: Widening Participation of Under-Represented Groups* (tables T1, T2, SP1), accessed at www.hesa.ac.uk/index.php/content/view/1174/141/

Hills, J. (1997) *The Future of Welfare: A Guide to the Debate* (2nd edition), York: Joseph Rowntree Foundation.

Hills, J. (ed) (1999) *Persistent Poverty and Lifetime Inequality: The Evidence*, CASEreport 5, London: London School of Economics and Political Science and HM Treasury.

Hills, J. (2001) 'Poverty and social security: what rights? Whose responsibilities?', in R. Jowell, J. Curtice, A. Park and K. Thomson (eds) *British Social Attitudes: The 18th Report*, Aldershot: Ashgate.

Hills, J. (2002) 'Following or leading public opinion? Social security policy and public attitudes since 1987', *Fiscal Studies*, vol 23, no 4, pp 539-58.

Hills, J. (2004) *Inequality and the State*, Oxford: Oxford University Press.

Hills, J. (2006) 'Financing UK pensions', in H. Pemberton, P. Thane and N. Whiteside (eds) *Britain's Pension Crisis: History and Policy*, Oxford: Oxford University Press.

Hills, J. (2007) *Ends and Means: The Future Roles of Social Housing in England*, CASEreport 34, London: London School of Economics and Political Science.

Hills, J. and Lelkes, O. (1999) 'Social security, selective universalism and patchwork redistribution', in R. Jowell, J. Curtice, A. Park and K. Thomson (eds) *British Social Attitudes: The 16th Report: Who Shares New Labour Values?*, Aldershot: Ashgate.

Hills, J. and Stewart, K. (eds) (2005) *A More Equal Society? New Labour, Poverty and Exclusion*, Bristol: The Policy Press.

Hilton, M. (2006) 'Measuring standards in primary English: issues of validity and accountability with respect to PIRLS and National Curriculum test scores', *British Educational Research Journal*, vol 32, no 6, pp 817-37.

Hirsch, D. (2006) *What Will it Take to End Child Poverty?*, York: Joseph Rowntree Foundation.

HM Treasury (1997) *Employment Opportunity For All – A New Approach*, HMT 8, London: HM Treasury.

HM Treasury (1999) *Tackling Poverty and Extending Opportunity*, no 4, London: HM Treasury.

HM Treasury (2002) *Long-Term Public Finance Report: An Analysis of Fiscal Sustainability*, London: HM Treasury.

HM Treasury (2007a) *Funding the Scottish Parliament, National Assembly for Wales and Northern Ireland Assembly: Statement of Funding Policy*, London: The Stationery Office.

HM Treasury (2007b) *PBR CSR: Public Service Agreements*, London: HM Treasury, accessed at www.hm-treasury.gov.uk/pbr_csr/psa/pbr_crs07_psagrowth.cfm

HM Treasury (2008a) *Ending Child Poverty: Everybody's Business*, London: HM Treasury.

HM Treasury (2008b) *Long-Term Public Finance Report: An Analysis of Fiscal Sustainability*, London: HM Treasury.

HM Treasury (2008c) *Public Service Agreement 15*, London: HM Treasury, accessed at www.hm-treasury.gov.uk./media/E/8/pbr_csr07_psa15.pdf

HM Treasury (2008d) *Pre-Budget Report – Facing Global Challenges: Supporting People through Difficult Times*, Cm 7484, London: The Stationery Office.

HMRC (HM Revenue and Customs) (2006) *HMRC Statistics*, London: HMRC.

HMRC (2007) *Child Tax Credit and Working Tax Credit Take-Up Rates 2004-05*, London: HMRC.

Hobbs, G. and Vignoles, A. (2007) *Is Free School Meal Status a Valid Proxy for Socio-Economic Status (in Schools Research)?*, CEE DP 0084, London: Centre for the Economics of Education, London School of Economics and Political Science.

Hobcraft, J. (1998) *Intergenerational and Life-Course Transmission of Social Exclusion: Influences of Childhood Poverty, Family Disruption, and Contact with the Police*, CASEpaper 15, London: London School of Economics and Political Science.

Hobcraft, J. and Kiernan, K. (2001) 'Childhood poverty, early motherhood and adult social exclusion', *British Journal of Sociology*, vol 52, no 3, pp 495-517.

Hodge, M. (2000) 'Equality and New Labour', *Renewal*, vol 8, no 3, pp 34-41.

Home Office (1998a) *Statistics on Race and the Criminal Justice System*, London: Home Office.

Home Office (1998b) *Rights Brought Home: The Human Rights Bill*, Cm 3782, London: Home Office, accessed at www.archive.official-documents.co.uk/document/hoffice/rights/rights.htm

Home Office (1999) *Stephen Lawrence Inquiry: Home Secretary's Action Plan*, London: Home Office.

Home Office (2000) *Code of Practice on Reporting and Recording Racist Incidents*, London: Home Office.

Home Office (2003) *Statistics on Race and the Criminal Justice System 2002*, London: Home Office.

Home Office (2004) *Recording of Stops Implementation Guide in Response to Recommendation 61 of the Stephen Lawrence Inquiry Report*, London: Home Office.

Home Office (2005) *Improving Opportunity, Strengthening Society: The Government's Strategy to Increase Race Equality and Community Cohesion*, London: Home Office.

Home Office (2006) *Race and the Criminal Justice System: An Overview to the Complete Statistics 2004–2005*, London: Home Office.

Home Office (2007) *Control of Immigration Statistics 2006*, London: Home Office.

Home Office (2008) *Asylum Statistics 2007*, London: Home Office.

Home Office and Vantage Point (2003) *Community Cohesion Pathfinder Programme: The First Six Months*, London: Home Office.

Horne, J., Bejtka, K. and Miller, S. (2008) *Trends in International Maths and Science Survey (TIMSS) 2007 – Highlights from Scotland's Results*, Edinburgh: Scottish Government Social Research.

House of Commons Public Accounts Committee (2007) *Sure Start Children's Centres, 38th Report of Session 2006-07*, London: The Stationery Office.

House of Commons Treasury Committee (2007) *The 2007 Comprehensive Spending Review: Prospects and Processes: Sixth Report of Session 2006-07*, London: House of Commons.

House of Commons Work and Pensions Committee (2008) *The Best Start in Life? Alleviating Deprivation, Improving Social Mobility and Eradicating Child Poverty: Second Report of Session 2007-08*, London: The Stationery Office.

Hsieh, C. and Pugh, M. (1993) 'Poverty, income inequality, and violent crime: a meta-analysis of recent aggregate data studies', *Criminal Justice Review*, vol 18, no 2, pp 182-202.

Iannelli, C. (2008) 'Expansion and social selection in education in England and Scotland', *Oxford Review of Education*, vol 34, no 2, pp 179-202.

ippr (Institute for Public Policy Research) (2006) *Irregular Migration to the UK*, London: ippr.

Ipsos-MORI (2007a) *Public Bodies' Response to the Disability Equality Duty: An Audit of Compliance with the Requirement to Publish a Disability Equality Scheme*, London: Ipsos-MORI, accessed at www.healthcarecommission.org.uk/_db/_documents/Equalities_publications_audit_briefing.pdf

Ipsos-MORI (2007b) *'What Works' in Community Cohesion*, London: DCLG.

Jackson, B. and Segal, P. (2004) *Why Inequality Matters*, Catalyst Working Paper, London: Catalyst.

Jansson, K. (2006) *Black and Minority Ethnic Groups' Experiences and Perceptions of Crime, Racially Motivated Crime and the Police: Findings from the 2004/05 British Crime Survey*, Home Office Online Report no 25/06, London: Home Office.

Jäntii, M., Røed, K., Naylor, R., Björklund, A., Bratsberg, B., Raaum, O., Österbacka, E. and Eriksson, T. (2006) *American Exceptionalism in a New Light: A Comparison of Earnings Mobility in the Nordic countries, the United Kingdom and the United States*, IZA Discussion Paper no 1938, Bonn: Institut zur Zukunft der Arbeit.

JCHR (Joint Committee on Human Rights) (2003) *Human Rights and Public Authorities*, accessed at www.publications.parliament.uk/pa/jt200203/jtselect/jtrights/67/67ap01.htm

JCHR (2004) *The International Covenant on Economic, Social and Cultural Rights*, accessed at www.publications.parliament.uk/pa/jt200304/jtselect/jtrights/183/18307.htm#a24

JCHR (2006) *Meaning of 'Public Authority' under the Human Rights Act*, accessed at www.parliament.uk/parliamentary_committees/joint_committee_on_human_rights/jchr231106pn03.cfm

JCHR (2007) *The Human Rights of Older People in Healthcare*, accessed at www. publications.parliament.uk/pa/jt200607/jtselect/jtrights/156/156i.pdf

JCHR (2008) *A Bill of Rights for the UK?*, London: Office of the High Commissioner for Human Rights, accessed at www.publications.parliament. uk/pa/jt200708/jtselect/jtrights/165/165i.pdf

Jenkins, S. and Rigg, J. (2001) *The Dynamics of Poverty in Britain*, DWP Research Report no 157, London: DWP.

Jha, P., Peto, R., Zatonski, W., Boreham, J., Jarvis, M.J. and Lopez, A.D. (2006) 'Social inequalities in male mortality, and in male mortality from smoking: indirect estimation from national death rates in England and Wales, Poland, and North America', *Lancet*, vol 368, no 9533, pp 367-70.

Johnson, P. and Falkingham, J. (1992) *Ageing and Economic Welfare*, London: Sage Publications.

Johnson, P., Disney, R. and Stears, G. (1996) *Pensions 2000 and Beyond: Analysis of Trends and Options*, vol 2, The Retirement Income Inquiry, London: Institute for Fiscal Studies.

Jones, F. (2008) *The Effects of Taxes and Benefits on Household Income, 2006-07*, London: Office for National Statistics.

JRF (Joseph Rowntree Foundation) (2008) 'Minimum living standards: public consultation shows what people find acceptable', Press Release, 1 July, York: JRF.

Kawachi, I., Kennedy, B., Lochner, K. and Prothrow-Stith, D. (1997) 'Social capital, income inequality and mortality', *American Journal of Public Health*, vol 87, no 9, pp 1491-8.

Kazimirski, A., Smith, R., Butt, S., Ireland, E. and Lloyd, E. (2008) *Childcare and Early Years Survey 2007: Parents' Use, Views and Experiences*, Research Report no DCSF-RR025, London: National Centre for Social Research.

Keating, M. (2005) *The Government of Scotland: Public Policy Making After Devolution*, Edinburgh: Edinburgh University Press.

Kelly, K. and Cook, S. (2007) *Full-Time Young Participation by Socio-Economic Class: A New Widening Participation Measure in Higher Education*, London: DfES.

Kelly, M. (2008) *Public Attitudes to Child Poverty*, DWP Research Summary, London: DWP.

Kendall, L., Rutt, S. and Schagen, I. (2005) *Minority Ethnic Pupils and Excellence in Cities: Final Report*, DfES Brief no Rb703, London: DfES.

Kenway, P. (2003) *Eradicating Poverty: A Target for the Labour Movement*, London: Fabian Society.

Kenway, P. (2006) 'Cameron's poverty challenge to Labour', *Bevan Foundation Review*, pp 36-37.

Kenway, P., MacInnes, T., Kelly, A. and Palmer, G. (2006) *Monitoring Poverty and Social Exclusion in Northern Ireland 2006*, York: Joseph Rowntree Foundation, accessed at www.jrf.org.uk/bookshop/eBooks/1814-poverty-Northern-Ireland. pdf

Kintrea, K. (2006) 'Having it all? Housing reform under devolution', *Housing Studies*, vol 21, no 2, pp 187-207.

Klug, F. (2007a) *A Bill of Rights: Do We Need One or Do We Already Have One?*, LSE Law, Society and Economy Working Paper no 2, London: London School of Economics and Political Science.

Klug, F. (2007b) *Memorandum Submitted to the Joint Committee on Human Rights*, accessed at www.publications.parliament.uk/pa/jt200708/jtselect/jtrights/memo/britishbill/contents.htm

Klug, F. and Wildbore, H. (2005) *Equality, Dignity and Discrimination under Human Rights Law: Selected Cases*, London: London School of Economics and Political Science, accessed at www.lse.ac.uk/Depts/human-rights/Documents/Human_rights_equality_and_discrimination.pdf

Koser, K. (2005) *Irregular Migration, State Security and Human Security*, Geneva: Global Commission on International Migration.

Kunst, A.E., Bos, V., Lahelma, E., Bartley, M., Lissau, I., Regidor, E., Mielck, A., Cardano, M., Dalstra, J.A., Geurts, J.J., Helmert, U., Lennartsson, C., Ramm, J., Spadea, T., Stronegger, W.J. and Mackenbach, J.P. (2005) 'Trends in socioeconomic inequalities in self-assessed health in 10 European countries', *International Journal of Epidemiology*, vol 34, no 2, pp 295-305.

Labour Party (1997) *Labour Party Manifesto: New Labour Because Britain Deserves Better*, London: Labour Party.

Labour Party (2001) *Ambitions for Britain*, London: Labour Party.

Labour Party (2005) *Britain Forward not Back: The Labour Party Manifesto 2005*, London: Labour Party.

Laible, J. (2008) 'The Scottish Parliament and its capacity for redistributive policy: the case of land reform', *Parliamentary Affairs*, vol 61, no 1, pp 160-84.

Law, A. and Mooney, G. (2006) '"We've never had it so good": the "problem" of the working class in devolved Scotland', *Critical Social Policy*, vol 26, no 3, pp 523-42.

Leitch, S. (2006) *Prosperity for All in the Global Economy: World Class Skills*, London: HM Treasury.

Lemos, S. and Portes, J. (2008) *The Impact of Migration from the New European Union Member States on Native Workers*, London: DWP.

Lester, A. (2003a) *The Human Rights Act 1998: Five Years On*, Lecture, 25 November, accessed at www.odysseustrust.org/lectures/227_law_reform_lecture.pdf

Lester, A. (2003b) *Stonewall Lecture: New Labour's Equality Laws: Some Are More Equal than Others*, accessed at www.odysseustrust.org/lectures/220_stonewall_lexture.pdf

Lester, A. (2006) *Thirty Years On*, accessed at http://83.137.212.42/sitearchive/cre/anthology_04.html

Lester, A. and Clapinska, L. (2005) 'An Equality and Human Rights Commission worthy of the name', *Journal of Law and Society*, vol 32, no 1, pp 169-86.

Letwin, O. (2006) 'Why we have signed up to Labour's anti-poverty target', *The Guardian*, 11 April.

Levacic, R. and Jenkins, A. (2004) *Evaluating the Effectiveness of Specialist Schools*, London: Centre for the Economics of Education, London School of Economics and Political Science.

Levitas, R. (2000) 'What is social exclusion?', in D. Gordon and P. Townsend (eds) *Breadline Europe: The Measurement of Poverty*, Bristol: The Policy Press.

Lewis, H. (2007) *Destitution in Leeds: The Experiences of People Seeking Asylum and Supporting Agencies*, York: Joseph Rowntree Charitable Trust, accessed at www. jrct.org.uk/core/documents/download.asp?id=203

Lewis, J. (ed) (1998) 'Introduction', *Lone Mothers in European Welfare Regimes: Shifting Policy Logics*, London: Jessica Kingsley.

Lewis, J. (2001) 'Orientations to work and the issue of care', in J. Millar and K. Rowlingson (eds) *Lone Parents, Employment and Social Policy: Cross-National Comparisons* (pp 153-68), Bristol: The Policy Press.

LGA (Local Government Association) (2002) *Guidance on Community Cohesion*, London: LGA.

LHF (London Housing Federation) (2004) *Think Big: Delivering Family Homes for Londoners*, London: LHF.

Liberty (2007) *Memorandum Submitted to the Joint Committee on Human Rights*, accessed at www.publications.parliament.uk/pa/jt200708/jtselect/jtrights/memo/britishbill/contents.htm

Lindsay, C. (2005) 'Employment and unemployment estimates for 1971 to 1991', *Labour Market Trends*, vol 113, no 1.

Lister, R. (2001) 'Doing good by stealth: the politics of poverty and inequality under New Labour', *New Economy*, vol 8, no 2, pp 65-70.

Lister, R. and Moore, R. (1997) 'Government must reconsider its strategy for more equal society', *Financial Times*, 1 October.

Love, J., Kisker, E.E., Ross, C.M., Schochet, P.Z., Brooks-Gunn, J., Paulsell, D., Boller, K., Constantine, J., Vogel, C., Fuligni, A.S. and Brady-Smith, C. (2002) *Making a Difference in the Lives of Infants and Toddlers and their Families: The Impacts of Early Head Start*, vol 1: Final Technical Report, Princeton, NJ: Mathematica Policy Research Inc, accessed at www.mathematica-mpr.com/PDFs/ehsfinalvol1.pdf

LSC (Learning and Skills Council) (2006) *Evaluation of the Adult Learning Grant Cohort 2* (Wave 1), accessed at http://readingroom.lsc.gov.uk/Lsc/National/alg-cohort2-wave-1.pdf

Lupton, R. (2001) *Places Apart? The Initial Report of CASE's Areas Study*, CASEreport 14, London: London School of Economics and Political Science.

Lupton, R. (2003) *Poverty Street: Causes and Consequences of Neighbourhood Decline*, Bristol: The Policy Press.

Lupton, R. (2005) 'Social justice and school improvement: improving the quality of schooling in the poorest neighbourhoods', *British Educational Research Journal*, vol 31, no 5, pp 589-604.

Lupton, R. and Sullivan, A. (2007) 'The London context', in T. Brighouse and L. Fullick (eds) *Education in a Global City: Essays from London*, London: Bedford Way Publishing.

Machin, S. and Manning, A. (1999) 'The causes and consequences of long term unemployment in Europe', in O. Ashenfelter and D. Card (eds) *Handbook of Labor Economics* (1st edition) (vol 3), Amsterdam: Elsevier.

Machin, S. and Van Reenen, J. (2007) *Changes in Wage Inequality*, CEP Special Report no 18, London: Centre for Economic Policy, London School of Economics and Political Science.

Machin, S. and Vignoles, A. (2006) *Education Policy in the UK*, CEE Discussion Paper no 57, London: Centre for the Economics of Education, London School of Economics and Political Science.

Machin, S., McNally, S. and Meghir, C. (2007) *Resources and Standards in Urban Schools*, London: Centre for the Economics of Education, London School of Economics and Political Science.

Mackenbach, J.P., Stirbu, I., Roskam, A.J., Schaap, M.M., Menvielle, G., Leinsalu, M. and Kunst, A.E. (2008) 'European Union Working Group on Socioeconomic Inequalities in Health: socioeconomic inequalities in health in 22 European countries', *New England Journal of Medicine*, vol 358, no 23, pp 2468-81.

Macpherson, W. (1999) *The Stephen Lawrence Inquiry: Report of an Inquiry by Sir William Macpherson of Cluny*, London: Home Office.

Manacorda, M., Manning, A. and Wadsworth, J. (2006) *The Impact of Immigration on the Structure of Male Wages: Theory and Evidence from Britain*, IZA Discussion Paper no 2352, Bonn: Institute for the Study of Labour, accessed at http://ftp.iza.org/dp2352.pdf

Mandelson, P. (1997) *Labour's Next Steps: Tackling Social Exclusion*, Fabian Pamphlet no 581, London: The Fabian Society.

Marcenaro-Gutierrez, O., Galindo-Rueda, F. and Vignoles, A. (2007) 'Who actually goes to university?', *Empirical Economics*, vol 32, no 2-3, pp 333-57.

Marshall, B., Duffy, B., Thompson, J., Castell, S. and Hall, S. (2007) *Blair's Britain: The Social & Cultural Legacy*, London: Ipsos MORI Social Research Institute.

McGhee, D. (2003) 'Moving to "our" common ground – a critical examination of community cohesion discourse in twenty-first century Britain', *The Sociological Review*, vol 51, no 3, pp 376-404.

McGregor, A., McDougall, L., Taylor, K., Hirst, A., Rinnie, S. and Clark, S. (2005) *Evaluation of the New Futures Initiatives*, Glasgow: Scottish Enterprise.

McKendrick, J., Sinclair, S., Irwin, A., O'Donnell, H., Scott, G. and Dobbie, L. (2008) *Transmitting Poverty: Media, Poverty and the Public in the UK*, York: Joseph Rowntree Foundation.

McKnight, A. (2000) *Trends in Earnings Inequality and Earnings Mobility: The Impact of Mobility on Long Term Inequality*, Employment Relations Research Report Series 8, London: Department of Trade and Industry.

McKnight, A. (2005) 'Employment: tackling poverty through "work for those who can"', in J. Hills and K. Stewart (eds) *A More Equal Society? New Labour, Poverty, Inequality and Exclusion*, Bristol: The Policy Press.

McKnight, A., Glennerster, H. and Lupton, R. (2005) 'Education, education, education…: an assessment of Labour's success in tackling education inequalities', in J. Hills and K. Stewart (eds) *A More Equal Society: New Labour, Poverty, Inequality and Exclusion*, Bristol: The Policy Press.

Meadows, P. and Metcalf, H. (2007) *Evaluation of the Impact of Skills for Life Learning: Longitudinal Survey of Learners*, Wave 3, London: DfES.

Melhuish, E. (1993) 'Preschool care and education: lessons from the 20th for the 21st century', *International Journal of Early Years Education*, vol 1, no 2, pp 19-32.

Melhuish, E. (2004) *Child Benefits: The Importance of Investing in Quality Childcare*, Facing the Future Policy Paper no 9, London: The Daycare Trust.

Merrell, C., Tymms, P. and Jones, P. (2008) *Changes in Children's Cognitive Development at the Start of School in England 2000-2006*, Durham: CEM Centre, Durham University.

Micklewright, J. and Schnepf, S. (2006) *Response Bias in England in PISA 2000 and 2003*, Research Report no 771, Nottingham: DfES Publications.

Middleton, S., Perren, K., Maguire, S., Rennison, J., Battistin, E., Emmerson, C. and Fitzsimons, E. (2005) *Evaluation of Education Maintenance Allowance Pilots: Young People Aged 16-19 Years: Final Report of the Quantitative Evaluation*, DfES Research Report no 678, Nottingham: DfES Publications.

Midwinter, A. (2007) 'The financial framework', in P. Carmichael, C. Knox and R. Osborne (eds) *Devolution and Constitutional Change in Northern Ireland*, Manchester: Manchester University Press.

Miliband, E (2005) 'Does inequality matter?', in A. Giddens and P. Diamond (eds) *The New Egalitarianism*, London: Policy Network.

Miller, J., Bland, N. and Quinton, P. (2000) *The Impact of Stops and Searches on Crime and the Community*, London: Home Office.

Ministry of Justice (2007a) *Race and the Criminal Justice System-2006*, London: Ministry of Justice.

Ministry of Justice (2007b) *The Governance of Britain*, Cm 7170, London: Ministry of Justice, accessed at www.official-documents.gov.uk/document/cm71/7170/7170.pdf

Ministry of Justice (2008) *The Governance of Britain - Constitutional Renewal*, London: Ministry of Justice, accessed at www.justice.gov.uk/docs/constitutional-renewal-white-paper.pdf

Modood, T., Berthoud, R., Lakey, J., Nazroo, J., Smith, P., Virdee, S. and Beishon, S. (1997) *Ethnic Minorities in Britain: Diversity and Disadvantage*, London: Policy Studies Institute.

Moon, D. (2007) *'Modernisation' vs. 'Progressivism': New Labour and the 'Progressive' Tradition*, Compass Thinkpiece no 20, accessed at www.compassonline.com

Mooney, G. (2006) 'Social justice in the devolved Scotland: representation and reality', Paper presented at the ESRC Social Justice and Public Policy seminar on devolution, University of Glasgow, 28 March.

Mooney, G., Scott, G. and Williams, C. (2006) 'Introduction: rethinking social policy through devolution', *Critical Social Policy*, vol 26, no 3, pp 483-97.

Mooney, G. (2008) 'Devolution: towards increasing divergence?', Paper presented at the Social Policy Association Conference, Edinburgh, 23 June.

Morelli, C. and Seaman, P. (2007) 'Devolution and inequality: a failure to create a community of equals?', *Transactions of the Institute of British Geographers*, vol 32, no 4, pp 523-38.

Morris, S., Sutton, M. and Gravelle, H. (2005) 'Inequity and inequality in the use of health care in England: an empirical investigation', *Social Science & Medicine*, vol 60, no 6, pp 1251-66.

Mullan, P. (2000) *The Imaginary Time Bomb: Why an Ageing Population is not a Social Problem*, London: I.B. Tauris.

Mullis, I.V.S., Martin, M.O. and Foy, P. with Olson, J.F., Preuschoff, C., Erberber, E., Arora, A. and Galia, J. (2008a) *TIMSS 2007 International Mathematics Report*, Chestnut Hill, MA: TIMSS & PIRLS International Study Center, Boston College.

Mullis, I.V.S., Martin, M.O. and Foy, P. with Olson, J.F., Preuschoff, C., Erberber, E., Arora, A. and Galia, J. (2008b) *TIMSS 2007 International Science Report*, Chestnut Hill, MA: TIMSS & PIRLS International Study Center, Boston College.

Mumford, K. and Power, A. (2002) *Boom or Abandonment: Resolving Housing Conflicts in Cities*, Coventry: Chartered Institute of Housing.

Mumford, K. and Power, A. (2003) *East Enders: Family and Community in East London*, Bristol: The Policy Press.

NAO (National Audit Office) (2007) *Performance of the Department for Communities and Local Government 2006-07*, Briefing for the Communities and Local Government Committee, London: NAO.

NAO (2008a) *HM Revenue and Customs 2007-08 Accounts: Report by the Comptroller and Auditor General*, London: HMRC.

NAO (2008b) *Widening Participation in Higher Education*, London: NAO.

NAO and DWP (2008) *Increasing Employment Rates for Ethnic Minorities*, London: NAO.

NEA (National Energy Action) (2008) *Fuel Poverty Set to Return to 1997 Levels*, accessed at www.nea.org.uk/Media_Centre/News_releases/?article_id=453

NESS (National Evaluation of Sure Start) (2005) *Early Impacts of Sure Start Local Programmes on Children and Families*, NESS Report no 13, London: NESS.

NESS (2006) *Cost Effectiveness of Implementing SSLPs: An Interim Report*, NESS Report no 15, London: DfES.

NESS (2007) *Family and Parenting Support in Sure Start Local Programmes*, Research Report NESS/2007/FR/023, London: DCSF.

NESS (2008) *The Impact of Sure Start Local Programmes on Three Year Olds and Their Families*, Research Report NESS/2008/FR/027, London: NESS.

NIACE (National Institute of Adult Continuing Education) (2006) *'More than a Language...': NIACE Committee of Inquiry on English for Speakers of Other Languages*, Leicester: NIACE.

Nickell, S. and Quintini, G. (2002) 'The consequences of the decline in public sector pay in Britain: a little bit of evidence', *The Economic Journal*, vol 112, February, pp F107-F118.

NNI (Neighbourhood Nurseries Initiative) Research Team (2007) *National Evaluation of the Neighbourhood Nurseries Initiative: Integrated Report*, London: HMSO.

North, D., Syrett, S. and Etherington, D. (2007) *Devolution and Regional Governance: Tackling the Economic Needs of Deprived Areas*, York: Joseph Rowntree Foundation.

NPI (New Policy Institute) (2007) *Monitoring Poverty and Social Exclusion in Scotland 2007*, London: NPI.

ODI (Office for Disability Issues) (2008) *The Disability Discrimination Act: Analysis of the ONS Omnibus Survey 1996-2006*, London: ODI, accessed at www.officefordisability.gov.uk/docs/dda-report.pdf

ODPM (Office of the Deputy Prime Minister) (2002) *Living Places: Cleaner, Safer, Greener*, London: ODPM.

ODPM (2004) *Neighbourhood Wardens Scheme Evaluation*, Research Report no 8, London: ODPM.

ODPM (2006) *Neighbourhood Management – at the Turning Point?*, Research Report no 23, Programme Review 2005-06, London: ODPM.

OECD (Organisation for Economic Co-operation and Development) (1998) *Employment Outlook*, Paris: OECD.

OECD (2000) *Education at a Glance*, Paris: OECD.

OECD (2005) *Babies and Bosses: Reconciling Work and Family Life*, vol 4 (Canada, Finland, Sweden and the United Kingdom), Paris: OECD.

OECD (2007a) *Education at a Glance*, Paris: OECD.

OECD (2007b) 'Main economic indicators', accessed at www.sourceoecd.org/database/OECDstat

OECD (2007c) *PISA 2006: Science Competencies for Tomorrow's World*, Paris: OECD.

OECD (2007d) *Babies and Bosses: Reconciling Work and Family Life*, vol 5 (A Synthesis of Findings for OECD Countries), Paris: OECD.

OECD (2007e) *Benefits and Wages*, Paris: OECD.

OECD (2008) *Growing Unequal? Income Distribution and Poverty in OECD Countries*, Paris: OECD.

OFMDFM (Office of the First Minister and Deputy First Minister) (2006) *Lifetime Opportunities: Government's Anti-Poverty and Social Inclusion Strategy for Northern Ireland*, Belfast: OFMDFM.

Ofsted (Office for Standards in Education, Children's Services and Skills) (1993) *Access and Achievement in Urban Education*, London: Ofsted.

Ofsted (2005) *Excellence in Cities: Managing Associated Initiatives to Raise Standards*, HMI 2595, London: Ofsted.

ONS (Office for National Statistics) (1997) *Population Trends*, no 90, Winter, London: ONS.

ONS (2002) *Student Achievement in England: Results in Reading, Mathematics and Scientific Literacy among 15 year olds from OECD PISA 2000 Study*, London: The Stationery Office.

ONS (2003) *Labour Force Survey User Guide – Volume 1: Background & Methodology*, London: ONS, accessed at www.statistics.gov.uk/downloads/theme_labour/LFSUG_Vol1_2003.pdf

ONS (2007a) *Government Actuary's Department's 2006-Based Projections*, London: ONS.

ONS (2007b) *Regional Accounts 2007*, London: ONS.

ONS (2007c) *Annual Survey of Hours and Earnings Results 2007*, London: ONS.

ONS (2008a) *National Population Projections 2006-Based*, Series PP2, no 29, London: ONS.

ONS (2008b) *Population Trends*, no 132, Summer, London: ONS.

ONS (2008c) *Regional Trends 40*, London: ONS, accessed at www.statistics.gov.uk/RegionalTrends40/

ONS (2008d) *Infant Mortality by Ethnic Group, England and Wales*, London: ONS, accessed at www.statistics.gov.uk/statbase/Product.asp?vlnk=15111

ONS (2008e) *Quarterly Labour Force Surveys, October-December, 2007*, London: ONS.

ONS (2008f) *National Accounts: Main Aggregates*, accessed at www.statistics.gov.uk/STATBASE/tsdataset.asp?vlnk=205&More=N&All=Y

Orton, M. and Ratcliffe, P. (2005) 'New Labour ambiguity, or neo-liberal consistency? The debate about racial inequality in employment and the use of contract compliance', *Journal of Social Policy*, vol 34, no 2, pp 255-72.

Orton, M. and Rowlingson, K. (2007) *Public Attitudes to Economic Inequality*, York: Joseph Rowntree Foundation.

Osborne, B. (2006) 'Devolution and divergence in education policy: the Northern Ireland case', in J. Adams and K. Schmuecker (eds) *Devolution in Practice: Public Policy Differences within the UK*, Newcastle: ippr North.

Page, B. (2008) 'Working class communities – fairness and access?, Presentation at the Ipsos MORI Social Research Institute, Cabinet Office, 10 June.

Pahl, R., Rose, D. and Spencer, L. (2007) *Inequality and Quiescence: A Continuing Conundrum*, ISER Working Paper no 22, Colchester: Institute for Social and Economic Research, University of Essex.

Palmer, G., MacInnes, T. and Kenway, P. (2008) *Monitoring Poverty and Social Exclusion 2008*, New Policy Institute on behalf of the Joseph Rowntree Foundation, York: JRF.

Pamuk, E.R. (1985) 'Social class inequality in mortality from 1921 to 1972 in England and Wales', *Population Studies*, vol 39, no 1, pp 17-31.

Parry, G., Van Cleemput, P., Peters, J., Walters, S., Thomas, K. and Cooper, C. (2007) 'Health status of Gypsies and Travellers in England', *Journal of Epidemiology and Community Health*, vol 61, pp 198-204.

Parry, R. (2002) 'Delivery structures and policy development in post-devolution Scotland', *Social Policy and Society*, vol 1, no 4, pp 315-24.

Parry, R. (2004) 'Devolution and social security in Scotland', *Benefits: The Journal of Poverty and Social Justice*, vol 12, no 3, pp 169-74.

Parsons, C., Godfrey, R., Annan, G., Cornwall, J., Dussart, M., Hepburn, S., Howlett, K. and Wennerstrom, V. (2005) *Minority Ethnic Exclusions and the Race Relations (Amendment) Act 2000*, Research Report RR616, London: DfES.

Paskell, C.A. and Power, A. (2005) '*The Future's Changed': Local Impacts of Housing, Environment and Regeneration Policy since 1997*, CASEreport 29, London: London School of Economics and Political Science.

Pawson, H. and Davidson, E. (2008) 'Radically divergent? Homelessness policy and practice in post-devolution Scotland', *European Journal of Housing Policy*, vol 8, no 1, pp 39-60.

Pemberton, H. (2006) 'Politics and pensions in post-war Britian', in H. Pemberton, P. Thane and N. Whiteside (eds) *Britain's Pension Crisis: History and Policy*, Oxford: Oxford University Press.

Pennell, H., West, A. and Hind, A. (2006) *Secondary School Admissions in London*, Clare Market Papers no 19, London: Centre for Educational Research, London School of Economics and Political Science.

Penrose, J. (2002) *Poverty and Asylum in the UK*, London: Refugee Council and Oxfam, accessed at www.refugeecouncil.org.uk/OneStopCMS/Core/CrawlerResourceServer.aspx?resource=7599496F-2448-4282-9065-540B7B659DDA&mode=link&guid=3a5ee26b4b4b4834b19425505b2fecbc

Pensions Commission (2004) *Pensions: Challenges and Choices: The First Report of the Pensions Commission*, London: Pensions Commission.

Pensions Commission (2005) *A New Pensions Settlement for the Twenty-First Century: The Second Report of the Pensions Commission*, London: Pensions Commission.

Pettigrew, N., Hardy, R. and Lee, A. (2005) *Specialist Employment Adviser Evaluation*, DWP Research Report no 365, London: DfES.

Pevalin, D.J. (2007) 'Socio-economic inequalities in health and service utilization in the London Borough of Newham', *Public Health*, vol 121, no 8, pp 596-602.

Phillips, A.W.H. (1954) *Report of the Committee on the Economic and Financial Problems of the Provision for Old Age*, Cmnd 9333, London: HMSO.

Phillips, C. and Bowling, B. (2007) 'Ethnicities, racism, crime and criminal justice', in M. Maguire, R. Morgan and R. Reiner (eds) *The Oxford Handbook of Criminology* (4th edition), Oxford: Oxford University Press.

Piachaud, D. (2001) 'Child poverty, opportunities and quality of life', *The Political Quarterly*, vol 72, no 4, pp 446-53.

Piachaud, D. (2008) 'Devolution and social security in the United Kingdom', in J. Midgely (ed) *Welfare Reform in the United States: Implications for British Social Policy*, CASEpaper 131, London: London School of Economics and Political Science.

Picketty, T. and Saez, E. (2003) 'The evolution of top incomes: a historical and international perspective', *AEA Papers and Proceedings*, May 2006, pp 200-5.

Pinkerton, C., McLaughlan, G. and Salt, J. (2004) *Sizing the Illegally Resident Population in the UK*, Home Office Online Report no 58/04, London: Home Office, accessed at www.homeoffice.gov.uk/rds/pdfs04/rdsolr5804.pdf

PMSU (Prime Minister's Strategy Unit) (2005) *Improving the Life Chances of Disabled people*, accessed at www.cabinetoffice.gov.uk/strategy/work_areas/disability/

Powell, M. (ed) (2002) *Evaluating New Labour's Welfare Reforms*, Bristol: The Policy Press.

Power, A. (1987) *Property before People: The Management of Twentieth-Century Council Housing*, London: Allen and Unwin.

Power, A. (1997) *Estates on the Edge*, London: Macmillan.

Power, A. (2004) *Neighbourhood Management and the Future of Urban Areas*, CASEpaper 77, London: London School of Economics and Political Science.

Power, A. (2007) *City Survivors: Bringing Up Children in Disadvantaged Neighbourhoods*, Bristol: The Policy Press.

Power, A. and Lupton, R. (2005) 'Disadvantaged by where you live? New Labour and neighbourhood renewal', in J. Hills and K. Stewart (ed) *A More Equal Society? New Labour, Poverty, Inequality and Exclusion*, Bristol: The Policy Press.

Power, A. and Mumford, K. (1999) *The Slow Death of Great Cities? Urban Abandonment or Urban Renaissance*, York: York Publishing Services.

Power, A. and Tunstall, R. (1995) *Swimming Against the Tide: Polarisation or Progress on 20 Unpopular Council Estates, 1980-1995*, York: Joseph Rowntree Foundation.

Power, A. and Willmot, H. (2005) 'Bringing up families in poor neighbourhoods under New Labour', in J. Hills and K. Stewart (ed) *A More Equal Society? New Labour, Poverty, Inequality and Exclusion*, Bristol: The Policy Press.

PPG (Pensions Provision Group) (1998) *We All Need Pensions: The Prospects for Pension Provision*, London: The Stationery Office.

PPI (Pensions Policy Institute) (2006a) *An Evaluation of the White Paper State Pension Reform Proposals*, London: PPI.

PPI (2006b) *Are Personal Accounts Suitable for All?*, London: PPI.

PPI (2008) *The Pensions Primer* (updated), London: PPI.

Prais, S.J. (2003) 'Cautions on OECD's recent educational survey (PISA)', *Oxford Review of Education*, vol 29, no 2, pp 139-63.

Rake, K. and Jayatilaka, G. (2002) *Home Truths: An Analysis of Financial Decision Making within the Home*, London: Fawcett Society.

Ramsay, M. (2005) 'A modest proposal: the case for a maximum wage', *Contemporary Politics*, vol 11, no 4, pp 201-16.

Ramsay, S.E., Morris, R.W., Papacosta, O., Lennon, L.T., Thomas, M.C. and Whincup, P.H. (2005) 'Secondary prevention of coronary heart disease in older British men: extent of inequalities before and after implementation of the National Service Framework', *Journal of Public Health*, vol 27, no 4, pp 338-43.

Rattansi, A. (2005) 'The uses of racialization: the time-spaces and subject-objects of the raced body', in K. Murji and J. Solomos (eds) *Racialization: Studies in Theory and Practice*, Oxford: Oxford University Press.

Redmond, G., Sutherland, H. and Wilson, M. (1998) *The Arithmetic of Tax and Social Security Reform: A User's Guide to Microsimulation Methods and Analysis*, Cambridge: Cambridge University Press.

Reed, H. and Latorre, M. (2008) *The Economic Impact of Migration on the UK Labour Market*, London: ippr.

RGCC (Recruiters Guide to Courses and Campuses) (2008) *Forecast: Implications for Employers*, accessed at www.rgcc.org.uk/page3.asp

Riccio, J.A., Bewley, H., Campbell-Barr, V., Dorsett, R., Hamilton, G., Hoggart, L., Marsh, A., Miller, C., Ray, K. and Vegeris, S. (2008) *Implementation and Second-Year Impacts for Lone Parents in the UK Employment Retention and Advancement (ERA) Demonstration*, DWP Research Report no 489, London: DWP.

Robinson, D., Reeve, K. and Rionach, C. (2007) *The Housing Pathways of New Immigrants*, York: Joseph Rowntree Foundation.

Rodriguez-Pose, A. and Gill, N. (2004) 'Is there a global link between regional disparities and devolution?', *Environment and Planning A*, vol 36, no 12, pp 2097-117.

Romeri, E., Baker, A. and Griffiths, C. (2006) 'Mortality by deprivation and cause of death in England and Wales, 1999-2003', *Health Statistics Quarterly*, no 32, pp 19-34.

Roney, J. and Cook, L. (2008) 'Migration impacts forum housing report' (unpublished).

Ross, J., Lloyd, J. and Weinhardt, M. (2008) *The Age of Inheritance*, London: International Longevity Centre.

Rowlingson, K. and McKay, S. (2005) *Attitudes to Inheritance in Britain*, York: Joseph Rowntree Foundation.

Royal Commission on Long Term Care (1999) *With Respect to Old Age*, Cm 4192-I, London: The Stationery Office.

Royal Commission on the Distribution of Income and Wealth (1979a) *Report No 7: Fourth Report on the Standing Reference*, Cmnd 7595, London: HMSO.

Royal Commission on the Distribution of Income and Wealth (1979b) *Report No 8: Fifth Report on the Standing Reference*, Cmnd 7679, London: HMSO.

Ruddock, G. (2006) *Validation Study of the PISA 2000, PISA 2003 and TIMSS-2003 International Studies of Pupil Attainment*, Nottingham: DfES Publications.

Rumbaut, R.G. and Portes, A. (eds) (2001) *Ethnicities: Children of Immigrants in America*, Berkeley, CA: University of California Press.

Runciman, W. (2006) 'What happened to the Labour Party?', *London Review of Books*, 22 June.

Rutherford, J. and Shah, H. (eds) (2006) *The Good Society: Compass Programme for Renewal*, London: Compass in association with Lawrence & Wishart.

Rutter, J. (2003) 'The experiences and achievements of Congolese children in Camden schools', London Borough of Camden (unpublished).

Rutter, J. (2006) *Refugee Children in the UK*, Buckingham: Open University Press.

Rutter, J. and Latorre, M. (2008a) *The Delivery of Public Services for Migrants in Rural Areas*, London: ippr.

Rutter, J. and Latorre, M. (2008b) *Migration, Housing and the Built Environment in Greater London*, London: London Housing Federation.

Rutter, J. and Newman, N. (2008) *Moving Up Together: Promoting Equality among the UK's Diverse Communities*, London: ippr.

Rutter, M. (2006) 'Is Sure Start an effective preventive intervention?', *Child and Adolescent Mental Health*, vol 11, no 3, pp 135-41.

Sassi, F. (2005) 'Tackling health inequalities', in J. Hills and K. Stewart (eds) *A More Equal Society? New Labour, Poverty, Inequality and Exclusion*, Bristol: The Policy Press.

Scarman, L. (1981) *The Scarman Report: The Brixton Disorders, 10-12 April 1981*, London: HMSO.

Scharf, T., Phillipson, C. and Smith, A.E. (2005) *Multiple Exclusion and Quality of Life amongst Excluded Older People in Disadvantaged Neighbourhoods*, London: The Stationery Office for the Social Exclusion Unit.

Scharf, T., Bartlam, B., Hislop, J., Bernard, M., Dunning, A. and Sim, J. (2006) *Necessities of Life: Older People's Experiences of Poverty*, London: Help the Aged.

Schmuecker, K. (2008) 'Social justice in the UK: one route or four?', in G. Craig, T. Burchardt and D. Gordon (eds) *Social Justice and Public Policy: Seeking Fairness in Diverse Societies*, Bristol: The Policy Press.

Schneider-Ross (2007) *The Public Sector Equality Duties: Making an Impact*, Hampshire: Schneider-Ross.

Scott, G. (2006) 'Active labour market policy and the reduction of poverty in the "new" Scotland', *Critical Social Policy*, vol 26, no 3, pp 669-84.

Scott, G., Williams, C. and G. Mooney (2008) 'Nationalism and social policy in Scotland and Wales: towards increasing divergence?', Paper presented at the Social Policy Association Conference, Edinburgh, 23 June.

Scottish Executive (1999) *Social Justice ... A Scotland where Everyone Matters*, Edinburgh: Scottish Executive, accessed at www.scotland.gov.uk/Resource/Doc/158142/0042789.pdf

Scottish Executive (2002) *Closing the Opportunity Gap: Scottish Budget for 2003-2006*, Edinburgh: Scottish Executive, accessed at www.scotland.gov.uk/Resource/Doc/46997/0024934.pdf

Scottish Government (2007) *The Government Economic Strategy, Edinburgh: Scottish Government*, www.scotland.gov.uk/Publications/2007/11/12115041/0

Sefton, T. (2002) *Recent Changes in the Distribution of the Social Wage*, CASEpaper 62, London: London School of Economics and Political Science.

Sefton, T. (2003) 'What we want from the welfare state', in A.R. Park, J. Curtice, K. Thomson, L. Jarvis and C. Bromley (eds) *British Social Attitudes: The 20th Report: Continuity and Change over Two Decades*, Aldershot: Ashgate.

Sefton, T. (2004) *A Fair Share of Welfare: Public Spending on Children in the UK*, CASEreport 25, London: London School of Economics and Political Science.

Sefton, T. (2005) 'Give and take: attitudes to redistribution', in A.R. Park, J. Curtice, K. Thomson, C. Bromley, M. Phillips and M. Johnson (eds) *British Social Attitudes: The 22nd Report: Two Terms of New Labour: The Public's Reaction*, Aldershot: Ashgate.

Sefton, T. (forthcoming) *Public Expenditure on Children*, London: Save the Children UK.

Seldon, A. (2007) 'Conclusion: the net Blair effect: 1994-2007', in A. Seldon (ed) *Blair's Britain: 1997-2007*, Cambridge: Cambridge University Press.

Sellen, D., Tedstone, A. and Frize, J. (2002) 'Food insecurity among refugee families in East London', *Public Health and Nutrition*, vol 5, no 5, pp 637-44.

SEU (Social Exclusion Unit) (1998) *Bringing Britain Together: A National Strategy for Neighbourhood Renewal*, London: SEU.

SEU (2000a) *National Strategy for Neighbourhood Renewal: A Framework for Consultation*, London: SEU.

SEU (2000b) *Policy Action Team Report Summaries: A Compendium*, London: The Stationery Office.

SEU (2000c) *Minority Ethnic Issues in Social Exclusion and Neighbourhood Renewal*, London: Cabinet Office.

SEU (2001) *New Commitment to Neighbourhood Renewal: National Strategy Action Plan*, London: Cabinet Office.

Sewell, T. (1997) *Black Masculinities and Schooling: How Black Boys Survive Modern Schooling*, London: Trentham Books.

Shaw, A. (2008) 'Kinship, cultural practices and immigration: consanguineous marriage among British Pakistanis', *Journal of the Royal Anthropological Institute*, vol 7, no 2, pp 315-34.

Shaw, C. (2007) 'Fifty years of United Kingdom national population projections: how accurate have they been?', *Population Trends*, Summer, no 128, pp 8-23.

Shaw, M., Dorling, D., Gordon, D. and and Davey Smith, G. (1999) *The Widening Gap: Health Inequalities and Policy in Britain*, Bristol: The Policy Press.

Shaw, M., Davey Smith, G. and Dorling, D. (2005) 'Health inequalities and New Labour: how the promises compare with real progress', *British Medical Journal*, vol 330, no 7498, pp 1016-21.

Sibieta, L., Chowdry, H. and Muriel, A. (2008) *Level Playing Field? The Implications of School Funding*, Reading: CfBT Education Trust.

Sinclair, S. (2008) 'What you see is what you get: media and public perceptions of poverty in the UK', Paper presented at the Social Policy Association Conference, Edinburgh, 23 June.

SPCT (Surrey Primary Care Trust) (2008) *Race Equality Scheme 2008-2011*, accessed at www.surreyhealth.nhs.uk/doc.aspx?id_Resource=713

Sriskandarajah, D. and Drew, C. (2006) *Brits Abroad: Mapping the Scale and Nature of British Emigration*, London: Institute for Public Policy Research.

Stern, N. (2007) *The Economics of Climate Change: The Stern Review*, Cambridge: Cambridge University Press.

Stewart, F. and Langer, A. (2008) 'Horizontal inequalities: explaining persistence and change', in F. Stewart (ed) *Horizontal Inequalities and Conflict: Understanding Group Violence in Multiethnic Societies*, Basingstoke: Macmillan.

Stewart, J. (2004) *Taking Stock: Scottish Social Welfare after Devolution*, Bristol: The Policy Press.

Stewart, K. (2005a) 'Towards an equal start? Child poverty and deprivation under Labour', in J. Hills and K. Stewart (eds) *A More Equal Society? New Labour, Poverty, Inequality and Exclusion*, Bristol: The Policy Press.

Stewart, K. (2005b) 'Changes in poverty and inequality in the UK in international context', in J. Hills and K. Stewart (eds) *A More Equal Society? New Labour, Poverty, Inequality and Exclusion*, Bristol: The Policy Press.

Stewart, M.B. (2004) 'The employment effects of the National Minimum Wage', *Economic Journal*, vol 114, no 494, pp C110-C116.

Stewart, M.B. and Swaffield, J. (1999) 'Low pay dynamics and transition probabilities', *Economica*, vol 66, no 261, pp 23-42.

Strand, S. (2008) *Minority Ethnic Pupils in the Longitudinal Study of Young People in England: Extension Report on Performance in Public Examinations at Age 16*, DCSF Report RR029, London: DCSF.

Strategy Unit (2002) *Inter-Departmental Childcare Review: Delivering for Children and Families*, London: Strategy Unit.

Straw, J. and Boateng, P. (1996) *Bringing Rights Home: Labour's Plans to Incorporate the European Convention on Human Rights into UK Law*, London: Labour Party.

Sutherland, H., Sefton, T. and Piachaud, D. (2003) *Poverty in Britain: The Impact of Government Policy since 1997*, York: Joseph Rowntree Foundation.

Sutherland, H., Evans, M., Hancock, R., Hills, J. and Zantomio, F. (2008) *The Impact of Benefit and Tax Uprating on Incomes and Poverty*, York: Joseph Rowntree Foundation.

Sylva, K., Melhuish, E., Sammons, P., Siraj-Blatchford, I., Taggart, B. and Elliot, K. (2003) *The Effective Provision of Pre-School Education (EPPE) Project: Findings from the Pre-School Period*, London: DfES.

Tanaka, S. (2005) 'Parental leave and child health across OECD countries', *Economic Journal*, vol 115, no 501, pp F7-F28.

Tanner, E., Welsh, E. and Lewis, J. (2006) 'The quality-defining process in early years services: a case study', *Children and Society*, vol 20, no 1, pp 4-16.

Tatton, S. (2007) 'Executive pay: fat cats or hungry tigers?', Presentation on IDS Executive Compensation Review to the Royal Statistical Society's SUF Annual Conference, 15 November, accessed at www.rss.org.uk/main.asp?page=2861

Taylor, B. and Newall, D. (2008) *Maternity, Mortality and Migration*, Birmingham: West Midlands Strategic Migration Partnership.

Taylor-Gooby, P. (2005) *Attitudes to Social Justice*, London: ippr.

Taylor-Gooby, P. and Hastie, C. (2002) 'Support for state spending: has New Labour got it right?', in A. Park, J. Curtice, K. Thomson, L. Jarvis and C. Bromley (eds) *British Social Attitudes: The 19th Report*, London: Sage Publications.

Taylor-Gooby, P. and Martin, R. (2008) 'Trends in sympathy for the poor', in A.R. Park, J. Curtice, K. Thomson, M. Phillips, M. Johnson and E. Clery (eds) *British Social Attitudes: The 24th Report*, Aldershot: Ashgate.

Team Hackney LAA (Local Area Agreement) (2007) *Putting Hackney First, Local Area Agreement 2007-2010*, accessed at www.teamhackney.org/team_hackney_ laa_2007_-_2010_final.pdf

Teasdale, P. (1998) 'Incidence and repeat spells of unemployment in analysis using claimant data', *Labour Market Trends*, November, pp 555-61.

Thiollière, M. (2007) *Quelle ville voulons nous?*, Paris: Éditions Autrement.

Thumim, J. and White, V. (2008) *Distributional Impacts of Personal Carbon Trading*, London: Defra.

Tikly, L., Haynes, J., Caballero, C., Hill, J. and Gillborn, D. (2006) *Evaluation of Aiming High: African Caribbean Achievement Project*, DfES Brief no Rb801, London: DfES.

Tomlinson, S. (1998) 'New inequalities? Educational markets and ethnic minorities', *Race, Ethnicity and Education*, vol 1, no 2, pp 207-23.

Townsend, P., Davidson, N. and Whitehead, M. (1992) *Inequalities in Health: The Black Report and The Health Divide*, Harmondsworth: Penguin Books.

Toynbee, P. (2003) *Hard Work: Life in Low Pay Britain*, London: Bloomsbury.

Toynbee, P. and Walker, D. (2001) *Did Things Get Better? An Audit of Labour's Successes and Failures*, London: Penguin Books.

Training and Development Agency for Schools (2006) *Corporate Plan 2002-05*, London: TDA.

TUC (Trades Union Congress) (2007) 'Midlands TUC welcomes minister's decision to drop "workfare" from welfare reform package', TUC Press Release, 13 December, accessed at www.tuc.org.uk/welfare/tuc-14096-f0.cfm

TUC (2008) *Closing the Gender Pay Gap: An Update Report for TUC Women's Conference 2008*, London: TUC.

Twist, L., Schagen, I. and Hodgson, C. (2008) *Readers and Reading: The National Report for England 2006 (PIRLS: Progress in International Reading Literacy Study)*, Slough: NFER.

UCAS (Universities and Colleges Admissions Service) (2008a) 'Latest university application figures show 9.1 per cent rise', Press Release, 16 July, accessed at www.ucas.ac.uk/website/news/media_releases/2008/2008-07-16

UCAS (2008b) 'Report on distance to HE, UCAS Research Team report prepared for the Participation Research Group', 24 January, unpublished.

UNCESCR (United Nations Committee on Economic, Social and Cultural Rights) (2002) *Concluding Observations of the Committee on Economic, Social and Cultural Rights: United Kingdom of Great Britain and Northern Ireland, United Kingdom of Great Britain and Northern Ireland – Dependent Territories*, 05/06/2002, UN document, E/C.12/1/Add.79, Concluding Observations/Comments, New York: United Nations.

UNCRC (United Nations Committee on the Rights of the Child) (2008) *Concluding Observations: United Kingdom of Great Britain and Northern Ireland*, UN Doc CRC/C/GBR/CO/4, 20 October, New York: United Nations.

UNHRC (United Nations Human Rights Committee) (2008) *Concluding Observations*, UN Document, CCPR/C/GBR/CO/6, 21 July, New York: United Nations.

UNICEF (United Nations Children's Fund) (2000) *A League Table of Child Poverty in Rich Nations*, Report 1, Florence: UNICEF Innocenti Research Centre.

UNICEF (2007) *An Overview of Child Well-Being in Rich Countries*, Innocenti Report Card 7, Florence: UNICEF Innocenti Research Centre.

Wadham, J., Mountfield, H. and Edmundson, A. (2003) *Blackstone's Guide to the Human Rights Act 1998*, Oxford: Oxford University Press.

WAG (Welsh Assembly Government) (2001) *A Plan for Wales 2001*, Cardiff: WAG.

WAG (2004) *Making the Connections*, Cardiff: WAG.

Wagstaff, A., Paci, P. and van Doorslaer, E. (1991) 'On the measurement of inequalities in health', *Social Science and Medicine*, vol 33, no 5, pp 545-57.

Waldfogel, J. (1998) *Early Childhood Interventions and Outcomes*, CASEpaper 21, London: Centre for Analysis of Social Exclusion, London School of Economics and Political Science.

Waldfogel, J. (2006) *What Children Need*, Cambridge, MA: Harvard University Press.

Waldfogel, J. and Garnham, A. (2008) *Childcare and Child Poverty*, Report prepared for the Joseph Rowntree Foundation Initiative on 'Eradicating Child Poverty: The Role of Key Policy Areas', York: JRF.

Walker, A. (2002) 'In praise of centralism', accessed at http://editiondesign.com/catalyst/pdf/walker.pdf

Wanless, D. (2002) *Securing Our Health Future: Taking a Long-Term View*, London: HM Treasury.

Wanless, D. (2004) *Securing Good Health for the Whole Population*, London: HM Treasury.

Warnes, A. (1996) 'The demography of old age: panic versus reality', in R. Bland (ed) *Developing Services for Older People and their Families*, London: Jessica Kingsley.

West, A. (2006) 'The pre-school education market in England from 1997: quality, availability, affordability and equity', *Oxford Review of Education*, vol 32, no 3, pp 283-301.

West, R. (2008) *Key Performance Indicators on Smoking Cessation in England: Findings from the Smoking Toolkit Study*, accessed at www.aspsilverbackwebsites.co.uk/ smokinginengland/ref/smokinginengland.ppt

Whiteside, N. (2006) 'Occupational pensions and the search for security', in H. Pemberton, P. Thane and N. Whiteside (eds) *Britain's Pension Crisis: History and Policy*, Oxford: Oxford University Press.

Whitty, G. (2008) 'Twenty years of progress? English education policy 1988 to the present', *Educational Management Administration and Leadership*, vol 36, no 2, pp 165-84.

Wildbore, H. (2008) 'Does Britain need a bill of rights?', *Politics Review*, vol 17, no 4, 4pp.

Wilkinson, R. and Pickett, K. (2006) 'Income inequality and health: a review of the evidence', *Social Science and Medicine*, vol 62, pp 1768-84.

Wilson, R. (2007) 'Rhetoric meets reality: Northern Ireland's equality agenda', *Benefits: The Journal of Poverty and Social Justice*, vol 15, no 2, pp 151-62.

Wincott, D. (2006) 'Paradoxes of New Labour social policy: toward universal child care in Europe's "most liberal" welfare regime?', *International Studies in Gender, State & Society*, vol 13, no 2, pp 286-312.

Wolf, A., Jenkins, A. and Vignoles, A. (2006) 'Certifying the workforce: economic imperative or failed social policy?', *Journal of Education Policy*, vol 21, no 5, pp 535-65.

Woods, L.M., Rachet, B., Riga, M., Stone, N., Shah, A. and Coleman, M.P. (2005) 'Geographical variation in life expectancy at birth in England and Wales is largely explained by deprivation', *Journal of Epidemiology and Community Health*, vol 59, no 2, pp 115-20.

Young, M. (1958) *The Rise of the Meritocracy 1870-2033*, London: Thames and Hudson.

Index

Page references for figures and tables are in *italics*